A Street in
Arnhem

The Agony of Occupation and Liberation

Robert Kershaw

Ian Allan
PUBLISHING

First published 2014
This paperback edition first published 2015

ISBN 978 0 7110 3828 8

Published by Ian Allan Publishing Ltd, Addlestone, Surrey KT15 2SF.

Printed in England

Visit the Ian Allan Publishing website at *www.ianallanpublishing.com*

Contents

Acknowledgements and thanks

My particular thanks go to Robert Voskuil who accessed a lot of information from the very helpful staff of the Oosterbeek Airborne Museum and from his own sources and memory. He has in addition provided photographs and valuable local advice throughout the writing and gestation period of this book. My thanks also to Robert Sigmond, Chris van Roekel, Wil Rieken, Berend Esvelt, Harry van Gorkum, Geert Maassen, Scott Revell and many other Dutch colleagues, who all stepped up to the mark in terms of information, interviews, photographs and remarkable stories. Colonel John Waddy (retired), ex-156 Para, was particularly helpful in tracking down very many unusual accounts and introducing me to many of the Dutch contacts mentioned above.

Pre-war Arnhem street plans label the road running from Oosterbeek to Arnhem as the Utrechtsche Straatweg – only the last section running from Oosterbeek to Arnhem Station is called Utrechtseweg. In the interests of narrative simplicity the modern road name, Utrechtseweg, is used when referring to the Street.

Post-war reconstruction has produced many different house numbers, so present-day address numbers are used, even though this is not always practical. Reconciling differences between 1944 and today was challenging, so my apologies for any inevitable errors that may occur. Tracking changes has been like trying to hit a moving target, with new houses being built every year. The changes would, I suggest, tax even a Dutch official, but with the aid of personal enquiries and access to a copy of the pre-war Oosterbeek telephone directory and address book, a reasonable stab at accuracy has been achieved. For example, Wil Rieken's wartime address of 160 Utrechtsche Straatweg is the converted fashion shop that can be found at the same location at No 178 Utrechtseweg today.

General published sources

Army Bureau of Current Affairs *Arnhem 2: Inside The Perimeter*, No 84, Dec 1944

Bauer, C. *The Battle of Arnhem* (Zebra, 1979)

BBC *War Report: D-Day to VE Day* (Ariel Books, 1985)

Cholewczynski, G. F. *Poles Apart* (Sarpedon, 1993)
Spanhoe's September (Walka Books, 2008)

Duyts, W. and Groeneweg, A. *The Harvest of Ten Years* (Oosterbeek Airborne Museum, 1988)

Eastwood, S., Gray, C. and Green, A. *When Dragons Flew* (Silver Link, 1994, 2009)

Fairley, J. *Remember Arnhem* (Pegasus Journal, 1978)

Fürbringer, H. *9.SS-Panzer Division. Hohenstaufen 1944* (Heimdal, 1984)

Gerritsen, S. (ed) *Geschichten, die Bleiben* (NL Bevrijdingsmuseum, 1944-45)

Gijbels, P. and Truesdale, D. *Leading the Way to Arnhem* (RN Sigmond, 2008)

Hees, A-J. van *Green On!* (Private Pub, 2007)

Junier, A., Smulders, B. and Korsloot, J. *By Land, Sea and Air* (RN Sigmond, 2003)

Kershaw. R. J. *It Never Snows in September* (Ian Allan Publishing Ltd, 1994)
Skymen (Hodder & Stoughton, 2010)

McKee, A. *The Race for the Rhine Bridges* (Stein & Day, 1971)

Maassen, G. *Oosterbeek Verwoest 1944-45* (Private Pub, 1980)

Margry, K. *Operation Market-Garden: Then and Now*, 2 Vols ('After The Battle', 2002)

Middlebrook, M. *Arnhem 1944* (Viking, 1994)

O'Reilly *From Delhi to Arnhem* (Thoroton, 2009)

Pijpers, G. and Truesdale, D. *Arnhem Their Final Battle* (RN Sigmond, 2012)

Ryan, C. *A Bridge Too Far* (Hamish Hamilton, 1974)

Sigmond, R. *Off at Last* (RN Sigmond, 2009)

Teesling, P. A. van (ed) *Over and Over* (Kontrast Oosterbeek, 2000)

Waddy J. *A Tour of the Arnhem Battlefields* (Leo Cooper, 1999)

Wilkinson, P. *The Gunners at Arnhem* (Spurwing Pub, 1999)

Zee, H. van der *The Hunger Winter* (Jill Norman & Hobhouse Ltd, 1982)

Periodicals

Note Oosterbeek Museum Mini-History publications are denoted MH with the number.

Baker, E. B. *'Bunny' Baker's Arnhem Story* (Eagle Magazine, Vol 9, No 10, Dec 2001)

Heijbroek, N. *Three Englishmen in Our Cellar* (MH No 66, May 2000)

Hofwegen, J. A. van *September 1944: A Month We Will Never Forget* (Eagle Magazine, Vol 9, No 8, Apr 2001)

Hol, J., *Memories of Oosterbeek* (MH No 52, Nov 1996)

Jong, A. de *War Evacuees in the Open Air Museum* (NL Open Air Museum, Arnhem, 2004)

Kessler, H. *Kämpfe im Raum Arnheim* (Die Weissen Spiegel, 2/85, 5/85 and 6/85)

Maassen, G. H. *Anxious Days at Dreijen* (MH No XXXV)
Daily Reports from the Municipal Police of Oosterbeek (Sep 17-20 1944, MH No XIII)

Meijer, C. *War in the Weverstraat* (MH No XXV)

Roekel, C. van *Sturmgeschütz-Brigade 280* (MH No 70, May 2001)

Tiemens, W. H. *The Only Female Prisoner of War in Arnhem* (MH No 39, Aug 1993)

Timmerman, H. *German Field Graves in Oosterbeek* (MH No 84, Dec 2004)

Veelen, H. van *Civilian Aid in the Schoonoord* (MH No 64, Oct 1999)

Voskuil, R. *The Wartime Adventures of an Arnhem Schoolboy* (Kees Bolderman, MH No 75, Aug 2002)
Between Bombs and Gliders (MH No XXVI)

Zanten, 'Willy' van *The Arnhem Diary of a Dutch Schoolboy* (Pegasus Magazine, Summer 2008)

Zonnenfeld, J. W. van *Volunteers Needed* (MH No 79, Aug 2003)

Published memoirs and personal accounts

Bankhead, H. *Salute To The Steadfast* (Ramsay Press, 1999)

Breman, R. *The Tommies Are Coming!* (Airborne Museum Oosterbeek, 1988)

Curtis R. *Churchill's Volunteer* (Avon Books, 1994)

Dover, V. *The Silken Canopy* (Cassell, 1979)

Frost, J. *A Drop too Many* (Cassell & Co, 1980)

Gibson, R. *Nine Days* (Stockwell, 1956)

Hackett, J. *I Was a Stranger* (Sphere, 1977)

Hagen, L. *Arnhem Lift* (Hammond, 1945)

Kent, R. *First In!* (Batsford, 1979)

Mawson, S. *Arnhem Doctor* (Orbis, 1981)

Powell, G. *Men at Arnhem* (Buchan & Enright, 1986)

Sims, J. *Arnhem Spearhead* (IWM, 1978)

Święcicki, M. *With the Red Devils at Arnhem* (Max Love, 1945)

Urquhart, R. *Arnhem* (Pan, 1972)

Vlist, H. van der *Oosterbeek 1944* (Society of Friends, Airborne Museum, Oosterbeek, 1992)

Zeno *The Cauldron* (Pan, 1966)

TV and Internet

Forever in Our Memory (video by H. Kardol, B. de Reus and R. Voskuil, Bal, Sep 1989)

Freedom's Trail Arnhem (internet, F. van Lunteren and W. Brouwer, Arnhem Council and Gelders Archive)

The Hunger Winter (M. Tosh, producer, BBC Timewatch, Elstree, MCMLXXXVIII)

The Lost Evidence: Operation Market Garden (Downing, T., Flashback TV, History Channel, 2006)

Victoria Cross (Pearson, R., BBC Midlands presentation on Major Robert Cain VC)

Unpublished accounts and memoirs

Arnhem secret APFU 'dope sheets', Sgts Lewis, Smith and Walker, 18-25 Sep 44, Imperial War Museum

Benest, D., 10 Para Research Notes, Airborne Assault Archive, Duxford: Benjamin Pick, 'Paddy' Stewart and Bert 'Taff' Wilmott, B Company

Esvelt, J. H. *Diary* (private account courtesy of Berend Esvelt)

Fullriede, F., Oberstleutnant Hermann Göring Division, Abshrift Tagesbuch, 31.8.44- 27.12.44

Harzer, *Gefechtsbericht*: Battle report and personal correspondence on the part played by the Hohenstaufen Division in the Battle of Arnhem, edited with notes by Th. A. Boeree

Hayden, W., Sgt, 1 Para, private account of Dressing Station experience

Krafft, S. *SS Pz Gren A.u.E. Btl 16 in den Kämpfen bei Arnheim 17.9 44-7.10.44*

Labahn, Obersturmführer *Gefechtsbericht der 7.(Stamm) Kompanie für die Zeit vom 17.9. bis 26.9.44* (2 Oct 1944)

Lippert M., Standartenführer *Abschrift*. Der handschriftlichen Aufzeichnungen des ehem. Staf. M. Lippert, letzter Kommandeur der SS-Unterührerschule Arnheim (Schneider Collection)

Maanen, A. van, *The Diary of Anje 17-25 Sep 44* (Oosterbeek Airborne Museum Archive)

Möller, H. *Die Schlacht um Arnheim-Oosterbeek. Der Einsatz des Pionier Battalion 9 Hohenstaufen vom 17. bis 26. September 1944* (Private account, Sep 1978)

Müller, P., Rottenführer, Pz Gren Regt 20 9th SS, Abschrift Arnheim

Tettau, H. von *Gefechtsbericht über die Schlacht bei Arnheim 17-26.9.44* (Bundesarchiv)

Ziegler, A, Rottenführer Panzerjäger Abt 9th SS Abschrift *Einsatz Arnheim* (Bamberg, 1976)

Interviews

Carson, K., Flt Sgt 512 Sqn RAF Flight Engineer, author interview 22 Sep 2007

Chatfield, H., Flt Lt 512 Sqn RAF, author interview 22 Sep 2007

Dombrowski, W., SS Rottenführer, 2 Kp. Pz Pi Btl 9th SS, correspondence and author interview 23 Oct 1987

Enthammer, J., Lt V1 Artillery, author interview 15 Jun 1987

Gorkum Van, H., Dutch Resistance helper, author interview 8 Jul 2009

Lindemann, R., Junker, SS Unteroffizierschule Arnheim, author interview 11 Jun 1987

Rieken, W., 160 (now 178) Utrechtseweg, child in Oosterbeek, author interview 27 May 2011

Schwarz, W., SS Hauptsturmführer, Div Ia 9th SS, author interview 16 Sep 1987

Shackleton, A., Glider Pilot Regt, Liddle interview, Second World War Experience Centre, Leeds, Jul 2002

Swan, J., Cpl, 18 Platoon C Company, 1st Bn Border Regt, interview R. Milton, Airborne Assault Museum Archive, Duxford

Waddy, J., Major, 156th Parachute Battalion, author interview 9 Aug 2007

Ziegler, A., SS Rottenführer, Panzerjäger Abt. 9th SS, author interview 23 Nov 1987

Introduction

Driving east-west to Arnhem along the Utrechtseweg, I am constantly reminded how much evidence relating to the events of September 1944 can still be seen left and right of the road. The first indication is the left turn into the Wolfheze road just before Oosterbeek; this is where the German Arnhem Stadtkommandant's car was shot up by advancing paratroopers. Woodland left and right was overflown by fleets of gliders and aircraft that were to disgorge thousands of airborne troops onto the Renkum Heath nearby. Within a couple of bends the leafy Arnhem suburb of Oosterbeek comes into view. Inside a minute and the entire 1-kilometre stretch of the ferociously defended airborne perimeter has passed. The grand mansion on the right overlooking green parkland was the embattled headquarters of the 1st British Airborne Division for those nine days. An obelisk memorial stands inside the triangular grass area on the other side of the road. Beyond the pillar are the houses that made up the northern edge of the perimeter.

Next to No 200 Utrechtseweg there is a crossroads. Two British medical stations were set up here, inside the Hotel Schoonoord to the right and the Hotel Vreewijk on the left. They were fought over and changed hands several times. If you turn left into the Stationsweg and continue over the railway bridge, the Commonwealth War Cemetery, where the Allied dead are buried, can be seen to the right. Back at the hotel crossroads the road continues into Arnhem. British soldiers marched and skirmished along that street, swamped by crowds of cheering orange-flag-waving Dutch civilians. Two days later they limped back in defeat, dragging their wounded past wrecked trams and a road overlaid with downed wires and shot-down tree branches.

Fighting ravaged the Utrechtseweg for nine days. Superficial damage inflicted during the swift Liberation became total during the siege. Dutch civilians had elected to stay in their houses. Like the British, they were to be caught unawares by the ferocity of the rapid German reaction. This one street saw or heard virtually every development that took place during the nine-day battle of Arnhem in September 1944.

Every year thousands of Dutch and British people gather to commemorate this pain and suffering at the Commonwealth War Cemetery just off the Utrechtseweg. The opening hymn, 'O God, Our Help in Ages Past', can be confusing to follow with both nations singing in their own language. The poignant setting becomes especially atmospheric when bathed in the last rays of a weakening autumn sun, seemingly floodlit by divine intervention. Hundreds of Dutch schoolchildren emerge during the ceremony, filing between the serried rows of white marker stones until there is a child opposite every grave. This is achieved amid fidgeting disinterest tempered by the mild curiosity that comes with all events organised by grown-ups. The assembly is done quietly and unobtrusively.

When the officiating clergy at last turn to the children, long bored with the lengthy ceremony, the mood becomes more serious and reverential. They are asked to read out the name of the soldier buried before them as they lay their flowers in an act of remembrance. Many of these soldiers lying before them, they are reminded, are still unknown. The act never fails to bring a lump to the throat, creating an atmosphere so tangibly emotional it could be cut with a knife. 'Age shall not weary them … at the going down of the sun. We will remember them.'

A special bond exists between the people of Arnhem and Oosterbeek and the airborne veterans. As a professional Parachute Regiment officer, I have experienced the link during many commemorative anniversaries. Little changes with the passage of time. Roelie Breman, a 15-year-old girl in 1944, wrote in the preamble to her wartime Oosterbeek Diary:

'Imagine how it must feel when your father or your brother is lying buried in a strange country and that you do not even know which grave to look for!'

Each year the schoolchildren are reminded about these 'unknowns'.

'You cannot even be sure if this is the right place to look for him, for even now the soil of our village hides the resting places of several unknown soldiers "Known unto God".[1]

This heartfelt reverence for the memory of soldiers killed defending this village in September 1944 has been passed onto subsequent generations. Dutch families have been known to pay English public school fees for sons of Arnhem veterans living in the United Kingdom. English families have 'adopted' Dutch children. The link has endured and even now associations are continually set up to perpetuate the memory after the last veterans have gone.

I wrote a book about Operation Market Garden from the German point of view[2]; although it was an original idea at the time, what more remains to be said? Many, many books are written about the battle of Arnhem. After speaking with Dutch, British and German veterans during many battlefield visits I have come to appreciate that nearly all of them stood on the Utrechtseweg at some time during the battle. Closer examination of this one road has started to unveil aspects of the battle not considered before. Interpreting all three national perspectives at this one street level has become conceivable with the wealth of material gathered over the years. What might these particular insights be?

The British

The prevailing British view on landing was disbelief that an operation could ever go as well as this. Most of the soldiers had not been in action for some time, and many not at all. One of the parachute brigades was largely veteran, but average casualty rates of 50% on former airborne operations did not leave many amid the replacements. As the plan unravelled they became increasingly dismayed. Very few of them saw much at all. The street – the Utrechtseweg – was often remembered as the main thoroughfare from Oosterbeek to Arnhem. After a promising start the plan flopped. This tended to erode the men's faith in leadership 'from on high', but they carried on. As it was obviously a cock-up in the making, they were not going to be blamed for not trying to fight it through. Just as well they were trained to be fighting fit because the battle became a very physical and cumulatively exhausting ordeal. Sleep deprivation had an insidious effect on psychological resolve. Information came via rumour control. Existence was at trench and cellar level. Tenacity saved the core, and the heavy construction of the well-built houses they defended did the rest. Although they were boxed in by the Germans, the buildings boxed the panzers out. I had not identified many of these threads before.

The Germans

The Germans, expecting a ground attack, found that unexpectedly it came from the air. The much vaunted SS Panzer Division was actually a shadow formation, with no tanks; indeed, in some cases even small arms had been handed in because they were entraining from Arnhem station to re-equip in the Reich. Some of the SS soldiers picked up Sten guns from dead British paratroopers. The remnants of the 9th SS Panzer Division fought mainly without armour at 25% strength, supplemented by as many pioneers, sailors and Luftwaffe ground personnel as they could get their hands on.

Two battalions, a German and paratrooper, fought each other to the death on the street. The Germans stood at the end because they had a few officers left; the British were pulled back, having lost all theirs. At no stage were the Germans confident of winning. Every time they gained the upper hand on the street another air armada flew over and inverted the odds. Only when the Arnhem Bridge was recaptured did the situation appear to stabilise, but by then the Allied ground advance was in Nijmegen, just 10 kilometres away, then Polish paratroopers dropped in their rear. It was the German General Staff system and inspirational leadership by individual commanders that kept the Kampfgruppen together. They neither liked nor trusted the Dutch, so there were few qualms about wrecking the street – better here than in the Reich.

That the Dutch hated the Germans becomes abundantly clear from the street-level perspective. This disdain lingers beneath the surface even today among the wartime generation. World War 2 had been kind to the leafy suburb of Oosterbeek thus far; it had been a pre-war tourist attraction. Tenacious resistance by the surrounded paratroopers destroyed it, but the Germans got the blame. So remorseful were the 'airbornes', as the Dutch called them, that when they returned in 1945 to recover their dead they were convinced the locals would resent them. On the contrary, they took them into their hearts where they have remained ever since.

The Dutch

The Dutch story of the street was one of Liberation with a few smashed windows followed by complete devastation when the Germans came back. Elation went through stages of optimism to shocked disbelief and then despair. Material damage became inconsequential against the more pressing need to survive pinned in cellars sheltering below the ground. The fortunes of battle overhead were discernible only through soldiers clumping across their floorboards, shooting, animal-like screams, then the sudden appearance of an armed German soldier at the cellar entrance. Or more often, a grenade tossed down the steps. The village became a devastated no-man's-land. In material terms the Dutch lost everything and many family members besides. During this ordeal the bizarre became the norm and any form of domestic order odd.

A Street in Arnhem chronicles this deterioration for the first time through the perspectives of Dutch civilians and fighters in the form of a docudrama. Ordinary Dutch people are tracked as they sought to survive their appalling predicament, as also are the British and German soldiers fighting through their houses, all on this one street. Fighting and surviving happened on three planes. The British were ensconced at house level with trenches in the gardens outside, the Germans had to move at street level, while the Dutch sheltered in cellars beneath. The participants had no idea about what was going on around them in big-picture terms. The individual horizon was left and right of the mark-one eyeball on the Utrechtseweg.[3]

A Street in Arnhem is the personal story of what it is like to fight a modern war in your own back yard.

CHAPTER 1

The Occupation of the Street

Prologue: Saving Bota

Fighting at night was never as intense as by day. Foot patrols clashed in the gloom. A sudden flurry of German spandau machine gun fire would rip through the darkness answered by stuttering British Bren guns. Flashes outlined rooftops, followed split seconds later by hollow-sounding booms and bangs. Shouts and screams accompanied such exchanges, setting off a crescendo of gunfire. Streaks of tracer flickered and whined off the brickwork of terraced houses, arcing high into the sky. Battle sounds were magnified by the close proximity of buildings and echoed around house blocks. A howling deluge of shellfire would then descend on the identified activity. Multiple crackling detonations spewed out fountains of glowing shrapnel until almost as unexpectedly stillness descended. Soldiers paused, exercising caution, reluctant to attract any more incoming fire. Flares popped into the night sky, producing lengthening shadows as they descended, an eerie curtain call curtailing the violence. Eyes strained to detect any movement within each dark crevice that changed shape as the flares fluttered down. An orange light bathed the ruined houses along the Utrechtseweg in a soft glow before the flare went out. Every shadowy angle was scanned and rechecked for victims worthy of further consideration as the inky blackness reasserted itself.

This was the time to move, before another firefight developed. Black shapes stirred and began to stagger laboriously, picking their way through indistinct back gardens. Every bundle of possessions carried by the awkwardly moving figures seemed to snag noisily against a fence or some other obstacle, further raising tension.

Nine-year-old Wil Rieken at No 178 (formerly 160) Utrechtseweg clutched her straw dog Bota as tightly as she could. She had been hugging him for six days. Her real dog Millie was too big and fat to carry. When the tram from Arnhem to Oosterbeek, running alongside No 178, had hit him, he was that rotund it biffed him out of the way. Wil smiled at the thought. Millie could be 'very naughty', she remembered. He had jumped through the window of the German-occupied Dennenkamp Park villa opposite her house 'and got all kinds of food' before the soldiers had shot him.

Wil felt safe as they picked their way through the ravaged gardens in the gloom because her Daddy was with her. It was the straw dog Bota that needed saving. 'One day I was very frightened,' she admitted; that was after the smoke from the massive explosion at the back of their house cleared to reveal 'the big chestnut tree split into several parts, leaving a big hole in the ground outside.' Part of the house had fallen in a slurry of collapsing brick and tiles. The enormous blast had created a small hole inside their cellar, through which they could see into the back garden. 'We thought the house was on fire because of the red dust,' she remembered. It was time to go.

A solitary German soldier led the way through the gardens, but it had been a grisly start. 'There was a pile of killed German boys in camouflaged jackets up to the wall with our neighbour,' Wil recalled, 'and we had to step over four or five dead Tommies as far as I remember.' The combatants had seemed so very young. She called them all 'boys'. Like the neighbours, the Riekens had bred rabbits to supplement meagre ration coupons. 'My father wanted to open the door of the hutch to let them out,' she remembered, 'but he couldn't undo the door, because there was a dead British boy leaning on it.'

Johan Rieken was heavily laden; Wil walked. Her mother, Jacoba, stumbled alongside carrying what possessions they could manage. Wil held Bota tight because he was obviously scared. 'If you lived in Oosterbeek,' the beautiful leafy suburb bordering Arnhem, she recalled, 'you were prosperous.' But the tree-lined Utrechtseweg with its elegant villas and massive houses and attractive terraces had been transformed into a bleak façade of skeletal ruins, whose cadaverous silhouettes were lit from within by smouldering fires. The pungent smell of burned wood and damp brick-dust permeated everything. Familiar and once friendly-looking house fronts had all their windows and doors blown out, and collapsed roofs

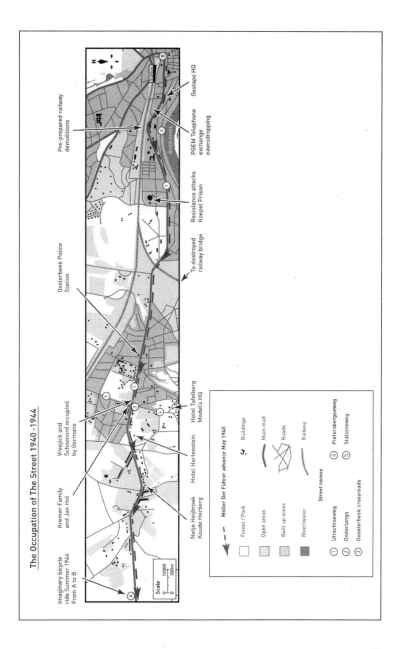

The Occupation of The Street 1940 - 1944

Imaginary bicycle ride Summer 1944 From A to B

Kremer Family and Jan Hol

Vreejick and Schoonord occupied by Germans

Oosterbeek Police Station

Pre-prepared railway demolitions

Gestapo HQ

PGEM Telephone exchange eavesdropping

Resistance attacks Koepel Prison

To destroyed railway bridge

Hotel Tafelberg Model's HQ

Hotel Hartenstein

Netje Heijbroek Koude Herberg

Scale
0   1000ft
0   300m

Möller Der Führer advance May 1940

Forest / Park

Open areas

Built up areas

River/water

Street names

Buildings

Main road

Roads

Railway

① Utrechtseweg
② Onderlangs
③ Oosterbeek crossroads
④ Pietersbergseweg
⑤ Stationsweg

burning inside gave them the appearance of Hallowe'en masks with no eyes. 'We passed the house of one of my friends,' Wil remembered, it was hardly recognisable; Oosterbeek was hardly recognisable. Up ahead, the nervous German soldier challenged every shape that reared up as they wound their way through the shot-up back gardens paralleling the Utrechtseweg. He did not want to be shot by his own men.

'We then crossed the street and went up the Norderweg,' Wil remembered. They climbed the higher ground. 'We could look back down our road and there we saw a flame-thrower moving.' She clutched her straw dog even more tightly. The transformation of the street was startling. The flame-thrower had reached No 178, belching great gouts of flame like a fairy-tale fire-breathing dragon. 'You could see it by the flare and the lights,' she recalled. 'From there we left Oosterbeek and had to walk all the way to Apeldoorn to my grandparents.' They spent a night with friends in an electrician's shop and another in the coconut-mat factory at Beekbergen.

The street she left would never be the same, she reflected. 'Seven Tommies were burned by the flame-thrower in the restaurant nearby. It stopped next door and that's when the Germans came to our house.' The Riekens turned away and trudged on into the night.[4]

*

Wil's street, the Utrechtseweg, was an unnamed dirt road in 1570 that led from Arnhem to Utrecht. The village of Oosterbeek along its route derived its name from the settlement that had coalesced alongside the Ostbac stream, which since Roman times had flowed through the Zweirsdal. In the 10th century a small church was built on the banks of the Lower Rhine River flowing nearby. Commercial activity came from the river, the main transportation artery for huge log-built rafts. After 1600 the road became busier, and oak and beech trees were planted along its verge, providing welcome shade for travellers going through Oosterbeek. By 1820 it had been paved with bricks, and its modern route is clearly identifiable from an 1867 map. Trees were then cut down to the north to make way for the railway line that paralleled the village and the Lower Rhine, flowing

1,000 metres further south. Oosterbeek's first buildings were along the Benedendorpsweg, the road hugging the polder next to the river bank. Next came large mansions and villas built on the high ground to the north of the riverside settlements by ex-colonials who had profited from fortunes made in the Dutch East Indies. In the middle of the 19th century the Utrechtseweg was the road dividing the more wealthy upper northern part of Oosterbeek from the lower southern part. By 1845 Oosterbeek had its own railway station. By the turn of the next century the Utrechtseweg had developed into a charming shopping avenue, forming the town centre. Its beauty and charming prosperity attracted an artists' colony that, preceded by J. W. Bilders and his son Gerard, was to include Paul Gabriël, Joseph Israels, the Matthijs and Mauve brothers, and many others.

During the early 1900s Oosterbeek was a popular tourist venue offering walking tours and exclusive and expensive restaurants. The delightful Westerbouwing patio overlooked pleasure steamers plying their trade on the Lower Rhine. Marching bands paraded along the tree-lined boulevard on Orange Day, the Queen's birthday. The 1920s and early 1930s were the heyday of these popular hotels: the Tafelberg, Wolfheze, Schoonoord and Vreewijk. The Dutch poet van Lennep often stayed at the Schoonoord. 'It was a charming house,' remembered Hendrika van der Vlist, the owner's daughter. 'It breathed repose and tranquillity on the road that in later days was to have so much traffic.' Oosterbeek was a prosperous and exclusive suburb and remained so until the Germans came. Ms Van der Vlist described the white statue of Ceres that stood on the semi-circular hotel lawn of the Schoonoord as 'a sign of a good harvest and prosperity', giving the hotel 'a certain distinction'. Nobody in their wildest imagination living along the street during this balmy period could imagine that one day a battle would be fought here and that the Hotel Schoonoord, a medical dressing station, would be at its very centre.

*

Five-year-old Wil Rieken lived safely in these picturesque and pleasant surroundings. Her father was a baker and local employer. 'We were only allowed to play on this side of the road,' she recalled at No 178 Utrechtseweg, 'opposite a big estate called the Dennenkamp. There was a big lawn between the house there and the road, with deer.' Her father was a well-known local chef and was often asked to cook on Sundays for the big estates around the town. His baker boys were supposed to collect the bills, but the wealthy were often slow to pay. 'Tell the baker next week,' was a common response.

During the Depression the excuse became more commonplace. Hendrika van der Vlist remembers 'difficult years' when 'many guests went abroad; the guilder was strong! A trip along the Rhine cost much less than staying in a Dutch hotel.' Many hoteliers went bankrupt. 'By working hard and by doing things themselves my parents managed to keep their heads above water' and tried to do what they could for their former employees. Women turned up during the slump to earn what little money they could for their families. Hendrika recalled:

> 'In the afternoon they would sit in a big circle in the back garden, peeling potatoes and cleaning vegetables. The slices of bread and butter that they received in the evening they always wrapped up, mostly in newspaper, to take home for the children.'[5]

In the late 1930s economic tensions transitioned to diplomatic. Hitler's Germany reoccupied the demilitarised Rhineland in 1936 and Austria in 1938. Dutch vigilance heightened during the Munich Crisis and increased after Germany annexed the rest of Czechoslovakia in the spring of 1939. A partial Dutch mobilisation was called in April and fully implemented on 24 August 1939, just before Germany declared war on Poland in September. Holland maintained its neutrality despite British and French entry into the war, but invested 900 million guilders in new defence equipment. Some was ordered from Germany, which delayed delivery.

Oosterbeek and the street remained untouched in its quiet rural backwater. The restraint exercised by the Allied Entente and Germany in 1914 was expected to be replicated in the event of another general

European conflict. Potential invasion routes through southern Holland, which were likely to be used to attack France, were ignored. So was the Mechelin incident of January 1940 when German war plans were exposed after one of her aircraft crashed in Belgium. The Dutch convinced themselves that war would not come.

Military preparations were never in evidence along the street, even though Oosterbeek was near the German border. The only conceivable military objectives nearby were the two bridges that spanned the Lower Rhine. The road bridge at Arnhem, finished in 1935, had taken three years to build and replaced the floating pontoon structure that had traditionally accommodated the traffic flow south to Nijmegen. The rail link to Nijmegen crossed the Lower Rhine near Oosterbeek. The town's thrifty inhabitants were more concerned with trade and tourism than with the military, which was rarely seen. Dutch army manoeuvres in 1932 and 1936 had been cancelled as a savings measure. No longer were horse-drawn Dutch artillery trains pulling up outside the Ginkel Inn opposite the heath as they had in 1935. Indeed, only a minority of those eligible for army service in the street were actually called up, and those that did only served 24 weeks. Dutch civilians were in denial over what was happening in Europe, even after Hitler's invasion of Scandinavia in April 1940, which was not preceded by any declaration of war. Holland, unlike north-west Europe, had missed the devastation of 1914-18. An illusion of safe neutrality persisted. The government only began to take the threat seriously when it was too little and too late.

Occupation, May 1940: 'Like Thieves in the Night'

War came suddenly on 10 May 1940 and passed quickly through Oosterbeek. At 04.25 two sharp cracks reverberated across the polderland between Nijmegen and Arnhem. The central span of the road bridge at Nijmegen, completed just four years before to link with the Arnhem road bridge, rose momentarily into the air and collapsed into the River Waal below. The rail bridge alongside also exploded, rocking the entire city. At about the same time the road and rail bridges at Arnhem, the latter well in sight of the Utrechtseweg, followed suit. With a loud crack the

23

KEMA railway viaduct exploded over the Benedendorpsweg alongside the street, and masonry blocked the road, but left the tramline section next to it clear. Everybody on the Utrechtseweg near the Stationsweg was warned to stay indoors when the Dreyense road bridge spanning the railway line at the Oosterbeek-Hoog railway station was blown up. A little seven-year-old blonde girl, Jannie de Weijert, was outside on the Graaf van Rechterenweg nearby, scrambling about in her back garden looking for her cat. She was mortally wounded by the flying debris.

German Fallschirmjäger (paratroopers), peering through their windows as streams of Junkers Ju52 transport aircraft roared overhead, viewed the destruction as senseless. What was the point of raising the drawbridges of 'Fortress Holland' across its waterways, rivers and canals when they could simply fly over? All that the explosions below signified, recalled Hauptmann (Captain) Karl-Lothar Schulz with Fallschirmjäger Regiment 1, was that they were now over enemy territory:

> 'Ahead of us, parallel to our course, is a great waterway. Two bridges span it, a railway bridge and a road bridge. We have hardly glimpsed these bridges when both disappear in a gigantic flash. Grey-black clouds of smoke come rolling up. The bridges are down, the Dutch have blown them. This display is repeated at nearly every bridge we pass. Down there, they seem at last to be aware that the war has begun.'[6]

Thirteen-year-old Dick van t'Land, living in Wolfheze, a mile north of the Utrechtseweg, remembered the 'German aircraft coming over very early'. His parents switched the radio on and they heard 'Warning, Warning, German paratroopers have jumped over The Hague and Rotterdam'. They were on edge the entire day, opting to lie on the living room floor rather than go to bed 'because they expected even more unforeseen things might happen'. The next day they were reassured to see French soldiers passing through Wolfheze en route to Wageningen and the Grebbeberg. 'At first we thought they were French coming to our help,' he remembered, 'but it was the German troops!'[7]

The Germans came from the east, crossing the River Ijssel at Westervoort. Brandenburg commandos disguised as Dutch bicycle infantry attempted to take the bridge by guile, but were arrested and detained. An armoured train, which was a 'Trojan Horse' crammed with German soldiers from the 207th Infantry Division, was shot up by the Dutch defenders manning the old Westervoort fort. It squeaked to a halt, emitting steam in all directions, when the bridge ahead was abruptly blown. Dutch defensive fire was neutralised by two tanks during the costly dinghy river assault conducted by infantry motorcycle combination soldiers from the SS Standarte Der Führer Regiment. The SS troopers clambered across the wrecked bridge superstructure even though it was under fire. Dutch defenders had anticipated holding for days – instead it was all over in 5 hours. By 09.30 the Germans were across. The road to Arnhem, 2½ miles away, was completely open. By 11.00 the lead elements of the SS Der Führer would be on the Utrechtseweg.

At the eastern extremity of the street, nearest the approaching Germans, the local inhabitants were woken by squealing and crashing sounds. There was intense locomotive shunting activity in the De Berg railway marshalling yard. Steam locomotives puffed up and down to the accompaniment of metallic screeches as sections of goods trains were shunted up to the high point of the yard and released piecemeal to crash into assembled goods wagons piled up below.

Bep Bolte, a supervisor with NS (Nederlandse Spoorwegen – Dutch State Railways) lived at No 48 Utrechtseweg overlooking the scene. He recalled 'being given the order to wreck the whole lot'. Organised by the yard's Chief Clerk, Ravenbergen, groups of railwaymen drove locomotives over open points and shunted goods trains into each other. One steam engine was derailed on the turntable east of Arnhem station. 'Just behind my house you have, I reckon, twelve tracks radiating diagonally across,' Bep Bolte recalled, and these were utilised to create the mayhem desired. 'We set up a goods train section there' and, by utilising the natural slope from the Utrecht direction, 'let them run down' onto sections of rail that had been split open below. Soon there were wrecked goods wagons 'piled three on top of one another, as sweet as a nut'. They worked on 'until the whole lot was smashed'. It was anticipated the Germans would not even begin to work out where to start untangling the mess.

Dutch railway staff were carrying out the pre-prepared destruction plan, which was to be conducted in the event of hostilities. This orgy of destruction was replicated at Dutch stations throughout southern Holland. Railway emergency electrician G. Pijkeren watched the destruction from No 91 Noordelijke Parallelweg, where he lived, on the other side of the Arnhem shunting yard. Locomotives bulldozed sections of goods wagons, urgently puffing clouds of dirty grey smoke into the sky as they created mayhem 'piled three wagons high'. Station clerk Pietersma watched the loads being spilled in all directions. 'Turmac tobacco products were scattered everywhere,' he recalled, which 'for me, a railwayman, was a dreadful sight.' Wagon Master D. Dekker watched a locomotive shunter 'working hard to bring about extreme destruction'. German troops were expected within the hour. The locomotive puffed and wheezed back and forth hissing steam, its wheels squealing and slipping as it pulled 25 goods wagons up the slope. Once there they were 'disconnected one by one to smash into goods wagons standing in a dead-end siding'. It was all too much for the wagon shunter working alongside Pietersma – he turned his head away and began to cry.[8]

Platoon commander Oberscharführer (SS Staff Sergeant) Hans Möller recalled his first sight of leafy Oosterbeek. The mission 'was to force a crossing of the Ijssel near Arnhem and then clear snipers from the route of advance Arnhem-Oosterbeek and Renkum.' Essentially his task was to sweep up any resistance along the Utrechtseweg, moving east to west. His platoon was part of the 16th Pionier (Engineer) Company of the SS Der Führer Regiment. There had been a sharp fight to get across the Ijssel River, 5 miles short of the street. Möller's men assisted helming and paddling the inflatable dinghies, a daring enterprise in the face of intense Dutch fire. On reaching Arnhem they stole every Dutch bicycle in sight, which the camouflaged SS troopers continued to do as they swiftly rode along the Utrechtseweg through Oosterbeek. Houses bordering the road were methodically scanned for snipers. Anxious civilian onlookers twitching curtains raised tension. There was no firing until they got beyond Oosterbeek. Following the bloody Westervoort river crossing, there was little compunction about opening fire. Opposition was not to be tolerated – they had to quickly push through. Behind them the ponderously marching infantry of the 207th Division followed up.[9]

Two miles further along the street the first gunfire sounded at Heelsum. The Germans were engaged by Dutch Hussars, who opened fire again at Renkum, another mile beyond. The Hussars formed part of a thin crust of Dutch resistance screening the main Grebbe line, sited across the small foothills of the Utrecht hill ridge. The Grebbeberg was a 165-foot-high Ice Age moraine feature, between Lake Ijssel and the Lower Rhine. The Dutch Army intended to stand here, and soon machine gun fire and artillery inflicted casualties on the III Battalion of Der Führer Regiment. By nightfall the regiment was through the street and closing on Renkum, pushing against the outer limits of the Grebbe line. They were held there for three days.

At the confectioner's shop of No 178 Utrechtseweg, five-year-old Wil Rieken recalled that 'there was a little space between the curtains and the floor in the living room' through which she was able to peer. 'The curtains were too short,' she remembered. 'I was on my knees, by myself, looking through the gap.' Along the road came the lead marching elements of the German 207th Infantry Division. It was early afternoon, Wil recalled,

'…or something like that – we hadn't had lunch and the shop was closed. The thing I remember best, and I still don't like to think about it, is marching legs. They had boots and gaiters and that was the part I saw.'

The arrival of multiple legs was incongruously accompanied by deep singing.

'I liked the singing, but I don't like marching legs, still today. I started crying because I was alone in the room. My Dad came in, because my Mum was always in the shop. The sounds of marching outside in the road had frightened me.'

Johan Rieken comforted his disturbed daughter. She was not the only onlooker depressed at the arrival of the Germans. Seventeen-year-old Harry van Gorkum remembers 10 May, 30 minutes by car away, to the north, at Apeldoorn.

'It was totally demoralising, it was one of the worst things. I'll never forget all these Germans marching in. And of course they were all in frightfully good order whereas the Dutch Army was not in such a terribly good state. That was monstrous. We thought it wouldn't last very long. Optimism really – but what was reality? Nobody knew. We hadn't been involved in the First World War and this was the first war since Napoleon!'

The occupation of Oosterbeek was soon over. Farmer J. Peelen was hit by a stray bullet 3 miles further along the street at Renkum, having left to milk his cows at 5 o'clock in the afternoon. At Heveadorp, a mile south of the Utrechtseweg near the Westerbouwing, Corrie Geerink was hit by a machine gun round on his way to meet his girlfriend. Because they had been spared the devastation of the 1914-18 war, the Dutch stayed at home, unlike the French and Belgians, and impassively watched the Blitzkrieg roll by. There was no resistance in the street. Only at Renkum did the skirmishing become so dangerous that a few villagers fled their homes. By the evening of Saturday 11 May the first Dutch prisoners from the Grebbe line were walking back through the street at Oosterbeek on their way to Arnhem railway station and transportation to Germany.

'Everyone was talking about it,' remembered Wil Rieken at No 178, 'and everyone thought it would not last long because our army was in Wageningen [8 miles away] and fighting was going on.' Her parents were visibly upset 'but they didn't like to discuss nasty things in front of the children'. Nobody knew what was going on. 'You could hear them talking about it when I was in bed,' she recalled. Before long 'the Germans came to the shop and marched through the house.' She did not like this peremptory entry. They wanted Johan Rieken's cooperation. 'I do know they offered some food so that they could use the bakery, but my father refused it of course.'

They were in a hopeless predicament. Holland capitulated four days after the Germans marched down the street. 'Sometimes you can't refuse,' Wil Rieken insisted. Might had become right. 'The Germans wanted to do some baking in our oven and they forced Father to do so – he was never friendly with them – but sometimes you just can't refuse.'

'It was dreadful to hear that the Queen had left,' recalled Harry van Gorkum. 'We were pleased she had gone to England – we were total anglophiles, especially my family.' The inhabitants of the street were left directionless. News came from the radio, which was avidly followed. 'We had that strange period of not having a government, but we were used to that' in Holland, van Gorkum claimed. 'We had so many parties that we often had months of no government.' The bewildered inhabitants of Oosterbeek carried on much as before.[10]

In Wolfheze, a mile north of the street, Dick van t'Land remembered that one of the local Nederveluwe clinic buildings was commandeered for use as a field dressing station. Wounded from the Grebbeberg fighting were brought back, 'but remained only a short time'. Refugees from Wageningen stayed only momentarily. 'On the whole life in the occupied Netherlands carried on completely as normal,' he recalled. 'It was actually a very quiet period.'[11]

War swiftly passed them by. Nijmegen to the south was the first city to be captured by the Germans and they took it within hours. Sixteen-year-old Miep Minis-Dijkstra, living at the customs post at Beck, remarked that 'there were hardly any Dutch soldiers in sight'. After a brief period of gunfire the Germans passed through, then 'there was nobody to see'. The Blitzkrieg was impressive. German soldiers seemed imbued with superhuman martial qualities and were natural organisers, unlike their own government.

G. Pijkeren watched the Germans promptly clear up the mess in the shunting yards opposite No 48 Utrechtstraat. 'Some rolling stock with broken axles can't be put back on the tracks, so the Germans just dumped them next to the railway line.' Once the troops had passed along the street, German railway officials turned up and took over the depot.

'Clearing the derailments only took 11 days,' Pijkeren remembered. The main part of the havoc was cleared in less.[12]

Twenty-year-old Jaap Jansen had only served four months' conscription with the Dutch infantry when 'the Germans struck on May 10th, like thieves in the night'. His experience was atypical, before coming back to Oosterbeek to resume his work as a garage mechanic in Arnhem. 'The enemy didn't show up,' he recalled. They chased German phantoms near a large expanse of flat land near Bussum, which could have been used as an airfield. 'We hung about twiddling our thumbs' and did not see a single German. When a local civilian pipe-layer dug up the field, Jansen's unit was sent toward Amsterdam. 'Whether it was meant to be a strategic fallback or part of some brilliant offensive plan I never learned.' The Army had already capitulated. 'It was all over. Just like that. Very disappointing.'[13]

The Utrechtseweg was simply an east-west conduit for the German advance towards Utrecht and the coast beyond – an unremarkable, if pretty, village that singing German infantry marched through during the glorious 'Führer-weather' that characterised the Blitzkrieg campaign in the west. The only other traffic was Dutch prisoners coming back. Dutchmen were indignant at this breach of their cherished neutrality, but they were a pragmatic people. German soldiers did not attract immediate opprobrium; besides, their military performance had been impressive. National Socialist sympathisers like Jan K. living in Arnhem observed that 'German soldiers showed themselves to be extremely fair and disciplined, that was the case, and my memory of it remained just the same until the end'.[14] They docilely queued alongside Dutch women in confectionery shops at Arnhem to buy chocolate, which was rationed in Germany. 'I do remember the uniforms,' recalled young Wil Rieken. 'They were really gentle toward the children, it was not really frightening.' Her fear had been their unexpected entry, 'those legs, the streets were OK to play for me.'

Concern among adults transitioned to the business of purloining the basic necessities for life. Wil's family profited from their semi-rural location because they were able to procure extra food from local farmers.

Her aunt provided a large Gouda cheese. 'It was kept in a room upstairs and sometimes my Mum cut a little piece off,' she recalled. 'If we were forced to evacuate it was my job to carry it in a pillow case to go to my grandparents in Apeldoorn.' There was less chance the Germans would bother to stop and search a little girl. 'It was very heavy to carry for a nine-year-old, I can tell you.'

Dutch hotelier Jan Kilkens remembered that the Germans 'were not the immediate enemy' during the early days, 'so long as we did not bother them'. Hitler ordered the release of Dutch prisoners of war as a conciliatory gesture and people started to relax. Jan K.'s family had been in the National Socialist NSB (Nationaal Socialische Beweging) since its founding in the early 1930s. 'We were real "Orange-fans",' he claimed, and 'very nationalistic'. So 'we were very disappointed to discover that the Royal Family had already disappeared in a few days, with the government in tow.' The NSB would quadruple to 80,000 members after the occupation, but only 1% of the population would ever join. The newly installed German occupation authority, headed by the former Austrian Chancellor Arthur Seyss-Inquart, promised to retain living standards and improve employment. Some people like Jan K. accepted the changed circumstances. 'The Netherlands were occupied,' he recalled, 'but actually not much happened to disturb us.' Others, like an interpreter who placed an advert in the local Arnhem newspaper as a 'German Translator' immediately grasped opportunities. Civil servants not prepared to accept foreigners 'giving orders' resigned or were sacked. Hotelier Jan Kilkens explained the degree of pragmatism that reigned:

'The doorman opened the door for anybody, like he had for years before. The bell boys did the things they had to do, the porter did the things he had to do, everybody from the highest to the lowest did the job that he did.'[15]

Nothing changed along the Utrechtseweg. The trams still ran and people commuted along its length to Arnhem or Renkum. It looked much the same as it had before the war.

Occupation, Summer 1944

An imaginary bicycle ride along the Utrechtseweg four summers later provides a useful marker of what changed during four years of German occupation. As Harry van Gorkum pointed out, the journey by this time would not have benefited from the comfort of pneumatic tyres. 'We had bicycles,' he recalled, 'but no tyres; little wooden blocks acted as tyres, attached with pieces of wire.' The condition of the ubiquitous Dutch bicycle by this fourth year of the war mirrored the shortages, discomfort and irritations that now prevailed along the street.

Riding from west to east the cyclist had first to ensure he had an identity card, which contained a photograph and fingerprint. He might be stopped at any moment to show it after they were introduced on 1 October 1940. A large letter 'J' stamped inside identified if the holder was a Jew. The Germans thereby managed at a stroke to register all the Jews in Holland by guile, because the ID card was accepted without any thought of sinister implications. By May 1942 Jews were obliged to display a yellow Jewish star on their clothing. Dutch Jewish teenager Rita Boas-Koupmann recalled that her mother had ignored her eldest son's advice to get out in 1940. 'I must wait for the man who brings the laundry,' she insisted. 'What would you want me to escape from? I want to stay in my house.' Politics was not her concern. 'What should the Germans do to me?' her mother asked. She did not survive the war.[16]

In the wooded area at the western end of Utrechtseweg, there was a sign showing the turn off to Wolfheze, just outside Oosterbeek. It read: 'Municipality of Renkum. Restricted freedom of movement for Jews.' Other signs in the walking areas around the Bildeberg woods were ripped off, and someone once altered the sign to read 'Prohibited for Germans'. Another occupation landmark was the railway spur constructed along a 5-mile stretch from Wolfheze station to Deelen airfield to the north. This 'bomb line' was completed in 1941 to carry building materials but primarily ammunition, bombs, anti-aircraft guns, aircraft parts and aviation fuel to the German airbase.[17]

When the cyclist rode along he might look up on hearing a low droning noise. High above were the distant vapour trails of four-engined Allied bombers heading east towards the Ruhr and Berlin. They were en route to Moffrica, the Dutch nickname for Germany, whose inhabitants were derisorily called Moffen. The street was under the main Allied flight route. German fighter interceptors from Deelen would seek to engage them, and the heavy flak around the airbase would invariably crash out as the high-flying bombers traversed this outer ring of the Reich's air defences. An aircraft had made an emergency landing near Castle Doorwerth nearby, and a British bomber had crashed near Heelsum in July 1942, killing two crew.

'The first couple of months of the German occupation wasn't too bad,' recalled Harry van Gorkum, living just to the north at Apeldoorn, 'then it started.' The implications of this would not be lost on the cyclist. 'It was bad,' van Gorkum explained, 'because you weren't allowed to do what you wanted to do. There were all sorts of rules and regulations and then the terrible thing with the Jews happened.' The cyclist saw arrays of signs and posters that told him about blackout and curfew measures. Everyone had to take care not to expose light from houses between sundown and sunrise. Propaganda posters warned people to stay indoors because 'British airmen have no mercy for peaceful citizens'. The Queen's Birthday on 31 August was often surreptitiously celebrated in subtle ways. Three bathing suits were hung on the washing line on the Kerkpad, just south of the Utrechtseweg, one red, and the others white and blue, displaying the Dutch national colours. Orange ribbons and bows were often confiscated by the Germans. Another common symbol was the 'V For Victory' sign, celebrating Churchill's iconic gesture. German 'V' posters were pasted up as a response, proclaiming 'Victory on all Fronts'. But this was becoming less plausible from late 1943 onwards. Dutch Police Constable Venema at the Heelsum end of the street was told to remove all the 'V' posters, which he did, including the German ones. Amusing though this harmless psychological sparring was, it did not cloak the extent to which life had become increasingly grim for the inhabitants of the Utrechtseweg by the fourth year of occupation. One man in Oosterbeek was arrested and imprisoned for two years for being in possession of a large number of photos of the Dutch Royal Family.[18]

Little was happening or indeed did happen along the leafy stretch of the street where it entered Oosterbeek. There was virtually no traffic, only the odd wood-gas-burning lorry or car passing by. The scarcity of petrol and the German penchant for abruptly commandeering cars and buses kept traffic to a minimum. People generally travelled by train. During the first three years of the occupation rail passenger numbers more than doubled from 95 to 232 million. Lorry-loads of German soldiers occasionally moved past on their way to the Harskamp training area to the north, coming from the SS Unterführerschule Arnheim based at the Willemskaserne (Barracks) at Arnhem. The primary road users remained cyclists.

Many of the hotels the cyclist passed in Oosterbeek town centre had been taken over by the local authorities to house first evacuees, then German soldiers. When the Germans began to fortify the Netherlands coastal regions in 1942, the inhabitants were evicted. These included 135,000 people from The Hague alone, forcibly evacuated when their homes were demolished to make way for defence works. Elderly folk and incomplete families unable to move themselves found themselves arriving at Arnhem station on special evacuation trains, where in December 1942 they were taken to the Schoonoord and Tafelberg hotels. As Hendrika van der Vlist recalled:

> 'Our house was requisitioned by our government to provide a home for aged people in The Hague. At that time we thought it terrible… The hotel was crowded with aged people. From time to time father went there to have a look. When he returned he was always in low spirits; the house was getting into a terribly run-down condition.'

The family was obliged to leave and take refuge in accommodation opposite. Then in April 1943 the Wehrmacht took over the Schoonoord and installed a telephone exchange. The Van der Vlists were told to continue furnishing it.[19]

As the cyclist rode on more and more tangible signs illustrated the extent to which the street's inhabitants were clandestinely exploited to support the Reich's war effort. There were German boarding schools and health resorts for women from the bombed-out cities in the Ruhr. Oosterbeek temporarily supported a Mütterheim (maternity home) for expectant German mothers, so they could enjoy the final six weeks of confinement in relative peace, comfort and safety. The inhabitants of the street were increasingly frustrated as each new measure took a cumulative toll, with still little sign of Allied progress. Harry van Gorkum described the interminable stand-off:

'After the 1940 invasion we thought it would be a couple of months. That it lasted so long was an enormous disappointment. It didn't look like the Allies were going to win for a couple of years. All the good Allied ships were sunk, the Americans did not want to come into the war and the British were very brave but not very successful. The only success started in Africa.'[20]

The cyclist would have monitored events with growing optimism on his illegal radio. Five times each day the BBC broadcast Radio Oranje, a 15-minute Dutch language broadcast with news and commentary. Jaap Jansen, living in Wolfheze, described the transmissions as 'getting an earful of freedom'. Listening to London was forbidden by the Germans from 4 July 1940, but could not be effectively monitored so in May 1943 all radio sets had to be handed in to the authorities. They were stored in the Arnhem synagogue at Pastoorstraat, the ultimate indignity. 'We were sitting in Holland and officially we could not hear the English news,' remembered Harry van Gorkum. 'We did – but that was another thing.' Jansen claimed that 'Radio Oranje kept our hope alive.' His family bypassed the edict by delivering his 'written-off' radio to Pastoorstraat in Arnhem and 'kept our new one, a huge Phillips'. Ironically the requisitioned radios were carefully stored from floor to ceiling in the synagogue and properly administered. The aim was to give them back to their original owners at Endsieg, or 'Final Victory'. 'In our house,' Jansen remembered, 'the clandestine receiver was hidden in a dummy compartment within one of the deep closets separating the main rooms.' 'Finding a forbidden radio set brings a severe punishment with it,' recalled Hendrika van der Vlist at No 186 Utrechtseweg. It could cost two years in prison or a swingeing fine of 100,000 guilders (45,000 euros) and the radio would be impounded. 'The thin rag of paper on which the BBC news has been typewritten has become a most dangerous thing,' she claimed.[21]

As the cyclist rode by the Utrechtseweg crossroads in the centre of Oosterbeek, there was little ostensible sign of the occupation apart from uniformed comings and goings from the requisitioned hotels. Most memories of the occupation years recall long periods of uneventful normality interspersed with interfering minor notices that announced the latest petty restriction. 'We lived normal lives,' explained Wil Rieken, 'until just now and then something would happen.' Those sinister happenings were more apparent the nearer one got to Arnhem. She remembered:

> 'Young people think something is happening all the time. It was not like that. There would be a long time and then something bad would happen.'[22]

The sheer monotony of the occupation was depressing. 'The Black Market is thriving,' observed Hendrika van der Vlist at No 186. 'Is there anyone who still lives on the rations he gets for his coupons?' She doubted so – gentleman's shoes cost 150 guilders (£50), a pound of butter was 50 guilders (£17) and a single egg might fetch 1 guilder 50 cents (50p). 'A lot of people did become dejected' with the stultifying German presence and lack of Allied progress, recalled Harry van Gorkum, 'and depression sets in easy if you are hungry and cold.' Life was tedious, then suddenly the 'something' would occur. 'A knock on the door may bring the fatal message "Dress and come!"' recalled Van der Vlist. 'Many fellow villagers have already been roused from their beds by the Quisling militia or some other hostile authority.' Only those who have lived through an occupation can appreciate the constant anxiety, vulnerability and dread that can accompany the unexpected nocturnal knock at the door.

On approaching the bridge where the Nijmegen railway crosses the Utrechtseweg before traversing the massive rail bridge over the Lower Rhine, the cyclist had reached the point where the leafy suburb of Oosterbeek transitions to the suburbs of western Arnhem. To the right the chimney stacks of the Nijmegen power station can be clearly seen 11 miles away across the flat polderland in between. On 22 February 1944 a vast pall of smoke would be seen billowing up into the sky from across the Nijmegen-Waal waterfront. This was Oosterbeek's first unsettling glimpse of what war could mean for them. The American 446th Bomber Group mistook the Munster, Goch and Kleve enclave along the River Rhine for that of Entschede, Deventer, Arnhem and Nijmegen along the Lower Rhine and River Waal. Eight hundred people died, as many as the Luftwaffe had killed at Rotterdam. What lay beneath the awful column of black oily smoke could only be imagined. Miep Minis-Dijkstra, who witnessed the catastrophic destruction of Nijmegen town centre, knew:

'Everyone tried to help, but where to go? It was complete chaos. One saw people in open carts because there was nothing else available – there were no ambulances. Everything we had had been requisitioned and taken to Germany. And then we saw people all over the place missing bits of arms and legs. It was a real misery!'[23]

The overspill from this massive bombing error hit the gas works in Oosterbeek and van Ommeron's paint and glass company to the south of the street and Arnhem. Seventeen houses were destroyed and 21 others badly damaged, with 57 people killed. The war breathed lightly on the street, giving its inhabitants much food for thought.

Who could the cyclist truly trust? Jews were certainly more vulnerable the nearer one got to Arnhem. The round-ups had begun in the autumn of 1942, and 105,000 of Holland's 140,000 Jews were to perish. The Arnhem civil register and Red Cross records reveal that a total of 2,256 Jews lived in and around Arnhem during the occupation. The major arrests occurred on 10 December 1942, when 959 were picked up and held at ten local assembly points. Johan van der Kamp saw one of the groups being taken away. 'They stood by the Dommering café – a long line of people. But we were not allowed to get any closer.' They spent the night in a school at the western end of the Utrechtseweg. He recalled:

'We dashed to Sonsbeeksingel. Don't ask me why. We saw the train pass by. Of course it was pointless.'

The arrests and detentions continued into 1943, so that at the war's end some 1,300 had been murdered or died of starvation and disease in concentration camps.[24]

The cyclist had to be wary of being plucked from his bicycle during the random mass arrests that accompanied the German searches for forced labour, which began in early 1942. Any public place was vulnerable, including church congregations and particularly railway stations like that at Arnhem, where haphazardly selected pressed men were spirited away to Germany. One enduring memory for Hendrika van der Vlist was the sight of 'the many, many men dragged from their work to do slave labour in Germany against their wishes and against their conscience'.

When Mr H. M. Otten arrived by train at Arnhem station 'shortly before eight o'clock' on 12 June 1944 on his way to work he was confronted in the station concourse by a German soldier 'with his rifle at the ready [who] ordered me to stand against the wall with my hands up.' He joined a group that rapidly ballooned with more casual arrests, 'exactly how many I don't know'. Otten managed to spot a colleague getting off the train from Ede and urgently asked him to alert Otto Prins, managing the shipbuilding company for which he worked, to intercede on his behalf. 'After about 45 minutes he turned up and, after a conversation with the soldiers, he collected me.' Otten was lucky. He was in a reserved occupation, but some 30,000 of his countrymen were not, and were taken away during the occupation. More than six million of these labourers were to be press-ganged from all over Europe to provide the cornerstone of the German economy. Western Zwangsarbeiter, or forced labourers, were treated better than their eastern counterparts, who endured slavery conditions in concentration camps. They were at least housed in spartan barracks that boasted a bunk and wardrobe, but there was little or no pay. Tens of thousands of Dutchmen went into hiding 'like criminals', as Ms Van der Vlist described it, to escape conscripted labour, obliged 'to conceal themselves and avoid the daylight'. All along the street were men aged between 18 and 40, who kept out of sight by day.[25]

Bep Bolte, the railway supervisor who lived at No 48 Utrechtstraat next to the Arnhem shunting yard, recalled that 'all those trains came past carrying the people who had been taken prisoner' to Germany. 'They threw small notes from the train.' Corrie, his wife, 'had seen what was going on and took the dog for a walk alongside the track, where she recovered the scraps of paper,' which normally had an address. They had to be cautious. Envelopes were stamped and addressed but 'posted at another location, never in Arnhem,' so that the anxious families had at least an inkling of what had happened to their missing loved ones. 'We made no mention of the sender,' he emphasised. 'You can understand, you didn't do that'.[26]

After passing the St Elizabeth Hospital, the Utrechtseweg continues to Arnhem Station square. Immediately before the hospital the cyclist would see the distinctive 19th-century dome of the Koepel prison rising above the rooftops. This is the point along the street beyond which unpleasant things could happen, where the shadowy world of the Resistance was more apparent. The Koepel prison was used to remand criminals and detain suspects for the Geheime Staats Polizei, or German Gestapo, before they were moved to Germany by train. Two Dutch resistance raids were carried out against the Koepel on 18 February and 11 May 1944. In the first raid a small group of Dutchmen disguised as SD (Sicherheitsdienst) security men bluffed their way inside to free a resistance man they claimed was wanted 'for questioning'. He was released into their custody. Incredibly a similar ploy was successful three months later. Two men disguised as Dutch policemen entered with a 'captive', pulled pistols and took two important Resistance men from their cells. The group drove off along the Utrechtseweg to Oosterbeek, where they split and went into hiding.[27]

The shady Resistance struggle worked both ways. National Socialist sympathiser Jan K. recalled his school class teacher being murdered in Arnhem 'as retaliation' following another NSB killing in the same neighbourhood days before. 'Generally,' Jan K. explained, these were NSB sympathisers who played no particular role, so their killings were 'completely senseless'. He had two brothers among the 25,000 Dutchmen who served with SS Freiwillige units on the Eastern Front. Only half of them came back; his oldest brother was killed, and the other lost a leg. 'Actually we were fighting against Communism, something that happened before the war,' he explained. The cyclist would have sensed these conflicting undercurrents in the street. Much was left unsaid because opinions were dangerous. Harry van Gorkum's viewpoint was crystal clear: 'The Germans did everything possible to make themselves thoroughly hated,' he claimed. 'They had very little chance not to be hated,' which echoed the majority view. When Wil Rieken's father, running the bakery at No 178 Utrechtseweg, discovered that one of his female assistants was dating a German boy, she was told that her future employment depended on her giving him up.

Past the Museum at No 88 Utrechtstraat was Gestapo HQ at No 85, with the Gelderland Provincial Electricity Board (PGEM) offices opposite.[28] The cyclist would have been wary approaching this sinister area because the SD interrogation rooms were in the cellars at No 85. An Arnhem Resistance group had been rounded up very early at the end of 1940 and the beginning of 1941. Names and addresses had been swiftly uncovered, resulting in 30 people being executed or sent to concentration camps. Nobody trusted anybody. John Wunderlink recalled that the golden rule in his group after this unfortunate experience was:

> 'No one knows anyone else's name; if I had to contact someone I
> was never given a name, only a distinguishing mark or password.'

Unbeknown to the Germans, the Dutch Resistance was listening in to the telephone exchange inside the PGEM building. People on the 'wanted' list – Jews or suspected resistance members – were brought to the same location for interrogation.

The infamous SD or Gestapo headquarters was dreaded, and a part of the street to be avoided. Phillip X. Olivier worked in the Huis van Bewaring remand jail in Walburgstraat nearby, and was familiar with the SD staff, who worked at both locations. He recalled SS Oberscharführer (Staff-Sergeant) Mack, who tended to dispatch all his detainees – whatever the excuses – to Germany via Amersfoort concentration camp. 'Young and old, sick or fit, it made no difference to him. Es gibt nur ein weg … Amersfoort – there was only one way, to Amersfoort, he used to say,' Olivier recalled. 'We had to hear it umpteen times a day.' The Sonderkommando or Special Action head was Walther Beck, an 'intensely vicious and suspicious' man who, according to Olivier, 'on his own admission had scrapped the word "pity" from his vocabulary.' Beck spoke Dutch well, having worked as a waiter in the Netherlands before the war. 'He thought it wonderful if or when a group of Dutch people were shot,' which as far as he was concerned 'should happen more often, then perhaps they might learn.'[29]

A man who chose not to follow the advice was Johan Penseel, who began his resistance career filling Wehrmacht vehicles with water mixed with petrol when they passed through in May 1940. In March 1943 he was severely beaten in the SD cells as a Resistance suspect. 'I was questioned by the SD at Utrechtseweg, after which I was thrown unconscious into my cell in the Huis van Bewaring' on Walburgstraat. A young 17-year-old shared his cell. 'He was a plant,' Penseel recalled, 'put in each cell in turn to try to worm information out of prisoners. Penseel 'told him the same lies I had told the SD,' which meant with no incriminating evidence he was released a few weeks later. He was an electrician and a member of the Arnhem LKP Resistance, who organised safe houses for Jews, sabotaged German electrical installations and gathered valuable intelligence.[30]

The raid on the Huis van Bewaring jail on Sunday 11 June 1944 was the most successful freeing of political prisoners during the Dutch occupation. It illustrated the unseen and little-known nature of the activity that was occasionally conducted along the street. Planning took place at Wolfheze and at the t'Hemeldal villa, at the western extremity of the Utrechtseweg, near the Koude Herberg crossroads, while its execution was in Arnhem's western suburb. Three attempts were aborted during May and early June until, on the 11th, nine people in civilian clothes forced an entry through the Jail Director's office. They were led by a bogus Pastor and 'wife'. Pistols were pulled out and the group got inside, but as one of the raiders, Joop Abbink, recalled, they burst into the day room 'and everywhere were ladies in negligees'. Not only was this unexpected, 'I was terribly shocked,' he explained, 'because at the time such things were highly unusual.' It was a quaint chivalrous statement that belied the brutality of the times and situation. 'As a gentleman, you shouldn't see such things,' Abbink insisted. The ladies were requested to dress and the cell doors opened. The raid was coolly organised and conducted. They got the political prisoners out through the director's office and presented each one with an envelope containing 10 guilders and a vital ration card. Fifty-six of them walked out, mainly Resistance people, mingling with the Sunday church worshippers leaving the Saint Eusebius Church nearby.[31]

Thus far the war had been long, monotonous and uneventful for the people of the street. Jaap Jansen travelled its length each day from his house in Wolfheze to the garage in Arnhem where he worked, repairing mainly German vehicles. By the end of 1943 he was beginning to appreciate that the German propaganda claim of 'winning on all fronts' was 'painting too rosy a picture'. He found himself converting ever more German vehicles to run on wood-gas. 'I thought this could mean only one thing: Herr Hitler was literally scraping the bottom of the fuel barrel.' Rumours and propaganda abounded with few certainties. 'At last in June 1944, the event we had awaited for so long came to pass,' Jansen remembered. 'The Allied forces had landed in Normandy!' Radio Oranje transmitted the news. There was now a second front on the mainland of Western Europe.

> 'We hoped they would soon break out. But they were still far away. And the Germans were still here. No signs of panic or impending change.'[32]

Life on the street carried on much as before.

CHAPTER 2

Anxious Days

Coming or going? The Germans

Although it remained quiet on the street in late August, the SS NCO
School Arnheim was suddenly dispatched 'in double-quick time'
to the River Waal, according to its commander SS Standartenführer
(Colonel) Hans-Michael Lippert. His task was to sweep up German
troops fleeing Belgium and check the retreats flooding across the road
bridge at Zaltbommel and the steam river ferry at Gorinchen. After two
months of bloody stalemate in Normandy, the whole tenor of the western
campaign had changed. Lieutenant Colonel Fritz Fullriede, commanding
a Hermann Göring Training Regiment spread across Holland, wrote in
his diary that 'the whole West Front has collapsed, the others march
where they will, and us and our big mouth over our Atlantic Wall'.
When the SS NCO School drove along the Utrechtseweg in its mixed
bag of commandeered transport to go to war, the young NCOs probably
thought they would never return to their familiar comfortable haunt, the
Willemskaserne Barracks at Arnhem. The street remained unremarkable,
simply the way to somewhere: Belgium or the Channel coast.

The SS trainees were faced with a sobering scene on arrival at
Zaltbommel and Gorinchen. The 34-year-old Lippert was reminded of a
similar catastrophe in 1918 as he took in the scenes of panic unfolding
before him. The width and depth of the fast-moving Waal River aided
their mission. It could only be crossed via the existing bridges or by ferry.
'At these two crossing places,' he recalled, 'fleeing troops pushed and
shoved and became dammed up in a chaos of countless vehicles loaded
with all sorts of goods, and not just military hardware.' Every person,
civilian or military, was obliged to show a valid movement order. Some
3,000 soldiers who could not were gathered at Woudenburg nearby. Self-
contained and complete units were passed on to the Netherlands High

Command chain. Lippert gave a rallying address to the dubious flotsam he had collected in the market place at Thiel. Disturbing explanations were offered about their flight. 'Their commanders had advised them to throw their weapons away because fighting and dying was senseless,' Lippert recalled. These excuses could not be checked or condemned 'because I myself had seen officers trying to flee over the Waal'. By the end of August the traffic flow had normalised, petering out with each passing day.[33]

Fritz Fullriede's diary entries for the first two weeks of September 1944 give an insight into the mindset of the German soldier in southern Holland faced with impending catastrophe. He was the commanding officer of a Training and Replacement Regiment 12,000 strong, penny-packaged into battalion-size detachments that were spread about to dam the retreat. His personal role became to move around southern Holland to advise and coordinate the deployments of these units. The loss of Paris then Brussels, two months after an attempted assassination attempt on Hitler in July, suggested that the war may already be lost. Fullriede discussed future prospects with a group of officers at one of the barracks. 'The Western Front is finished,' he confided to his diary on 2 September. 'The enemy is already in Belgium and on the German border; Romania, Bulgaria, Slovakia and Finland are asking for peace.' The auguries were disturbing: 'It's exactly like it was in 1918,' he concluded. Whether the Führer was supported or not, the scale of the latest set-backs was testing the resolve of the German soldier. It was difficult to comprehend that only two years had passed since the Wehrmacht had dominated Europe from the North Cape to the Caucasus, and that now the border of the 'Thousand-Year Reich' itself was under threat. The implications of all this had yet to sink in.

There had been mistrust inside the German High Command ever since the plot on Hitler's life. Fullriede was especially cynical about his superiors, complaining that his II Battalion was 'falsely deployed and stabbed in the back by its neighbour'. This resulted in its encirclement and a three-day battle during which it was 'practically wiped out'. Only a few shattered remnants got out and 'it was all the absolute fault of this joke of a higher command'.[34]

Many German soldiers, like 19-year-old newly commissioned Leutnant Joseph Enthammer, part of a V2 rocket inspection team, were on the run through Belgium. His men, recently trained at Peenemünde, commandeered a rubbish collection cart to escape being overrun by US troops. They drove for Nijmegen but crashed into a Luftwaffe lorry en route, which killed seven of their 12-strong group. Enthammer was knocked unconscious and left behind to recover. Mindful of the ire his rocket unit status would attract, he stole a horse on awakening and followed on; he later traded the horse for a moped, tying it to the spot in exchange. He made it to Nijmegen after being filled up by German panzers en route, and reported to the Sammelstelle, or 'collection point', where he was told that his unit was setting up in a small 'well-to-do' village called Oosterbeek outside Arnhem.35

The cream of the German western combat leadership and troops had perished in Normandy. Fullriede recalled that 'from Germany one heard only distressing news about bombed-out cities and so on.' The Russians were closing in on the Reich's eastern borders. Fullriede was bitter, complaining that it was 'unbelievable to hear laughing and jokes at the First Fallschirmjäger Army HQ at Vught about the loss of so many of our soldiers.' Encircled pockets fought on, trusting to relief, 'but our luckless Higher Command Headquarters left the gallant fellows in the lurch' and 'wounded officers and men who had given up were mainly shot by the Belgians with the permission of the English.' The bridges at Grave and Nijmegen he noticed were insufficiently protected and not properly prepared for demolition. The front appeared to be collapsing. 'It was criminal,' Fullriede reflected, and 'it was just as well that those in Germany do not appreciate how senselessly and irresponsibly their young were offered up for sacrifice.'

'I do not know what is wrong with the Moffen,' wrote Father Hermanus Bruggeman on 5 September near Johannahoeve Farm, 2 kilometres north of the Utrechtseweg:

'The Amsterdamseweg was crowded; Moffen cars, horses with wagons, all different sorts of vehicles, even prams, and they were all heading for Arnhem. People say that the Germans are running and that the English are already at Wijchen. We heard a couple of explosions in that direction; could that be the English? We can hardly believe it. Who knows, we may be free tomorrow. Why not? Belgium was freed in a couple of days.'

On 2 September Seyss-Inquart, the Reichskommissar in Holland, ordered all Reichsdeutscher German civilians to return to Germany. This immediately caused a panic among the NSB pro-German Dutch inhabitants, who gathered their wives and children and fled. Fullriede recalled 'a sad train of Dutch National Socialists moving through Utrecht by night, evacuated to Germany to avoid the hatred of the Dutch. Many women and children.'[36]

'Dolle Dinsdag', or 'Mad Tuesday', signified to the Dutch that Germany had probably been defeated. Dutch National Socialist Jan K. watched endless columns pass by on the Velperplein in Arnhem, just across from the main road bridge. 'I was pretty sober about these things,' he recalled, 'but thought the Germans had definitely lost the war.' Processions of vehicles were pouring north up the road from Nijmegen to Arnhem, where they turned east for Germany. Unruly groups of soldiers stole horses, wagons, cars and bicycles. Dutch spectators watched trucks, farm wagons, hand carts and even prams pass by, piled high with loot ranging from furniture to lingerie, filched from France, Belgium and Luxembourg. On the Utrechtseweg, 38-year-old chemical engineer Jan Voskuil saw 'utter confusion' as dozens of German trucks, dangerously overloaded, drove by. Soldiers on bicycles accompanied them, 'pedalling furiously, with suitcases looped over their handlebars.' The Moffen were in retreat.[37]

Appearances could, however, be deceptive. These men were the Tross, or baggage, of the defeated armies in Normandy. They had got out while the hinges of the Falaise gap had been held open by the combat troops. Mixed among them were German civilians and Dutch National Socialists fleeing inevitable retribution from the resurgent population. They looked like a totally defeated force, but the fighting soldiers had already been siphoned off from the retreating columns at the Waal bridge and ferry sites.

The gap torn in the German line by the rapid Allied advance into Belgium was filled by a swift insertion of the so-called First Fallschirmjäger (Parachute) Army commanded by General Kurt Student. They were a hodge-podge of air force technical and ground personnel and other units swept up during the retreat and cadred within infantry companies and battalions led by Fallschirmjäger veterans. A new German front rapidly coalesced in southern Holland populated by the final intakes taken from the final reserves of available German manpower. There were teenagers mixed with father-figure older age groups released from previously protected civil occupations. 'Stomach and Ear' units were formed from men with dietary disorders or hearing problems, or recovering from wounds. Scattered among them were the so-called Veruckte-Helmuts, or 'Crazy Helmuts', men who had lost loved ones or entire families to Allied bombing and the Russian advances in the east. They were bitterly determined to sell their lives dearly. German veterans by this stage of the war fought for each other, rather than for the regime, and were bonded together within Kampfgruppe or combat groups personalised by the name of their commander. Men fought for the Kampfgruppe Lippert, Chill, Wossowsky or Möller. Although the war was lost in strategic terms, soldiers had yet to countenance a 'year zero' scenario, when the Thousand-Year Reich might be overrun by foreign invaders. The urgency of the moment allowed scant time for reflection in any case. Failing all else, draconian discipline held them together. Anyone who wavered might be shot.

The day after 'Dolle Dinsdag' a Spitfire reconnaissance aircraft flown by Flight Lieutenant L. J. Scargill from 541 Squadron RAF made a low photographic pass over the Arnhem road bridge. It recorded little or no activity, and none of military consequence. The middle section of the pontoon bridge was caught mid-channel in the Lower Rhine to enable barge traffic to pass. Scargill completed his run flak-free, startling river crew men who looked up in fear as he powered past and climbed rapidly into the haze on the far side. There was not a soldier or military vehicle in sight. German military efficiency was reasserting itself.[38]

Battle-winning units and specialised key weapons personnel such as panzer and artillerymen or their units, were urgently passed through to the rear for future refits. These trained personnel were virtually irreplaceable. After the 'Tross' came coherent withdrawing formations, the remnants of the rearguard fighting units. On 7 September, two days after 'Mad Tuesday', a steady stream of battle-damaged armoured vehicles came up the road from Nijmegen. Heavy half-tracks and tanks towed disabled assault guns, clattering and gouging up the road as they squeaked past with no caterpillar tracks. These vehicles, festooned with tree branches, were packed with grim-faced soldiers wearing the distinctive short Waffen SS camouflage smocks, the remnants of the 9th SS Hohenstaufen Division. The 10th SS Frundsberg survivors with their parent II SS Corps moved off to the south and east of Arnhem. The Meldekopf Reporting Centre for the Hohenstaufen was in Arnhem. Their vehicles were encumbered by extra military equipments rather than loot. After reporting in they were redirected to the north of Arnhem, where they settled into the villages spread along the Ijssel River.

Fourteen-year-old Cornelis, or 'Kees', Bolderman, living at the eastern end of the Utrechtseweg, watched the battered traffic coming up from the south. Every lorry had one or two German soldiers sitting on the mudguards with their feet on the running boards with rifles at the ready, scanning the skies above for any signs of Allied aircraft. Like all youths of his age, Kees was transfixed by the technical power exuded by the huge panzers. They passed through the Willems Plein and Nieuwe Plein (squares), past the railway station and turned north under the railway bridge heading for Apeldoorn. Four German tanks parked in the Haarhuis Hotel park opposite Arnhem station. Their armoured plating showed considerable evidence of battle damage. These men had fought their last rearguard action at Cambrai eight days before. As the tired and dishevelled crews stood by their panzers, Kees watched them burning documents in a hole they had dug in the park. The uncommunicative crews regarded him as a meddling brat. There were no unit recognition signs on the vehicles. After some failed attempts at conversation, one of them did let slip that they were Hohenstaufen men. At nightfall the tanks moved off.

The teenager was impressed by the deep ruts the caterpillar tracks carved through the asphalt. They swiftly drove off, a manifestation of naked power, knocking off brick paving corners as they clattered by.[39]

Allied intelligence had lost all trace of the II SS Corps during the tumultuous retreat through Belgium. Dutch Resistance had watched them pass through southern Holland. The Albrecht group sent a message from 'Richard' in Roermond on 7 September reporting 'large units SS panzer troops passed here, coming from the direction of Maastricht and marching northward along Maas and Waal.' The traffic rumbled throughout the night. Montgomery's G2 Intelligence Officer recorded in his diary that 'Dutch resistance report of battered panzer formations sent to Holland to refit with Eindhoven and Nijmegen as reception areas.' When their symbols disappeared from the Allied situation maps in front of First US Army, the Intelligence Officer could afford to remain sanguine – after all, Brussels and Antwerp had fallen. The whole German front appeared to be withdrawing and the two panzer divisions 'were last identified in the great retreat of First US Army front'. He was near the truth when he wrote in his intelligence summary that 'there cannot be much left of them'. General der SS Wilhelm Bittrich's II SS Corps was down to about a dozen or so tanks and 20% to 30% of its established strength. In Allied terms, it had been fought to annihilation. 'What there is, is out of the line and may perhaps have found its way into Holland,' the report read.

German norms concerning unit reconstitution after heavy casualties differed from those of the Allies. Dutch Resistance spotted unit identification boards on the northern side of the Arnhem bridge reading 'Meldekopf [reporting centre] Hohenstaufen'. This confirmed that the unit was reforming. London was informed on 15 September by Dutch Resistance that:

'SS Div. Hohenstaufen along Ijssel. Units from this division noticed from Arnhem to Zutphen and along the road Zutphen-Apeldoorn.'

This very accurate report did not impress Second British Army intelligence, planning on the eve of launching the biggest airborne operation of the war to date. These identified locations were 30 minutes away from Oosterbeek by truck, or 2 hours on foot.[40]

'Arnhem and Oosterbeek were amazing sights,' declared Alfred Ziegler, a motorcycle dispatch rider with Panzerjäger (anti-tank assault gun) Abteilung (battalion) 9 with the Hohenstaufen. 'I was astonished to see such a beautiful town and village.' They had lost all their self-propelled guns in France. The few crews left formed a composite infantry company commanded by SS-Hauptsturmführer Klaus von Allwörden. Ziegler's motorcycle combination had stopped a cannon shell in the engine block from a low-level strafing run by an Allied fighter bomber and he had been towed to Arnhem, where workshop vehicles had repaired his bike. The SS troopers could hardly comprehend the peaceful scenes they met after the carnage they had experienced in France. People here were still going about their daily business.

'France had been a virtual desert for the Germans' trying to procure food and drink, recalled Leutnant Joseph Enthammer as he regarded Oosterbeek. 'Here the inhabitants were very friendly.' He wondered why. 'You could buy everything in Holland, cheese, tomatoes, everything!' Ziegler also appreciated his more convivial surroundings. 'Fine gardens and houses neatly laid out' he found as he familiarised himself with the Utrechtseweg, the main through route to Arnhem. The whole area he discovered was criss-crossed with tarmac, cobbled or 'quaint little tracks'. Bicycle tracks alongside the main roads were especially welcome. 'I used to drive along these with my motorcycle,' he remembered, 'because they provided better protection from the air.'[41]

The SS men began to unwind and readjust to an environment that was tempo-free from the normal exigencies of combat. 'The division was virtually burned out in the Normandy fighting,' recalled 19-year-old Rottenführer (SS-Corporal) Wolfgang Dombrowski. He was with the 2nd Kompanie of Panzerpionier (armoured engineer) Battalion 9. They had barely got out through the last 2-kilometre-wide gap in the Falaise pocket, after which they had the 'constant unenviable task of providing the division rearguard'. Dombrowski became separated during the chaotic retreat, but managed to rejoin his battalion's remnants three days later. 'We believed that once we got over the German border it would be all over.' He had his doubts whether the division would ever be reconstituted, but the General Staff had grasped the nettle and things began to happen. They were warned that they would be returning to Siegen in Westphalia in the Reich, where they would be re-equipped with new tanks. The 'Tross' rear-party elements had already departed by train on 13 September. Soldiers were instructed to hand in their personal weapons, confident that they would receive new ones on arrival, itself a statement of the continuing ability of the German General Staff system to function efficiently, despite the carnage inflicted on its field army. Surviving half-tracks had to be handed over to their sister division, the 10th SS Frundsburg. They would remain in situ, to feed the front with reserve armoured battle groups. 'We were accommodated in Brummen, about 30 minutes drive from Oosterbeek, and despite some grumblings of artillery fire in the distance we were happy living in virtual peacetime conditions,' Dombrowski remembered. 'We believed the war was probably over, but we lower ranks were all about 18 or 19,' while their officers averaged between 24 and 29 years. 'We were not too concerned about life's deeper issues – we were prepared to simply fight on.'[42]

Alfred Ziegler, billeted south of Apeldoorn nearby, recalled that 'morale was good, but there were no illusions that the war was not already over.' Soldiers joked that this was the west, not Russia, 'so instead of a little wooden hut in Siberia, they would be more likely better off in a camp in Canada.' Few soldiers had the time or inclination to reflect too much on the future. 'One of my friends confided in me,' Ziegler recalled. '"Don't be a hero," he said, "the war is lost".' There was something to look forward to, at least, a refit in the Reich. Units were warned off entraining for Siegen. As they waited they were regrouped into infantry 'Alarm' companies, just in case, as always in war, the unexpected should occur.

An anxious wait: the Dutch

It had been a glorious summer on the street, where events in France were viewed through a pleasant hazy vacuum. Fifteen-year-old Roelie Breman often went swimming in the municipal swimming pool in the Lower

Rhine, in sight of the railway bridge nearby. The arrival of the German soldiers was unsettling. People remembered the awful pillar of smoke rising from the devastated centre of Nijmegen after the mistaken Allied bombing in February. The Germans would attract more air raids. 'People are in a state of tension now that the war is getting nearer to our country,' she wrote in her diary on 1 September:

> 'Many people have started to pack their clothes and valuables. Mummy is also going to pack some suitcases, but she has not yet started; we will do so as soon as the English troops have reached our borders. Most of our neighbours have already packed their things.'

Everybody was vying to comment on the latest news. 'It really is amusing,' Roelie thought, 'the way they all claim to know more than the others.' By 5 September some parents in the street were stopping their children from attending school. Roelie's teacher, Mr Van de Velde, 'tells us to go home and stay there till things have quietened down a bit.' This was on 'Mad Tuesday'. There was no swimming that evening for Roelie, and the following day they started to pack. It seemed that more Germans were coming than going.[43]

Hendrika van der Vlist in the Hotel Schoonoord at No 186 Utrechtseweg recalled 'my father's hotel which a year ago already was requisitioned by the Deutsche Wehrmacht and in which we are allowed only a few rooms, is packed to the very roof.' Many of her neighbours also had Germans quartered on them. Groups would only stay for two days when 'everything in the house is turned topsy-turvy' then move on. Cupboards were taken from the first, then the ground floors and thrown out into the garden to make more room. The unhappy Van de Vlist family could only look on in consternation as the next group arrived 'like a swarm of locusts, settles on the dirt of the previous group, and again the removal takes place'. The soldiers were unimpressive, in stark contrast to their 1940 predecessors. Despite the filth caused by their comings and goings, they found time amid all the urgent activity to 'schmücken [beautify] their rooms, as they say'. Ms Van der Vlist was disdainful, commenting that they 'don't look manly any longer'.

Allied air activity became increasingly active. A goods train coming up from Nijmegen was strafed on the embankment north of the Lower Rhine railway bridge. It was seen from the street, and 18-year-old J. A. van Hofwegen in Weverstraat watched as 'the locomotive was hit and came to a standstill hissing leaking steam'. Within the hour another locomotive puffed up and dragged the train into Arnhem. 'If it is not necessary we don't take the train,' recalled Van der Vlist, a problem because it was the main civilian mode of travel. Her brother's holidays had just finished; he was due to return to his school in The Hague, but yielded to general advice 'to wait a bit'. He stayed in the hotel.

The German Army may be going soft, but more and more of it was arriving. On 8 September truckloads of German troops turned off the Utrechtseweg at the Oosterbeek crossroads into the Stationsweg. Sitting in the back obscured by branches of camouflage foliage were serious-looking teenagers with outsize helmets. They belonged to SS Panzer Grenadier Depot and Reserve Battalion 16 commanded by 37-year-old Sturmbannführer (SS Major) Sepp Krafft. The unit had been moved from its coastal defence positions to Oosterbeek by SS General Hans-Albin Rauter, the Supreme SS and Police Commander in the Netherlands. Rauter suspected that the Dutch, like the French Resistance in Paris, were on the verge of revolt and would do so once the Allies crossed the border. Field Marshal Model's Army Group Headquarters was located in the Hotel Tafelberg in Oosterbeek, and Krafft was dispatched as additional insurance. His men took over the Berg en Dal building in the Graf von Rechterenweg, around the corner. The priests staying inside were told to leave, their second move after the Wehrmacht had already ejected them from Arnhem. These young men were of a different calibre from those who had decorated their hotel rooms with flowers at the Schoonoord. Krafft's battalion provided replacements for front-line SS units and had previously been a feeder for the SS Hitlerjugend Division in Normandy. They felt threatened by the developing situation and would have scant sympathy for any Dutchmen who got in their way.

J. A. van Hofwegen watched five German half-tracks pulling up under the trees in Dr Brevee's garden at No 144 Weverstraat, a turning off the Utrechtseweg. Brand new Fiat trucks followed, basing themselves in the school opposite Van Hofwegen's house at No 154. They unloaded desks, files, office equipment and radio transmitters. Unbeknown to the locals, they were providing the administrative back-up to Model's Army Group B Headquarters, settling into the Hotel Tafelberg nearby. Oosterbeek was in the middle of the rear combat zone supporting the German armies defending southern Holland – a safe place for headquarters and front reserves, 2 hours' drive time from the front. Those living along the street started to appreciate that, unlike the scenes of panic witnessed days before, these units were composed, efficient and likely to stay. 'Round the [Schoonoord] hotel the soldiers are digging machine gun emplacements,' observed Hendrika van der Vlist:

'Telephone cables are run everywhere through the house. From the upper sides of the doors small squares are sawn to pass them through.'

It seemed like considered vandalism. 'In front of the hotel there are two German guards, and they are walking up and down.'[44]

Increased German activity was evident along the entire length of the street. At its western extremity, 17-year-old Netje Heijbroek's family lived in the stately house known as 'Valkenburg', where the road bends at the Koude Herberg, opposite the Sonnenberg estate. A tracked vehicle towing a 75mm gun drove up during the second week in September. It was positioned to shoot west down the road towards Heelsum, and its eight-man crew joined them in the house. 'All the hotels were full,' Netje remembered. 'The Bilderberg with "grey mice" [female Luftwaffe staff], the Tafelberg with high-ranking officers and even a Field Marshal was expected at the Hotel Hartenstein.' On 10 September Mr and Mrs Pekelharing came to live with them. 'They had been evacuated to the Hotel Hartenstein, but the Germans had now taken over the hotel.'

Netje's father was a former Dutch officer and it was clear to him that something was about to happen. 'The organisation began to roll,' she remembered:

'Every member of the family had a job. Pack a suitcase with clothing and important papers; put a chair in a pre-selected safe spot in the little passageway near the cellar along with a blanket and warm coat. Fill the bath, fill bottles with clean water, etc.'

Allied air activity was just as evident here. Netje's father wrote in his diary about 'a beautiful attack by Typhoons... They fired at anything that moved on the roads, and in Wolfheze [just to the north] they set a train on fire that continued exploding for three hours.' Seventeen-year-old Dick van t'Land, living nearby, saw the seven aircraft strafe the station where there was an ammunition dump. 'Not much happened afterwards but the explosions went on for hours,' he recalled.[45]

Schools started up again but attendance was haphazard; parents were erring on the safe side. 'I hear that all schools will be officially closed from next week,' wrote Roelie Breman in her diary on Saturday 9 September. 'They will apparently all be requisitioned.' The occupation remained menacing. On Sunday 'German soldiers are again rounding up the men, so you see only women going to church.' Only the Minister and old men attended while German soldiers stalked the streets. 'Manhunting', Ms Van der Vlist called it. 'In Arnhem women stand and weep in front of the concert hall, Musis Sacrum; they were walking in the street with their husband or fiancé and then suddenly there was a raid.' They were loaded on trucks. 'Was it Deelen? Or the Ijssel?' she wondered. People thought the British would likely march straight through the street as the Germans had in 1940. She asked a German truck driver parked outside the hotel whether he thought Germany would still win the war. 'Just wait for our new weapons,' he responded. The Germans were constantly ratcheting up the pressure and showed no sign of leaving. 'Bad news is sent to the men working in the Arnhem offices,' Van der Vlist recalled:

'All the men aged between 18 and 50 have to be at the station "tomorrow at 7am". They have to be provided with a spade, a blanket, a plate, a spoon and a fork; the work they will have to do: digging. In the event of disobedience to this order the wives and children will be turned out of their houses and the furniture will be burnt.'

An explosion shattered the stillness of Arnhem during the night of 15 September. The Dutch Resistance had sabotaged the Plattenberg railway viaduct. The local *Arnhemsche Courant* newspaper printed a warning the next day in stark lettering: 'If the culprits don't report before tomorrow, September 17th 12 o'clock, a number of citizens will be shot.' Many men went into hiding on Saturday in anticipation; most did not go out of doors. The ultimatum would expire after church the next day.[46]

Sunday 17 September gave every indication of being a beautiful day. 'The sun is shining and there is no cloud in the sky,' recalled Roelie Breman, living in the Benedendorpsweg near the railway bridge. In other words, 'a typical day for many aeroplanes to come over,' she observed. At 7 o'clock Dutch policeman G. Huijgen took over the daily reports book from his colleague W. Maassen at the Police Station at No 107 Utrechtseweg. There was nothing to report; by mid-morning most people in the street were on their way to church.

'It was soon very restless in the air,' observed Dick van t'Land at Wolfheze. His family had decided against going to church because of the recent air raids on the railway station. He recalled that in any case 'the preacher ended mass pretty quickly to give the congregation a chance to get home because there was so much activity.' Hendrika van de Vlist, attending mass at the local Protestant church near the Schoonoord, thought that 'it is good flying weather, we can't expect anything else'. The congregation became uneasy when they heard distant bomb explosions and the rattle of aircraft machine guns. 'There is booming as never before,' she later recalled. What could the targets be? Church congregations along the street faced the same dilemma as that voiced by Ms Van de Vlist: 'Shall we venture to go home again or remain in the shelter of the building?'

At Wolfheze Dick van t'Land remembered that the disturbance was less about aircraft, more about the German anti-aircraft batteries at Deelen airfield shooting up everything they had into the sky overhead. His mother was preparing the midday meal in the kitchen with his younger sister and wheelchair-bound aunt, while his father was listening to the illegal English radio in the pavilion behind the house. Dick was outside with his older sister and brother counting a large approaching aircraft formation, 'which in my estimation released about 30 bombs'. He was part of a curious audience outside doing the same, until Dick realised that 'things were a bit too hot' and ran inside the house. 'There goes a dud,' he thought after the approaching whistle, and dived to the ground, which saved his life.

The raid was quickly over. 'You couldn't see through the dust,' he recalled, 'but as this settled and I stood up, my sister and brother, and the others, were dead on the ground.' He crawled through wreckage following the sound of his younger sister's screams, who had already been pulled out from beneath his dead mother by his crippled aunt; she was 11 years old. Part of her arm had been torn off, she had shrapnel in her stomach and her shoulder was badly burned. His Dad had caught the full force of the blast coming out of the pavilion. The mental asylum and clinic was burning furiously. Shell-shocked patients wandered about in bloodied long nightshirts. There had only been a few Germans in the clinic, 'perhaps 20 soldiers,' Dick remembered, manning a gun and securing an ammunition dump nearby that was now exploding. They counted 45 dead at first, 'but after a few days the number rose to 81'. Many more wounded were to die during the evacuation. 'About 100 dead,' he reflected. 'Quite a lot for such a small village.' He managed to get his seriously injured young sister and aunt out of the house. 'My aunt was, as I said, disabled and she rolled her wheelchair into the bomb crater outside.' Dick had to leave her while he urgently sought help for his sister.[47]

On the Utrechtseweg to the south, near the Koude Herberg, Netje Heijbroek saw 'the sky was full of aircraft on that beautiful Sunday… Everywhere about us was being machine gunned and bombed, especially at Wolfheze.' Pillars of black smoke began to lazily rise above the woods surrounding the village. At 12.35 police officer Huijgen at No 107 Utrechtseweg recorded a 'fire near Bilderberg'. Fifteen minutes earlier, the assistant station master at Wolfheze had telephoned reporting a direct strike on the station, and four houses hit, 'everywhere rubble and dust'. People remained cowering in their shelters. 'Ambulances drove hither and thither' along the western end of the street, remembered Netje Heijbroek. 'Many refugees began to appear, laden with what little they had been able to take with them.'[48]

Nine-year-old Wil Rieken at No 178 Utrechtseweg, the confectioner's shop, remembered that her father, a member of the 'Orange' Resistance group, was called to Wolfheze to help fight the fires at the mental asylum. He was shocked at the slaughter he found. 'When he came back,' Wil recalled, 'for the first and only time in my life I saw my father cry.' He came and embraced her mother and said, 'Coos, it's going wrong, it's going very wrong,' and wept. 'That made me almost cry, seeing my big Dad – he was not tall, but a very strong man.'[49]

Anje van Maanen, like many 17-year-old teenagers, was sleeping in, feeling 'terribly lazy and comfortable' on this fine Sunday morning at No 8 Pietersbergscheweg, next to the Oosterbeek crossroads. 'We were not going to church today, so I have all the time in the world.' The sound of distant booms and cracking detonations accompanied the sudden entry of her brother, who announced, 'They are bombing.' They rushed upstairs and looked out of the attic window. Aircraft were flying past in formations of sixes. Despite the haze she saw with a start that Wolfheze was burning and, looking the other way, could see that Arnhem was burning too. She got dressed.[50]

Just before the German resistance ultimatum expired in Arnhem, pandemonium broke out. At around 10.45 Mitchell bombers were over the city bombing anti-aircraft positions. Jan Hol at No 10 Stationsweg remembers 'like a bolt from the blue, the German flak guns opened up, followed immediately by loud explosions from the Arnhem direction.' He watched as huge columns of smoke rose into the air – the town was being bombed. Hiding from German labour press-gangs, Hol had to 'keep away from the windows during the day', then get a little exercise in the back garden at night. The Jansens, the family hiding him, came hurrying back from church. 'Something was happening on the Utrechtseweg,' they said. 'They didn't know what exactly, but it seemed safer to stay indoors.' They could go back to church in the evening when things had quietened down. The Jansens started to prepare Sunday lunch. 'We wondered what the air attacks were all about, because the front line was still far removed from Oosterbeek.' Lunch was going to include milk pudding, a rare treat at this stage of the war, a product of the good relations the Jansens had with local farmers. 'Let's eat it up now,' Jan suggested, or 'one bomb and it's gone'. A sour joke, because within seconds they were scurrying into the cellar as swarms of low-flying aircraft zoomed over, firing rockets and machine guns. 'I never did get to eat any of that pudding,' Jan Hol remembered.[51]

Nine Mosquitoes flew very low over Johannes van Zonnenveld at No 76 Utrechtseweg at about 12 o'clock 'and made a great impression on me,' he recalled. They were heading for the Willem Barracks and the Royal Hotel in the Arnhem Willemsplein. Anje van Maanen involuntarily ducked while watching the swarm of Mosquitoes pass overhead from the maid's window. 'They fire on Arnhem – Oh, and Arnhem burns like hell. Awful! Something must be happening,' she recalled, 'but what??' The raid was over in 15 minutes, leaving the Willems Barracks ablaze, but the SS NCO School was gone. Two aircraft were shot down.

One terrified young schoolgirl sheltering in a cellar nearby saw the 'horrifying' impact of the bombs. 'People were falling down dead right next to you,' she recalled, and 'I ran home as fast as I could.' Mr Ripperda Wiertsma turned up at the barracks on his bicycle and saw 'many Germans wandering about like orphans, their hair and clothing covered in dust and rubbish.' General Küssin's offices of the Ortskommandant of Arnhem were nearby. The destroyed barracks had been famous. Designed in 1836, they had been home to the famous Dutch Royal Horse Artillery Gele Rijders until May 1940. They burned furiously for the rest of the day and into the night.[52]

'Suddenly we hear a whizzing sound and a loud bang,' recalled Roelie Breman on the Benedendorpsweg near the railway bridge. 'We all go and stand in the corridor – Granny is very frightened.' When the noise died down they ventured outside. 'The entire railway-dyke is covered in thick smoke. That's where the bombs have fallen,' Roelie realised. All around the ground was covered in shell splinters and 'four or five windows have gone'. Jan Esvelt watched the spectacle unfold from the other side of the Lower Rhine in Dotterlaan, where he had an unobstructed view towards the west across the railway bridge to the wooded area on the high ground north of the river. He saw bombs fall on the anti-aircraft battery near the brick factory opposite the St Elizabeth Hospital on the Utrechtseweg. His own street was also littered with shrapnel, and the inhabitants were intimidated by the 'ear-shattering noise of falling bombs, the house is shaking'. He had no idea what was going on. Fires were clearly visible in Arnhem, but caused by bombs or something else?[53]

Police officer G. Huijgen, manning the Police Station at No 107 Utrechtseweg, heard a report that bombs had hit the Steenenkruis street near the railway bridge. There were apparently two dead and wounded. German anti-aircraft guns sited in the Rosande Polder east and west of the railway dyke had been bombed, as observed by Roelie Breman. Overshoots had struck No 48 Steenenkruis, killing 36-year-old Mr Albertus Willemsen, and 21-year-old Willem van Brummeln at No 32. Their houses were burning. The police officers began to log an increasing litany of devastation: the Sanders brick kiln was blazing, 20 cows had been cut down by bomb splinters in the meadows near the Oosterbeek railway station, and Maassen – Huijgen's colleague – heard that his house on the Benedendorpsweg had been hit, thankfully with no casualties.[54]

'This must be something special,' decided Hendrika van de Vlist, hurrying home from the Protestant church. 'It has never been as bad as this.' During pauses between raids 'people can leave the church at last and run towards their homes,' observed Roelie Breman. 'Nobody need tell us what war means, now we know, they say.' 'Everywhere along the roads people are watching the sky,' Van der Vlist recalled, including the Germans 'seeking shelter under a tree, afraid they may be noticed by a hostile plane.' Eighteen-year-old J. A. van Hofwegen remembered that the scramble from church started after women and children began wailing in the St Bernulphus church on the Utrechtseweg. RAF Mosquitoes swooped over 'making a hell of a noise', scattering people seeking cover in the shop doorway opposite the church. 'Women and children were screaming and crying and we were all quite upset by this confrontation with acts of war.'[55]

Anje van Maanen's father was a doctor and their painter, Myholt, came looking for him at No 8 Pietersbergscheweg. He breathlessly described the devastation he had seen at Wolfheze – help was urgently needed. 'It is terrible there,' he reported:

> 'About one hundred killed and blood everywhere. Nobody is allowed to leave Wolfheze and nobody can reach it, doctors can't do anything. The Germans have lost their heads and are flying about in chaos – firing around, on everybody and everything. Arnhem has been hit too, amongst others the barracks and the Willemsplein.'[56]

The spectre of war had returned and was gnawing at both ends of the street like a dog with a bone. Scores of people were dead and houses on fire, totally unlike the previous experience of May 1940.

There was a lull between the air raids around the blazing buildings of the mental asylum at Wolfheze. German anti-aircraft ammunition stored between the buildings was 'cooking off' in the intense heat, alarming those trying to recover the injured and sending into further hysterics the mental patients wandering around in their nightshirts. Former Dutch soldier and garage mechanic Jaap Jansen, serving with the LBD Air Raid Defence Service, had been called out by the Police Station to assist with the recovery of bodies and the injured from a terraced block of four houses hit near Wolfheze railway station. When another formation of Stirling bombers was detected by their droning approach from the south-west, a general panic broke out as patients and helpers fled into the woods. 'Oh no,' Jansen recalled saying, 'not again!'

German soldiers walking with their girlfriends in the woods and across the Renkum Heath in their best uniforms looked up when the bombers crossed the Utrechtseweg over Heelsum. Raids were not especially significant, despite the morning's activity. But these hostile aircraft were flying lower than usual. Then one of the crews bailed out through the bomb bay. It was normally the job of the Arnhem NCO School to crash out and pick up crews that abandoned their aircraft. Soon the air was filled with scores of parachutists who kept coming. 'Scheiss! Fallschirmjäger! [Shit! Paratroopers!]' muttered German onlookers, as they ran for it.[57]

The fly-in: the British

Navigator Flying Officer Reginald Lawton, peering from the cockpit of one of these 190 Squadron Stirling bombers, recalled that 'the day was cloudless'. They were dropping the airborne pathfinders of the 21st Independent Parachute Company. 'We had no difficulty in finding our drop zone,' he remembered. They had already crossed the two prominent river lines of the Maas and Waal and were approaching their third, the Lower Rhine. The outline of the green woods east and west, and purplish heathland beyond the railway line, conformed to the familiar air photographs they had so laboriously studied. Beneath them was the village of Heelsum with the street running through it, indistinguishable beneath its tree-lined canopy. Much of Oosterbeek was also screened by trees, but further to their right was the distinctive urban mass of Arnhem, bordered at its southern edge by its two prominent bridges. They were in the right place.

The pathfinders in the back had cursed the absence of the comfortable Dakota seats they were more accustomed to. This was their first Stirling jump, even though most were veterans. They sat, lay and leaned against the fuselage and each other in the dimly lit aircraft interiors. Light only came from the front and rear gun turrets. With 5 minutes to go the lids of the coffin-shaped bomb bay apertures were folded back, and slipstream noises buffeted and swished around them. No 1s crouched in the forward stoop intently watching the chequerboard of green fields racing by 700 feet below. 'Red on!' was called, and a red jump light glowed. A ribbon of silver flashed beneath – the river – followed by a few seconds' pause and the light changed to green. 'Green on! Go!' Paratroopers plunged through the former bomb bay doors, emptying the fuselage in seconds.

'We could see Dutch civilians waving and starting to cycle towards the paratroops,' Lawton observed. In all, 186 pathfinders were dropped. They had 20 minutes to mark two glider landing sites and one parachute drop zone.

'On the way back we flew over the main force of tugs and gliders and parachute aircraft, supported by fighters, who were shooting up the few ack-ack batteries that opened up. All these aircraft made a continuous stream 280 miles long.'[58]

Stirling pilot Douglas Smith boosted his engines to get above 'the thousands of planes that were coming in'. It was the most impressive air armada anyone had ever seen. Aircraft were leaving the English coastline even as the first were approaching the drop zones. Smith recalled saying to his friends that 'if Hitler could see what I can see now he would throw in the towel'. They felt invincible. 'We were absolutely the masters,' he declared. They were the lead element of the 1st British Airborne Division, which was part of the 1st Allied Air Corps. The Air Corps was spearheading the ground advance of the Second British Army led by General Horrocks's XXX Corps across the major waterways of southern Holland. The long-awaited Liberation of the street was at hand.

Operation Market was an 'airborne carpet' of paratroopers from the American 101st and 82nd Airborne Divisions laid across the main water obstacles from Eindhoven to Nijmegen on the River Waal, to link up with the British airborne force 60 miles behind enemy lines across the Lower Rhine at Arnhem. The Utrechtseweg lay at the northern fringe of the proposed operation. All this was to precede the ground offensive named Garden. The aim of Market-Garden was to link the airborne pockets to form a corridor through which XXX Corps would advance to force the Rhine, then break into the German Ruhr industrial heartland and on to Berlin. It was anticipated that the war could be over by Christmas. Allied planners had not appreciated that two badly battered SS panzer divisions were refitting to the north and east of Arnhem. The 9th SS Hohenstaufen Panzer Division's remnants were nearest to the Utrechtseweg. They had 19 'Alarm' companies totalling about 2,500 veteran SS infantry with some tanks and armoured vehicles, all within a 30-to-45-minute truck drive from the street.

Thundering across the Dutch countryside 20 minutes behind the pathfinder insertion was the main aircraft stream, a mass of approaching aircraft and gliders some nine wide. This was the tangible manifestation of the Allied planners' dream to end the war. The First Airborne Army was to be described by the official US history as an unused strategic resource 'burning holes in SHAEF's pocket'[59]. There were two aircraft streams, the smaller northern British contingent and the southern stream flying two American airborne divisions, 1,545 aircraft supported by 900 fighters. The British stream led with 358 tugs towing gliders carrying the 1st Air Landing Brigade followed by 155 parachute aircraft with the 1st Parachute Brigade.[60]

'Your men are killers,' General Horrocks, commanding XXX Corps, had confided to Major General Urquhart commanding the 1st Airborne Division during preliminary briefings. British airborne soldiers were specially chosen volunteers who regarded themselves as an elite. Selection for airborne forces was a brutally hard physical and mental process designed to prepare soldiers to operate behind enemy lines, where it was presumed they would be surrounded at the outset – as would these men dropped 60 miles into the enemy's rear-combat zone. On average only 40% of volunteers passed to reach parachute training. The process produced fit, confident, resilient and highly aggressive soldiers. Glider soldiers were also subjected to rigorous physical selection like glider pilots, taught under the 'Total Soldier' training concept to operate as infantry on landing.

Gliding was dangerous because a myriad of things could go wrong. They might undershoot, stall and prematurely dive, become prematurely released or trapped in an involuntary spin. One glider infantryman recalled that 'there was a definite difference between us and the parachute brigades', sarcastically adding it was a case of 'expert killers versus only glorified infantry'. Paratroopers received 2 shillings per day jump pay, while glider men got 1 shilling, 'so we were downgraded'. British paratroopers were dismissive about their glider colleagues until Sicily in 1943, when they went into action alongside the 1st Air Landing Brigade. 'To go into action in a glider is worth four [shillings]!' declared a 1st Brigade paratrooper.

'The first glider I ever saw cast off in the air at 5,000 feet immediately nose-dived to earth and killed the entire passenger load.' Glider familiarisation flights were detested. 'Trusting myself to an apparatus constructed mainly of plywood did not appeal to me in the least!' commented Sergeant Eddie Hancock with the 2nd Parachute Battalion.[61]

Inside the hundreds of gliders and parachute aircraft of the northern aircraft stream were 8,000 airborne soldiers with the first lift. They slept, munched on sandwiches, read the Sunday papers, told stories, or simply sat. Many were flying into battle for the first time, or not for a very long time. The paratroopers had seen more action than the glidermen, but the division had not fought since 1943. As airborne actions traditionally experienced an appalling 50% casualty rate, by September 1944 many of these men were replacements. Combat veterans had not fired a shot in anger for 14 months.

The 1st Airborne Corps was the last remaining strategic reserve, and as the German front collapsed in Normandy it was on stand-by for a string of postponed airborne insertions, nullified by swift Allied ground advances. Glider pilot Arthur Shackleton, flying in a 2nd South Staffords infantry platoon, recalled the string of abortive operations preceding this one:

'Most people don't know this – the original was called Comet and the British 1st Airborne were going to take all the bridges. The Americans were not involved in the original one. We were scheduled for the Arnhem Bridge – our squadron. It was postponed and postponed and postponed and in the end it was scrubbed… They cobbled this thing called Market together, whereby the Americans were coming in and the 1st British Airborne were just going to take the Arnhem Bridge.'

Lieutenant Alexander MacKenzie, the Intelligence Officer flying in with the glider-borne 7th Kings Own Scottish Borderers (7 KOSB) had been relieved when Comet was cancelled. Their objective had been the huge bridge at Nijmegen and was dependent on retarding parachute brakes to reduce landing speeds when their gliders set down on the muddy river banks alongside. 'It was expected that when the gliders touched down they would go "arse over tits" with horrendous consequences.' Seventeen cancelled operations after D-Day on 6 June had tested to the absolute limit the patience of the mentally prepared airborne troopers. Fights down-town were becoming a regular occurrence around the billets of the 'still-born division', as they called themselves. With the fall of Paris, Brussels and Antwerp, the war seemed to be passing them by. 'We were all frustrated,' recalled artillery Captain Paddy de Burgh, flying in a glider. 'We wanted to get in and join the battle – we were quite pleased when we went, despite all the hindsight about the Germans being to the north of Arnhem'.[62]

Tension was high among the glidermen over the North Sea until with some relief the flooded Dutch coastline came into sight at Schouwen Island off the Scheldte Estuary. The glider battalions of the South Staffords and 7 KOSB had suffered awful losses at Sicily the year before, when much of the glider force had been prematurely released too far out to sea. Of the 605 officers and men lost by the 1st Air Landing Brigade and Glider Pilot Regiment, 300 had drowned. Landing in the sea in a glider at 80 to 90mph was the equivalent of touching down on loose shale. Any irregularity in the approach meant the glider flipped over or dug in nose-first.

Soldiers had little to do except dwell on the hazards coming up, while commanders mulled over their plans. Major General 'Roy' Urquhart was pleased that his division was at last in action, but uneasy about the scant intelligence. Everything depended on the Germans collapsing, when most veterans never underestimated their ability to reconstitute in a crisis. Urquhart's combat power was fragmented over two aircraft lifts. This was worrying. He was confident in the potential ability of Horrocks's XXX Corps to arrive in time, but previous airborne operations had been a litany of failed ground-force relief deadlines. His glider-borne infantry battalions were also being inserted piecemeal, but the 1st Parachute Brigade force, earmarked to seize Arnhem and its two bridges, was arriving intact with as much artillery and anti-tank division support as he could muster. Fifty percent of his offensive force was going to be left behind to secure the second and third lift landing sites and drop zones.

Lieutenant Colonel John Frost, commanding the 2nd Parachute Battalion, was further back in the huge airborne stream. He too considered his options, staring out of the open Dakota door as it flew over the flooded Dutch countryside. Thus far the operation had been totally unreal. Breakfast with bacon and eggs had been a leisurely affair in the Mess; it was a late start, even time to peruse the Sunday papers. This was totally unlike earlier experiences of last-minute changes, dashing off to find non-existent transport and meals at extraordinary hours. There had been a mess-up with the tea lorry at the airfield – nothing to serve the tea with.

Frost, a highly experienced parachute commander, considered this operation to have some 'glaring snags'. They were the furthest away from the relieving ground forces' start line and the drop zones were too far from the bridges. All this entailed a long approach on foot through unpredictable closely wooded and built-up areas. Experience at Oudna in North Africa in 1942 had taught him that surprise was a rapidly depreciating commodity. They would have to move quickly. One of the paramount lessons from costly bridge-taking operations in Sicily was that it made sense to parachute on both sides of any bridge. Here they were only approaching from the north side, after a time delay. Why couldn't the RAF start earlier and fly two lifts in one day? Frost was feeling vulnerable, knowing only too well how quickly the Germans could recover in a crisis. Arnhem was a division objective in itself, yet his brigade was doing it alone: 1 Para was to take the north, 3 Para the west, while his 2 Para was going to penetrate along the south to secure the key bridges. Frost was confident that he and his battalion would get their bridge, but what about everyone else? Information on the enemy was sparse, but 'we were assured there was nothing to worry about'. The ground forces would get through. 'Our own army was on the crest of the wave,' he recalled. They had rested and reorganised and were 'poised for the final run in, and we had every confidence in their ability to finish it off.'[63]

The vast majority of the soldiers in this aircraft stream would at some stage in the future battle walk the Utrechtseweg. Yet there is virtually no mention of it in the myriad of written orders and documents preceding the operation. It was designated route 'Tiger' in the 1st Parachute Brigade

Group Plan and allocated to the 3rd Parachute Battalion. 'Leopard' was the name given to the Amsterdamseweg to the north, earmarked for 1 Para, and Frost's battalion would use 'Lion', the southerly Benedendorpsweg route into Arnhem alongside the river. Like the German May 1940 experience, the Utrechtseweg was simply the main east-west route from Arnhem. Scant notice was taken of its inhabitants. 'Civilians must not be trusted,' briefed the 7 KOSB Commanding Officer on 16 September. 'Fraternisation will be strongly discouraged' and 'no movement of unauthorised civilians will be allowed.' The division's view was similar. 'There is no reason to suppose that they are not collaborationists,' RASC briefing notes emphasised. 'All local inhabitants will be regarded with suspicion until proved friendly.' Frost had been told that the Dutch Underground 'was said to have been penetrated by the Germans, who had planted their own adherents, so it was not to be relied upon.'[64]

Concern at soldier level was less sophisticated. James Sims, flying with Frost's battalion, had seen gliders explode or prematurely cast off into the sea, and recalled:

> 'It suddenly struck me how much danger I was in. Here I was in this slow fragile aircraft (hadn't I already seen two blow up?) and we might well meet flak or enemy fighters. I wondered what the German reception committee was preparing for us. Cannon fire? Machine guns? Tanks? Cold steel? "What the hell am I doing here?" I asked myself. I must be bloody mad!'

For those who had not been in action before there was a feeling of elation mixed with the dread of the unknown. 'I was still wet behind the ears in lots of ways in terms of knowing what it is like to be under fire,' admitted 25-year-old Captain John Killick, an infantry field security officer flying with the Parachute Brigade.

> 'One knew well enough what war was all about I suppose and one knew in theory at least what one was called for, but it all

seemed, I have to confess, it sounds a bit *Boy's Own Paper*-ish. It all sounded like great fun.'

They crossed the flooded coastline, 'a long ridge of land, not unlike the spine of some extinct prehistoric reptile,' James Sims observed. The dark skeletal mass contrasted starkly with the sunlit water. 'Looking out of the windows we could see that the RAF had marked the trail to Arnhem with one blazing flak tower after another.'[65]

Every soldier in this 280-mile-long stream was to undergo the typical airborne cold shower immersion from peace to war. Unlike conventional soldiers, there was no gradual growing consciousness of approaching battle. There are no enemy positions to study with binoculars prior to the off, or preliminary bombardment. They were straight in from the start. The first chance of death or mutilation came with the landing itself, even before the enemy was seen. They put aside the Sunday papers, woke up and began to compose themselves for whatever would come. It was unreal.

So confident were they of success that there was even a public-media glider flying in with the division staff. Sergeant Gordon Walker, a Dunkirk and desert veteran, had trained the previous June to be a cine cameraman at Pinewood Studios just outside London. He was filming from the glider cockpit from the start. His colleague, Sergeant Denis Smith, had been on the same course and was flying in another glider; he even filmed some flak as they flew over the Scheldte Estuary. There was another Army Film & Photo Unit (AFPU) cameraman jumping with the parachute brigade. Sergeant Mike Lewis, wounded twice, had been with airborne forces since the early days of 1941, and Arnhem was his 18th jump. They were all keyed up, as were the gaggle of journalists and war correspondents accompanying them, to record this final decisive action of the war in film and print. Like everyone else, they had first to face an uncertain landing.

At the western end of the Utrechtseweg Dutch civilians noticed a strange deep droning noise that slowly rose in volume until it became a pulsating roar. Nobody had ever heard its like before. British pathfinders watching intently in the distance saw the first tell-tale specks high up and over to the east. Then more dots came into focus towards the west. Fighters suddenly roared in overhead, banking away in all directions seeking any interference with the coming landings. Observers caught their breath – the whole sky across the Lower Rhine and beyond was steadily filling up with more and more aircraft, hundreds of planes as far as the eye could see. The intimidating mass pushed a rising wake of sound ahead of it, much like a wave about to crash on the seashore. For the next hour wave after wave of aircraft rolled over the street, to the absolute delight of the watching Dutch, who had to shout to make themselves heard.

Major Ian Toler with the Glider Pilot Regiment flying the command group of the 2nd South Staffords glider infantry spotted the distinctive bend in the Lower Rhine River. It was the recognition signature to release the tow – Landing Zone (LZ) 'S' was just beyond the approaching railway line

'…and we were off. Speed back to 90 knots: half flap until almost up to the LZ then full flap and nose down. The stick was fully forward but still the speed kept at 80: terrific juddering as if stalling, but we dropped fast, going straight for the LZ. The landing was OK but well short of the overshoot boundary. I took off full flap and ran on, but halfway across the LZ we ran into soft plough and this pulled us up rapidly. I undid my straps, clambered out and lay panting on the ground, as the other gliders swished in and landed all around us amid plumes of dust; but some crashed into trees or collided with other gliders.'[66]

Toler's experience typified the unpredictable laws of chance that governed any mass glider landing. Artillery staff Captain Paddy de Burgh was quickly down, 'one or two bullets flying around but nothing very serious'. Glider serials seemed to separate in unison, swooping down like swans, beautiful in flight but clumsy and awkward in the final seconds of touch-down. 'I remember my glider pilot, Robbie Boyd, suddenly shouting, "God – I've bogged it!",' recalled Captain David Allsop, landing with the jeeps of the 1st Division Reconnaissance Squadron. 'He was coming in too steeply for the soft ground. Just then the floorboards came up and hit us in the face.' 'For between 15 and 20 minutes,' Lieutenant John Stevenson, one of his platoon commanders, recalled, 'there was the constant crashing of those things coming down – great woofted birds, all over the place.' Lieutenant Alan Green, landing with his 1st Border Regiment platoon, remembered

> '…a burst of automatic fire from the ground and the nasty sound of bullets winging their way through the belly of the glider. There was an awful moment when everyone wondered what damage had been done; then came a surprise comment from Private Ron Stripp: "I've been hit in the arm."'

No one else was injured, the glider still responded to its controls, and 'everyone gave a sigh of relief'.

Arthur Shackleton, flying with the 2nd South Staffords infantry, remembered it as 'a beautiful trip – the landing was like an exercise. Sunday lunch-time people strolling about in their Sunday best.' Sergeant Gordon Walker, the AFPU cameraman, was swiftly down and out of his glider on LZ 'Z', west of Wolfheze, to film the landings. With one glider coming in every 9 seconds he had to watch out. He filmed whole glider serials swooping in, raising spirals of dust behind them as they jinked up and down, as if testing the going before ploughing in heavily amid great spumes of dust.[67]

General 'Roy' Urquhart orientated himself as he flew in, recognising the line of the Lower Rhine with its two distinctive bridges. His attention was attracted by the chimney stack of the Wolfheze hospital, well ablaze, as also were the German barracks at Ede. Only the day before his senior operations officer, Lieutenant Colonel Mackenzie, had been quizzed by the American Air Force about the morality of bombing the asylum. Were they sure only the Germans were occupying it? 'On your head be it,' was the response when they were given the 'go-ahead'. Urquhart did not know that close to a hundred civilians and patients had already perished in the preliminary bombing, and terrified asylum patients were roaming the very woods he was now observing.[68]

Shortly before 14.00, and almost an hour into the landings, the noise level rose by several decibels. A huge block of C47 Dakota aircraft came in, flying a V-shaped formation nine aircraft wide, wing tip to wing tip. The 1st Parachute Brigade jumped onto LZ 'X' alongside the glider landing site, the climax of the landings – some 2,280 men from 145 aircraft. Dutchman Jaap Jansen, who had been assisting the recovery of the dead and injured from the first bombing, recalled the sound of different engines, which 'rose to a thunderous roar'. He described how:

'The men from the nearest plane jumped first. Then those from the centre one. Then those from the third plane. And so forth. Man, what a sight that was! When I think of it… Hundreds, many hundreds of parachutes. The sky was full of them! It was … it is … unbelievable. That moment… I still have no words for it. Overwhelming, that is what it was.'[69]

Corporal Reg Curtis, jumping No 13 with the 1st Parachute Battalion, towards the end of his stick, 'had never seen so many planes in the air at one time' and 'wondered where the heck all these men and aircraft came from.'

They had to stand in the doorway with up to 100lb of equipment strapped to their legs. Leg muscles strained as the aircraft rose and fell, battered by multiple slipstreams on the final approach. There was always the last-minute bravado during the run-in, when nervous smiles resembled grimaces. James Sims, jumping with Frost's 2 Para, recalled someone plucking at his parachute and declaring, 'Blimey, cowboy, this isn't a chute, it's an old army blanket.' With the slipstream sucking at the faces of those looking out and ruffling the scrim netting of camouflaged helmets, James Sims intently regarded the red jump light until the green finally winked on:

'"Go!" The Lieutenant vanished. We shuffled along the heaving deck of the Dakota … three … four … five … an

American crewman had set up a cine camera and was filming our exit … six … seven … eight … a chap from Maidstone half turned and shouted something with a grin, but it was lost in the roar of the engines … nine … ten … eleven … through the doorway I could see a huge Hamilcar glider on tow right alongside us; one wing of it was on fire but the glider pilot gave us the thumbs up sign … twelve … thirteen … fourteen … the man in front of me hunched over slightly as he went out. Almost before his helmet disappeared I jumped but the slipstream caught me and whirled me around, winding up my rigging lines.'

Reg Curtis remembered:

'Being No 13, I had a bit of a wait, not long: I shuffled forward, then everything seemed to happen so quickly. I felt a slight pat on my parachute pack, and next I found myself tumbling out of the doorway into that familiar open void again.'

He was out 'and now in enemy-occupied territory'. Sims remembers the familiar experience on exit; the deafening engine roar of the past 2 hours was gone. 'For the first time since leaving England I could distinguish other sounds.' There were a few cracks from shots, shouts from below, punctuated by bursts of machine gun fire in the distance. 'I found myself in a blizzard of silk,' he recalled as he drifted to the ground, 'which a moment before had seemed so far beneath me and came spinning up at an alarming rate.' AFPU cameraman Sergeant Mike Lewis threw off his parachute on the ground and began to film other parachutists landing about him and unloading containers. Then his camera jammed. An irritating start to an unmissable scene.[70]

In the woods around the Hotel Wolfheze, about a kilometre or two beyond the nearest landing gliders, SS troopers gazed skyward and involuntarily gulped. What they were witnessing and continued to watch for an hour was in reality a harbinger of doom. Nobody had anticipated that the Allies would arrive by air – they were expected on the ground. The grumbling front line in southern Holland was still 2 hours' drive away by car. They were aghast at this intimidating spectacle. They had to shout at each other as parachute aircraft, gunning their engines after the drop, howled away with a higher engine note, climbing left and seeking more height to avoid heavy flak ahead at Deelen.

Their commander, 37-year-old Sturmbannführer Sepp Krafft, kept his presence of mind and issued a string of directives. They had been on manoeuvres in the woods all morning to avoid the Allied bombing in and around Arnhem. What the hell were the British doing here in any case, Krafft wondered. There was no immediate objective close at hand. Model's headquarters was in Oosterbeek and the Arnhem bridges were 8 miles away.

Krafft had about 300 men in situ, his 2nd Kompanie in the immediate area, while his 4th was a just over a mile away near the Utrechtseweg, at the Berg en Dal location. He called up his 9th Kompanie in Arnhem to join them as soon as possible. Krafft was not going to pull back. 'It would be wrong to play a purely defensive role and let the enemy gather his forces unmolested,' he determined. He would fight. Experience had taught them that 'the only way to draw the tooth of an airborne landing with an inferior force is to drive right into it.'[71]

By 15.00 most air activity had ceased. A major part of the 1st British Airborne Division was on the ground only a mile or so from the Utrechtseweg. Within an hour the first British boots would be on the road and the Liberation of the street could begin.

CHAPTER 3

The Liberation of the Street

Alarm! The Germans

At Brummen, 20 miles away to the north, Hauptsturmführer (SS-Captain) Hans Möller was out walking with his aide Obersturmführer (Lieutenant) Erwin Grupp, following Sunday lunch, admiring 'a wonderful blue sky and cirrocumulus clouds hovering above the western horizon'. They were not the only ones captivated by the unfolding spectacle. Everyone, including passing civilians, had stopped and was staring in the same direction. Surly these cannot be clouds – were they flak bursts? More and more 'fluffy' clouds were materialising. Parachutes, they realised – 'but so many of them?' Möller wondered. 'Without interruption, stick after stick, wave on wave, they came down silently and peacefully, presenting a fascinating view.' Streams of aircraft were noiselessly transiting left to right in the distance, ejecting more and more parachutes. What was all this about? Möller abruptly snapped into action, appreciating the dire threat. 'For Christ's sake, Grupp, Fallschirmjäger!' he muttered between clenched teeth. 'Let's get back – fast!'

He drove off to division headquarters as his battalion was alerted for action. The arithmetic for an effective response did not add up to much – his three weak 'Alarm' companies only amounted to about 80 men. Reports alerted them to landings in the Renkum Heath and Heelsum area. The reconnaissance platoon was sent off – it could get there within 35 minutes. 'That's all right by me!' he announced to the division staff. 'I knew Arnhem and Oosterbeek quite well.' He had advanced down the Utrechtseweg once before on 10 May 1940, as a senior NCO with the SS Der Führer Regiment. More recently he had driven the route again. History was about to repeat itself. 'Same old routine,' he declared, 'and it really happened that way, only a lot worse than the first time!'[72]

SS Rottenführer (Corporal) Wolfgang Dombrowski with Möller's Pioneer unit saw 'a gigantic smoke cloud over Arnhem, but not any paratroopers'. As is often the case with sudden call-outs, there was scant time for briefings. 'Load up and get to Arnhem' was the order. Dombrowski and his company drove off in four Opel-Blitz lorries, blissfully unaware of the true situation. 'When we set off for Arnhem, we thought we were on our way to Germany,' he recalled. They were on stand-by to depart by train to Siegen in Germany, which would mean welcome leave. He only had his pistol.[73]

Obersturmbannführer (SS Lt Col) Walter Harzer, the commander of the 9th SS Hohenstaufen Kampfgruppe, was lunching at Hoenderloo, 9 miles away. His 19 'Alarm' companies were billeted between 20 and 40 minutes' drive away from the street. 'We saw the first British parachutes in the sky over Arnhem,' he later recalled. The aircraft stream was turning away to avoid flak at Deelen airfield like any other bombing raid heading for the Reich. He had just decorated his reconnaissance commander Gräbner with the Knight's Cross and was walking to the mess for lunch. 'It could not be deduced at this stage that a large-scale operation was under way,' he remembered, 'and we sat down quietly to lunch.'[74]

Alfred Ziegler, the dispatch rider with the Panzerjäger (anti-tank) 'Alarm' company south of Apeldoorn, about 20 miles away, recalled that his quarters, shared with his commander von Allwörden, 'were located on top of a small rise from where you could see all the way to Arnhem'. He had been watching the late-morning air bombardment, 'but nobody had the faintest idea of what was coming'. Ziegler was an idealist, 'an imaginative fellow, always contemplating things', which did not endear him to his first sergeant. He had picked him up on inspection for stitching coming apart on the seat of his camouflage trousers, so leave on that wonderful Sunday afternoon could not be assumed. Just before judgement, they saw gliders under tow coming into view. 'See them,' he remarked to

3 Para is blocked short of the Hotel Hartenstein at Koude Herberg by Krafft's SS Battalion during the first night, and is unable to liberate the street until the following day.

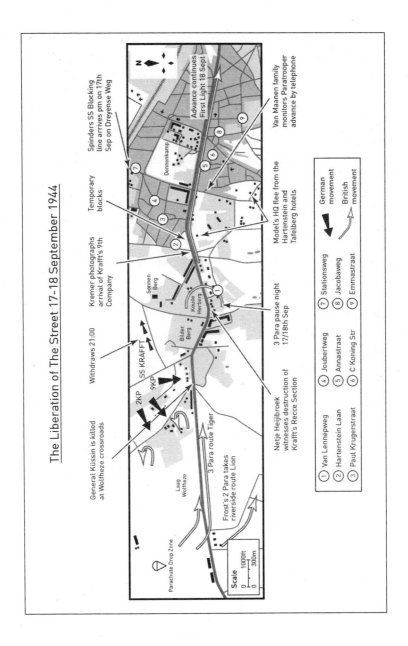

The Liberation of The Street 17-18 September 1944

General Küssin is killed at Wolfheze crossroads

Withdraws 21:00

Kremer photographs arrival of Krafft's 9th Company

Temporary blocks

Spinders SS Blocking line arrives pm on 17th Sep on Dreyense Weg

Advance continues First Light 18 Sept

Van Maanen family monitors Paratrooper advance by telephone

Model's HQ flee from the Hartenstein and Tafelberg hotels

3 Para pause night 17/18th Sep

Netje Heijbroek witnesses destruction of Krafft's Recce Section

2KP

9KP

SS KRAFFT

Sonnen Berg

Koude Herberg

Bilder Berg

Dennenkamp

3 Para route Tiger

Frost's 2 Para takes riverside route Lion

Laag Wolfheze

Parachute Drop Zone

N

German movement

British movement

① Van Lennepweg
② Hartenstein Laan
③ Paul Krugerstraat
④ Joubertweg
⑤ Annastraat
⑥ C Koning Str
⑦ Stationsweg
⑧ Jacobaweg
⑨ Emmastraat

Scale
0   1000ft
0   300m

his sergeant. 'They are coming down from the sky, whereas we are going up to heaven.' He was sent off to 'assemble all my mates immediately' and orders came within the hour. 'Much as I disliked it, I had to take the point of the column again with the commander in my sidecar,' he recalled.[75]

Field Marshal Model was sitting down to lunch at the Hotel Tafelberg, just off the Utrechtseweg. The landings were clearly visible only 3 miles away. His staff were astonished. General Christiansen, the Wehrmacht Supreme Commander in Holland, telephoned about the landing reports. The only response he got was from an excited staff officer who shouted, 'We're getting out of here!' followed by silence. A second call to re-establish telephone contact with the Tafelberg headquarters failed completely.

'The Moffen are running away very fast indeed,' observed 17-year-old Anje van Maanen, living on the Pietersbergscheweg opposite. 'Model, the western front General at the Tafelberg Hotel, passes us in a beautiful staff car; he has red patches [General Staff] and red stripes along his trousers.' The Field Marshal's car turned right onto the Utrechtseweg and sped off towards Arnhem. 'Lots of Germans follow his example,' Anje noticed, as did J. A. van Hofwegen on the Weverstraat nearby. Headquarters personnel 'stationed opposite our house loaded their trucks and drove off,' he remembered, 'as did Field Marshal Model's staff at the Tafelberg.' 'We wave a cheerful goodbye to them,' recalled Anje, 'terribly happy never to see them again.'[76]

The story of Model's suitcase theatrically bursting apart when he hastily departed the Hotel Tafelberg is probably the stuff of fiction. Model was the consummate professional, admired for keeping his head in a tight spot. Hitler saw him as an adept trouble-shooter, nicknaming him the 'fireman of the Eastern Front'. Model was feared and renowned among his subordinates for demanding precise situation reports in the midst of a catastrophe. He acted swiftly on facts, not conjecture. He called in at Feldkommandantur 642 in Arnhem, where the Stadtkommandant, General Küssin, was ordered to radio the latest developments to Hitler. Model did acknowledge that 'he had escaped through the eye of a needle,' barely avoiding capture by the paratroopers. The obsequious Küssin even relayed the comment to the Führer. Model had been surprised – his intelligence had anticipated an Allied ground offensive straight into the Ruhr, maybe with a feint towards Nijmegen, but not an ambitious airborne operation across the five river lines to Arnhem. His next port of call was Doetinchem, where he needed to confer with General Bittrich, commander of the II SS Corps.

Küssin thought he had better drive out to the front through Oosterbeek, and establish the facts. As the Germans had 'owned' the Utrechtseweg throughout four long years of occupation, being the officer responsible for its security he arrogantly felt he was not in need of an escort. He departed in his camouflaged Citroën staff car with just his driver, Gefreiter Josef Willeke, and an aide, Unteroffizier Max Köster. Küssin's administrative command only included a few field police, security guards and the flak detachments around the Arnhem bridges. He stopped off along the Utrechtseweg during the late afternoon and spoke to sentry posts manned by convalescent soldiers and men from Krafft's SS battalion. Nobody had seen anything; he was assured that all was well.

There was a flurry of German activity around the Stationsweg off the Oosterbeek crossroads, when Krafft's 9th Company drove up. Mrs Anna Kremer-Kingma, at No 8, took photographs of an empty side road suddenly filling with heavily camouflaged lorries packed with SS soldiers in open compartments in the back. There was much shouting and gesticulating as hurried instructions were issued by the battalion guides waiting to direct the newly arrived reinforcements behind Krafft's positions, using the back roads along the railway line. Jan Hol, hiding next door at No 10 to avoid enforced labour, had an anxious moment when he saw that 'outside on the Stationsweg strange things were happening'. His position was perilous enough, but Mrs Kremer-Kingma would be shot out of hand if she was spotted taking pictures. 'Cars and lorries full of Germans and "grey mice" [female women auxiliaries] were racing past on their way to Oosterbeek station just up the road. Anna Kremer-Kingma took a whole sequence of pictures. She captured images of guides stepping up onto the running boards of the trucks and clinging to the doors as they drove off through clouds of exhaust smoke towards the railway line.[77]

The Germans were 'jumpy' and obsessed with the notion of 'fifth column' collaborators, likely to harass their rear when they moved forward to deal with the British. They were indeed billeted at Oosterbeek to protect Model's headquarters from just such a threat. Krafft was especially sensitive about 'the attitude of the civilian population' because 'they will surely side with the enemy and will be particularly dangerous on the appearance of the enemy'. Mr J. P. Kelderman, living on the Mariaweg, south of Krafft's 4th Company billet at Berg en Dal, decided he would take a look at what was happening as it grew dark. His son-in-law, G. H. Maassen, living with him, 'told him not to, it might be dangerous,' but to no avail. Within minutes there was an outbreak of gunfire and the sounds of people running.

'My father-in-law came staggering into the house, holding his hand on his thigh,' recalled Maassen. Blood squirted out between his fingers, which he had clamped over an arterial haemorrhage. It had been a rash act and he barely escaped with his life. 'He told us that somebody had called him in German, but instead of answering the voice he had started running back, at which the Germans had shot him.' He now required urgent treatment. 'There were few telephones in this district adjoining Paul Krugerstraat,' just north of the street, Maassen recalled, so the message was relayed 'from one house to another, people shouting to their neighbours, till the nurse was reached.'

Sturmbannführer Krafft recalled a very similar incident. His young, idealistically schooled and motivated recruits could be ruthless. When threatened, they had little compunction about shooting civilians who got in the way. 'As a matter of fact, we did have trouble with Dutch terrorists about 200 to 300 metres from the battalion's original defence position,' he recalled. 'They were suitably dealt with!'

General Küssin arrived at Krafft's headquarters at the Hotel Wolfheze at 17.15, sited between his two forward companies. Considerable battle noises were echoing throughout the woods as he drove up. The SS controlled two of the primary routes into Arnhem, the Amsterdamseweg to the north and the Utrechtseweg in the centre. Krafft had set up his command post in the middle of an old people's home run by two sisters. These aged residents, compulsorily evacuated from The Hague, now found themselves at the centre of a battle. The 2nd Company had just been beaten back and Küssin was briefed accordingly. Trees ahead had masked the extent of the drop zones so the strength of the enemy air-landed forces could not be accurately pin-pointed, but they were assessed as considerable. The 2nd Company's positions ran all the way down to the Utrechtseweg, so Krafft's staff were rather surprised to see the general suddenly emerge from that direction. A reconnaissance troop sent down there earlier had not made it back, and fighting had been going on for nearly 2 hours. Küssin was able to tell Krafft that the II SS Corps was now in overall command, and was from where he would receive future direction. He elected not to accept his subordinate's advice to drive back along the railway line and instead drove off, back down the way he had come. After a few minutes 'we hear a burst of machine gun bullets,' Krafft commented, 'and we have lost a gallant soldier and his companions.'[78]

Krafft's heavy-weapon 9th Company now began to emerge from the woods near the railway line and drive up to the position. With his 2nd Company covering the Utrechtseweg forward left, clearly under pressure as witnessed by the outburst of fire after Küssin's departure, it appeared that the British might be turning his left flank. It was decided to block this primary approach route into Arnhem with the newly arrived 9th Company. They were ordered to counter-attack towards the crossroads where the Wolfheze road entered the street, with flak and 37mm guns. He intended to pinch off the British advance.

Two hours earlier, Model had arrived at the II SS Corps headquarters at Doetinchem. General 'Willi' Bittrich, the commander, had already issued warning orders, and by 17.30 issued the key order by telephone that was to create the conditions for future German success along the street, even though it was about to be liberated. Clear directives were given. Harzer's 9th SS Hohenstaufen was to advance from Arnhem to Oosterbeek and take on the British landings north of the Lower Rhine. The bridge across the Waal at Nijmegen was correctly identified as being the Schwerpunkt, or main point of effort. The 10th SS Frundsberg was to occupy it and secure a bridgehead south of the Waal to prepare for subsequent offensive operations. Above all, any link-up between the advancing Allied ground force and the 'airborne carpet' laid across the intervening river lines was to be prevented. The British landings at Arnhem had clearly overextended themselves; once ring-fenced, they could be destroyed at leisure. In a few crisp orders Model and Bittrich had ensured that the whole length of the street was likely to be contested by both sides. Both its Dutch inhabitants and the advancing British were blissfully unaware of the significance of what had been agreed. They did not foresee a battle – they were caught up in the elation of Liberation.

Harzer had already appreciated what he had to do. First, he had to block the three routes leading into Arnhem, which Krafft's SS battalion had already started to do, on the northern Amsterdamseweg route and the central approach on the Utrechtseweg. Harzer's operations officer, Hauptsturmführer Wilfried Schwarz, had already arrived at Siegen in Germany to begin coordinating the issue of new panzers for the divisions' planned reconstitution. 'I received a signal from Harzer,' he recalled, which was a terse, 'Get back, airborne landings.' He drove all night and arrived at dawn. 'Arnhem was still relatively quiet as I arrived, although there was some shooting.'

Schwarz remembers that 'the soldiers were thinking about their families as everything had been virtually packed for the move to Siegen.' But it was not to be. At first there was disappointment, then a resigned acceptance of 'here we go again'. Nineteen-year-old SS-Rottenführer Paul Müller was billeted at Harskamp training area with the remnants of Panzer Grenadier Regiment 20. 'Our luggage had already been assembled in a pile to be picked up by a lorry,' he recalled, 'because we were scheduled to depart for Germany at 20.00 hours.' Instead they were immediately placed on stand-by to move. 'Everybody got a carbine and 90 rounds of ammunition, which we stuffed into our pockets or haversacks, because we no longer had our ammunition pouches, steel helmets or entrenching tools.' The rest of their equipment would be brought up in lorries later. A 20-truck roving convoy was set up by the division staff, which began to ferry units forward. Müller with his unit waited their turn.

Harzer's 9th SS men, like the 10th SS, were responding in accordance with the specialist anti-airborne training they had received the previous year. Commander of Panzer Corps West, General Geyr von Schweppenburg, had introduced the training in France in 1943 while the newly formed corps was waiting for its tanks to be issued. Both divisions were created to repel future Allied landings expected as part of an envisaged 'Second Front', likely to be preceded by airborne landings. By June 1944, however, the Corps was serving in Russia. Tactics had been developed for rapid and deep attacks from the move before newly landed parachute troops could form up. Disconnecting water and power supplies and cutting telephone lines was all part of this specialised training. The few surviving armoured vehicles belonging to the 9th SS were therefore immediately pushed down the roads to the west of Arnhem to disrupt airborne troops forming up after the drops. Harzer ordered his artillery commander, SS-Obersturmbannführer Ludwig Spindler, to set up a so-called 'Sperrlinie', or blocking line, on the western outskirts of Arnhem. These units began to fill in a line that gradually established itself north to south along the Dreyenseweg, just north of Oosterbeek Hoog railway station, 2,000 metres from the Utrechtseweg. Alfred Ziegler was at the head of the Panzerjäger (anti-tank) 'Alarm' company column led by Klaus von Allwörden, leading the deployment 'with the assault guns clattering down the road behind us'. They presented a formidable spectacle to any advancing airborne troops. 'Soldiers who had been on leave from the town were streaming back,' Ziegler recalled, elated at their rapid progress. 'I waved them off the road as we sped past.'[79]

The rapid and aggressive response by the 9th SS 'Alarm' companies moving into Arnhem from the north and pushing out westwards towards Oosterbeek was not matched by the German effort to the west of the landing zones. SS-Standartenführer Michael Lippert had watched the fly-past from his command post at Schoonrewoerd, north-west of Zaltbommel, between the Waal and Lower Rhine. Hundreds of aircraft flew by from east to west 'and with my binoculars it was clear to see the planes' doors were open and that an air landing was imminent!' As he monitored the aircraft stream he noticed that 'after a short time the aircraft went lower and great numbers of paratroopers began jumping out.' He calculated that they were dropping about 40 kilometres away, somewhere around Ede, Wageningen and Arnhem. His SS NCO School Arnheim did not have its own integral transport, so he immediately began to requisition vehicles locally from the Dutch. 'Everyone knows that the success of an airborne landing is dependent upon the first 24 hours,' he anxiously reflected, but no word came to move. By 18.00 he had virtually given up any prospect of likely deployment until finally, at 19.00, '6 hours after the first landings,' he was ordered to report to Major General von Tettau's staff in Grebbeberg. 'My first impression,' he remembered on arrival at 21.00, was 'that this improvised command staff was one unholy cock-up, where bedlam reigned supreme.'

'Tettau and his staff give the impression of being like an old gentleman's club,' commented Lieutenant Colonel Fritz Fullriede, called upon to provide a battalion from the Hermann Göring training regiment. The west group was loosely formed in the wooded area around Wageningen during the first night after the landings. At daybreak a loose screen began to move eastward. From north to south they were the Dutch SS concentration camp guards from Wach Battalion 3, alongside Eberwein's SS training unit from Lippert's school. In the centre were Luftwaffe technical ground crew acting as infantry with Fliegerhorst Battalion 2. Standartenführer Lippert's SS NCO School Arnheim provided the core, bolstering Schiffstamm Abteilung 10, sailors converted to infantry advancing alongside the Lower Rhine to the south. A unit of artillery crews with small arms from Regiment 184 provided a nebulous reserve. It was a very slow-moving, ponderous and hesitant advance.

SS-Junker Rolf Lindemann, a 20-year-old officer cadet with Lippert's school, recalled that 'it took two days for the move, which started on 18 September, to arrive complete in Arnhem.' He belonged to the most experienced element following the Utrechtseweg from east to west, with the sailors on their right. 'We had a couple of wood-burning civilian trucks at first, which we requisitioned,' he recalled, 'but they broke down because nobody knew how to work them.' As a consequence the unit arrived piecemeal at Grebbeberg during the night, dogged by low-flying Allied aircraft that had strafed them en route. 'It may sound stupid, but only the company and platoon commanders had a map – I never saw one during the entire battle.' Eventually the unpredictable wood-burning lorries were abandoned, and two fire engines were confiscated at the small village of Leerdam. The unit looked like a travelling circus, with 'one large fire engine with its ladders and a small one'. Heavy weapons were loaded aboard the fire engines while the remainder of the heavy equipment came by horse and cart. With the infantry riding on stolen bicycles, the indignant Lindemann quipped that the move 'was less like a military operation, more like Napoleon's retreat from Moscow!'[80]

British boots on the Street

On Renkum Heath the landings appeared to have been a great success. 'The drop zone was like a giant intersection, with jeeps calmly bouncing over the plough' as they dispersed from landed gliders, recalled Reg Curtis with the 1st Parachute Battalion. 'Gliders were coming in to land like an inter-city service.' Soldiers collected heavier equipments from containers and ran off to join their respective units. An air of unreality pervaded this bustling scene. No operation goes as well as this, thought some of the veterans.

Private James Sims, with the 2nd Parachute Battalion, wryly regarded a group of captured Germans. 'Dressed in their best Sunday uniforms, they were, at that moment, probably the most embarrassed soldiers in the German Army.' They had been captured walking out with their girlfriends. Irene Reimann, a Luftwaffe Signals Corps female Luftnachrichtenhelferin, had the unfortunate distinction of being the only female PoW picked up by the British. She was apprehended in uniform on the landing zone, in the company of a German soldier. AFPU photographers Sergeant Gordon Walker and Mike Lewis immediately scooped pictures of her being offered a cigarette by a glider pilot. Reimann was predictably fearful. War correspondent Alan Wood remembered her as 'half cheeky, half in tears and extremely ugly'. Sims meanwhile was chortling at the acute discomfort of the German prisoners:

> 'They had been caught in the fields where we landed, snogging
> with their Dutch girlfriends, and their faces got redder and
> redder by the minute as they caught the drift of some of the
> remarks the grinning paratroopers flung at them.'[81]

The first British boots were on the street by late afternoon. In the west, local dentist J. Barents photographed glider soldiers from B Company the 1st Borderers outside what is today No 130 Utrechtseweg in the village of Renkum as they took up blocking positions. They had quickly covered 3 kilometres from glider landing zone 'Z' south-west of Wolfheze. In the photograph a Bren gunner was lying prone, providing cover from the garden entrance, while other soldiers were moving along the hedge line. Jen Emmen, the owner's young son, can be seen standing upright, staring at them from the garden path – an incongruous image taken in the midst of war, in an area that platoon commander Lieutenant Alan Green with B Company described as 'clean and tidy – spotless'. It would soon change.[82]

The 3rd Parachute Battalion marched fast along the Utrechtseweg, having entered route 'Tiger' via Heelsum. The lead platoon commander, Lieutenant James Cleminson, took risks in the absence of 'no real opposition' to maintain speed. He accepted the channelling effect of the high fences on both sides of the road. 'All that we could do,' he recalled, 'was to string out on either side of the road and keep moving as fast as possible.' So intent were they on getting to the bridge that they did not realise until too late that 'a German staff car had swept down the road from Wolfheze and into the middle of my front section.' Soldiers, keyed up with all the tension, fired and fired into the car with Stens and Brens until it looked like a sieve. Nobody seemed able to stop.

Küssin's driver, Josef Willeke, grabbed his rifle while still at the wheel, but had no chance. The General pulled out his pistol but was caught full in the chest and neck by withering bursts of Sten and Bren fire. One bullet flung his head violently back, exiting the top left side of his skull, scalping the front of his hair line and covering the terrified Max Köstler in the back with the General's blood and brains as he too was mortally hit. 'We were all keyed up,' Cleminson recalled, 'so everyone let fly at it, stopping it dead and killing all the occupants.' Willeke, his leg bent into a grotesque angle by the impact of a bullet, and the General were unceremoniously pulled from the front seats of the car. Cleminson and his men realised that they had just dispatched a high-ranking officer. This outburst of shooting, shattering the silence of the country lane, had spoiled Model's tidy division of responsibilities for the defence of the Arnhem bridge. The 9th and 10th SS had tasks on either side of the bridge – they were not concerned with its defence, which was Küssin's job.[83]

British soldiers emerged onto the street further along near 'Valkenburg', Netje Heijbroek's house, by No 254 Utrechtseweg. She was sheltering with her mother and younger sister in a shelter trench that had been dug at the back. From here she observed 'columns of Tommies approaching from the direction of Wolfheze'. Two English patrols had already passed them by, and thankfully the German 75mm gun covering the Koude Herberg bend had been withdrawn. Her father recalled that two lorries 'full of fleeing Germans appeared', probably Krafft's missing reconnaissance patrol beating a hasty retreat. Heijbroek saw:

'The Englishmen shot all the tyres to shreds and the Germans fled into the gardens of van Borsselenweg and the grounds of the Sonnenberg, whereupon a battle ensued.'

British fire directed from the house windows cut down the Germans and the survivors were winkled out and killed. Krafft was later to confirm in his report that 'we found out later that the recce troop of 2 Company had been wiped out on the Wageningen-Arnhem road.'

Netje saw that a young German soldier had been shot dead by a lime tree. 'He lay there so peacefully,' so incongruous, she observed, 'as if he was part of the natural surroundings.' The war had reared its grisly head at the western sector of the street. 'It was the first of the dead I saw,' she reflected, 'and I had to think of his young life… The Englishmen told us we would have to go back indoors' as it was getting dangerous. Larger columns of British troops were now coming into view, following the first dispersed groups and 'visibly tired from the long march and dangers'.

They offered them water and fruit.[84]

Further east along the Utrechtseweg at the next crossroads, Cleminson's lead element came under fire from a German self-propelled gun. The armoured vehicle 'drove straight down the road into my lead section, knocking out the platoon PIAT [Projectile Infantry Anti-Tank].' They scattered into the gardens at the side of the road and tried to work their way around the gun. A fierce firefight ensued and 'the Germans pulled back, taking their wounded and some of ours'. They quickly reformed and pushed on.

Further north, on 'Leopard', the Amsterdamseweg route, the 1st Parachute Battalion was being impeded by Krafft's SS. Corporal Reg Curtis remembered 'hit and run jabs by the enemy'. The woods constantly echoed with bangs and explosions accompanied by shouts and screams. 'Mortar bombs started whining and bullets slashed the undergrowth.' Armoured cars appeared and 'eventually the whole battalion lay doggo for a while to try to avoid further detection.' The appearance of self-propelled guns and armoured half-tracks was starting to unnerve them. 'We lay up in the woods for what seemed hours,' Curtis remembered, 'pushing on occasionally but cautiously.'[85]

Alfred Ziegler, with the 9th SS Panzerjäger 9, was part of Spindler's rapidly coalescing 'Sperrlinie', or blocking line, along the Dreyenseweg. 'We were supported by a towed 40mm gun and a Sturmgeschütz IV self-propelled tracked gun.' They had an overabundance of MG-42 machine guns – 'practically every man had one, picked up during the retreat from France.' They ambushed the first group of paratroopers that emerged by the 6 kilometre marker stone on the road to Arnhem. 'We opened up with a concentric fire that cut the first lot down,' he recalled. There were not many SS troopers, but 'we boasted a terrific firepower'. The SS men were unimpressed at this 'too cock-sure' an advance. 'I ask you!' Ziegler recalled:

> 'They came marching down the road in company file – what a nonsense! Maybe they were determined to get to Arnhem quickly to show what they could do.'

Krafft's 9th Company led by Obersturmführer (Lieutenant) Leiteritz launched an attack at 17.30 through the woods towards the Utrechtseweg, aiming for the Wolfheze intersection. Brigadier Gerald Lathbury, who had paused with 3 Para at this location, recalled 'a few ranging rounds of mortar burst in the trees overhead shortly followed by heavy mortar fire.' Machine gun fire lashed A Company in the battalion's rear. Despite committing his flak gun, two 37mm guns and more than seven mortars for fire support, the SS attack could not physically reach the road. More than 750 mortar bombs were lobbed over in an assault that, as Krafft described, 'has not succeeded in taking the position but is successful in pinning the enemy down so that he cannot push on to Arnhem for the time being.' General Urquhart, the division commander, came up, impatient at the delay, only to have his jeep 'stonked' and his driver wounded. 'I could now hear the plop and whine of mortars,' he remembered, 'and some of these bombs were falling with unsettling accuracy on the crossroads and in the woodland where many of the 3rd Battalion men were sheltering.' Soon there were 35 wounded down and no forward movement. 'With typical Teuton thoroughness,' Urquhart appreciated, 'they had assumed our line of advance and had accurately ranged their mortars on this important crossroads from some 2,000 yards away.' Krafft had effectively blocked the Utrechtseweg.[86]

Lieutenant Colonel John Frost meanwhile pushed on rapidly with the 2nd Parachute Battalion along the southern route 'Lion'. The sounds of gunfire to his left and his own extensive experience made him acutely aware that, despite the surprise they had achieved, the Germans would soon respond. He was prepared to take risks and expend a few lives now, appreciating that he would save many in the long term. His route was initially through wooded roads and tracks, ideal ambush territory. Despite the dense undergrowth of gorse and birch he forced the pace. 'We had no time to spare for flank guards,' he decided, 'so trusting everyone to do the right thing if attacked we pressed on ventre à terre, merely leaving very small parties to cover the more important roads leading into our own.' Short firefights occurred ahead while opposition was bypassed through and across gardens. 'Crowds were now greeting us as liberators as if the war was already over,' recalled Private James Sims. His officer threatened to shoot 'one young Dutchman, charging about on a bike completely drunk, waving on high a stone bottle of gin from which he was offering swigs to one and all.' The officers drove them mercilessly, 'a crutch-rot of a march,' as platoon commander Mick Flavell remembered. They were losing time and the soldiers started to appreciate, like Sims, that 'this semi-triumphal entry into Arnhem would not last much longer'.

Up ahead Sims heard 'shouts, screams, cheers, single shots, the rapid fire of enemy machine guns and the slower reply of our own Bren guns [which] came echoing back as the battle for the railway bridge was joined.' A reverberating crack and boom shattered all glass in the windows around them. Lieutenant Peter Barry, who had actually climbed onto the railway bridge, remembers there was

'…a flash and a massive explosion. The iron plates on the deck heaved up in front of me; we had stopped just short of disaster. The centre span then collapsed into the river with a huge splash.'

Frost had been relying on C Company crossing the bridge so he could attack the Arnhem road bridge from both sides. Frustrated, the 2nd Battalion pressed on. Major Victor Dover, who had commanded the abortive attempt to seize the railway bridge with C Company, remembered that 'the strange nagging feeling that things were not going as planned became stronger'. His men were starting to share his concern. 'They were old campaigners and could "smell" the course of a battle.' Private Sims, coming up behind and carrying the battalion's heavy mortar tubes, saw that one of the riflemen had been left behind. He was a young boy, helmet off and legs buckled under. He had been propped up against a wooden seat in a clearing overlooking the river. 'The front of his battle blouse was soaked with blood, and someone with rough well-meaning had stuffed a white towel inside the front of his shirt in a vain attempt to staunch the wound.' Some of the Catholics crossed themselves as 'we crept by as quietly as possible as though afraid of waking him from that dread sleep'. They pushed on, passing the evidence of further skirmishes. Up ahead came the sound of shouts, bangs, the rip of spandau fire and pauses as soldiers struggled across garden fences to bypass the opposition. A flurry of fire, calls and the dull crump of grenades followed by cries of pain accompanied short sharp contacts. Bodies of German soldiers and whimpering wounded beside wrecked and smoking vehicles provided mute testimony of rapid forward progress.[87]

Küssin's death now paid a premium because his absence had created a command and control vacuum around the Arnhem road bridge. Both the 9th and 10th SS Divisions had assumed that Küssin was coordinating its defence. Harzer briefly called by during the afternoon to tie up defence measures, but Küssin was away; he would be back, he was told. As Frost's men approached the bridge at dusk, the unsuspecting German defenders were watching the road approach, where the main threat was anticipated. SS-Standartenführer Harmel, the 10th SS commander, later tasked with recovering the bridge, recalled that 'the youngsters had not paid sufficient attention'. Frost's paratroopers climbed the stairs to the bridge from the river level below and in a brief but fierce exchange overwhelmed its old men and teenage flak defenders. 'They had not expected Frost to get there so soon,' Harmel remarked, 'and he surprised them.' Frost's composite force consisting of two-thirds of his battalion and division attachments occupied the houses around the northern ramp of the bridge during the night with about 740 men.[88]

Major Victor Dover's C Company, separated from the 2nd Parachute Battalion, had turned off the southern river route onto the Utrechtseweg. His secondary mission was to capture Küssin's headquarters. Theirs were the first British boots to emerge in large numbers at the eastern end of the street, short of the final approach to Arnhem railway station.[89] Once the Gestapo headquarters was found to be abandoned, Dover decided he should join Frost's force at the bridge.

Hans Möller's Engineer battalion drove through the northern outskirts of Arnhem at about 16.30. 'There was a lot of confused running and shooting around,' he remembered. 'Nobody knew what was going on.' The enemy, they were told, was where the sounds of shooting could be heard.

His reconnaissance platoon could confirm that the Utrechtseweg on the eastern edge of Oosterbeek was still clear. Möller knew the way because it was familiar territory. He decided to drive out to the area of the railway viaduct near the Den Brink Park, which he knew to be a defensible position.

When Dover's company observed Möller's men debussing from their vehicles, where they had paused in front of the St Elizabeth Hospital, they assumed they were prisoners from Frost's advance. They were shuffling themselves into loose ranks. 'What the hell are these Germans doing with their rifles?' he asked the battalion Intelligence Officer, moving with them. 'Suddenly the penny dropped,' Dover recalled. Ian Russel, his leading platoon commander, had already worked out the significance of the rifles. 'Kill those bloody Huns before they kill us!' he shouted. 'For Christ's sake, hurry! Fire, Fire!' and the first two Bren guns began to lash the unsuspecting German ranks. 'Bodies were flung in all directions,' Dover remembered, 'and the wounded were moaning and one of the vehicles caught fire.'[90]

SS-Corporal Wolfgang Dombrowski and his comrades were coming to terms with the unpleasant realisation that they were not going to Germany. They had driven straight past the railway station. When the first tracer bullets started zipping across the road he thought, 'Idiots! They are on exercise!' 'No – the Tommies have landed!' shrieked a Wehrmacht Major from across the road, 'and that's live ammunition!' Möller recalls both advancing companies 'were suddenly hit by such a heavy volume of fire that my spearheading engineers were forced to take cover.' They were on the 'high road' part of the Utrechtseweg, in the area of the St Elizabeth Hospital. All he could see was a deserted tramcar at the junction of his road and the Onderlangs 'low road' coming in from the river's edge to their left. 'The enemy was invisible,' he recalled. Dombrowski felt naked, with just a pistol. Lying in front of him was an abandoned British Sten gun. 'I frantically grabbed it,' he remembered, thinking, 'Thank God – I've got a gun!' Möller's men felt distinctly vulnerable, as he recalled:

'Civilians were running back and forth and acting strangely. Something seemed fishy there. There were also scared people

in the houses around us who cast confused looks at us. That
was not so good, civilians among us at the same time, are they
with the enemy? Were they neutral or resistance fighters? It
looked like things were going to be funny!'

In the middle of all the confusion 'a huge detonation sounded from the
banks of the Rhine, and everything shook under its pressure wave.' It
came from their left – the railway bridge had exploded. 'Why so? What
was going on there?' Möller wondered. When Bittrich, the SS corps
commander, turned up at his command post, 'like he habitually did, to
obtain a first-hand impression of what was going on,' nobody was the
wiser. Bittrich had no idea about any plans to blow the railway bridge
'and was quite concerned about what was going on in our rear.' He
promised reinforcements.[91]

The war had embraced the eastern end of the street, engulfing all three
participants, Germans, British and Dutch, who were either determined
opponents or unwilling bystanders in an emerging battle. Möller's 2nd
Company under Voss had suffered the first casualties, but began to move
through the gardens leading to the railway line on the right. Contact was
established with the SS flak 'Alarm' company under Obersturmführer
Gropp. He had turned up towing an 88mm gun and a 20mm cannon from
Deelen airfield and could now dominate the Utrechtseweg from the high
ground north of the railway cutting. Gropp's unit formed the northern
extremity of Spindler's blocking line that ran through the Den Brink Park
and north along the Dreyenseweg. Steinart's 1st Company started to
move left of the street down towards the river. Möller described that 'we
were deadlocked in this jungle of gardens and mansions, of hedgerows
and fences, of flower gardens and vegetable patches with terraces and
pavilions.' Frost had got through, but the main thoroughfare, the
Utrechtseweg, was now blocked. 'The wide Utrecht street with the
deserted tramcar had turned into a death zone,' Möller commented.

At the western end Lieutenant James Cleminson reached the Hotel
Hartenstein at about 18.00, where they discovered it had been used as a
German officers' mess. 'Lunch had been left on the table,' he recalled, 'and

with my hungry platoon we tucked in until the company commander moved us on.' They did not progress far, stalled by enemy armoured cars that fired at them from the edge of the Hartenstein park. The main body of his parent battalion, 3 Para, was still well behind, stopped at the Wolfheze crossroads by Krafft's SS trainees. There would be no further progress along the street that night, even though Krafft's battalion withdrew under cover of darkness. The vanguard called a halt and dug in short of the Hotel Hartenstein. 'Reports from in front were discouraging,' General Urquhart rationalised. 'The leading company was in contact with the enemy, and being held close to the Hartenstein hotel, on the outskirts of Oosterbeek.' Meanwhile Lathbury, the 1st Parachute Brigade commander, 'heard from the brigade major on the wireless that the 2nd Battalion had captured the bridge. Splendid!'[92]

Sergeant Gordon Walker, the AFPU cameraman, met his two companions Smith and Lewis by the PR glider after the drop and decided to head for Arnhem. 'We got as far as the slight rise in the hill outside of Oosterbeek before being stopped by machine gun fire.' Krafft's battalion had pinned down the 3 Para vanguard. 'We realised the Germans must have come in force and cut the road.' They moved forward and 'the infantry troops there were saying "It's no good, we can't get through" – so that was that.' They returned to Wolfheze.[93]

Liberation! The Dutch

The Dutch, with their local knowledge, knew more than anyone else what was going on at this early stage, but were mistrusted by both sides. The lead elements of the 3rd Parachute Battalion digging in around the street, short of the Hotel Hartenstein, were unable to evacuate their 35 wounded, some of whom were serious. Patrols had identified enemy activity both front and rear. Brigadier Lathbury remembered that 'the battalion MO, Captain Rutherford, telephoned the St Elizabeth Hospital on the civil line' using one of the local houses on the Utrechtseweg, and discovered that the British were already using it. This unique opportunity to garner vital information after the drop was never exploited. A local Dutch Resistance man pointed out that the Gelderland Provincial Electricity Board telephone system (PGEM) was working. The paratrooper response was that their own field transmitters would do, but they were failing to get through. Even though Möller, commanding the German road block to the east of the street, was convinced that 'the sympathy of the population was clearly and understandably with the liberators,' the British had reservations. Corporal Reg Curtis with 1 Para, fighting his way into Arnhem from the north, even assumed 'maybe fifth columnists were busy', because according to his pre-drop briefings:

> 'We knew that in the area, working in cooperation and collaborating with the Germans, were quite a number of the Dutch National Socialist Party, with a large contingent of fifth columnists. Although none were caught red-handed in conflict with our troops, the element of suspicion was there, of the collaborators.'

Glider-borne infantry from the 7th KOSB had already skirmished with Dutch SS troops on the fringes of the Ginkel Heath drop zones. 'We were warned by the Dutch underground movement to be wary of these elements,' Reg Curtis remembered.[94]

This failure to communicate with the Dutch was to have consequences. The PGEM telephone network was reliable. When the Germans evacuated the exchange they disconnected nearly all the private telephones. Reliable Dutch girls remained behind and restored the circuits that connected them to equally reliable friends in the surrounding area. Mr A. H. Becker, sheltering in the cellar of the PGEM exchange, remembered that although 'our occupier changed a few times, the telephone line was still working throughout, and regular messages were being sent through.' Civilians who had been unable to make use of their telephones for some time were pleasantly surprised to find them ringing again.[95]

'Telephone!' announced Anje van Maanen, living at No 8 Pietersbergscheweg near the Oosterbeek crossroads. 'Hallo, yes?' she asked, and heard the Tromp family calling from Heelsum, who announced, 'We are free, the Tommies have dropped behind our house and they are on their way to Oosterbeek.' Sounds of jubilation could be discerned in the background. 'They are so nice,' the Tromps said. 'We're smoking Players and eating chocolate!' The Van Maanens were left excited and overjoyed, but became 'terribly impatient' when nothing was heard until 6 o'clock, when the phone rang again. This time it was the Sanders family on the line, who said, 'The Tommies are very near Oosterbeek.' Speaking over a crackling line, they told them 'there is a fight going on around their house,' and they had all gone into the cellar. Anje listened intently, and recalled that 'we can hear some shooting in the distance'. There was a pause and the telephone rang again. This time the Sanders declared that 'they are liberated, and the Tommies are in their house.' With the British on their way, the Van Maanens settled into a period of excited apprehension, listening out all the time for the sounds of shooting, which were coming nearer and nearer.[96]

Roelie Breman on the Benedendorpsweg, on route 'Lion' next to the Lower Rhine, heard German soldiers running down the Weverstraat shouting, 'Die Engländer, die Engländer!' They ran off towards Arnhem. Voices were heard outside and Roelie peeped out and saw 'a lot of soldiers'. Lieutenant Colonel Frost's 2nd Parachute Battalion was speed-marching urgently by, strung out along the Benedendorpsweg. 'They are very tired and thirsty,' Roelie remembered. 'We give them water and they go on.' Their purposeful advance, urged on by officers and NCOs who forced the pace, made a deep impression. 'The English soldiers are very well equipped,' she noticed, unlike the shabby Germans. Vehicles towing guns and equipment came at the end of the column – 'You can see the long aerials swishing behind,' she remembered. More and more marched by and then 'a heavy fight follows' when 'a large group of them goes toward the brick works and the railway bridge.' Information was shouted from house to house. The Van Maanen family heard from the Gerritsens next door that 'the Benedendorpsweg of Oosterbeek is liberated and the English have reached Station-Laag.' They waited impatiently, but there was still no sound of British boots on the Utrechtseweg.[97]

Four long years of occupation had made the Dutch astute observers of German behaviour. Any troop movements were an implicit threat. The

Krema-Kingma family had watched Krafft's 9th Company assembling on the Stationsweg that afternoon, even taking photographs. Jan Hol, hiding with the Jansen family next door at No 10, got the news from their brother at around 16.30. 'I've seen them,' he claimed:

'...Hundreds and hundreds of parachutists. I met them as I was going to milk the cows near the Rhine. I even shook hands with some of them. And look... English cigarettes!'

Being inquisitive could be dangerous. Anje van Maanen's parents decided to keep the family indoors as it grew dark. 'In the darkness the Germans and the English will fire onto anything they see or hear,' they were warned. There was fighting around the Koepel prison near the St Elizabeth Hospital at dusk. British paratroopers from the 3rd Battalion clashed with Möller's SS men in the Wilhelminastraat, where they had linked with the SS flak detachment on their right to block the Utrechtseweg. Gatekeeper Frederik Michels, who commuted daily from Nijmegen to the Koepel, slid back the small hatch in the prison gate to view the commotion outside. As soon as his face was momentarily silhouetted against the light shining from behind, British paratroopers shot at the exposure. Michels toppled backwards, mortally wounded.

Jan Hol on the Stationsweg 'spent most of the evening and night with my nose pressed to the window pane, staring into the darkness, awaiting their arrival.' No movement could be discerned. Further along, at No 48 Utrechtseweg, Bep Bolte, the railway supervisor, remembered that 'on Sunday evening we heard voices coming from the direction of the railway'. He stood in the back garden with his wife and stepdaughter and peered down into the gloomy railway cutting beneath. There were signs of movement. They could just see the outline of British soldiers moving in single file along the tracks, going towards the railway station to their right. Elements of 3 Para, having been driven off the road by German armoured vehicles, were seeking to get into Arnhem along the railway tracks.

Cees Meijer at 20 Weverstraat, just south of the Utrechtseweg, had watched the Germans pull out. 'They waved at us, so we got the impression that they thought the war for them had ended and that they could go home.' Much later two Germans scurried past, one 'half undressed,' Cees recalled. 'His comrades had apparently forgotten to warn him when they rushed off.' Much of the contemporary evidence suggests that by late afternoon, as Cees observed, 'it was rather quiet'. There were no Germans, which 'gave us the impression that things were going well for the English'. British paratroopers had already marched by through the Benedendorpsweg alongside the river. Many locals had gone down to watch. An air of normal behaviour started to manifest itself, at odds with the rapidly diminishing German presence. Johannes van Zonnenveld watched heavily armed SS troops in battledress retiring eastwards at the same time as people were coming back from the lower village heading for home. 'They were already smoking English cigarettes.'[98] Apart from Krafft's blocking action just west of the Hotel Hartenstein, there did not appear to be an appreciable German presence anywhere on the street as far as the Den Brink Park to the east. Any isolated stay-behind groups had no idea what was going on and certainly were not incorporated into any defensive blocks forward of SS-Obersturmbannführer Spindler's 'Sperrlinie', or blocking line, filling in along the Dreyenseweg north of Oosterbeek station. By opting to dig in for the night short of Oosterbeek, the British missed an opportunity to push more substantial elements of 3 and 1 Para straight down the Utrechtseweg to Frost's 2 Para at the Arnhem bridge. Kees Bolderman, living at the east end of the Utrechtseweg, remembers walking through 'virtually deserted streets' after his evening meal. 'Here and there are small knots of people,' he recalled, 'busily talking to one another.' Away to the west he could 'hear the uninterrupted sound of rifle and machine gun fire in the distance'. He went back home 'because there is nothing special to see'.[99]

Towards evening the previously feared offices of the SD and Gestapo at No 85 Utrechtseweg were in turmoil. They had decided to flee. Martin Bokhoven, living at No 72, noticed 'at about 7 o'clock on Sunday evening the Germans burned their complete archive in the cellars, and the people who were still imprisoned there were loaded in a truck and driven off.'

This was one of the psychological high points of the Liberation. 'Shortly afterwards, the entire SD (Gestapo) apparatus headed off towards the station too.' The locals breathed more easily, but it was not all over yet.[100]

General Bittrich, the commander of the II SS Corps, sat in his Doetinchem headquarters like a spider in its web. The strands were provided by the Dutch telephone system, which linked him to his superior, Field Marshal Model, and his subordinates, the 9th SS under Harzer, Harmel's 10th SS and the Luftwaffe communications network. They could in turn effectively communicate with their 'Alarm' units by telephone. By contrast, the British were experiencing radio transmitter problems, to such a degree that Urquhart, the division commander, like Küssin, felt he should go forward and see what was happening himself. As a consequence he was going to cut himself off from his command during a crucial phase of the battle. Harzer subsequently recalled that 'it was an advantage for our command that an excellent telephone system existed in Holland and particularly in Arnhem.' The British chose not to use it. As Harzer explained, 'This made it possible to dispense almost entirely with radio communication during the battle, especially as our signals section possessed very few transmitters that were of any use,' because most of their signals equipment had been lost during the retreat from France.[101]

Bittrich drove into Arnhem that night and discovered that 'the situation in the Arnhem area was completely obscure'. Avoiding the turmoil of the confused fighting, he went back to Doetinchem and stayed by his telephone. Two Blitzmädchen female telephone operators resolutely decided to stay on and man the Arnhem switchboard that night. They made it possible for the subordinate German commanders to be constantly updated on the progress of the fighting, and it was they who told Bittrich late that night that the Rhine bridge had fallen to the British. This partly explains the speed and effectiveness of the German countermeasures, whereas the Dutch, who knew a great deal, were largely ignored by the British.

The situation at the far eastern end of the street around the St Elizabeth Hospital and Museum was fluid and dangerous, unlike the relative oasis of peace around the centre of Oosterbeek. Jan Hendrik

Esvelt, living on the south bank of the Lower Rhine, could see 'fires in Oosterbeek and along the Utrechtseweg near the St Elizabeth Hospital'. Nobody had any idea what was happening. 'Are the British advancing?' he wondered. 'In the evening we could hear cheering in the city – because of the liberation?' His daughter Berend recalled her father trying to pick out the detail with binoculars. German armoured cars were passing beneath, making for the Arnhem bridge. 'A passing German soldier shouldered his rifle,' she recalled, 'and shouted to put the binoculars away.'[102]

Hans Möller's engineer Kampfgruppe was fighting amid flame and smoke against Victor Dover's C Company from 2 Para at the far eastern end of the Utrechtseweg, less than a mile from the Arnhem road bridge. 'This was like a "wild west shoot-out",' recalled one of his section commanders, SS-Rottenführer Wolfgang Dombrowski. 'There was no front – it was a case of sections and groups fighting scattered actions against British groups of similar size.' In the middle were the terrified Dutch. 'There was no discernible "front" on the English side either.'

Rinia van Nauta lived next to No 54 Utrechtseweg[103], occupied by Dover's men. 'This poor man, his wife and children found themselves on a warm Sunday evening suddenly trapped in their home and surrounded by Parachutists,' Dover recalled. 'It was a beautiful house, splendidly furnished and certainly not intended to be a fortress for troops with hobnailed boots.' Van Nauta's house was 'torn apart' as 'windows were being knocked in and his furniture was being piled to form barricades.' Dutchman H. Buhrs, who had joined with Dover's men as a guide, remembers that 'the huge mansion was packed with soldiers, with the staff officers in the cellar.' Möller's 2nd Company commander, Voss, had identified this 'large mansion at the corner where we had met such heavy resistance'. His other company commander deployed to provide fire support for a break-in. They had no idea of the British numbers packed inside.

'Silently, like cats, and under the cover of darkness,' Untersturmführer (Lieutenant) Erhard Voss and another group under Oberscharführer (Sergeant) Pötschke crept into the park area bordering the mansion. Möller recalled 'hugging the hedgerows and the clumps of bushes for concealment'.

They kept off the gravelled paths reflected in the ambient light in order to be 'careful to avoid all sounds'. Tension rose – 'not a sound was heard, no resistance, no sign of the enemy – eerie'. Rottenführer (Corporal) Maas dashed forward at the prearranged signal, raced up the stairway, deftly hung an explosive device on the door knob 'and pulled the fuse igniter'. A massive explosion blew in the door and Voss, accompanied by five SS engineers, sped through the ruined gaping entrance. They were confronted by a large hall and wide marble stairs, and even noticed the expensive carpet.

> 'Then four tall figures appeared on the first landing. Everybody pulled up his SMG [sub-machine gun] and fired. A terrible hail of bullets and hand grenades resounded in the hall. Two Canadians dropped and rolled down the stairs. Voss stumbled and collapsed; everyone had fired at the same time.'

Hand-to-hand fighting broke out and Möller described how 'more paras came down from the rooms on the upper floor and up from the cellar like disturbing a hornets' nest.' Pötscke and his group rushed the door but could do little except retrieve the mortally wounded Voss and two others who had gone down, before beating a hasty retreat. 'We had underestimated the enemy completely,' admitted Möller. 'Obersturmführer Steinart plastered the mansion with a hail of fire from the other side of the street.' The pulverising fire from the 20mm cannon mounted on the two half-tracks enabled the group to be extracted.

'To be caught in the middle of a battle with your family around you is the worse kind of horror,' Victor Dover recalled. 'Rinia van Nauta was a brave man, but however hard he tried to conceal his feelings the anguish in his eyes was plain to see.' Dover's unsentimental paratroopers agreed that 'there was not a man in the company who did not feel concern and share some of the anguish of this Dutchman. War is madness gone mad!' They managed to get the Van Nautas out of the house during a lull in the fighting, but they were not the only ones caught up in the violence. One young lad, H. Verkerk, living nearby at No 83 Utrechtseweg, remembered that:

'About ten in the evening, as if by agreement, a hellish noise of gunfire and machine gun fire began. We heard the British in the porch, smashing at the door. Heavy firing was coming from the front and rear. The house shuddered under the fire aimed at it by the Germans using light flak guns, thinking it was full of British. Maybe it was: we had no way of knowing. If so they must have come in at the rear!'

The Verkerk family had only just been telephoned by friends from Oosterbeek saying that they were about to be liberated. They were a little dubious, bearing in mind what was going on around their house.

'It is not difficult to imagine the atmosphere and the feelings of the inhabitants of the Utrechtseweg during that night,' Dover reflected. Despite German property requisitions about them, 'most of the residents were living in their own houses' and these were being fought through. Liberation was proving to be more painful then anticipated. Dover's company was being cut to pieces in a series of fragmented actions. 'To fight an armed enemy is one thing,' Dover declared, 'but to be involved with civilians in a confined area, civilians who were both friendly and frightened, is another matter.' Verkerk remembered the Henzens, living ten houses down the street at No 67, telling him that 'the Germans were in his cellar firing through the ceiling at the British on the floor above, and the British were replying to the Germans in a similar manner,' firing through the floor.

Dover was then 'hit in the backside with something; exactly what it was I shall never know'. The fragment passed through both cheeks of his bottom, leaving four small holes. 'Sir, you'll get your discharge with this one,' was the ribald comment from one of his soldiers, who dressed the wound. 'You'll be no bloody good in the Army, but the Navy will have you – you've got five of 'em.' Dover had to smile. 'The humour of the soldier is frequently lewd,' he accepted, 'but unquenchable in times of stress.'[104]

Stress there now was as Dover sought to extricate his hard-pressed company from the trap in which they now found themselves. Möller was driving a wedge into his company at street level, while all movement was engaged by Gropp's flak group on the high ground on the other side of the railway cutting. High walls and garden fences impeded all progress. 'These walls slowed down the pace of the withdrawal and lost us the surprise of a sudden departure,' Dover admitted. Paratroopers moving in small dispersed groups fell easy prey to the intense German fire. 'The Germans soon reacted to the slowness of our withdrawal. Half-track vehicles kept abreast with us along the Utrechtseweg, pumping in fire. Snipers seemed everywhere.' Dover's men were split up as they pulled back to No 72. 'Without any form of communication and surrounded by brick walls and buildings, to say nothing of the Germans, the company was disintegrating,' Dover realised. All his platoon commanders were down and there were only 25 men left with him, responding to orders. They became pinned down at No 72, with the caretaker Bokhoven and his son.[105]

Armoured half-tracks crawled right up to the house once they realised they had only to contend with small arms fire. 'It was like shooting peas at a barn door,' recalled Dover, while the Germans returned 20mm cannon fire, pounding away at point-blank range. The house soon filled with smoke and it became difficult to breathe. 'The noise of the armoured vehicles in the confined area was magnified by the crunch of shells.' Dover's wounded, stranded on the other side of the road, called for help, but it was impossible to reach them. 'Those who have never lost a battle are fortunate,' Dover reflected, 'because they have not had to face the decision whether to fight to the last man and the last round, or whether to surrender – and just when.' His men 'were very steady,' he recalled, but 'they knew that this was a battle they would not and could not win'. The Germans brought up flame-throwers and tried to flame them out, 'adding fuel to the buildings already burning'. Dover had little recourse except to accede to the ultimate humiliation and call out 'Cease firing!' Bokhoven, the caretaker, was also taken prisoner and was to die in a concentration camp in Germany. 'Young Bokhoven, however, survived,' Dover remembered, and lived to tell the story.[106]

Liberation remained an intoxicating thought for the Dutch living in the central part of the Utrechtseweg that night. They could hear the intermittent sounds of battle near the bridge, but there was nothing to suggest that anything was amiss. Even as the sounds of battle wafted eerily across the eastern side of the street the policemen at No 107 Utrechtseweg continued to fill in the Daily Reports Book. They recorded that at 20 minutes to midnight 'police officer Nauta from Renkum reports that two patients from the Wolfheze Psychiatric Hospital have been found in Renkum'. A new dawn emerging over the Oosterbeek crossroads seemed to herald the end of four years of occupation. The police reports continued to exude a perplexing normality. At 7 o'clock an air raid warden came into the Police Station and handed in a 'British gun and helmet'. An hour later a hand grenade was left at the counter, 'found in the garden of the Villa Eikenhorst'. A few windows had been broken in Oosterbeek on top of the damage from the bombing raids on Sunday morning, but little else. Some of the residents had even filled in the mortar bomb craters in their pristine lawns. It appeared the good times were coming back.[107]

At dawn the 3rd Parachute Battalion quickly moved along the Utrechtseweg and closed up to the area of Den Brink and the St Elizabeth Hospital. Contrary to their own patrol reports, the Dutch could have told them the previous night that the coast was already clear. Reconnaissance squadron jeeps set out early to prove routes to the bridge. The Oosterbeek crossroads by the Schoonoord and Vreewijk hotels remained relatively peaceful. Crowds gathered to wave at the reconnaissance jeeps driving by, the paratroopers seated sideways with their legs dangling over the sides. They waved back.

'My father told me England was a very different world from here,' remembered eight-year-old Jan Berenden. 'Everyone was free and you had a lot of food there, so a lot of people were crying.' Jan 'was totally out of my mind' when he watched the parachutes descending the day before. His enduring memory of the first British soldiers that marched by was that 'they smelt very different'. The heady smell of freedom. 'The Germans always smelt a bit sour because of their food, their würst [sausage], whereas the British smelt a little sweet, like cigarettes and chocolate.' Young Wil Rieken at the baker's at No 178 Utrechtseweg remembers that 'we saw the Tommies coming'. She was completely caught up in the excitement. 'We saw the jeeps and everyone was trying to shake hands; it was so good to see them, almost like a festival.' G. A. Versteeah gave one lone airborne signaller a lift on his bike. 'He had got separated from his unit during the night' and made it clear that he must get to the bridge. When they got as far as the Marienberg at the eastern end of the street 'he suddenly got into contact with his unit on his walkie-talkie' and off he went. 'He was delighted,' Versteeah fondly recalled, 'thanking me very much.'[108]

Jan Hol at the Stationsweg caught his first glimpse of the British between 3 and 4 o'clock in the morning. 'A subtle movement in the darkness attracted my tired eyes, and there they were.' Long silent files were moving quietly by. He dashed outside gushing with enthusiasm, seeking to welcome them. 'Foolishly enough,' he recalled, 'all I could think of saying was "Do you speak English?" They simply laughed and continued on their way.' G. H. Maassen left his home in the Mariaweg and came down to the Utrechtseweg. There he saw 'Tommies, we called them', standing at the end of his road at the Paul Krugerstraat junction. 'They stood looking around as if they were on holiday,' he recalled, 'now we had been liberated!' His exhilaration was somewhat tempered when he noticed the British and German bodies lying near the fire station on the Utrechtseweg. British soldiers were striding by, marching in the direction of Arnhem.[109]

An air of peaceful unreality reigned – the Liberation appeared all but over. Johannes van Zonnenveld noticed that in the Jacobaweg, opposite the Police Station at No 107, there was 'a family sunning themselves in their front garden, would you believe!' German snipers were still active. 'We told them it was probably healthier to stay inside.' Eight-year-old Willy van Zanten's grandmother, Opoe Zoetekouw, in Cornelis Konigstraat nearby, insisted on sticking to her normal Monday washing day. Oblivious to the sounds of fighting, she stood defiantly by her washing line and declared that 'they're not going to hit me'. Willy had actually seen that there was a German sniper 'hidden in a large beech tree, about 50 metres north of our house' targeting the Utrechtseweg from its south side. When four British soldiers came down the road in a jeep his 17-year-old brother pointed him out.

'The British asked him to surrender. He shouted "Nein" and fired his rifle. Then he was shot with a burst of machine gun fire and fell out of the tree. I saw it and, thinking back, I still see it before my eyes.'

Fifty-nine years later, an older Willy van Zanten was to show British veterans around the same area. Stopping at the site of the old beech tree, he explained that he lived only about 100 metres away and started to tell the sniper story. 'Over there was a large beech tree,' he started to explain, 'with a German sniper,' one of the veterans interrupted. The perplexed Willy finished his story and veteran Bob Paisley explained, 'I did it.' He was not proud of what he had done, simply stating that 'it was my job which I was paid for'. 'Just imagine,' declared the astounded Willy, '59 years after the battle I met that British soldier – unbelievable.'[110]

Anje van Maanen thought she had spotted British soldiers in the street below, but their attitude and bearing was somehow different. They 'must be Tommies,' she thought. 'They move so silently and quiet.' Calling out was not a good idea because they might shoot back if Germans. 'We got a fright,' Anje recalled when her aunt settled the issue by flinging open her bedroom window and shouting out a cheerful 'Good morning!' The equally startled paratroopers quietly responded, fingers to lips, 'Ssh – ssh, good morning.' 'Tommies, and so we are Free! Free! Free!' celebrated the delighted Anje. People poured into the street wearing their pyjamas and dressing gowns.

The war had not brutally emerged in central Oosterbeek like it had to the east of the street. 'A characteristic of the British soldier I had seen in other battles, was his respect for the property and the houses of the people over whose land he fights,' remembered the division commander General Urquhart. 'Now, I saw it as a time-waster.' It seemed to verge on dalliance bearing in mind the need to get to the bridge as soon as possible. Avoiding trampling across flower beds had not been a feature of the 2nd Battalion advance, now defending houses around the northern ramp of the bridge. Such civilised behaviour was impeding progress. 'I was told that they were even knocking on doors and asking permission to search a house,' declared the exasperated Urquhart. 'They soon lost this politeness.'[111]

The Dutch were accustomed to more boorish German behaviour. 'You were all so gentle,' recalled newly married Jo Crum-Bloemink, 'and we were not used to that.' Corporal Jim 'Spud' Taylor, proving routes with A Troop of the division Reconnaissance Squadron, was tasked with taking out a troublesome German sniper, hidden in a blind spot that was difficult to reach. He recalls how, intent on his kill:

'I went up the path, carrying my Bren gun, and knocked at the front door. When the lady opened, I asked if I might come in, in order to shoot a German. I was shown into a room in the house, with a table in the centre of the floor. I removed the cover from the table, replacing it with my camouflaged face-veil, so that the front metal legs of the Bren gun would not scratch the polished surface. Quietly, I opened the window and returned to the table, from which position I could see the sniper clearly in my sights. I fired and hit him, then gathered up all the empty cartridge cases. I helped the lady to put back her cloth and left the room just as it had been, but remembered afterwards that I'd forgotten to close the window.'

Lieutenant John Marshall with D Troop was laughed at by a Dutchman for knocking at the front door 'instead of kicking in the glass as the Germans would have done'. The perplexed Marshall was told, 'What a funny lot you English soldiers are!'[112]

The residents of the street were not used to the sights and sounds of war. Unlike soldiers, they did not appreciate the menace of the whispering approach of a mortar bomb. Anje van Maanen was in a crowd opposite their house when it was fired upon from the Dennenkamp Park. There was 'a whistling noise, which we can't place', then:

'A moment later again, the same noise just above our heads. It's most queer and then suddenly we realise, it's bullets going over our heads. They're firing at us!'

Snipers were alien. Anje described them as 'Germans who fight in trees and on top of roofs until they are dead'. They 'try and kill as many people as they can, and they are practically out of reach'. An interesting civilian perspective on a threat they had yet to come to terms with. Bodies also came as a shock. Anje rode her bike by several 'queer-looking lumps' near the Hotel Hartenstein. 'There he lies,' she recalled at the terrible realisation, a 'pale drawn face, closed eyes, a little bit of blood on his temples and his hand stretched backwards carrying a shell.' He was killed in action. Though these corpses were German, she was overcome by the pathos of the scene and confessed, 'I cry a little on my bicycle.' She was aggrieved that 'people could walk around talking and laughing and not minding the dead'. After all, 'this man too was a young man who lived his life, who loved and did not want his life ended this way.'[113]

The veneer of ostensible normality was still maintained in the police Daily Reports ledger at No 107, despite the obvious noise of battle to the east of the street. At 10.00 a woman was reported shot dead near the railway line, but 30 minutes later two ownerless bicycles were reported by Mr de Swart at his factory. Reports of missing evacuees came in, and a health warning that 'loose fragments' were dropping off the water tower next to the street, which 'may be dangerous for people walking beneath'. Live shells continued to be handed in, and spare beds offered at a local school, later to be burned out. At 12.00 Mr Bax announced that one of the Wolfheze psychiatric patients had walked into his house. 'She does not possess any papers,' the report read, 'and wears a man's overcoat.' Mr Klaver, a plumber, complained that his wallet had been stolen from his house after it had been bombed. Yet there are no entries about any of the intense military activity occurring along the length of the street. Fierce fighting was crackling at its eastern end, where the Germans appeared to be ominously regrouping again, but there is no mention in the report book. The Dutch residents in the centre of Oosterbeek seemed blissfully unaware of the awfulness of what was happening around them.[114] They had just been liberated.

CHAPTER 4

Street Blocks

Western screen: the Germans

Generalleutnant Hans von Tettau, the commander of the improvised division being hastily formed west of Oosterbeek, was not reassuring when SS-Standartenführer Hans-Michael Lippert turned up at his headquarters at Grebbeberg. 'He greeted me by saying, "Now we're in the shit, we're finished!"' Lippert's SS NCO School Arnheim was inbound and due to arrive over the next few hours. His was a more phlegmatic response: 'Herr General,' he offered, 'the English haven't got us yet and if we are supposed to go under, let's not make it easy for them.' What did dismay Lippert was that nobody on the General's staff seemed to know anything about the enemy situation. 'The only thing I could find out was that English troops had landed west of Arnhem and Nijmegen,' he recalled.

Neither was Lippert impressed with the hodge-podge of units forming up that would support him in the projected eastward advance on Arnhem. His immediate southern neighbour was Schiffstamm Abteilung 10, a naval manning battalion under Kapitänleutnant Zaubser, due to advance along the line of the Lower Rhine River. They were men who had crewed the naval guns and observation bunkers in the 'Atlantic Wall', which had been bypassed by the Allied invasion, then hastily converted to infantry. 'Zaubser's first request was to have some experienced officers and NCOs attached to his unit,' Lippert recalled, 'as was the case with the Fliegerhorst battalion,' made up from former air force technical personnel. Forty-eight-year-old Bootsman (Boatswain) Alfred Steckhan was one of the seamen, with the 2nd Company of Schützen Battalion 250, also with Von Tettau's composite 'division'. He had written a brief letter to his wife on the day the paratroopers landed, capturing the mood of these somewhat disorientated ad-hoc units, awaiting the move forward. 'My dearest Liess,' he wrote:

'I am pleased that you are still in the land of the living. Nowadays you mustn't be surprised if things suddenly change. Maybe your letters will get through anyway. If the new weapons are not used in action soon I don't know how this struggle will end. In spite of everything I am still hopeful because if we throw in the towel now we are done for.'

Steckhan had no idea the airborne armada was on its way when he penned his letter. Nor did he appreciate that this would be his last communication with his wife. He had barely three days left to live. Lippert swiftly grasped that 'it was obvious to me, that the companies of the NCO School would be the only worthwhile unit among the other attached units under command.'[115]

Rolf Lindemann, an officer cadet attached to Lippert serving as a heavy weapons section commander, was, like many of his men, an eastern front veteran. The majority were young soldiers with about one year's service who had served for short periods at the front. 'But a soldier with one year's service is not really experienced,' Lindemann assessed, but they were more so than the accompanying collection of sailors, airmen and SS concentration camp guards under command. Lindemann's men had been selected from the best of the recruit intakes and sent back to the school for NCO training after a short period at the front. 'They were more aggressive and adventurous than normal soldiers and felt they belonged to an elite.' Alfred Steckhan was by contrast a mature 48-year-old, married with two daughters and prepared to do his national duty, but in reality he wanted to go home. Once the 'Atlantic Wall' had been breached, Steckhan knew the future would be far from rosy. Lippert's men were more motivated than most. 'They were not necessarily fanatic national socialists,' Lindemann recalled, 'because Himmler was not loved at all by the Waffen SS.' Lippert's uncompromising views made him disdainful of Von Tettau's apparent pessimism, and this was to create command frictions. 'Tettau was an SS hater,' Lindemann claimed. 'We really disliked him because of his attitude to us, but we loved Lippert,' a charismatic leader.[116]

Wach Battalion III Nordwest, commanded by Sturmbannführer Anton Helle, was rather dismissed in effectiveness terms by Lippert as 'consisting of companies without any battle experience'. The soldiers included Dutch volunteers, Ukrainians, soldiers convalescing from injuries, and Dutchmen seeking to avoid 'arbeitsatz', or pressed labour, in Germany. Most were medically unfit concentration camp guards and personnel, because fit soldiers had been sent off to regular SS units long ago. Unit motivation was poor and any effective soldiers had been weeded out more recently to supplement hastily formed combat units attempting to stem the Allied advance through France and Belgium. Guarding static camps was their only military experience apart from reluctantly enforcing local security against the Resistance. They also formed 'Alarm' Einheiten 'call-outs', dispatched to track down shot-down Allied air crew. Only a few officers and NCOs had combat experience; the rest were insufficiently trained and underequipped.

Lieutenant Colonel Fritz Fullriede, the commander of the Hermann Göring Training Regiment, was ordered to relocate his Wossowsky Battalion from Katwijk-on-Sea to Ede. Herbert Kessler, an NCO with the battalion, recalled the day when 'the air was filled with the noise of engines' as they watched the awesome fly-past over the coast. 'The soldiers looked at each other in amazement,' Kessler recalled, 'when they noticed that the engine-powered planes were towing gliders.' The battalion assembled in a forest where their commander, Oberleutnant Artur Wossowsky, delivered an evocative 'pep-talk'. 'Kameraden, the time has come,' he began. 'I demand an unrelenting commitment until this operation is brought to a complete success.' Soldiers were fired up, but 'the awfully young soldiers with their 18 years of age had known neither death nor injury so far.' Unfortunately the advance with their commander's final 'I know that I can rely on you' ringing in their ears was less inspiring than the atmospheric speech delivery. Wossowsky led in a staff car, but the rest of the battalion rode behind on bicycles, 'the only means of transportation available'. The 26-year-old Wossowsky had been plucked from Fullriede's regimental staff; he was an anti-aircraft commander and knew absolutely nothing about infantry combat operations. As Kessler recalled, it 'was not easy to keep the companies together using this means of transportation'. The deployment descended into a form of cycle rally, conducted by night to avoid low-level Allied strafing attacks. 'They succeeded in gathering the men in during regular breaks,' Kessler remembered. 'Some of the soldiers even rode by day to re-establish contact with their unit.' This was not the idealistic baptism of fire for the Fatherland that many of the young recruits, fed a diet of Blitzkrieg propaganda, had been anticipating.[117]

Von Tettau's division 'screen' approached the British landing zones on a five-battalion front from the west. Inexperience produced caution. Lippert remembers that the first outbreak of firing on the Utrechtseweg began at Renkum at about 03.00 on 18 September. Reconnaissance troops had been dispatched towards the brickworks next to the river. B Company of the 1st Borderers glider infantry, holding a forward blocking position at the brickworks, suspected that they were going to be bypassed and surrounded by Von Tettau's eastward advance. Lippert had already identified 'heavy rifle and machine gun fire in the area of the chimneys south of Renkum'. The first German reconnaissance elements were already there, milling around a motorcycle combination in the courtyard facing the Borderer outposts, oblivious to the danger. 'No doubt they were interested in learning what was going on,' recalled Lieutenant Hardy with the Borderers, who sprang the ambush. 'With such a target presented to our men, it was too good to miss... War is a filthy rotten business,' he reflected, accepting that they were probably 'nice young fellows' as they opened up with two or three Bren guns and 10 to 16 rifles. 'The crowd that clustered around the motorcycle were probably much the same, but at that moment they had no parents, brothers, sisters, wives and children.' Many were cut down in the initial burst of fire. 'They were just a target, for this was war,' Hardy concluded. Pandemonium reigned as the inexperienced German soldiers scattered and sought to reorganise, 'but when they did start to return fire, it was obvious there were a large number of them in the area.'

Schiffstamm Abteilung 10 advanced toward the brickworks. They were unsure of themselves; this was to be a baptism of fire for the inexperienced sailors. Private Jim Longson, a Vickers machine gunner attached to B Company, had tracked their approach from his hay-loft position over the brickyard stables. He could see that they 'were led by an officer who appeared unsure of his route, as he made constant reference to a map he was carrying.' Commanders like Zaubser were more attuned to plotting coastal artillery shoots against ships out to sea. Eventually Longson saw that the officer 'pointed in the direction of the brickworks and led his men towards it – the target was again too good to be true.' At 200 yards the column of advancing Germans was lashed by concentrated .303 machine gun fire. The first dead and dying had fallen at the western end of the street, and the shocked and disorientated survivors scrambled for cover in the houses alongside the road. The brickworks was not to be fought clear until 15.00. Lippert remembers that the 'bitter attack resulted in heavy casualties – confusion and indecision reigned'. He managed to move up heavy machine guns and mortars from the NCO School so that the sailors could reach the western edge of Heelsum, a mile and a half beyond. This enabled them to catch up and line up with the rest of the general advance moving slowly eastwards.[118]

Just before 15.00 the heavy drone of a mass of approaching aircraft began to be heard from the south-west. This was accompanied by a crescendo of noise rising up from the north and west of Wolfheze as a storm of German flak opened up, dwarfing the more muted sounds of skirmishing heard by Dutch locals on the fringes of Oosterbeek. Soon the leading serial of 36 Dakotas hove into view, a phalanx of aircraft flying nine wide in V-shaped 'vics' of three. Puffs of smoke began to cluster ahead of the swarm, which flew steadily on through flashing webs of tracer, wispily draping themselves among the aircraft in the stream. Two aircraft were smoking, peeling out of the tight formation that seemed almost reluctant to part and let them through. Escorted by diving and wheeling Spitfires and Typhoons, 127 aircraft passed over at 700 feet and dropped 2,300 men from the 4th Parachute Brigade in less than 10 minutes. Glider serials competed for space amid the crowded glider zones of the first lift. Corporal Jim Swan, fighting for possession of these landing sites as the aircraft came in, recalled Hamilcars and Horsas landing behind him. 'One Horsa we saw going up again after touch-down and turning over completely before crashing to earth, upside down – it was nasty.'[119]

Inside minutes the eastward impetus of the Division von Tettau was checked by this sudden and alarming inversion of odds, another major enemy air landing. Von Tettau reported later that approximately a regiment landed in the rear of some of his units and their impact 'had certain crisis dimensions'. The Dutch, unable to see much beyond being deafened by the sudden peak in the intensity of shooting, were quietly satisfied. Liberation was on course.[120]

Fifteen-year-old Roelie Breman remembered that the British soldiers around her on the Benedendorpsweg near the railway bridge were 'very anxious for some reinforcements to arrive'. When 'at last' the 4th Parachute Brigade was seen dropping in the distance 'the soldiers are very pleased'. Everyone was ecstatic at the 'magnificent sight', she recalled. 'We went and stood on the road to the brickworks to have a better view.' Anje van Maanen, near the Oosterbeek crossroads, saw that 'everybody is thrilled, and people wave and jump around like mad monkeys'. Geert Maassen, living at No 32 Mariaweg, next to the Oosterbeek crossroads, remembered:

'In the afternoon we saw aeroplanes again, diving towards the ground. By now we knew that these were gliders, and again there were hundreds of parachutes. From our back garden we had a good view of what happened in the air, but not what happened on the ground.'[121]

Lippert, caught up in the move to recapture the area of the drop zones, had been optimistic. 'Many Engländer were fleeing towards the east to Wolfheze and Oosterbeek.' The Germans had taken many prisoners and 'captured hundreds of gliders, heavy weapons, ammunition, rations and taken away jeeps'. Completely focussed on the forward battle, he missed the pandemonium going on to his rear. When he drove back through the drop zones to his headquarters at about 16.00 'I could see that there were gliders now standing in places where before there had been none.' Within minutes his vehicle came under fire and his driver was seriously wounded. He had to try and get back on foot through newly landed and abandoned gliders all around. Hans Möller, to the east of the Utrechtseweg, recalled that 'we had to watch, unable to intervene as wave on wave, thousands of parachutes descended 15 kilometres away from us.' The situation to the west of the street had changed. 'The enemy got new reinforcements,' Möller realised. 'What would that mean for us?'[122]

Street block east: the British
Major John Waddy from the 156th Parachute Battalion was the No 1 in his aircraft standing at the door.

> 'I could lean out and I could see this massive aircraft flying in front of me, the black puffs of flak, and the thing that fascinated me was that you saw a black puff ahead of you, it seemed to hang in the air and suddenly it whipped past your door. I didn't realise that we were travelling at about 100 knots and then we started to get machine gun fire and you could see the tracer coming up through the formations.'

The first thing that Company Sergeant Major George Gatland with 11 Para heard was 'a sound in the plane like someone was throwing a handful of hard peas against the belly'. Looking out of the window 'we suddenly saw little puffs of black smoke appearing in the sky around us'. The barrage of flak was unexpected. The RAF had silenced German ack-ack sites around Rhenen for the first lift the day before, enabling a fly-in with no opposition. During the night a heavy anti-aircraft battery under Hauptman (Captain) Schulz had been set up around Von Tettau's headquarters in the same area, one of many anti-aircraft units now arriving from the Ruhr. The 4th Parachute Brigade drop zone at Ginkel Heath was also being attacked by Helle's Dutch SS Wach Battalion III under Von Tettau's command. Gatland, feeling nervous as his aircraft approached the crossing point of the street at 800 feet, with its underside lashed by shrapnel near-misses, remembered 'then it started coming through'. With vicious cracking reports 'you could see the tracers coming up and just going through the floor'. He was No 3 in the stick, and even at this stage during the final run-in to the drop zone 'the flames already tried to get through the fuselage'. When he jumped and his chute opened 'I looked around and saw that both engines of our plane were alight'. Private Joe Berry looked across the brief gap from the open door of the aircraft flying directly alongside. 'I was in the plane next to Company Sergeant Major Gatland's plane,' he remembered. 'I saw the plane he was in going down with the port engine on fire and people bailing out.'[123]

The Dutch residents of the Utrechtseweg had little comprehension of the frightening conditions aboard the aircraft. They simply witnessed the majestic fly-past at a distance or were attracted by the sudden flurry of shooting that announced its arrival. All that J. W. van Zonnenveld at No 76 Utrechtseweg saw was 'a sky full of gliders coming in to land followed by parachutes of all colours'. Jan Esvelt, with a grandstand view from the southern bank of the Lower Rhine near the Arnhem road bridge, was more concerned about 'raging fires in Arnhem, more and more'. 'What is going on?' he recorded in his diary, noting 'more parachute drops and gliders'. Netje Heijbroek, at the west end of the street near the Koude Herberg crossroads, noticed that 'when the second group of "Airbornes" came by on the Monday evening the mood was much less high-spirited.' These men 'had landed in the midst of the German tanks and artillery'. The Dutch remained broadly optimistic, but 'we could also see that things were not going according to plan.'[124]

Many of the paratroopers had been reading newspapers during the flight, trumpeting the successes of the day before. 'Great Sky Army Opens the Battle for Rhine' headlined the *Daily Mail*, which commented '…early today there was every indication that the first stage of the great airborne invasion of Holland had gone entirely to plan.' This was not the impression shared by Major John Waddy, standing at the aircraft door:

> 'I saw an aircraft, one of ours, pass beneath the door and it
> was ablaze nose to tail. I watched it as it went down, sort of

port wing down, and it burst in a great ball of white flame.
I thought to myself, "This is getting bloody dangerous".'

His signaller jumped out behind him amid 'the crack-crack of machine gun fire ... and got a bullet straight through his radio.'[125]

Private Leonard Moss, with 11 Para, jumped No 2 from his aircraft, struggling with a heavy PIAT anti-tank launcher 'under pressure from the eager men behind' pushing up against him, anxious to clear the aircraft under fire. The distractions resulted in an appalling exit:

'I fell, twisting like a bullet ... out of control. I realised I was
in trouble, turning and twisting my rigging lines so much
that my canopy almost closed. Bullets whizzed past me from
the ground and anti-aircraft shells continued to explode all
around.'

His kit bag needed to be swiftly released before he hit the ground with such a heavy load, otherwise it might snap his leg. More focussed on surviving his entanglement than on the sounds of battle around him, he managed to clear his rigging lines at the last moment, but landed heavily with the enormous PIAT still attached to his parachute harness. 'I swung the right way up and landed really hard on my back,' he recalled. 'I was winded and in agony.' Only as he painfully staggered to his feet did he appreciate that 'men were being hit, wounded and killed; the air was alive with flying lead.' A gust of wind inflated his parachute and pulled him over, dragging him along the ground 'as bullets tore through the canopy material'. He eventually disentangled himself and moved towards the marker smoke designating his rendezvous point.

It was an inauspicious entry for the 4th Parachute Brigade. Six aircraft had gone down, five managing to drop most of their sticks before making forced landings. Men were wounded in the aircraft lined up ready to jump, while others were hit in the air. The loss of these aircraft, in addition to men killed and wounded fighting their way through the equally surprised Dutch SS battalion caught in the middle of the drop, cost more than 200 men. Almost 10% of the brigade were casualties before they had even gone into action.

One of John Waddy's platoon commanders had his legs shattered by a burst of machine gun fire during the descent. Even more tragically, 'he got hit in the pouches' at his waist, which contained 'a phosphorous grenade that went off'. Having landed 'shot through the legs, he was burning to death' in a fountain of white phosphorous that blossomed out into the burning heathland. Unable to get up or walk, he begged all those passing by to put him out of his misery. Phosphorous burns brightly on contact with air, so the conflagration could not be slapped out. Somebody gave him a pistol and a single shot rang out. 'After the war, when I came back from prison camp, his family kept writing to me and asking me to tell them how he got killed,' Waddy sadly remembered. 'Of course, I couldn't say.'[126]

Meanwhile, away to the east of the street, in the Lombok suburb of industrial terraced housing by the St Elizabeth Hospital, Arnhem, General Urquhart, the 1st Airborne Division commander, was marooned at No 14 Zwarteweg. He had been unexpectedly caught up in street fighting in a side road off the Utrechtseweg. Gerald Lathbury, the 1st Parachute Brigade commander, had been with him unable to move, having been shot and wounded near the spine. He was sheltered by a Dutchman around the corner at No 135 Alexanderstraat. A German self-propelled gun pulled up outside Urquhart's house, which meant that both he and his leading brigade commander were going nowhere. Much like the German General Küssin's demise 24 hours before, key leaders had been taken out at a crucial point in the fighting.

A group of 27 civilian prisoners was being transferred from Deelen military airbase that morning to the Koepel prison, just two streets away from Urquhart. Gropp's SS flak detachment on the high ground north of the railway cutting immediately fired on them. Wearing khaki overalls, they looked like British soldiers, coincidental with the 3rd Parachute Battalion push through the Lombok district, trying to reach the Arnhem bridge. Prison governor A. Zondag faced a dilemma. Intimidated by the ever-growing noise of fighting around the bridge, he decided he should open the cell doors for the less serious offenders. Twenty or so prisoners elected to leave the prison at once, dressed in clogs and khaki overalls because their civilian clothes were in the prison store under fire. Groups fleeing into the Alexanderstraat came under intense fire from Möller and Gropp's SS men, who assumed they were the vanguard of yet another British foray toward the bridge. Some were killed in the road and the rest scattered. Among them was 59-year-old Joseph van Vijnck, who had been imprisoned for handling stolen goods in Amsterdam. His group was turned away by the British. Nobody, it seemed, was prepared to shelter the unfortunate prisoners marooned in a terrifying no-man's-land, shot at by both sides. Van Vijnck and a friend walked north into the Mariëndaal estate in Oosterbeek. What happened to them is unknown, except that both their bodies were found after the fighting and buried in a field grave in the woods.[127]

Corporal Reg Curtis with 1 Para had encountered heavy machine gun and mortar fire nearby as the unit fought its way beyond the factory to the right of the Utrechtseweg, just short of the Lombok district. 'Wham – a mortar bomb landed very near, near enough to feel the draught,' he recalled. 'Snipers were taking pot-shots at us, dodging and weaving through gardens and back yards.' Shrapnel pinged off a nearby rooftop and sounded 'like a pea on a drum as it hit my helmet,' he remembered. They were caught up in the 'absolute bedlam' of close-in street fighting. 'In the heat of battle men were shouting curses, lobbing grenades through open doors and windows, to follow up with a further shriek of contempt for the enemy with "Waho-Mahomet!"' Sticking out from the gateway of a Dutch house was a pair of feet, one incongruously with the boot blown off, but the foot was completely intact. 'I had a horrible feeling that my battalion was being cut to pieces,' he remembered. 'Fire was coming from my left behind a row of houses and from the rooftops and windows.' Inside the factory on their right 'men were scrapping like gangsters with grenade, Sten, .45 Colt pistol and the fighting knife'. Then an explosion 'just beneath me' left 'the lower part of my right leg in a most unusual position'. Bleeding heavily, he was stretchered out to a nearby wooden shed. 'The medics cut the boot from the foot of the shattered leg and it looked awful,' he remembered. All he could do was shelter where he was and watch through a demolished gateway as the fighting continued. 'I lay helpless as the clatter and confusion of battle went on.'[128]

Hauptsturmführer Hans Möller had been fighting off English attacks all day along the Utrechtseweg. 'The street was soon littered with broken glass and branches,' he recalled. 'The tramcar was riddled with bullets and ricochets' with dead Dutch civilians lying about. Möller was unsettled by the 'noise of the bitter fighting' coming from behind as Frost's 2 Para battled off all the attacks thrown at the road bridge. He had consolidated his own defence, moving up flame-throwers and panzerfaust hand-held anti-tank rocket launchers. He had stock-piled smoke grenades, 'indispensable tools of house clearing and street fighting, which we had practised so often in training and now tested in battle.' The Hohenstaufen SS troopers were veterans and were holding their own. 'Again and again and with great determination the enemy tried to break through our lines.' At the same time SS-Obersturmbannführer Ludwig Spindler's blocking force men were arriving, and filling in gaps leading down to the Lower Rhine.

Paul Müller, earmarked to depart the previous evening on the 20.00 train to Siegen in Germany, instead moved down with elements of SS Panzergrenadier Regiment 20 to the river bank. 'As we moved,' he recalled, 'we encountered more and more signs of battle: destroyed British light guns and other equipment, as well as British casualties in the streets and in front of houses.' The defence line was being systematically strengthened and would require more than a hastily mounted attack to break through. The battle situation had fundamentally changed: it was apparent that the British were not up against the previously anticipated line of communication troops. Frost's men had burst through with the benefit of surprise. Now a consolidated defence network was barring all approaches to the bridge. 'Quite obviously they were probing for a soft spot,' Möller surmised. But there were none. The Utrechtseweg was effectively blocked.[129]

With Urquhart cut off from his headquarters and his lead parachute brigade commander lost, a creeping command paralysis now began to afflict the conduct of the British advance along the Utrechtseweg to the Arnhem bridge. Brigadier Hicks, the Air Landing Brigade commander, assumed control as acting division commander. His first directive was to order the newly arrived 4th Parachute Brigade commander 'Shan' Hackett to change his original plan and detach the 11th Parachute Battalion to aid the badly mauled 1st Brigade's attempts to close on the bridge. Likewise, the newly arrived 2nd South Staffordshire glider infantry contingent was also dispatched, to join the rest of the battalion that Hicks had already sent to reach Frost. This meant that three dispersed groups were making their way along the street to reach the bridge.

Hackett was displeased but, being new to the situation, immediately complied. The air-landed 7th KOSB, which had already been fighting for 24 hours around the drop zones, was attached to his brigade as compensation. Hackett began to move his brigade eastwards toward the high ground north of Arnhem, 'towards the centre of divisional activity as quickly as would be compatible with the retention of its coherence'. Hackett would try and coordinate the offensive capability of the 4th Parachute Brigade, but there was no senior officer to coordinate the vanguard's attempts, nearest the bridge itself.

'What could possibly go wrong now?' Private Frederick Hawksworth with B Company the South Staffords recalled. 'Four or five young Dutch children came running up and stood in front of us and started to sing a Dutch song for us.' The men formed up and marched off. But as Private Robert Edwards with D Company remembered, 'The whole pace of the operation for some inexplicable reason now became very slow, and deceitfully easy – it was just like setting out on a route march back in England.' Waving Dutch crowds along the Utrechtseweg added to a holiday atmosphere. 'We even marched for 50 minutes and rested 10 minutes,' Edwards remembered. Group photographs were taken by Dutch photographers at the corner of Annastraat and the Utrechtseweg, lots of smiling faces and men leaning up against tree-lined metal railings as they signed autographs. Corporal Arthur Stretton, in the same company, remembered that 'shortly before midday we stopped just outside a café where a lady took our pictures, which was rather amusing.' Lieutenant

Roebuck, one of the platoon commanders, remarked: 'I at least had my photograph taken before I was killed in Holland.' This was to prove a prescient remark, because Roebuck was to be dead within 24 hours. Stretton's and Edwards's platoons were to be ambushed further along the street near Den Brink, shortly after their images were captured.[130]

Sniper activity increased as they moved east. Major Robert Cain, commanding B Company the Staffords, remembered that 'we soon came to know and regard these as an integral part of the landscape, but at first we were oversensitive.' They steadily moved past 'streets with houses and rows of shops' along the Utrechtseweg. Private Rodney Hall with D Company was covered by debris from tiles and chimney pots after a sniper shoot near the water tower on the Molenweg. As he brushed himself down, realising he was unwounded, two ladies owning a small bungalow invited some of the men inside. 'Would you believe it?' Hall recalled. 'They served us cakes and sang the national anthem.' They were jolted back to reality on leaving when they discovered that their 19-year-old companion Lance Corporal Edward Hunt, a boy soldier since 17, 'was killed as he was trying to locate a German machine gun nest'. 'There was plenty of evidence that the way ahead had not been without a price,' Private Jack Lane in the Pioneer platoon surmised, because 'debris and bodies were scattered all around'.[131]

'We started to notice things were not quite right as we approached the end of Oosterbeek,' remembered Wilfred Salt with A Company the Staffords. 'Snipers were active and there were quite a few houses on fire.' Companies were approaching the German resistance line in dispersed columns, oblivious of the strength of opposition, still to be precisely located, up ahead. 'I vividly remember that when we were advancing some houses on the side of the road were burning,' Salt observed. 'From one of the houses we could hear shrill screams.' There was nothing they could do. 'We were unable to stop to assist because there was a lot of enemy fire directed at us and we had to keep moving on.'

Further back, Leonard Moss, who had injured his back jumping with 11 Para, was following up, hours behind. At first their experience was 'columns of troops hiking along country roads' with a few farmhouses burning and smoking in the distance. At 19.00 they paused at the Hotel Hartenstein for 3½ hours, consolidating the dispersed groups and being briefed by Brigadier Hicks, the acting division commander. By 23.00 the battalion was approaching the western outskirts of Arnhem. 'We could hear explosions and artillery, sporadic mortar fire and the occasional crack of a rifle.' Jeeps rushing back in the dark from the opposite direction parted the marching columns 'like a boat's wave,' Moss recalled. 'Though no one said anything, each man was wondering just what lay ahead of us.'[132] They came across the Staffords companies dispersed along the eastern end of the Utrechtseweg. The first group was held up by Den Brink and the Mariëndaal, and another was further ahead, pinned down at the junction with the Klingelbeekseweg. Adding to the confusion were stragglers from the 1st and 3rd Parachute Battalions, swept up in the approach towards the German defence line. The four battalions were gathering by dribs and drabs.

One of the basic tenets of command in battle is to frequently assess and readjust the plan if the enemy situation changes. The British could no longer benefit from the shock impetus of surprise. Offensive momentum in street fighting is only possible if mobility is maintained. Flanking movements through gardens or other areas can unnerve a determined defence into withdrawing. More systematic and deliberate attacks utilising all forms of fire support are needed to break an organised defence. It was clear that the piecemeal and uncoordinated company-size attacks from the 1st and 3rd Parachute Battalions had run out of steam. There needed to be a pause in order to develop a deliberate attack plan. The Germans controlled a 300-yard-wide choke point between the railway cutting of the Arnhem shunting yard to the north and the Lower Rhine to the south. Access through this was only achievable through an even narrower avenue of two streets. One was the Utrechtseweg, or 'high road', beyond the St Elizabeth Hospital, and the second was the Onderlangs, or 'low road', south of it, next to the Lower Rhine.

Obersturmbannführer Walter Harzer, commanding the 9th SS, had set up his command post in the villa 'De Heselbergh' on the Apeldoorn road the previous day. He took over Küssin's defunct town headquarters, which had been a communications centre for years and was at the hub of all telephone traffic. Wolfgang Dombrowski, fighting with Möller's Engineer battalion, later commented, 'By now the defence appeared more organised and coordinated, with orders being sent down from above.' The four British battalions converging at the choke point were less well organised. The deputy commander of the Air Landing Brigade, Colonel Hilaro Barlow, had been sent forward to do this, but was killed by a mortar bomb when he arrived. They were up against a consolidated German defence that had created a three-sided 'valley of death'. Gropp's flak men were on the high ground to the left, north of the railway cutting. Möller's Engineer battalion reinforced by Spindler's men blocked the centre. To the right, in the brickworks across the Lower Rhine, were 20mm cannon mounted on the reconnaissance battalion's half-tracks. The British intended to punch through in a series of hasty attacks. Only a deliberate systematically planned and conducted assault could hope to pierce this narrow defence front. The imperative for the British was to reach Frost at all costs. The problem was that nobody was clearly in charge.

An improvised British orders group hastily convened in the Arnhem Garage at the corner of the Utrechtseweg and Oranjestraat. Lieutenant Colonel Dobie, CO of 1 Para, and Lieutenant Colonel McCardie, commanding the Staffords, were joined late by the 11 Para CO, Lieutenant Colonel Lea. Ironically they were just around the corner from where General Urquhart, the division commander, was pinned by a German self-propelled gun outside No 14 Zwarteweg. It was agreed that Dobie would be in charge. The setting, as described by Major Ian Toler with the Glider Pilot Regiment, was strained and atmospheric. Wrecked British and German vehicles were strewn along the street outside.

> 'The house is dark save for a single candle in the front parlour, which might be the same as in any house in any British suburb. The furniture is all over, as the owners have left it, and yet this is in the middle of a battle, the only evidence for this at present being a hole in a window blind where a bullet came in a little while before.'

Dobie was explaining that 'they had been trying to get to the bridge all day, but that the town was strongly defended by machine guns, artillery and some tanks.' McCardie, having just run the gauntlet of fire to reach the 'O' Group, recalled that 'this fact was becoming very apparent to me'. Dobie's battalion was weak, down to about 70 or 80 all ranks, 'all of them very exhausted' having fought all night and day. There were conflicting reports as to whether or not Frost was still holding at the bridge. Hicks at division headquarters was assuming he had been overrun, but the assembled COs thought differently. 'The atmosphere was tense and dramatic,' Toler recalled:

'McCardie knows Frost is still there as he is in wireless contact with him and knows his plight. He decides he cannot let him down. We all go out and McCardie and Dobie make the decision to advance to the bridge at all costs.'

Just as the 'O' Group was about to break up, the 11 Para CO arrived and was told that the remnants of 1 Para were going to advance with those of 3 Para along the 'low road', while McCardie's Staffords would attack along the street on the 'high road'. Lea, having just arrived, recalled that 'from about 23.30 until 03.30 hours order and counter-order reigned supreme'. It was agreed in a new plan that 11 Para would follow 1 Para. What was required, however, were orders for a deliberate attack, not a hasty advance. 'No sooner had one "O" group been held, then different instructions would come from division headquarters,' the frustrated Lea recalled. Unknown to the three battalion commanders, the fourth missing battalion commander, Lieutenant Colonel Fitch with 3 Para, and his men had left their houses up ahead in the darkness and at 02.30 launched a hasty assault up the 'low road' towards the bridge. There was no time to brief the other three battalions to do anything other than attack. As clearing even a single house could generally swallow up a platoon, there was not enough manpower to mount a deliberate attack synchronised with fire support. The crescendo of shooting that suddenly broke out in the darkness ahead seemed to dictate a single imperative – less advance, more charge! This was launched by 04.30.[133]

Advancing from the Lombok street network required the Staffords to congregate, then dash across the open stretch of the Utrechtseweg dominated from the high ground by Obersturmbannführer Gropp's SS flak detachment. 'Suddenly all hell broke loose,' remembered Private Robert Harvey with D Company. 'I suspect they were just waiting for us.' There was virtually no cover. 'I saw on the left side of the road a file of our men just mowed down like corn.' Glider pilot Sergeant Arthur Shackleton, attacking with the Staffords, remembered:

'We had to cross the tops of these streets. Down each one, the Germans were firing on fixed lines, which was the machine guns coming down the middle of the road. What we remembered afterwards was an 88mm gun, firing air bursts as they called them – shrapnel. We lost three maybe four of our pilots.'

'Since we had virtually no cover on the open road,' recalled Harvey, 'I just ducked, set up my Bren gun and fired off a few mags.'

Private R. Edwards with D Company recalled 'a wide riverside stretch of road in front of the St Elizabeth Hospital', where 'all hell seemed let loose on us'. D Company started to falter. 'Jerry was firing at us with tracer bullets, which came whizzing past,' Robert Harvey continued. 'One of the chaps in my platoon got into a bit of a panic and I had to shut him up,', whereupon he was blown off the road by a grenade or mortar bomb. He rolled down the slope. By now Edwards was beginning to feel their situation was untenable:

'We were out in the open and must have been like targets in a shooting gallery. All Jerry had to do was line his guns and mortars along the gap, a quarter of a mile wide, and fire. He could not miss.'

Captain Ernest Wyss, his company second-in-command, ran up and down the men shouting, 'On, on, on D Company, on, on!' with a voice growing ever hoarser. 'Where men flagged, faltered or hesitated, he was there,' Edwards recalled. 'You could not crawl on your stomach and watch him standing upright – you had to follow his lead.' The survivors managed to reach the Municipal Museum up ahead, some sheltering in the grassy dell at its nearside. Edwards 'put my head down and ran like a harrier' for the beckoning cover. 'I stumbled over the dead and dying, slithered in pools of blood, until I reached the partial shelter afforded by the houses and buildings.'[134]

Down on the 'low road', the 1 Para attack had caught up with the 3 Para remnants, without realising they were ahead. At the same time they were being hit by overheads winging over the 'high road'. They shot back in the mistaken belief they were being engaged by aimed fire. Firefights developed with those occupied German houses in between and with the South Staffords on the 'high road', some of whom had not been told that friendly forces were attacking on their right flank.

By now the low-lying river mist was burning off the surface of the Lower Rhine. As it dispersed the German 20mm cannon established in the brickworks on the other side saw clusters of paratroopers filing along the 'lower road'. The flailing impact of 20mm multiple-bursting fire was sufficient to slice off limbs and heads in motion. The paratroopers scattered into the nearby houses, completely breaking up the impetus of their advance. 'Our situation is hopeless,' Lieutenant Colonel Dobie recorded in his battalion log. They were being fired at from 'the houses above us'. 'Anti-aircraft and machine guns are firing at us from across the river' and 'tanks are shooting from close range'. He charted the disintegration of his battalion through the radio situation reports: 'R Company – 6 men left. S Company – 15 men left (about). T Company – 8 men left. HQ Company – 10 men left (about)'. At 06.30 hours 'T Company was cut off and unable to fight its way out'. 'This was my last count,' states the war diary. 'No more radio contact with other companies.'

Lieutenant Richard Bingly with S Company recalled that the intensity of fire was such that 'it was impossible to move along the street so we had to go from one house to the next by blowing holes in the walls.' This was done 20 times until they found the last house in the row 'crawling with German tanks and artillery, which was firing straight into our houses'. They had penetrated almost to the Roermondsplein, about 900 yards from Frost's men still fighting at the bridge. 'Three days to cover 12 kilometres with virtually 100% losses!' the despairing Bingly reflected. 'It was a bitter pill.'[135]

The St Elizabeth Hospital was taking regular hits from 20mm shells. Dutch Red Cross volunteer Tonny Gieling remembers 'one round flew through the front of the building and ripped through the head of a patient as he was being fed by a German nun'. The experience was so surreal that Gieling could barely absorb what had happened. 'She sat there staring with the plate still in her hand.' Medical orderly William Roberts, with the 16th Field Ambulance, recalled that 'outside the noise was terrific, the rattle of machine gun fire and shell blasts, and down the road by the "Y" junction there was a crossfire.' They tried to pick up as many wounded as they could and drag them inside the hospital – 'soldiers were being mown down'. Walking wounded were sitting on the stairs inside the entrance. 'You could see the terrible torture on their faces, especially the ones with shell-shock – they did not know what to do or say.' An enduring memory was the pervasive smell, 'sour and rancid, what you get with dirt and blood and dead bodies'.[136]

Hans Möller, with the Hohenstaufen's Engineer battalion, heard 'some terrible noise of battle from the left, towards the Rhine and towards Spindler's men'. He watched flares spiralling over 'the open ground towards the Rhine' where 'the noise was increasing in intensity'. Paul Müller was down there with Panzergrenadier Regiment 20 covering the banks of the Rhine on the lower road 'with my two machine guns'. 'At 05.00 hours sharp the Tommies let loose with all hell to our right,' he recalled, starting with multiple low thuds as grenades detonated. 'It was still so dark and foggy,' he remembered, 'that you could barely discern the outline of a man walking upright 5 metres away.' The German line was bypassed and penetrated in places somewhere in the murky gloom. His machine gunners fell back, saying, 'It's all useless anyhow – they'll simply overrun us.' Müller remained behind with four others that he had persuaded not to run. 'This was their first time in action,' he recalled, 'and they had never heard the crack of a speeding bullet so close before.' Then, before he knew it 'approximately seven or nine figures loomed out of the fog in front of us.'

Private Brian Willoughby with R Company 1 Para, mixed up with the last attacking remnants of T Company, recalled that 'someone was being hit all the time, and while we continued advancing in battle order we lost even more.' This last attack was going in with fixed bayonets. Only six men were on their feet from the 40 that had started. 'Sadly it was impossible to stop to help the wounded' because extremely effective machine gun fire was cracking by and ripping up the ground about them. 'Take that gun out!' shouted an officer:

> 'There was a short pause; nothing happened; then a rush accompanied by shouts of "Waho Mahomet!". Followed by complete silence. No more machine gun. I was glad not to be involved in that.'

Paul Müller challenged the figures coming out of the mist and a hand grenade plopped down 2 metres in front of his fox-hole.

> 'Two bursts from my machine gun caused an explosion in the group of men. The effect was devastating: only one of the Tommies remained standing, the others were rolling and moaning in a heap on the ground.'

A terrifying duel developed with the lone survivor. Müller fired two more bursts directly at him to no effect until his machine gun ran out of ammunition. He excitedly called for another belt, but there was no answer – his companions had vanished. So he and the seemingly invincible Tommy threw grenades at each other. 'Tommy made a throwing motion followed by a bang in front of me, and fire and dirt flew into my face'. Müller hurled another grenade, stunned and blinded by the last, with the

Englishman barely 5 metres in front of his trench. 'You've got to get away fast now,' he thought, beginning to panic, 'or the Tommy will do you in completely.' His machine gun had been torn apart at the breech, his upper left arm was badly injured and 'warm blood was running into my eyes and mouth, and also down my body and into my boots.' A grenade fragment had lacerated his head. He was barely able to scramble out of the hole and as he did another hand grenade exploded within. 'My luck was that the Tommy did not fire after me, but just threw a couple more grenades, which did not really hurt me a lot.' Nevertheless the top of his back was peppered with shrapnel. Müller staggered off into the darkness towards the command post, to find the aid post, where he was sent off with the walking wounded to seek further treatment. 'I could only see the wounded rifleman walking ahead of me through a red veil of blood,' he remembered.

Willougby's group of six men realised they had breached the enemy line, because they were well forward of the Staffords up on the 'high road', to their left on the Utrechtseweg. Shattered 1 Para platoons gathered survivors together for a final push. 'There weren't many left,' Willoughby observed. Private James Shelbourne's group had suffered terrible losses to get this far. He was going to be forever haunted by the image of 'a young recently married officer' who had gone down in the fire and was 'cremated by his own phosphorous grenades'. They could advance no further because the way ahead was blocked by the entrance channel to a riverside dock, part of the small inner 'old' harbour. 'We could only wheel left, up the escarpment and into a row of houses' towards the Staffords, blocked on the Utrechtseweg. Led by just one officer, Willoughby's handful of men 'didn't get far'. He closed on his company commander, Major Timothy, who beckoned them over to regroup, at which point 'I walked into a shower of hand grenades coming from the upstairs windows of the houses in the row'. The Germans later picked him up and laid him on the rear deck of a self-propelled gun. There was a shout and roar of engines and the gun trundled off, squeaking and clattering its way towards the St Elizabeth Hospital.[137]

Hans Möller's block on the Utrechtseweg in the centre seemed impervious to pressure, bending, then coming back. He described the heavy attacks that bounced off his positions at first light. Steinart's 1st Company, occupying houses on the left-hand side of the street, 'fired without mercy – panzerfaust projectiles literally tore a group of paratroopers apart, the flame-throwers were belching flaming oil and fire at the attacking enemy.' Steinart's men were bolstered by fire support from Schmatz's 2nd Company, in turn supported by the 20mm cannon mounted on the armoured half-tracks of the 3rd heavy weapons company. The advancing paratroopers were advancing into a narrowing urban funnel, lashed by fire from the front and sides.

Sergeant Norman Howes with A Company the Staffords started to identify the outline of the Valley of Death they had penetrated. 'We passed the St Elizabeth Hospital, bodies and wounded were behind every tree, 20mm heavy fire was coming from our right across the river, machine gun fire from our front and from between the buildings on our left.' Street crossings were especially hazardous. Glider pilot Arthur Shackleton perceived how repetitive the incoming fire had become: 'They fired a 5-second burst' on fixed lines 'with a 5-second interval.' Crossing gaps became a lottery with death. 'We counted the bursts – five, five, run! – and most of us got across that way with them being methodical, and they never altered.' Once across:

> 'You would see a fleeting figure probably across the road, which we knew wasn't one of ours, so you would fire, but you never knew whether you hit them or not with it being dark.'[138]

The only way to get forward was by 'leap-frogging' in teams, using fire and movement.

As it grew lighter at about 07.00, B Company the Staffords had occupied the Municipal Museum. A Company led by Major Henry Lane was ordered to pass through and capture the PGEM buildings on the north side of the Utrechtseweg, opposite No 85.[139] The Verkerk family, who lived next door at No 83, had already been through heavy fighting when Major Dover's C Company 2 Para had been destroyed the day before. They sensed this further increase of military activity with distinct unease. Germans were moving about in the garden and had set up a machine gun. Another was established on their flat roof, and the front door was barricaded. Outside young H. Verkerk could see 'wounded Germans and British on the Onderlangs [the street below] sitting against the trees and dressing each other's wounds.' His father insisted they all go inside after 'my brother said he had seen a strange chap by our garden gate'. This was immediately followed by a short burst of fire in the garden, announcing that the tenancy of No 83 was in dispute again.

Lieutenant Hugh Cartwright, the Staffords Signals Officer, had spotted movement and recalled that 'we started by challenging each other, and almost immediately started firing at each other'. A bullet struck his shoulder and came out of his back, but 'countless hours of training probably saved my life as I instinctively crouched in the Sten firing position on my knees'. Any higher and he would have been dead. The bullet just missed his spinal chord and knocked him off the road; he rolled down the embankment where his momentum was arrested by some bushes. A few yards away he could hear wounded Germans dying, 'one of them calling out for his mother – it was rather sad.'

'The German on the flat roof shouted "Mother! Mother!" and was dragged away by his friend,' recalled Dutch boy H. Verkerk. 'When it came to dying the Germans were cowards,' he insisted, 'in contrast to the British – they always shouted and groaned.' The brief exchange of fire provoked uproar inside No 83. 'Suddenly one of the Germans shouted "Tommies! Tommies!" And the entire gang ran out of the house like madmen.' The Verkerks had no idea what was going on:

> 'There was a lot of wild shooting although not a single Tommy to be seen. All at once we heard a Kraut shouting from the top of the cellar stairs. "Tommies down there? Tommies come up quickly!" We dared not reply through fear. Furious, he came down, machine pistol at the ready, and shouted that we should have called out "Civilians!" because he had almost thrown a hand grenade into the cellar.'[140]

A Company briefly occupied the PGEM building opposite, but were soon driven out. Mr A. H. Becker, watching from the 'Kraton' cellars, remembered 'a group of eight men at the western wall of the PGEM held out for an hour against superior numbers before surrendering.' Forced back under pressure, A Company moved back to the houses grouped around No 72 opposite the Municipal Museum on the Utrechtseweg.[141]

It became clear that this would be the limit of the advance. Lieutenant Colonel Lea commanding 11 Para conferred with the Staffords and agreed that the plan needed to change. The only conceivable way of breaking the deadlock around the 'Monastery', as the Museum was being called, was to attack along the Renssenstraat, along the railway to their left. 11 Para started to regroup by moving into the streets to the left of the Utrechtseweg, around the Koepel prison and Lombok terraces. Such orders take time, and many of Lea's key officers, including his second-in-command, adjutant and signals group, were casualties. Just as this complicated move began to get under way, German self-propelled (SP) guns suddenly drove up onto the Staffords' forward positions.

Up ahead, Lt Col McCardie was heard to shout to Captain Oscar Wyss, the second-in-command of D Company, 'Oscar, can you do something about those bloody tanks?' 'Wight-ho, Sir,' he responded. Norman Howes recalled Oscar's endearing speech impediment that made him mispronounce his 'R's, producing a larger-than-life officer caricature hugely enjoyed by all ranks. 'Oscar Wyss was a character, well liked and respected by all,' Howes remembered. He had run back and reappeared at the A Company positions carrying a couple of PIAT bombs, firing at the SPs as he ran forward. Howes described:

'I then heard a terrible burst of spandau [machine gun fire] like ripping linen. I heard Oscar call out "Oh, oh, oh" then silence. I could not see his body but I guessed it was 10 metres away.'

The appearance of heavy German armour was the stuff of nightmare for lightly armed airborne troops. They had only PIAT anti-tank launchers available, with only a limited supply of bombs. Major David Gilchrist was with A Company 11 Para astride the Utrechtseweg in the area of the St Elizabeth Hospital. His PIAT anti-tank screen covered the vital junction between the high and low roads. 'I had PIATs but no bombs,' he recalled, because 'the Padre, bless his soul, had "borrowed" my jeep on which we had put the bombs during the night march.' The squeak and clatter of caterpillar tracks and distinctive crash-boom of 75mm guns firing point-blank into the defended houses could be clearly heard. Gilchrist's men watched the road, glancing anxiously at each other and over their shoulders to the rear. No PIAT bombs. They were caught completely naked on the road.[142]

In between: the Dutch

General Urquhart, released by the renewed attacks towards the bridge and making his way back through Lombok's side streets, would have seen the Koepel civil prison being subjected to shellfire. The Dutch, caught up in the emotion of the street's pending Liberation, were trapped in their houses, alongside the British. The prison governor, A. Zondag, felt that the prisoners should be offered an option to leave. 'Detainees were advised to remain temporarily in the institution for their own safety,' the prison register recorded. 'If they nevertheless chose to leave, it would be entirely at their own risk.' With khaki overalls as prison uniform, and unable to access their civilian clothing, it was indeed a risk. Yet only 57 of the incarcerated prisoners elected to remain. For the majority, it was an unhappy exodus. Most were immediately detained by SS soldiers advancing through Lombok and secured in a military police barracks in Arnhem. They were then taken by lorry to a penitentiary in Zutphen.

A number of those who took their chances among the British were shot at by the Germans, or caught in the crossfire. Major Cain with B Company the Staffords saw some of them emerging from the gaol as they retreated into the park at Den Brink. 'They looked very bleached and pale,' he recalled, 'as though they had been working in a bakery or flour mill.' About 50 prisoners got through to the Oosterbeek-Laag railway station via the Klingelbeekseweg. They were arrested by the British near the old Oosterbeek church. The Resistance tried to get them out when it was found the school where they had taken refuge was no longer safe. Ir F. de Soet telephoned the Police Station at No 107 Utrechtseweg, but they could do nothing. A few got across the Lower Rhine using the ferry at Driel and were never heard of again.

What the prisoners considered hazardous was haven for about 600 of Lombok's residents, caught up in the maelstrom of attacks around the Arnhem bridge. The domed roof and upper floors of the solid late-19th-century building could absorb mortar and shellfire. They took shelter in the cells on the ground and first floors. Once the Germans had passed through the district, the area became peaceful again. Four days later the Germans gave the anxious families just 60 minutes to get out.[143]

Telephones and power all along the street began to fail. 'Pity, you can't ring up any more,' wrote Anje van Maanen in her diary. Events were taking a sinister turn. No news stimulated rumour and the exchange of the same news, adding further to feelings of isolation and insecurity. Those Resistance men helping British soldiers and wearing orange armbands were encouraged to take them off. 'The British don't dare take the risk of letting them wear these bands yet,' Anje observed. 'Better to wait a little longer, till all is safe.' More and more refugees were fleeing the fighting to the east of the street, and told distressing stories about scrambling over gates and fleeing through gardens under fire. Suitcases were packed, just in case, and baths and all empty vessels filled with water. 'We are terribly disappointed,' Anje admitted. 'It is not alright with the Liberation, are we going to have the Moffen again – Oh No!'

These same uncertainties were becoming more pronounced up and down the Utrechtseweg and its surrounding streets. Then the unthinkable began to occur. 'This morning it is very noisy,' recalled Roelie Breman on the Tuesday. 'The English are still firing [their artillery nearby] towards Arnhem. They have warned us, however, that the Germans may begin to shoot back.' Sure enough, while she was visiting a neighbour the first shells started to fall. She fled back home, witnessing even more disturbing signs:

'We see people in the street, loaded with luggage and possessions. We ask them, of course, where they are from and they answer that they come from the Klingelbeekseweg. All people living there have been told that they must leave. More and more people are coming past, some also from the Benedendorpsweg. Nobody has told us yet to leave, so we stay, and besides, where are we supposed to go to? We might as well stay where we are.'

All these unsettling indicators were coming nearer and nearer with no direction or information. Roelie could also see that many English soldiers were coming back the same way. There seemed to be a general exodus of fleeing civilians and soldiers from east to west, appearing in the peaceful centre of the Utrechtseweg. 'We are afraid that they are retreating,' recalled an exasperated Roeli, 'but one cannot make out what they are doing.' 'I do remember that the boys walked back again from Arnhem, but very slowly,' recalled nine-year-old Wil Rieken at No 178 Utrechtseweg. 'They were whispering – I remember the shadows moving along the street.'

Eighteen-year-old J. A. van Hofwegen, living nearby at No 154 Weverstraat, just around the corner, was similarly perplexed. The day before, the crews of the four airborne howitzers shooting into Arnhem behind the old church had declared that 'in six weeks we will be in Berlin'. What was there to disbelieve? Especially as during the afternoon many newly arrived airborne troops had marched past, coming from Heelsum. But now it appeared that the South Staffords were coming back from Arnhem. A huge 17-pounder anti-tank gun was set up alongside the old church, pointing towards Arnhem. Jeep trailers were being set up criss-cross to form rudimentary road blocks, with anti-tank mines hidden beneath. It did not look good: 'The South Staffords settled in the school and smashed the windows with the butts of their rifles.' Van Hofwegen sat beside the police sergeant from No 107 Utrechtseweg behind the bakery, where they regarded the sky over Arnhem. It had turned red.[144]

Dutch Resistance activist Harry van Gorkum was at the east end of the Utrechtseweg trying 'to see what we could do for the Brits'. He had travelled from Apeldoorn the day before because 'hanging on the illegal radio, we had a fairly good idea of what was happening'. He had driven with his friend Lintwurst, allowed to use a wood-burning gas-driven car, because he ran a sausage factory. Any preconceptions he had about the situation vanished on arriving at the Lombok district. 'When we got there, we realised that it was not all that happy.' They wore Red Cross armbands and tried to pick up any British walking wounded they could find and transport them back to Apeldoorn, where they were handed on to the local Resistance. 'There was a certain amount of wishful thinking of course,' he admitted, 'but we never doubted for a moment that the Brits would not win.'

'We did a lot of running away,' Van Gorkum remembered. The situation had clearly changed. 'We didn't see much of the Germans, we didn't want to see them, because with the Gestapo offices [on the Utrechtseweg] nearby, we were in an illegal place anyhow.' As they picked up any British soldiers they could find, the Germans appeared to accept their Red Cross credentials 'and took comparatively little notice of us'. For three days they arrived in the morning, extracted who they could and drove back to Apeldoorn mid-afternoon. Then there was an abrupt change in British fortunes. 'On 18 September we couldn't consider anything could go wrong, even on the 19th there was fighting OK – but then we started to realise things were not going right at all… It was such a mess!' he recalled. 'Nobody wanted to be picked up, unless they had to, because they always wanted to stay together with their mates.' Most of the local Dutch had disappeared, adding to their feeling of vulnerability and isolation. 'I must admit we were pretty scared too,' he said. 'There was no heroism in it.' The fighting was not as they had anticipated. 'You didn't see anybody,' van Gorkum remembered. 'Fighting noises were always two or three streets away, very loud, a lot of shooting going on.' Safety depended on anonymity. 'A lot of the Brits were not interested in us'; they were fighting the battle, 'and no Germans were stopping us'. But this was to change: 'After the 21st it became a danger again, when you realised they had got back in control.'

'All right, there were no Gestapo checks', but they immediately ran if they saw a German uniform. There was the pervasive background anxiety of someone suddenly calling out, 'Hey! Hey! What are you doing here?' 'We tried to look terribly official with our red crosses, but…' there was little more they could do. Before long 'there were no more Brits wandering around needing our help and too many Germans'. Picking up the walking wounded was rather an impersonal process. 'Not a lot of conversation,' van Gorkum recalled, and never more than two in the car.

'The basic thing was that you had a cigarette, they were nervous and worried while my English was not fluent. We asked them to leave their weapons, otherwise we would have been shot straight away. On the whole they were despondent, it was going badly, but they were glad that they were alive.'

Van Gorkum spoke for the length and breadth of the street when he emphasised:

'We never considered it could go wrong. After all, the English had been thoroughly successful everywhere else, as far as we were concerned. We would probably not have listened if someone had said "It was not going right".'

After three days Lintwurst and Van Gorkum stopped making the journeys. 'It was too dangerous,' he decided. 'I had already been in prison once. If I got picked up, I wouldn't have a leg to stand on.'[145]

By midday on Tuesday 18 September the Daily Reports log at the Oosterbeek Police Station was recording fires and direct hits on a list of 12 properties, notified by residents on the east side of the village. The Germans had thus far prevented the fire service from tackling any of the reported fires. Fireman Theo Scholten recalled people standing helplessly in lines in front of their blazing houses while they burned, while frustrated firemen had to 'just stand there and not be able to fight the fires'. During the afternoon the tenor of reports in the log perceptibly changed. Multiple shell strikes were coming in on the hour and half-hour, producing injuries and deaths. Despite the catastrophe about to engulf

Oosterbeek, the two policemen wrote their reports in an understated and bureaucratic style, as if impervious to the events they were recording.

Mr George Vreede, a 71-year-old former cavalry captain living at No 37 Wolfhezeweg, reported in to say that there was ammunition behind his house. The next day Captain Vreede put on his old riding breeches and strode out into his garden brandishing a pistol. He had had enough of Germans and was going to take the war to them. They simply shot him down. Then on Tuesday evening the policemen took custody of two German girls, 'both resident in Amsterdam', who had been dropped off at the Police Station by the British for their own safety. The thin veneer of civilisation maintained by the seemingly mundane reports persisted. Parachute containers were appearing in gardens and a can of oil was handed in. The norm still vied for attention alongside the bizarre.[146]

Hospitals had been established in the centre of Oosterbeek at the Schoonoord and Vreewijk hotels on the Utrechtseweg, and in the Hotel Tafelberg just around the corner. Despite heavy fighting to the east of the street, many of its inhabitants, like auxiliary nurse Hendrika van der Vlist, working in her own home at the Hotel Schoonoord, could still believe 'it is absolutely clear that the Germans know they will be defeated'. Moreover, it might be worse. 'We should thank Providence,' she surmised, 'that Oosterbeek is not Arnhem and that our hotel has not been burned down.' A steady flow of wounded began to fill the straw-covered floor of her drawing room, and rows of beds had been set up in the big lounge. 'The inquisitive people, for whom there was no work, we have asked to leave.' She carried on washing the wounded, like one Dutch SS boy 'shot through the jaw and also close to the eye'. His whole face was thick and puffy, so young that one orderly remarked 'there is no sign of a beard'. After a few days Hendrika realised that 'it is clear to me that he is mentally defective,' and if so she indignantly wondered 'who made him join the SS?' Many of the wounded were embarrassed to be washed. One soldier, hit in the eye and with a terribly swollen face, had no idea what had happened to him – 'He only knows it is hurting terribly.' A few days earlier Hendrika van der Vlist would have recoiled at such an ugly wound. Her home, previously a genteel hotel, was now permeated with 'the strong sickly smell of blood

139

everywhere'. The wounded paratrooper asked the one universal question she was to come to dread over the coming days: 'Am I going to die?'

Netje Heijbroek, living at 'Valkenburg' in the west of the street, by the Koude Herberg crossroads, sensed the rise in tension around her. 'More and more Englishmen dug themselves in around our house,' she recalled, 'and a machine gun had been positioned on the flat roof of our kitchen.' News was sparse. The British, she noticed, were having problems with their radios. Information came only from the increasing number of refugees from Wolfheze, unable to get home. 'We had no idea what was going on in the village,' she remembered. 'The electricity had been cut off, so no more radio.' They were feeling increasingly vulnerable and isolated. 'In our small neighbourhood we lived as if on an island.'[147]

Domestic norms were becoming increasingly compromised. Home was no longer the secure haven it once was. Blitzkrieg had passed by quickly in May 1940, but not this time. Basic securities were gone. It was no longer safe to sleep in your bed because the war had crossed the Nijmegen railway line and was knocking on the door at the eastern fringes of Oosterbeek. There was equal uncertainty to the west. One hope remained. A British soldier on the Benedendorpsweg attracted Roelie Breman's attention and pointed towards the river polderland to the south. 'Towards Nijmegen we saw a large glow of fire and we heard the noise of heavy artillery.' The day before, Anje van Maanen had been assured by a group of British soldiers at the Oosterbeek crossroads that 'Monty' was due 'within a quarter of an hour – we just heard it from the radio'. On Tuesday night the citizens of Oosterbeek regarded the red sky over Nijmegen. The main road from Arnhem to Elst was clearly visible from Anje van Maanen's bedroom windows. 'There are an awful lot of lights there,' she remembered. 'That must be Monty now.' Hendrika van der Vlist at the Hotel Schoonoord around the corner also heard that 'Montgomery's army is quite close'. Everyone remained confident about the outcome. 'I'll have a shave and a bath next week in England,' remarked one of the wounded soldiers. Eleven miles away the 10th SS was tenaciously defending all the approaches to the road and rail bridges at Nijmegen against the determined Allied XXX Corps advance.

War was proving to be an ugly, untidy and messy business. Oosterbeek residents no longer sought to fill in the mortar craters that spoiled their immaculate lawns. Pervasive insecurity was having an insidious effect on normal standards. 'We do look untidy,' 17-year-old Anje confided to her diary. 'We can't be bothered with looking in mirrors – not now!' An influx of refugees had swelled their household to 11, and 'with such a crowd, you can't expect luxury'. She had been shocked at the refugees' stories of being shot out of their houses and climbing over fences. It opened up all sorts of unpleasant possibilities. The family decided they should pack some suitcases 'in case we must fly too, one never knows'. Packing bags added to the sense of vulnerability, a tangible sign of prevailing insecurity. They might have to leave at any time. Not to spend another night in the domestic bliss of a cosy home where everybody and everything belonged was an unsettling prospect, completely taken for granted 48 hours before. 'I go up to my room and get it ready,' Anje recalled. 'A small city bag in which I put a lambswool cardigan, new black shoes, woollen socks, stockings, underwear, a toothbrush and so on.' That night they would sleep on mattresses in the cellar, with candles because there was no power. All along the Utrechtseweg that night people's domestic routines had irretrievably altered. 'We don't undress any longer when it is night,' recalled Hendrika van der Vlist, 'and our shoes we keep close at hand, in case anything should happen.' The awfulness of their predicament was starting to become apparent because 'we are living and sleeping at the front'.[148]

CHAPTER 5

Boxing-in the Street

Tanks! From the east: the Germans

PK (Propaganda Kompanie) Berichterstatter Jacobsen, an official war photographer dispatched to Arnhem by Luftwaffe Command West, paused to take pictures of dead paratroopers outside No 63 Utrechtseweg. Being at the far eastern end of the street, Jacobsen assumed that these men had been killed during the fighting that morning, but only Major Victor Dover's C Company 2 Para men had got that far. Young H. Verkerk's older brother had spotted the corpses that same morning, peering out of No 83. One body, that of one of Dover's scouts, Lance Corporal William Loney, 'lay near our porch, a pleasant-looking young chap with red hair'. Private Norman Shipley was sprawled on the pavement further along, 'a very big fellow face down'.

> 'You could only see from his helmet where he had been hit. The helmet had fallen from his head and a bullet had gone straight through it. He could not have suffered. The Germans didn't move the bodies until Friday, having first robbed them. By that time they were in a state of decomposition.'[149]

The three British AFPU cameramen, Lewis, Smith and Walker, were pinned in houses to the west of the street, while Jacobsen and his Luftwaffe colleague Erich Wenzel were at the east end of the Utrechtseweg. Like their British counterparts, they were in Arnhem to record a victory, a rare event for German cinema audiences back home. They had more combat camera experience than their British opposites. Jacobsen had covered the Blitzkrieg in the west in 1940 and both had been in Russia and Normandy earlier that year. Arnhem was to prove the last German victory in the west and they were on hand to record it. Pictures had already been taken of tired and filthy wounded from 1 Para being trundled off in straw-covered hand-pulled carts. Anxious-looking Dutch refugees were photographed with their mattresses and possessions piled high on carts nervously hurrying by to take advantage of a pause in the fighting. When a column of menacing-looking camouflaged Sturmgeschütz III self-propelled assault guns clattered by Arnhem railway station, they were on hand to record the climactic arrival. Both followed on to investigate what may happen, anticipating dramatic material. By the time Wenzel and Jacobsen got to the eastern end of the street, ten of the growling monsters had halted in column, awaiting the order to move forward. Pictures showed that they were crewed by fresh-faced young teenagers.

Sturmgeschütz Abteilung (Brigade) 280 was commanded by Major Kurt Kühne. The unit had been refitting in Denmark when the crisis in the west broke, and was immediately entrained for Aken (Aachen/Aix-la-Chapelle) in Belgium. Twenty-two-year-old Gefreiter (Corporal) Wilhelm Rohrbach remembers that they had loaded 40 SPs (self-propelled guns) on the train. On arrival at Hamburg station the previous day they were suddenly re-routed to Arnhem. 'By chance an officer had heard a radio report that talked of airborne landings in Holland,' Rohrbach recalled. 'He was probably the only officer who knew where Arnhem was!' They offloaded at Bocholt in the Ruhr and drove via Apeldoorn through the northern suburbs of Arnhem. Jacobsen and Wenzel watched and took photographs as SS infantry groups began to assemble around two assault gun detachments forming up. Half of them moved off with squealing tracks and clouds of exhaust into Onderlangs, the 'low road', while the other five began to grind up the slope of the Utrechtseweg towards the Municipal Museum. The newly arrived gun crews observed Loney and Shipley's corpses with interest as they rolled by, alerted at the sight and watchful for signs of trouble ahead. Engine growls transitioned to whining gear changes as they ascended the crest of the hill and the first shots rang out. Commanders ducked down below their turret lids. Jacobsen and Wenzel followed a discreet distance behind – they had a battle to film.

'A shout of "Tanks!" went up' from Major Robert Cain's B Company Staffords positions around the Municipal Museum. They called it the

'Monastery' because of its distinctive dome-shaped roof. Bren guns opened up and 'looking down the steep slope we could see through the trees onto the lower road,' Cain recalled. 'A Sturmgeschütz was jolting along and stopping to fire its guns into our positions.' One of his platoon commanders rested a PIAT on a fence post and fired at it from the shoulder. 'I thought the twigs and branches might detonate the bomb,' Cain remembered, 'but it soared through and struck the side of the SP with a great clap of sound and a sheet of flame.' The 'monster' gun lumbered out of sight. A form of duelling followed with the armoured vehicles cautiously moving forward to blast suspect positions until PIAT gunners, protected by a pair of Bren gunners, worked their way around buildings and gardens to engage them from the flanks and rear through trees. 'It seemed to discourage them,' Cain remembered, 'as they withdrew' from his stretch of the road. 'We were now getting very low on PIAT ammunition and I went back to look for some.'[150]

Gefreiter Rohrbach with 280 Brigade's 3rd Battery was scared, like all the other inexperienced Sturmgeschütz crews. One hit in the rear from one of the light mobile PIATs was sufficient to wreck the lightly armoured fuel and engine compartments. They would be torched. The businesslike snub-nosed Sturmgeschütz IIIs were protected by ramshackle-looking 'schurzen', 5mm-thick steel plate skirts bolted to the sides. These provided protection against the PIAT hollow-charge bombs. The hull was also covered in 'zimmerit', a rough plaster coat to prevent the attachment of magnetic charges. Little could be seen from the armoured vision slits of the closed-down SPs lashed by Bren gun fire, and the 75mm guns had no meaningful traverse. The gunner-driver combination pointed the gun at targets by locking one track and swivelling the whole hull around to face the target and fire, whereupon the vehicle would rapidly reverse to cover. Protection was front and sides, while they were blind-sided and vulnerable to the rear – the very direction from which Rohrbach

The 1st Parachute Brigade is bloodily repulsed at the east end of the street, failing to relieve 2 Para at the Arnhem bridge. By midday on 19 September the remnants fall back along the street to Oosterbeek.

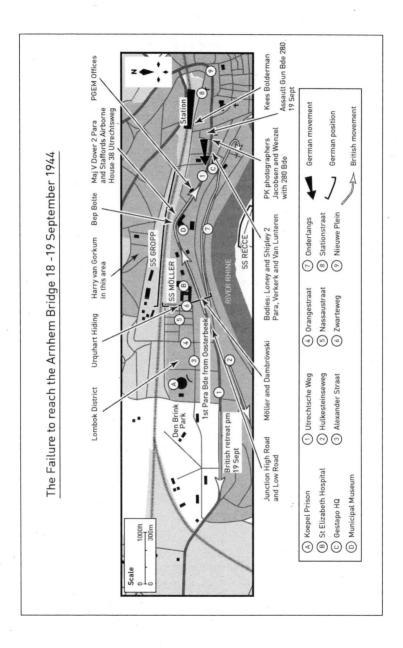

The Failure to reach the Arnhem Bridge 18 –19 September 1944

Lombok District
Urquhart Hiding
Harry van Gorkum in this area
Bep Bolte
Maj V Dover 2 Para and Staffords Airborne House 38 Utrechtsweg
PGEM Offices

Kees Bolderman
Assault Gun Bde 280 19 Sept

PK photographers Jacobsen and Wenzel with 280 Bde

Station

SS GROPP

SS MÖLLER

RIVER RHINE

SS RECCE

Den Brink Park

1st Para Bde from Oosterbeek

British retreat pm 19 Sept

Junction High Road and Low Road

Möller and Dambröwski

Bodies: Loney and Shipley 2 Para, Verkerk and Van Lunteren

Scale
0   1000ft
0   300m

Ⓐ Koepel Prison
Ⓑ St Elizabeth Hospital
Ⓒ Gestapo HQ
Ⓓ Municipal Museum

① Utrechtsche Weg
② Hulkesteinseweg
③ Alexander Straat
④ Orangestraat
⑤ Nassaustraat
⑥ Zwarteweg
⑦ Onderlangs
⑧ Stationstraat
⑨ Nieuwe Plein

German movement
German position
British movement

145

and other crew members were being stalked by paratroopers on foot emerging from behind trees and buildings.

Hauptsturmführer Hans Möller's engineer companies were engaged in a 'free for all' in the fighting around the houses bordering the Municipal Museum. 'The streets became death zones,' he recalled. 'The dead and wounded could not be retrieved.' Protecting the SPs that were attempting to manoeuvre and fire into houses along the narrow streets and intersections was dangerous for the accompanying infantry, easily run over by a suddenly reversing vehicle. 'Rubble was strewn everywhere,' Möller remembered during the battle for the Museum. 'Fences and walls had been flattened by the assault gun, while sharp gun reports spat fire at the enemy.'

The British positions were becoming untenable. Private Robert Edwards, defending with D Company, recalled the combination of 'the heaviest shelling and mortaring imaginable' with constant armoured attacks. 'Every time the shelling lessened the tanks would attack us,' he remembered. 'When they were knocked out or driven off, the shelling started up again.' PIAT ammunition started to run low. Edwards watched as the C Company commander and his headquarters disappeared 'under a welter of mortar bombs', leaving them leaderless. 'Not one officer present was left in any condition to give an order, and a sergeant, whose boots were squelching blood from his wounds, gave us the order to try and get out of it and make our way to the first organised unit that we came to.'

'Each time we opened up on Jerry, we got twice as much back,' recalled Private Sam Montgomery from A Company, pinned inside the 'Monastery', 'and the wounded would shout such things as "Leave the bastards alone!"' Major Cain with B Company saw that the end was approaching. 'The men were now being blown out of the ground at short range by 75mm fire from the tanks.' He passed the poignant sight of 'a grand little Welshman', one of the first soldiers to join his company, crumpled in a heap as he passed him by. 'Only his head and face were untouched', making him recognisable. 'Other pieces of him and his clothing were hanging on nearby bushes.' As the British started to pull back, Möller's men rushed the Museum through the holes they had blasted into the northern wall with SP guns, trapping and overrunning the paratroopers left upstairs.[151]

Möller sensed that by 10.00 'the enemy's momentum was spent'. Attacks were now 'fragmented, spread out and uncertain'. He urged on his combined assault groups of SPs and armoured engineers. 'Wounded civilians, who had tried to save what there was to save, were screaming, but what did that matter?' The battle had reached a climax. By 13.00 hours the momentum of the advance was with the Germans. 'Our fire became more and more vicious; we had plenty of ammunition and literally shot up the enemy – who bravely launched attack after attack – by carefully combining our weapons' effects.' Many of the houses along this stretch of the Utrechtseweg bordering the Museum and the St Elizabeth Hospital were now on fire, 'gobbled up by the flames,' Möller recalled. 'Dark pungent smoke drifted through the streets of this once elegant residential area.' Then suddenly it appeared that the self-propelled guns had cracked open the opposition. More and more prisoners were being taken. 'The British were completely exhausted,' Möller remembered, 'their strength overtaxed and confidence shaken by excessively high losses.' The Staffords began to quickly pull back down the road, confident at least that they would be screened and supported by the 11th Parachute Battalion coming up.

'It became apparent that something had gone very wrong in front,' recalled Major David Gilchrist with A Company 11 Para. 'Straggling groups of men of the South Staffords suddenly started coming back down the road.' As the 11th Battalion was forming up to move into the Lombok district, north of the Utrechtseweg, it was abruptly bracketed by heavy mortar fire, which scattered the troops into the surrounding gardens. At the same time German self-propelled guns came trundling down the road seemingly unopposed, machine gunning the disorientated 11 Para soldiers caught in their path. 'We had nothing with which to engage them except gammon bombs,' explained Gilchrist. His PIAT ammunition had been accidentally sent back to the rear in a jeep. A screen of 6-pounder anti-tank guns at the Klingelbeekseweg junction were out of the line of sight. Gammon bombs did not stick against the 'zimmerit'-coated assault gun hulls. Moreover, other SPs were emerging into the north of the Lombok area, having crossed the railway line and driven into Oranjestraat. The 11th Parachute Battalion was hit, completely unprepared from two directions, unbalanced and on the move. It was decimated.

The only impediment to the German advance was the grisly difficulty of maintaining forward momentum amid the piles of dead and wounded strewn across the street. An SP that exposed itself to the 6-pounder screen was struck and, being well ahead of their accompanying infantry, the remainder paused to take stock. The Germans had comprehensively shattered the four-battalion-strong charge to reach Frost at the bridge. 'The paratroopers had not expected this, to encounter elite SS divisions there,' reflected a grimly satisfied Möller. 'They had counted on an easy victory.' Only about 100 Staffords and 150 men from Lea's 11 Para were able to straggle back towards Oosterbeek. Clearly there was no prospect of Liberation for the Dutch inhabitants at this eastern end of the street.[152]

Erich Wenzel and Jacobsen, the two German PK photographers, followed up Möller's successful advance. They took a remarkable sequence of photographs on the Utrechtseweg 'high road' and Onderlangs 'low road', documenting the bitter British reverse. Sergeant Jim Drew with A Company the Staffords remembered a loudspeaker car appearing in front of the Museum. A metallic voice tonelessly called upon the British to surrender. 'Come on out you South Staffords, you are surrounded and there is no way out, come to the door with your hands up above your head.' As Jacobsen took pictures of German soldiers nonchalantly walking up to the Museum in the late morning sunlight, with rifles slung, Jim Drew's men had still not given up. 'Eventually the cellar was kicked open and a German threw an object on the cellar floor. We jumped to the other side.' Nothing happened, no explosion – it turned out to be a house-brick. 'He was indeed the finest German that I had ever met,' Drew reflected. It could have been a grenade – they would all have been killed or wounded.[153]

Quite by chance Jacobsen was on hand when the self-propelled gun was struck by one of the 6-pounder guns covering the Utrechtseweg from the Klingelbeekseweg junction. Major General Urquhart, the British division commander, had escaped his involuntary detention barely 250 metres from this point, at No 14 Zwartensweg, when the German SP gun moved off to avoid the Staffords pushing past. Jacobsen snapped a sequence of six photographs of German soldiers ducking for cover behind trees and bushes. Smoke from the impact rises up from the tank column ahead and German soldiers can be seen running, bent over, from one assault gun to the next. Jacobsen is taking pictures at sprocket level, in the lee of the armoured screen of a Sturmgeschütz. The assault gun crews were nervous. Gefreiter Wilhelm Rohrbach, edging forward with the 3rd Battery of Brigade 280 on the Utrechtseweg, recalled the 'murderous British fire', where it seemed every projectile fired by the British was on target. He recalls that six or seven assault guns were knocked out during the initial advance from the outskirts of Arnhem to Oosterbeek. Hauptmann Werner, one of the battery commanders, had already been killed, as also had Oberwachtmeister Josef Mathes, his own battery commander.[154] The advance was not easy. Jacobsen snapped off a photograph of one of the assault gun commanders cutting his way through downed tram lines with a bolt cropper, impeding progress at turret level.

Dutch civilians start to emerge from the houses along the Onderlangs to Jacobsen's left, waving white handkerchiefs. German soldiers barge past them and four paratroopers stagger into the street, two of them supporting a third injured comrade. His head wound is swollen and bleeding above the left eye. A dead paratrooper seemingly kneels, snagged and suspended by his torn smock like abandoned washing against the metal railings of the fence outside, in an attitude of despairing prayer. This poignant scene attracts a number of photographs from different angles.

On the other side of the street Möller's men are photographed bursting into the Arnhem Garage, with its distinctive 'Esso' sign outside. This is the very building where the Parachute Battalion commanders had held their fateful 'O' Group the night before. German soldiers peer anxiously around the abandoned and shot-up green NBM tram No 54. The sun reflects off the downed power line that has grotesquely spiralled across the street. Jacobsen did not catch the expression on Rottenführer (SS Corporal) Wolfgang Dombrowski's face as the drama of the entry unfolded. His task was to capture the garage with its attached house:

'One of my men reached it, opened the door and rapidly shut it. "There are loads of Engländer in there!" he exclaimed. At this moment, as I cocked my Sten, I realised it was not going to work. It had been damaged by splinters. What should we do? Surprise them and try and bluff our way through with the Sten? There were 10 to 15 Paras in there, exhausted after the jump and fighting. At the door was a Bren gun team with their finger on the trigger.'

Dombrowski knew that he faced a ferocious firefight, for which he was unprepared, as his men crowded around the garage door. 'They hesitated,' Dombrowski saw, 'and then surrendered.' It was a huge relief. There were more inside than he anticipated. Möller remembers that 'Dombrowski and his men discovered and captured 30 paratroopers who were hiding in a garage and hoping for an opportunity to get away again.' Both sides were equally relieved. Dombrowski picked up a new Sten, 'an excellent model with a wooden handle, which I held onto until almost the end of the war, when ammunition ran out.' They broke into the house next door and found the Dutch occupants. 'Any more British?' they demanded. 'Yes – wounded in the cellar,' was the response.[155]

Möller's SS veterans instinctively appreciated that the tide had turned. There were four jeeps and other equipment found in the garage, and 'aircraft recognition panels, which served us well later in the fighting,' Möller recalled. 'The poor blokes' they had captured 'were completely exhausted. They had been in action continuously for three days, but despite their bleak situation they believed firmly in their victory.' They would at least survive. 'The war was over for them.' The SS commander interrogated an Irish Captain, 'a very honest and brave man, who was very grateful for the cup of coffee and cigarettes I gave him as refreshment.' These men he appreciated were fought-out and surprised to encounter Waffen SS – 'what they least expected' – and they were 'embittered and disappointed with their command'. Möller was satisfied that 'we had managed to crack an important strongpoint', and with the Utrechtseweg secured at its eastern end the way ahead to Oosterbeek beckoned. 'And really you had to pity them, these brave lads.' The impetus was now back with the SS advance.

Jacobsen photographed one of the Staffords' mortar platoons being marched off to captivity. Lieutenant Jack Reynolds had spotted him, but was already in his viewfinder. 'Down the road I saw a German chap with a camera and a huge grin on his face,' Reynolds later recalled, 'and I thought what a bastard, and gave him the "V" sign.' His signaller, Lance Corporal George Parry, also appears in the same, now iconic photograph. Witnessing his officer's defiant gesture, he recalled, 'I was afraid that the Germans would have us shot for this, but luckily they didn't.' Reynolds was photographed again later by Jacobsen, sitting on a crate on the steps of the Municipal Museum, surrounded by a group of dishevelled, smoking and, in some cases, shocked-looking Staffords glider soldiers. Reynolds eloquently expressed the feeling behind the faces in this picture, visible 70 years after the event, snapped by chance by a German cameraman on the spot:

> 'The looks on the faces of the lads that were brought in after me surprised me. Some of the old regulars had a look on their faces as "another cock-up again", while the youngsters among them looked quite bewildered and scared.'[156]

Dutch civilian Wim van Lunteren had walked the stretch of the Utrechtseweg where Jacobsen had taken his pictures that morning outside No 63. His comments well describe the reason why the two PK photographers took them – a tangible image of the depressing British defeat. He observed 'two dead British soldiers' beyond No 63, again recalling 'one of them had reddish hair'. He walked further on to the high point of the Utrechtseweg between the 'Kraton' PGEM building and the Museum, and paused by the steep shrub-covered slope that descends to the Onderlangs below. It had been a catastrophe for the British:

> 'Standing nearby was a high-sided Opel-Blitz lorry with its front pointing in the direction of the station. German soldiers with

rifles at the ready allowed British prisoners to recover the bodies of their fallen comrades from the shrubbery. Then with a hefty swing the bodies were thrown over the high side into the lorry. This made a thudding sound.'

Not until Wednesday did the Verkerk family feel able to venture outside No 53 Utrechtseweg nearby, 'averting our eyes as we passed the corpses there'. Young H. Verkerk looked inside his house as they left the cellar. Sunday lunch was still on the table, he noticed, 'and the Germans had arranged my toy soldiers in battle order on the floor.'[157]

From the north: the lid closes on the box

The 1st Parachute Brigade, reinforced by an extra parachute and glider infantry battalion, had been shattered in just two days of fighting. The 1st and 3rd Parachute Battalions were down to remnants of a few score men each. The 2nd South Staffords was down to 375 men; more than half had already fallen on the Utrechtseweg. 11 Para had been caught unprepared in the open by the onrush of German self-propelled guns and decimated. Only about 150 were left – 62% had fallen in a matter of hours, leaving only shocked and fragmented groups to fall back to Oosterbeek. Exhausted men, separated from their units, fell asleep if they paused to rest. The enormous reverse and carnage wreaked amid companies and platoons that had joined together two years before and were as familiar with each other as family groups took a severe psychological toll. Private T. G. Coleman, with the South Staffords machine gun platoon, was told to drop off by his platoon sergeant Palmer and set up a hasty rearguard position with his pal Len Jordan, to delay the Germans. 'Probably seeing as we were pretty well buggered at the time he gave us a couple of Benzedrine tablets,' he recalled. 'They will help you to stay awake,' he said, emphasising that 'there would be no relief and when the position became untenable' they were to deactivate the gun and get back to Oosterbeek. They got behind their Vickers machine gun and Palmer departed with a 'cheery "Best of luck"', which they didn't feel, watching the flotsam of defeat file past in dribs and drabs.

As Sergeant Bill Kerr with 11 Para fell back towards Oosterbeek he recognised his surroundings. This was the road where he had been brought under fire advancing the day before. He had jumped into a ditch when the ambush was sprung and his helmet was sent flying with no chance of retrieval, the firefight having been too fierce. History appeared to be repeating itself when machine gun bullets suddenly tore up the same section of road. It was still there. Taking cover in the depths of the drainage ditch, he picked up an abandoned helmet, which he swiftly grabbed with some relief. On checking the liner he found his own name stencilled inside – it was the same ditch![158]

'More and more stragglers began arriving from the direction of Arnhem,' recalled Lieutenant Colonel 'Sheriff' Thompson commanding the glider-borne artillery, sited behind the old Oosterbeek church on the Benedendorpsweg. Jeeps accelerated by, refusing to stop, so Thompson positioned a jeep road-block next to the church. He saw that 'the morale of these men was very low', so swept them up and redirected them into new defensive positions in a row of houses that screened his guns from the Germans advancing from the east, handing out food, ammunition and cigarettes as they did so. 'The difficulty was that these men came from the 1st, 3rd and 11th Para battalions and 2nd South Staffords' who 'arrived in twos and threes divorced from their sub-units and without officers or means of communication.' There were very few rifles, as the men had exchanged or discarded them for Stens during the street fighting. The local inhabitants came out. 'People flocked around us, smiling and laughing and offering us fruit and drink,' remembered a clearly embarrassed platoon commander James Blackwood with 11 Para. 'When we told them the Germans were coming, their laughter turned into tears.' Blackwood got his men to dig slit trenches in the gardens against the backdrop of a 'melancholy procession of blanket-carrying refugees that began to move past'.

Coleman and his mate Len Jordan observed 'a lull in proceedings' as the procession of stragglers 'eased off'. Sniping and rifle fire went on around them for 3 hours, but little else. Then to their amazement a German lorry drove up, completely oblivious to what was going on, as if on a peacetime exercise. It motored into the small square they were covering.

'It had several soldiers aboard and they must have been so confident that, having us on the run with no opposition, they gave scant regard to the noise they were making. We opened fire at a range of about 200 to 300 yards. The driver tried to reverse, the soldiers were being hit and scattered in all directions, absolute shambles for 5 minutes or so, then of course it was our turn to come under fire.'

Quietly satisfied, they removed the breech block and other key parts from the Vickers and threw them away. They then moved back to Oosterbeek, where a thin defensive crust was forming. Lieutenant Colonel Thompson recalled deploying one recently arrived 11 Para NCO, who announced, 'Thank God, we've got some orders at last – now we'll be all right.'

The inhabitants of the east end of the street had been completely immersed in the intense fight that had occurred between the Utrechtseweg 'high road' and Onderlangs 'low road' on either side of the Municipal Museum. This severe battle could only be viewed with trepidation from central Oosterbeek, since the severity of the fighting was evident from the noise and distant smoke. The outcome in terms of their anticipated Liberation remained unclear. Even more pronounced was the sound of fighting to the north of the street, seemingly just beyond the Utrecht-Arnhem railway line. The 30-metre-high embankment prevented anything from being seen and to some extent deadened the noise. Those living in the streets north of the Utrechtseweg next to the Hotel Hartenstein noticed that the racket was becoming increasingly pronounced. The newly arrived 4th Parachute Brigade, seeking to move north-east into Arnhem on the other side of the railway line, was engaged in the 'battle of the woods'. Corporal Harry Bankhead, with the 156th Parachute Battalion, has always felt that 'the tranquillity of these woods holds a certain poignancy' because 'here lie probably the largest number of British and German dead without a known grave.' It was here that the last remaining cohesive element of the 1st Airborne Division clashed with SS-Obersturmbannführer Ludwig Spindler's 'Sperrlinie' blocking line. The Germans had deployed along the north-south Dreyenseweg, just beyond the road bridge next to the Oosterbeek-Hoog railway station, 900 yards north of the street. Harry Bankhead remembered that on Tuesday morning 'at first light, success was to play for', then 'by mid afternoon', after the failure to reach the Arnhem bridge and German blocking actions on the Dreyenseweg, 'the sky had fallen in'. Two companies from his battalion 'were wrecked within an hour'.[159]

Geert Maassen, living at No 32 Mariaweg, remembers the day. 'It sounded as if there was shooting from all sides.' The noise was growing in volume. 'We had the impression that the Germans were advancing, judging by the amount of shooting we heard,' he recalled. Another Dutchman, Jan Hol, on the Stationsweg nearby, remembers that 'the fighting had become fiercer outside; several shells from German guns had exploded close to the house.' There was a terrific battle being fought just beyond the railway line to the north – 'thick fat clouds of smoke hung in the air over north-west Arnhem'. But the fighting could only be heard, not seen. 'As the situation grew more and more dangerous, we knew we had to try and find better shelter than just staying indoors,' Maassen realised. The war had arrived. Across the railway line there was very little shelter for the advancing airborne troops.[160]

'As we neared the Dreyenseweg heavy gunfire rent the eerie stillness,' Corporal Harry Bankhead recalled. 'Red and yellow tracer, like fleeting glow-worms from a machine gun on fixed lines, sparked venomously over our heads.' The advancing paratroopers were taken aback by the ferocity of the opposition that mowed down the leading sections. 'The amount of ammunition being used by the Boche was astonishing,' recalled C Company commander Major Geoffrey Powell. 'We pressed on with this attack in three separate single company attacks,' recalled Major John Waddy with B Company. It was a repetition of the hastily mounted attacks that had happened earlier that morning along the Utrechtseweg. On their left the 10th Parachute Battalion was delivering similarly brave but fragmented quick attacks. The hapless 'Shan' Hackett was not being allowed to fight his formation as a brigade. Coordinated brigade-level actions appeared subsumed by an overriding imperative to close with the Arnhem bridge as soon as possible. Hackett had launched only two of his parachute battalions;

the newly attached 7 KOSB glider infantry battalion was required to secure Landing Site 'L' to his rear. Hackett suspected that the situation had changed. He was not up against line of communication troops, but Waffen SS. This required either a change of direction or a pause before mounting a deliberate brigade attack, supported with all available firepower. Direction from division headquarters with Urquhart's absence was unclear and indecisive. The plan was to capture the high ground to the north-west of Arnhem and enter the city alongside the 1st Parachute Brigade. 'That was the plan,' Waddy remembered, 'but we had no idea what opposition was ahead of us.' All Hackett got was a vague 'Press on'.[161]

The SS troopers holding on the Dreyenseweg were equally nonplussed. 'We were never absolutely certain where our men and the British were,' remembers Alfred Ziegler with the 9th SS Panzerjäger deployed in the light woods. 'We were so close that once I heard the Morse code – dit dit da da dit dit – and ran, because we knew we did not have any radios, so it had to be the British sending.' They had been heavily mortared and had beaten back attacks the day before with heavy losses. 'We got no rest throughout this day,' he recalled, 'but we stood firm.' The onus was on the British to move; all the SS had to do was hold in place in order to block access to Arnhem.[162]

Waddy was instructed to follow the A Company attack. 'There's not much opposition, just a few snipers,' he was assured by his commanding officer, Lieutenant Colonel Richard des Voeux, which 'is the thing I've never understood to this day,' Waddy recalled. Expecting to simply 'pass through' A Company, Waddy soon 'passed bodies and wounded men that I now know to be A Company, lying in the woods.' The clusters of corpses became so heavy that 'at one time I passed a complete platoon headquarters, the commander, sergeant and two men all killed.' In hindsight, Waddy felt 'Shan' Hackett, the brigade commander, had pressured his CO into a 'premature and hastily organised' assault, impressing the importance of speed and emphasising that 'we must get through to these chaps of ours on the bridge'. Normally his CO was a stickler for deliberately employing supporting fire, which was not happening now. 'There was machine gun fire from all directions,' Waddy appreciated. German armour was racing up and down and firing from the Dreyenseweg road, wreaking havoc on the advance. '20mm fire from their multiple flat guns was deadly, because it's high explosive and hits the trees and bursts and causes casualties.' Men were dismembered as if in slow motion by the heavy-calibre shells as they sprinted forward. Others, crawling for cover on the ground, were still being peppered by shrapnel and wood splinters from multiple tree bursts. 'Then we came up close to the road and all hell let loose,' Waddy remembered. They were being chopped to pieces by heavy guns mounted on armour.

Major John Pott with A Company managed to storm across the Dreyenseweg after concentrating his fire, followed up by a ferocious bayonet assault. They reached the Lichtenbeck high feature just beyond, but in the process his company was reduced to 14 men. All were wounded, there were no officers, and only six men were actually able to stand on their feet. Pott, a committed Christian, gathered his most seriously wounded beneath a bush and stood in the open, amid the battle, and prayed for them. 'Lord,' he confessed, 'I am sorry that I have only led the company to pain and death, but there is another commander who is the way, the truth and the life.' Pott was characteristically placing more faith in God than his steel helmet. 'I am committing you into His hands as I leave you now,' he concluded. 'Lord Jesus, watch over them please.'[163]

Alfred Ziegler, the dispatch rider with the 9th SS Panzerjäger (anti-tank unit), saw 'the first signs of cracking' following these 'terrible' attacks. 'In some places,' he recalled, 'our men had to assume hedgehog all-round defence positions when some groups of the enemy managed to infiltrate through our lines.' His Panzerjäger had been attached to a Kampfgruppe led by a Wehrmacht Captain Bruhns. 'He ordered me to drive towards Arnhem' to the rear 'because reinforcements were supposed to be on the way – who, how many and what, I didn't know.' Ziegler sped off on his motorcycle combination and 'found them in a forest outside Arnhem, where they had just arrived.' The armoured monoliths included so called Möbel-Wagen, 37mm flak guns, commonly called 'furniture vans' because of their high-sided box construction, mounted on Panzer IV chassis. They rolled along the tracks behind him.

Corporal Harry Bankhead turned to fellow signaller Ted Girling and shakily remarked, 'We are still going forward, Ted.' 'Don't talk rot, Harry,' Girling grimly responded. 'We are being hammered.' Out to their front 'we could hear the throb of powerful engines, either tanks or self-propelled guns.' This point represented the deepest penetration the 4th Parachute Brigade was to achieve in its attempt to fight through to the Arnhem bridge.

Ziegler had found a veritable arsenal of rapid-firing flak guns mounted on tracks. He was guiding a company of self-propelled flak guns commanded by a Fähnrich officer cadet and elements of an anti-aircraft battalion, with twin and quadruple armoured anti-aircraft guns mounted on armoured chassis. 'These units started to attack immediately', clattering along the Dreyenseweg, heading in the direction of the fiercest gunfire. 'They caught the enemy by surprise and forced him to withdraw,' he remembered. The tide had irreversibly turned on the Dreyenseweg.[164]

'By the time I came through,' Major John Waddy, leading B Company 156 Para, recalled, 'my company was being shot at and killed by this very intense fire.' Spotting a twin-barrelled 20mm flak gun on an armoured chassis firing directly down the forest ride on his advance, he 'foolishly, instead of concentrating on commanding my company, went forward with two or three men to try and knock it out'. They came under fire from a German tree-sniper and Waddy was hit and out of the battle, carried out under intense fire. His battalion had lost 50% of its strength, especially heavily among officers and NCOs. Only one rifle company was still relatively intact.

With the battle visibly climaxing and momentum inexorably slipping away, Major Geoffrey Powell suddenly received the 'startling' order from the battalion Signals Officer to fall back. 'We were all to withdraw to Wolfheze in 15 minutes time,' he heard. 10 Para, to their left, received the same terse message. 'At first it was hard to believe,' Powell recalled, 'that he had not made a mistake'. The clamour of battle to their north had become increasingly obvious 'and the risk of our retreat being cut off was plain, but this was a suicidal way to withdraw.' At present they were literally hugging the enemy in a life or death embrace. 'One could not just stand up and walk away from an enemy on one's heels,' declared the shocked, frustrated and dismayed Powell. 'Things over in the north must be bad indeed for the Colonel to be rushed in this way,' he thought. They were indeed, but news had also been received of enemy advances coming in from the west to their rear. When Powell told his second-in-command to get moving, 'his face registered shocked disbelief'. Captain Nick Hanmer, the Adjutant of 10 Para, was also incredulous, shouting to his CO, 'We can't withdraw from here – the Jerries are all around us.' Lieutenant Colonel Ken Smyth retorted, 'We've got our orders, let's get going.' But this was not easy. 'Peter Warr of B Company,' Hanmer remembered, had 'reported that he was being overrun by tanks, and was engaged in hand-to-hand fighting.'[165] The plan was already beginning to unravel.

There was no time to brief the normal practice of falling back through a number of secured rendezvous points. Only one was given: get to the other side of the Wolfheze level crossing. The problem was the railway embankment that separated them from the northern edge of Oosterbeek. Its steep embankment was an obstacle to vehicles. If Wolfheze to their rear was overrun by the western group of advancing Germans they would be unable to get the jeeps and towed anti-tank guns across the level crossing. There was only one alternative, an underpass beneath the embankment, with a treacherous sandy bottom, through which vehicles might squeeze. This was half a mile short of the level crossing. Congestion on the narrow track along the embankment leading to that tunnel and the level crossing was inevitable.

One of the reasons why the 4th Parachute Brigade was unable to pierce Spindler's block on the Dreyenseweg was the need to leave one-third of its strength behind. The glider-borne 7th KOSB battalion had remained in reserve, securing Landing Site (LS) 'L'. They were also ordered to retreat. It was feared that the Germans may have pushed beyond Wolfheze, following the west-east line of the street and potentially cutting them off from Oosterbeek. 7 KOSB had its own problems because it was being attacked from the north by Sepp Krafft's newly reorganised SS Training and Replacement Battalion. These Germans were bearing down on the left flank of Hackett's brigade while it was pinned against the Dreyenseweg to its front. Krafft, coordinating the north-south advance, had 642 Naval

Battalion and the 1st Marine Cadre, another regiment of sailors, in extended line to his right. His mission was to close the lid of the German box from the north, linking with Von Tettau's division on its west side and Harzer's 9th SS coming from the east. It was intended to compress the British Airborne Division from three sides, while it had its back to the river, and crush it. More urgently there was an opportunity to destroy this overextended British force north of the railway line before it could escape into Oosterbeek. The paratroopers were desperately fighting around the open ground bordered by woods to the north and east of the earmarked Landing Site at Johannahoeve, 2,000 yards north of the street. Just as the lid was being closed on this box by the Germans, and with a hasty British withdrawal under way, the Polish brigade's glider-borne heavy weapons lift began to land in between.

Low-lying mist at British airfields had prevented the main part of the reinforcing Polish Brigade from taking off. Its glider-heavy weapons element, transporting vitally needed anti-tank guns, did so, but only 28 of the 43 gliders setting off actually arrived. Seven suffered mishaps between England and the coast, and another seven were either shot down or had tow ropes parted by flak over Holland. They started to land right across the withdrawal line of the 10th Parachute Battalion, adding chaos to an already confused situation. 'As we withdrew across the open ground,' Captain Nick Hanmer recalled, the battalion was flailed by 'murderous fire' coming 'from the line of trees north of the LZ'. Brigadier Hackett anxiously watched their approach. They were moving across the LS under pressure from the rear but 'appeared deployed by companies and in very fair order'. They were mistaken for the enemy by many because they were preceded by the German fire that was slashing through their ranks and passing over the heads of other assembled brigade troops also seeking to retreat. Hanmer described the reality of the perilous predicament, sanitised by Hackett's distant observation. 'Men all around us were being hit,' he recalled, 'and all bar the walking wounded and those who could be supported by comrades had to be abandoned.' Geoffrey Powell, caught up in the pell-mell retreat, despairingly remembered that 'the landing zone was already a battlefield and the wretched Poles were about to land in the middle of it!'[166]

Lieutenant Jerzy Halpert, with the 2nd Polish Anti-Tank Battery, gazed anxiously through the cockpit of glider 131 flying into LS 'L'. 'It's bad!' he called back to the anti-tank gunners behind him. Directly ahead were clusters of puffy smoke balls, vicious flak, emanating from what was obviously going to be a 'hot' landing site. A shell bursting beneath the plywood Horsa peppered Bombardier Nosecki's trousers with red-hot shrapnel, which caused them to smoulder, but miraculously he was untouched. The pilot groaned and clutched his chest before replacing bloodied hands on the control column. 'Get ready!' he called, as he took them in. Nosecki, glancing through the port hole, saw a glider going in 'lit up like a fireball', and through the cockpit ahead he saw smoke streaming from a stricken Stirling in the distance. When the glider struck the ground and skidded to a halt, they were 'greeted by a shower of machine gun fire'.[167]

For the most part the Dutch inhabitants of the street were oblivious to the drama being played out on the other side of the railway embankment. They heard rather than saw it, mainly due to the ever greater densities of German anti-aircraft guns that constantly arrived to be deployed around the local area. Jan Esvelt, watching from across the south bank of the Lower Rhine, simply wrote in his diary that 'around 5pm a few gliders are landing again.' 'In the afternoon there were some more gliders,' recalled Roelie Breman, just south of the street. 'One huge glider has fallen down at the other side of the river – there was an enormous fire.' She erroneously thought that 'there were a hundred soldiers in it, none of them survived.' The technical panoply of modern war was lost on the inhabitants of Oosterbeek, thus far largely removed from the war. Only now was appreciation growing about what may be dangerous and what not. Most people assumed that these were Allied reinforcements and that the Liberation, despite some difficulties, was broadly on course. Anje van Maanen, living by the Oosterbeek crossroads, mentions that more 'droppings' have occurred and that 'this time the Germans have fired frantically, so we practically could not look – too dangerous.' Care was required. Young Sjoert Schwitters living at No 5 Cronjéweg, some 300 metres from the street, had an unimpeded view of much that was going on from his bedroom window. He watched as a German anti-aircraft gun blazed away from the rooftop of a nearby house:

> 'I saw one of them hit. There was an explosion – the nose of the glider seemed to have been shot off – and I saw soldiers and items of equipment, a jeep perhaps, and other items all falling out.'

He looked away in anguish. 'It was a terrible sight, and I hated the Germans for what they were doing – all those young men dying.'[168]

Over the Landing Site a strange harmonious whining superseded the low-cadence droning of the approaching multi-engined towing aircraft. It was not the fighter escort; the whine came from a flight of Messerschmitt Me 109 fighters that had overhauled the ponderous formation from behind. They tore through it, their distinctive 20mm cannon thumping out luminous trails of smoking tracer that bored into the fragile plywood glider hulls. Polish war correspondent Marek wiȩcicki, who had landed with the first lift, recalled that 'the German air force was the most unpleasant surprise of all', because it had long been assumed that the Luftwaffe was a spent force. 'One of the gliders broke up like a child's toy, and a jeep, an anti-tank gun and people flew out of it,' he remembered. 'We had never expected things to be so bad, so very bad.' It was going to get worse.[169]

Two of SS-Sturmbannführer Krafft's Reserve Battalion 16 companies were directly opposite in the wood line, converging on the retreating 10th Battalion, when the gliders landed. They crossed the Ede-Arnhem road 'and inflict considerable losses again on the British,' Krafft recalled. Marek wiȩcicki saw them after the low-level strafing runs were over:

> 'When they stopped the forest opened up. Skirmishing Germans, looking in the distance like rabbits jumping, or field mice, moved rapidly and inexorably forward, striking at the numerically much weaker British guards, throwing them back and forcing them to withdraw.'

The landing site was soon in German hands and the young, ideologically zealous SS troopers were not particularly chivalrous. Incensed by 10 Para's delaying tactics, which had cost them time and considerable casualties, they vented their frustration on the group of 20 paratroopers they managed to overrun. Private Ralph Shackleton was captured with his wounded PIAT No 2, Private Youell. The SS lined them up and mowed them down from a distance of 6 feet. Shackleton, who survived but played dead, watched as the injured Youell lying on the ground nearby was dispatched by a shot between the eyes. Shackleton managed to crawl off and was taken prisoner again.[170]

Nick Hanmer with 10 Para was thankful that the landing gliders had attracted much of the German fire away from them. The 9th SS quickly advanced forward from the Dreyenseweg, inexorably pressing on the heels of the chaotic retreat. 'I saw a German half-track,' Hanmer recalled, 'moving among the Horsas, firing into them at point-blank range.' What saved the majority of the fleeing paratroopers during the sudden collapse was the practical difficulty the Germans were having in closing the lid on the trap. They sought to advance as fast as the British could retreat with the same limited control. Coming in from two adjacent directions, they had to check fire for fear of hitting their own troops. Krafft offered an understated explanation in his obsequious later post-combat report. He admitted that the 9th Company commander under Obersturmführer Leiteritz 'has some very bad luck with his tactics, the company suffering heavy casualties in consequence.' Leiteritz had been responsible for the decisive block on the Utrechtseweg on the first day. It appears he may have been shot down in a blue-on-blue confrontation with the advancing 9th SS, charging in from his left flank. All this was scant compensation for 10 Para. Captain Hanmer remarked, 'I doubt if half of us who set off across the landing zone made the cutting under the railway.'[171]

The glider landings turned the retreat into a shambles. 'The crew of one must have been killed or badly wounded at the controls,' David Dagwell with 156 Para recalled, 'because it ploughed across the field, hitting at least two others that had already landed, before it cart-wheeled into oblivion.' Of ten anti-tank guns that set off from England, only three were driven off the landing site. The Germans began 'saturating' the glider landing zone with mortar and machine gun fire. Anti-tank crews managing to disembark their guns were shot down. 'The others who had survived the landing must have thought that they were completely surrounded by enemy forces and quite naturally began firing indiscriminately in all directions.' Amid the confusion Dagwell and his companions shouted themselves hoarse to attract a Polish group running towards the Germans. They were mown down. Language difficulties were unhelpful. 'Come! Come!' sounded too much like the German 'Komm! Komm!' to convince the Poles not to fire at their rescuers. The withdrawing British were equally confused. Corporal Doug Holt with 7 KOSB, 'being in the rear' during the withdrawal, 'saw many of A Company captured as they met up with the so-called Poles who were really the enemy.' Jimmy Coupland, with the anti-tank platoon, shook out air recognition panels at the edge of the wood to guide in the Polish guns. 'The firing then stopped,' he recalled, 'and we were waved out of the woods expecting to meet the Poles, but instead there were loads of Germans with machine guns all around.' The three solitary guns that escaped destruction were directed back to division headquarters at the Hotel Hartenstein on the Utrechtseweg. They joined the five other Polish guns that had landed with the earlier lifts and positioned themselves around the corner on the Oranjeweg, north of the street.[172]

Retreating British soldiers had to either climb the 30-foot railway embankment or get across the level crossing at Wolfheze to reach Oosterbeek. Generalleutnant von Tettau's advancing western group were already in Wolfheze. An SS battalion under Eberwein, part of Lippert's regiment, was clearing the woods on the approaches to Wolfheze. To his right was a Fliegerhorst battalion filling the void between the other SS NCO School battalion under Günther Schulz, attacking broadly west to east along the Utrechtseweg. Ahead was a widely dispersed British screen to the west of Oosterbeek, held by the 1st Border Regiment Battalion of glider infantry. They had just retired eastward to shorten their line to a 1-mile frontage, with thick woods in between. A Company was north of the Utrechtseweg, C Company astride it, D on the van Borsselenweg nearby, and B Company forward on the high ground of the Westerbouwing, next to the Lower Rhine. Without appreciating it, the Borderers formed the east side of the emerging British airborne perimeter, compressed now from west through north to east. They were blocking the west end of the street. Their withdrawal left a vacuum around Wolfheze, which the Germans promptly filled.

The return of the 'Moffen' to the west of the street was a shock for the Dutch inhabitants. At 1 o'clock on Tuesday 19 September the Kelderman family, living near the Wolfheze level crossing, saw a line of heavily camouflaged soldiers emerge from the woods towards them. It was a regular line with 1.5 metres between each man, bearing down on Wolfheze. They had 'their guns at the ready,' recalled eight-year-old Cees Kelderman, 'as if they were hunting some animal.' Eberwein's SS troopers demanded to know if there were any 'Tommies' in their house. They were told none, but they insisted on looking, reminding Cees's father that his family would be shot if it was a lie. The recovery of English parachutes produced shouts and threats, which were allayed when it was explained that they would be converted into clothing. Losing interest, they began to search for loot among the abandoned gliders nearby before low-flying German fighters shot them into flames.

Dick van t'Land was still sheltering in the cellar of his wrecked house near the Wolfheze mental asylum, where his parents and brother had been killed on the first day and his sister seriously injured. 'The Tommies are driving through the village with a white flag,' he heard. 'We could hardly believe it,' he recalled, 'but it was so – the Germans had come back.' They were flushed out of the cellars. 'Suddenly they were standing in front of us, about six soldiers with rifles, and we heard "Raus! Raus! Out! Out! Papers!"' They suspected they were hiding 'Tommies', but moved on, leaving a very confusing situation:

> 'At one time you saw Germans and on other occasions you met Tommies. I can't remember when it all changed but eventually you didn't see Tommies any more, and our hopes vanished.'

They thought they had been liberated. 'It was a heavy blow and a huge disappointment for us,' Dick remembered, while more and more refugees kept coming from Oosterbeek. 'The cellar was completely filled with refugees, and one night there was even a baby born, with naturally no doctor to be found.'[173]

Heading towards Wolfheze, oblivious to the emerging German threat, were shattered elements of the 4th Parachute Brigade. They retreated along the sandy track of the railway embankment, chased by half-tracks firing at a distance from the rear and right. Corporal Harry Bankhead with 156 Para remembered that 'the pace quickened almost to a run as men sought shelter,' ducking as higher shots ricocheted off the railway line. Companies became mixed up in the flight. Bankhead's battalion had already lost two-thirds of its strength, reduced to about 200 men in 30 hours. Soldiers became surly and insubordinate under the pressure of a string of reverses: the setback on the Dreyenseweg, a scant 15 minutes notice given to retreat, followed by their total inability to even protect the Polish glider landing. 'One bold Boche armoured car could be seen cruising amongst the chaos,' Bankhead recalled, 'shooting up any crews still struggling to free loads.' Dutch informants were heard saying that the Germans were closing on Wolfheze, 'quicker than expected'. Bankhead reflected:

'Clearly the enemy were pouring in fresh reserves while our numbers dwindled. Outwardly, at least, the senior officers were unruffled. The older men appeared to have greater resilience, but I noticed that younger soldiers, more easily drained, often stumbled on the uneven ground.'

Major Geoffrey Powell commanding C Company suspected that 'as I expected, little by little cohesion was starting to break down'. Even the men of the mortar platoon carrying heavy base-plates and tubes had caught up and were among his retreating riflemen. As spandau bursts passed harmlessly overhead, 'men were looking apprehensive and flinching'. The precipitate retreat was no longer orderly; it 'was taking the nature of a horde of men seeking safety'. Powell was convinced that 'soon discipline would crack and everyone would start to run'. Major Page, commanding Headquarters Company, realised this too and abruptly stopped in the middle of the track with his arms outstretched. 'I will shoot any man who runs past me,' he sharply announced. The pace slowed.[174]

Private Robin Holburn with the KOSB 'heard comments that the Wolfheze crossing "was closed"'. Realisation that the Germans were up ahead coupled with the increase of harassing fire dictated a change of direction. It was decided to go over the steep railway embankment where they were now and rendezvous inside the woods beyond. Vehicles were soon jammed up around the underpass beneath the embankment as infantry started to clamber over its completely exposed slopes. 'Confusion became pronounced,' recalled Holburn, with the general exodus of soldiers climbing over, and jeeps and handcarts becoming stuck on the slope. Geoffrey Powell slipped and clutched at bushes to get up the black cinder shale. 'This was a little like clambering across the firing butts on the range in the middle of a machine gun practice,' he thought. Fire slackened off as they scrambled and tumbled down the solid cover on the other side. There was still the odd mortar explosion, which convinced Powell that 'this was not a place to linger'. Many soldiers did not receive the word and continued on to Wolfheze, where they were surrounded and went into the bag. 'Around this area were scenes of very heavy fighting,' recalled Lieutenant Charles Doig, a 7 KOSB platoon commander, as he was marched away by the Germans.

> 'I saw the burned body of one of our officers, but couldn't recognise him as the upper part of the body had received the full blast of a flame-thrower. All one could distinguish was a bit of tartan flash on the shoulder.'[175]

...and west

The only stability to the west of the street was provided by the line held by the 1st Battalion the Border Regiment glider infantry. It had withdrawn slightly east of the Wolfheze crossroads, a vital conduit for the retreating parachute brigade to get into the perimeter gradually taking shape. But the effect had been to strengthen the line. Platoon commander Alan Green, with D Company in the woods near the van Borsselenweg just south of the street, recalled that 'the county was so heavily wooded that it was always possible that the two sides could get within 10 yards and neither be aware the other was there.' SS Junker Rolf Lindemann, advancing along this sector of the Utrechtseweg with Lippert's SS NCO School, recalled the difficult nature of the approach. 'Nobody knew where the British were' and it was difficult to maintain control with platoons going missing in the woods. Lindemann sent a 'messenger' to find them, a 32-year-old regarded as more 'expendable' because he was old. 'Off he walked,' Lindemann recalled, 'with his rifle shouldered, walking along one of the sandy tracks until two British soldiers stealthily rose up behind him in the bushes.' Having slung his rifle there was little he could do apart from sheepishly raise his hands in surrender. 'After a short interrogation he ended up in the tennis courts "cage" at the back of the Hartenstein hotel.' Alan Green remembered that 'the woods contained lots of dense cover provided by shrubs and tall grasses and weeds; it was only by being constantly alert and keeping good observation that anyone could be aware of what was going on in front of the company.'[176]

Strong German probing attacks came in once Lippert's battalion, commanded by Schulz, had located the extent of the line. 'We dug in and prepared for anything that came,' recalled Corporal Jim Swan with C Company. '18 platoon was the first to be hit hard with mortars and machine gun fire' on the 19th, just as the perimeter was forming, 'and was practically wiped out'. The Germans side-stepped this resistance and came upon Swan's position:

> 'We managed to hold our ground but it was touch and go. We were nearly overrun. One German fellow got to within just a couple of yards from Major Neil's slit trench. The Bren had fired that much, the barrels were red hot. They tried to change barrels and found the second barrel had been hit on the gas regulator and was useless, so we finished up with rifles. 15 Platoon had a bashing.'

Above *A pre-war view of the Oosterbeek crossroads, looking east toward Arnhem. Stationsweg is to the left in the foreground and the Hotel Schoonoord to the right.* Voskuil

Left *Looking west towards Heelsum before the war. Wil Rieken lived at the baker's shop on the left, opposite the Dennenkamp Park on the right.* Voskuil

Below left *The Hotel Hartenstein, a German HQ until it was captured, when it became General Urquhart's 1st Airborne Division HQ.*

Above *A view of Arnhem burning to the east, as it may have appeared to residents of the street.*

Below *Mrs Kremer in German-occupied Oosterbeek took this picture of an apparently deserted road from No 8 Stationsweg, at great personal risk. A lone German soldier is walking toward the Utrechtseweg on the far pavement.* Mrs A. L. A. Kremer-Kingma

Above *The Stationsweg suddenly filled with lorries that turned in from the Utrechtseweg to the right, transporting Sturmbannführer Krafft's 9th Heavy Company.* Mrs A. L. A. Kremer-Kingma

Below *The SS infantry in lorries move off, heading west to reinforce Krafft's blocking position. Mrs Kremer would have been shot if discovered taking these pictures.*
Mrs A. L. A. Kremer-Kingma

A Street in Arnhem

The street was only to be liberated for 24 hours before the Germans were fighting their way back again.

At first it was like May 1940, but this time the Germans appeared powerless to react as the British rapidly advanced.

General Küssin, the Stadtkommandant of Arnhem responsible for the defence of the Arnhem bridge, was killed at the junction of the Utrechtseweg and Wolfhezeweg by the lead elements of 3 Para.

Right *Sturmgeschütz Brigade 280 assault guns were filmed by Erich Wenzel lining up behind Möller's Kampfgruppe at the eastern extremity of the street, prior to attacking the Staffords at the Municipal Museum.*

Below *Wenzel took this picture of Dutch civilians fleeing the fighting as the Sturmgeschütz Brigade 280 SPs moved west along the street.*

Above *Dutch civilians are forced out of their houses by Möller's men on the Onderlangs.*

Below *On Ginkel Heath at 1400 hours on 18 September, Helle's Dutch SS Wach Battalion shoot at descending paratroopers from the 4th Brigade second lift.*

Above *Corporal Harry Bankhead with 156 Para remembers that the battalion was 'hammered' during the desperate retreat into the Oosterbeek pocket.*

Above *Major John Waddy with 156 Para was wounded during the abortive attempt to bypass the street and enter Arnhem from the west. He was again wounded awaiting medical treatment at the embattled Hotel Tafelberg.*

Above *The lightly armed 4th Parachute Brigade was shot to pieces by a line of German vehicles. This half-track is blocking the north-west approach to Arnhem on the Dreyenseweg, north of the street.*

Facing page top *A German assault group nears its objective.*

Facing page bottom *A British defender's view of infiltrating German soldiers.*

Right *Sturmbannführer Sepp Krafft delayed the liberation of the street by 12 hours, a decisive contribution to the eventual outcome of the battle.*

Below *Hauptsturmführer Hans Möller advanced down the street from east to west as an SS NCO in Der Führer in May 1940 and returned to fight the same route as a 9th SS Battalion commander in September 1944.*

Above *Obersturmbannführer Walter Harzer commanded the 9th SS Hohenstaufen Kampfgruppe attacking east to west along the street.*

A Street in Arnhem

Above *SS Rottenführer Wolfgang Dombrowski's section is breaking into the Arnhem Garage to the right of the tram, photographed by Kriegsberichter Jacobsen. Much to their surprise they found 30 paratroopers and four jeeps inside.*

Below *Lt Jack Reynolds and members of the South Staffords Mortar Platoon pass Erich Wenzel, photographing Möller's men mopping up the Municipal Museum on the Utrechtseweg.*

Above *Reynolds passes Jacobsen and gives a derisory 'V' sign. Lance Corporal George Parry, following behind, thought they were going to be shot*

Below *Reynolds, on the box on the left, sits with his shell-shocked men as they smoke to calm their nerves.*

Above *Jacobsen's poignant picture shows a dead paratrooper suspended by his smock from the railings in an attitude of prayer on the Onderlangs 'low road', as his companions are taken prisoner.*

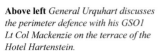

Above left *General Urquhart discusses the perimeter defence with his GSO1 Lt Col Mackenzie on the terrace of the Hotel Hartenstein.*

Above right *Lt Gen von Tettau commanded the hastily assembled units trying to advance from west to east along the street, in order to link up with the 9th SS on the opposite side of the Airborne perimeter.*

Above *Leutnant Giesa's flame-thrower tank from Panzer Company 224 was knocked out near the Koude Herberg crossroads at the western end of the Utrechtseweg, near Corporal Jim Swan with C Company the Borderers.*

Below *This is Corporal Jim Swan's trench-level perspective photographed by Sergeant Dennis Smith near Van Lennepweg with C Company the Borderers.*

A Street in Arnhem

The three AFPU photographers: Sergeants Dennis Smith (left), Gordon Walker (centre) and Mike Lewis (right)

As the fighting around the street drew to a close on 16 September the forcible evacuation of the local population by the Germans began. The street became a prohibited war zone for eight months.

Once the street was forcibly evacuated it was systematically looted by the Germans and the residents' possessions distributed to bombed-out German civilians in the Ruhr.

Above *British troops force a re-entry into the Gestapo HQ during the final liberation of the street in April 1945.*

Below *As in the previous September, the British fought back along the Arnhem Utrechtseweg, attacking from east to west towards Oosterbeek in April 1945. Infantry advance through smoke.*

Above *Wil Rieken's baker shop home at No 178 Utrechtseweg is seen shortly after the family's return after May 1945. About one-eighth of the buildings in Oosterbeek village were totally destroyed, with hardly a single house undamaged. The street was the centre point of the devastation.* Rieken

Above *Wil Rieken today with 'Bota', the straw dog to which she clung throughout the battle.* Rieken

Left *Wil Rieken laid flowers with the other schoolchildren during the first poignant ceremony of its kind in September 1945.* Rieken

The AFPU cameramen, Smith, Walker and Lewis, had got together with the Borderers after failing to reach Arnhem. Sergeant Gordon Walker wrote in his photographic 'dope sheet' sent back with his pictures that 'things are pretty tough, we are completely surrounded and the casualties are extremely heavy'. They were in a house overlooking the Koude Herberg crossroads on the Utrechtseweg. 'We have given up all idea of photographs and are fighting now for our lives,' he reported. 'The machine gunning, mortar and shellfire is hellish, the worst I have ever been in.'

Tenacious resistance and the obstacle value of thick undergrowth enabled the line to be held. It was a dangerous and unpleasant arena in which to fight. 'Many of the shells burst on impact with the tree branches and trunks,' Alan Green recalled, 'giving the effect of air bursts, thus causing many more casualties.' This was hard close-range fighting, which made it difficult for the Germans to exploit their numerical advantage. 'Hardly ever was a gun fired at more than 50 yards range, and very often it seemed that the enemy was sitting on the muzzle of each rifle or Sten gun.' Sergeant Walker felt 'it seems the enemy knows where we are but can't pin-point us, but he is attacking everywhere hoping to break the perimeter somewhere.' He was pessimistic: 'If XXX Corps doesn't come soon, it will be just too bad for us.' SS-Standartenführer Lippert was trying to identify the hold-up.[177]

Bootsman Alfred Steckhan, who had written to his wife Liess 72 hours before, was shot in the stomach in the woods just to the north of the Valkenburglaan. It took two months before Alfred's wife was notified that he was missing. 'Your husband was sent into action a few weeks ago,' his deputy company commander wrote, 'and following his recovery was not returned to his present unit.' This was misleading information – he had been picked up on the battlefield but little else was known. His personal belongings were sent home and Steckhan's wife received a distracting assurance that 'we hope that you had good news about your husband in the meantime'. Alfred Steckhan died of his wounds on 20 September, but his remains were not identified for another 60 years. By this time his widow had passed away, leaving his two daughters to be contacted by the investigating Dutch military graves unit.[178]

SS-Standartenführer Lippert instinctively knew that he must 'keep the pressure on Oosterbeek from the west'. Resistance needed to be collapsed before the British could form a perimeter. 'It was my main task,' he recalled. Unable to infiltrate the woods, he decided to force the Utrechtseweg at the Koude Herberg with tanks.

Oberleutnant Alfred May arrived at Von Tettau's headquarters late in the day on 19 September with Tank Company 224. His command had 132 men equipped with 18 French Char B1 tanks, converted to flame-throwers. The turrets kept their 47mm cannon but the 75mm gun originally mounted in the front hull was replaced by a flame spray tube. May's unit had first been alerted at Ypenburg Airport near The Hague. He was not allowed to use the motorway connection, but was directed to move mainly by night along narrow minor roads to avoid Allied fighter-bombers. This developed into a torrid two-day journey, the low point being when one of the tanks toppled into the harbour at Romeijnbrug, trying to negotiate the narrow streets of Oudewater in pitch darkness. Two crew members drowned. May's patience snapped following this mishap and he ordered the heavily camouflaged tanks to drive direct to Arnhem. His 17 remaining tanks were broken down into three sections of five or six tanks each, and one of these was attached to Lippert's SS NCO School.

Lippert, held up at the Koude Herberg crossroads, had his own problems. The western jaw of the German pincer advancing to threaten the retreating 4th Parachute Brigade was as haphazard in its conduct and progress as the British retreating before it. Lippert found he was unable to coordinate his regiment's movements with the other attacking units as 'agreement with Von Tettau's command staff was impossible, because there was no radio or telephone contact available.' This meant that 'during the early days the battalions belonging to Von Tettau's battle group were operating independently of each other.' Rolf Lindemann, one of Lippert's heavy weapons section commanders, was derisory about the effectiveness of these supporting units. 'The other units were no unit at all,' he disdainfully recalled. 'They had no idea of fighting, as was also the case of the Arbeitsdienst [Labour Service] Navy and Luftwaffe.'

Lippert's men were not even being resupplied. 'Cooperation with Von Tettau's staff was in fact a catastrophe,' Lippert complained. 'In my opinion it was thrown together too quickly and was dysfunctional, there were no weapons, ammo, heavy weapons, communications equipment, rations, transport, military police, doctors and ambulances and what have you.' But for the personal intervention of SS-Oberstgruppenführer Rauter, the Netherlands SS and Police Chief, Lippert would have received nothing. Rauter visited daily to find out what was going on and provided requisitioned vehicles to pick up the wounded and bring up food and ammunition. Lippert's NCO School was a barracks-based organisation and did not therefore have its own integral transport or logistic resupply. His men proved resourceful. Rolf Lindemann described how they developed the habit of 'watching the Allied resupply drops every afternoon; they were expected at about 16.00.' Having worked out the key to signalling the aircraft with marker panels, 'every afternoon we set them out... The aircraft always dropped onto the signs,' he commented with some relish. 'We always had sufficient supplies – the English got nothing!'[179]

It was Leutnant Siegfried Giesa's 2nd Section that lost the tank in the Oudewater harbour, and they were the ones committed against the Koude Herberg crossroads on the Utrechtseweg. Moving through the trees in close support was Eberwein's SS battalion from Lippert's regiment. Giesa dispatched Unteroffizier Jacob's tank to the left to outflank the position. As it trundled down the Sonnenberglaan beyond the crossroads, a 17-pounder armour-piercing round bored through its front glacis plate at 2,900 feet per second. It burst into flames. This was the most powerful velocity gun fielded by the airborne, carried inside the huge Hamilcar gliders. The gun had just escaped across the railway line at Wolfheze and had been incorporated into the Borderers' defence. Sergeant Horace 'Nobby' Gee immediately pumped another round into the flaming monolith. Gee's crew had been alerted to the sound of tanks revving up and moving around ahead. The screaming crew were unable to get out.

'18 and 17 Platoons were soon in the thick of it,' recalled Corporal Jim Swan. 'Mortar plus self-propelled gun and flame-thrower.' The men manning the houses at the crossroads were badly frightened when they saw flames spurting out from two more of Giesa's tanks squealing and clattering their way down the Utrechtseweg. They began to vacate their positions; some men panicked and ran into the houses occupied by D Company on the south side of the street. 'It got really nasty,' remembered Jim Swan. Although the 32-ton tanks were obsolete, they were hugely menacing and encased in armour more than 50mm thick. The ball-mounted spray tube spat flame out to a fearsome 140 feet, too much for some of the Borderers. The flammable liquid bounced off walls and ceilings, spraying inside the blind spots. There was no defence against flame. 'As if he can't do enough with the other stuff, he is now using flame-throwers,' wrote Sergeant Gordon Walker in his 'dope sheet'. An angry Lieutenant Alan Roberts with D Company ordered the sheepish-looking C Company men back. Major Neil, the C Company commander, 'led us toward the crossroads,' recalled Corporal Jim Swan. 'He was carrying a Bren gun, and a few spare magazines stuck in his smock.' The small section pressed home a counter-attack. 'We arrived at the crossroads in the driveway of a house right on the crossroads,' Swan recalled, 'and all fired at the self-propelled gun, the flame-thrower and troops behind.'

Captain Peter Chard was commanding C Troop of the light regiment 75mm pack howitzers in the open field along the Valkenburglaan nearby, just north of the Utrechtseweg. When Eberwein's SS infantry supporting Giesa's Flammpanzer were dispersed by the fire, Chard moved forward with a PIAT to kill off the tank. When it misfired he ran to the rear of the tank with pockets full of grenades, intending to lob one into the turret. As he broke cover he was engulfed by a spurt of flame, sucking the air from his lungs and coating his clothing in thick viscous burning fluid. He ran like a mad man back down the road towards his men, shrieking for someone to shoot him and put him out of his agony. Nobody could bring themselves to do it. They pulled him onto the ground and rolled him over in the sand to extinguish the flames. APFU cameraman Sergeant Smith was there and photographed the awful effects. The picture turned out to be the only image taken by the team during the Arnhem fighting to be embargoed by the censor. It was never made available to the Imperial War Museum collection after the war. Chard lingered on for nearly three more agonising weeks before succumbing to his burns at Apeldoorn Hospital on 9 October.

Set back in the gardens around the Koude Herberg crossroads were three of the Borderers' 6-pounder anti-tank guns. Two of them had no line of sight to the flame-thrower, but the third, 'Gallipoli II', manned by Corporal Lever and located in the garden of No 17 Van Lennepweg, had an unobstructed shoot. The multiple crack and boom sent a 6-pounder armour-piercing shot through the front glacis plate of Leutnant Giesa's own tank at about 2,700 feet per second. Sergeant Gordon Walker briefly filmed the moment: 'I managed to get a shot of the 6-pounder before it knocked out the SP,' he later wrote in his 'dope sheet' – 'a beautiful shot'. Giesa was slightly wounded by the impact but he and his men were able to bail out and found cover among the accompanying SS infantry. With two tanks down and a storm of fire aroused around the crossroads, Lippert's men fell back and plastered the location with mortar fire. Swan was blown off his feet in the driveway and hit in the face and left arm. His companion 'really got the worse of it – he was in a daze and the bandolier around his body was burning and his inside leg wounded.' They were recovered.[180]

Cameramen Sergeant Lewis caught only part of the desperate action. 'A self-propelled gun was 80 yards from me, but I could not see it.' He described the fighting as 'very close-in due to the nature of the woody countryside', and the enemy 'is heard often and rarely seen'. The situation around the Koude Herberg crossroads was precarious, but the Borderers were holding. 'Attack and counter-attack is the order of the day and night,' Lewis wrote. 'Jerry is a matter of a score of yards from here, and one vital crossroads has changed hands several times.' 'The troops are very tired, little sleep and food; no time for either. Benzedrine tablets help in combating fatigue.' They were effectively blocking the German advance pressing along the western Utrechtseweg. Some stability was essential at this point to enable the embattled and retreating 4th Parachute Brigade to get back inside the forming perimeter.[181]

The 7th KOSB moved off from its rendezvous point south of Wolfheze at 18.00 and managed to reach the Utrechtseweg in the fading light, benefiting from the protection the stiff Borderer defence had given its right flank. By nightfall about 270 of its men reached division headquarters at the Hotel Hartenstein, where they were directed to occupy a line of houses north of the street. Hackett wanted to move the rest of his depleted brigade into Oosterbeek that night, but division headquarters advised no move before first light. The staff had little comprehension of the magnitude of the disaster on the other side of the railway as the Germans had closed the lid on the box enclosing the perimeter. A textbook brigade withdrawal by secured rendezvous points controlled by division was now impractical. Friendly fire accidents paled into insignificance compared to the desperate running retreat that the 156th and 10th Parachute Battalions had just conducted. Brigade commanders did not question division orders, so Hackett's remnants were left outside the forming perimeter until it got light, when ironically both sides would see each other. At midnight on 19 September Krafft's SS battalion reported that 'our right flank contacts the left flank of the Division von Tettau, thus closing the pocket.' At dawn Krafft assumed that 'the battle group has only small pockets of enemy in the woodlands to mop up in the new attack at 06.00 hours.' Unbeknown to them there were about 520 British paratroopers still marooned just outside the pocket they had created. It was to prove a surprise.

Both 10 and 156 Para attempted to push south in the morning along the line of the Breede Laan to gain access to the Utrechtseweg, by making a wide circle through the woods to the west. Running battles soon developed. Krafft's men had been quite complacent. 'Units of the Division von Tettau have leapfrogged past us,' he observed, moving west to east. 'Being temporarily free of action' meant that they could relax and reorganise. Suddenly everything changed when a break-out attempt appeared to materialise. 'All previous orders are rescinded and the two Marine Regiments are ordered to close the gap,' Krafft reported. The survivors of the 4th Parachute Brigade clashed with Lippert's NCO School pressing in from the west, then with Krafft's battle group to the north, when the British changed direction to bypass growing opposition. 'The enemy put up a spirited defence, especially the snipers in the trees, so that the Marines cannot advance any further,' Krafft reported. Far from a routine mopping-up action, Krafft's battle group now had a real fight on its hands. The impetus of the British fighting retreat had changed again. 'The enemy now increases pressure on our right flank neighbour,' Lippert's men, Krafft recalled, 'threatening to break through to the east.' Lippert, in advancing west, was applying pressure like the coils of an anaconda, but he was unaware of the true nature of the British fighting retreats. 'Only a small area was won on the 20th September,' he later remembered. 'Cut-off English groups were constantly surfacing behind our line, which had to be attacked and taken out.' By 12.00 the remnants of the 250 men from 10 Para who had crossed the railway line reached the Valkenburglaan; they had been separated from 156 Para and were down to about 100 men. They saw their chance and attacked straight down the road, emerging onto the Utrechtseweg just behind the Borderer positions at 13.30. Only 60 men emerged onto the street.[18s]

The sad disintegration of the brigade continued. Soldiers with 156 Para had become thoroughly disorientated by the constant changes of direction taken in the woods to outflank or outfox the enemy who was beating a clearance operation across. NCO Ron Lintern recalled that by now 'the unwashed men in his section, besides smelling most vilely, were exhausted, thirsty and hungry'. No one had brewed or eaten for two days. Gaps were sought in the German lines by listening out for and gauging the revving engines and metallic clattering signatures of self-propelled guns, ponderously stalking them in the woods. Arthur Keating with A Company became impatient with the sergeant skirmishing alongside him, lying prone and aiming his rifle instead of moving. One glance confirmed that half his face had been blown away by a 20mm shell. 'The woods were simply full of Germans,' Corporal Harry Bankhead recalled. When 10 Para made its sudden break-out, the remnants of 156 with about 150 men, including brigade headquarters, was pinned in a hollow. They were fighting a veritable 'Custer's Last Stand' from a number of adjoining holes in a depression 15 feet deep, 50 feet wide and about 100 feet long. Surrounded by hordes of Germans, there appeared no escape. Bankhead described their nightmare predicament:

'The enemy had suffered heavily too as small groups of men clashed unexpectedly with each other in savage fury. At one point four 156 Battalion men lay still, facing an equal number of large dead Germans. The cries of the seriously wounded were harrowing.'[183]

Fighting around the hollow feature went on for 4 hours, until by 17.00 some 50% of the men who had survived were dead. Among them was Major Mike Page, the Headquarters Company commander and a close friend of Major Geoffrey Powell, shot in the head by a sniper. There had been so few officers left. Powell could not bring himself to look at the body:

'Michael could not be dead. They could not have killed Michael. Everyone else, yes. One after another friends had died, but I never believed that this could happen to Michael, so vast, so indestructible, the humorous gentle Michael.'

Ammunition was all but expended. Brigadier 'Shan' Hackett was not going to surrender. They could just discern the tantalising outline of houses through the trees and perhaps a British line about 400 yards away. The men silently lined the eastern side of the hollow with fixed bayonets, awaiting the order to break out. One man, Corporal Noel Rosenberg, was left at their rear with 12 full magazines for his Bren together with six Mills and six phosphorous grenades. 'It could have been the start of a race,' Geoffrey Powell recalled:

'Then, at his shout, the hundred of us rose to our feet and exploded in a solid mass over the lip of the hollow. In front was the Brigadier himself, leading the way. Behind came the yelling, screaming men, filthy and blood-stained, weapons in their hands, bayonets dull and menacing, a fearful sight to anyone in our path.'

The Germans were taken aback at the speed and ferocity of the charge. Before they knew it the paratroopers were among them. Private Bill Hurst fired his Bren gun from the hip. German soldiers ran or were shot. Hurst paused and raked one group of Germans cowering beneath some bushes. 'Better than being shot in the back once I'd passed,' he explained. Powell dashed past a wounded German, shot through both legs, 'silent, his face imploring us not to kill him'. German fire came from all directions, but only five or seven men fell. 'I saw no one hit,' recalled Powell. 'We were rushing downhill, along a lane, a solid human battering ram.' Possibly 70 made it out, about 50 from the 156th Battalion. It had been fought to virtual annihilation.

'We had done it!' declared an exuberant Powell as suburban houses came into sight.

> 'We had been running for rather more than a quarter of a mile, and now we fell into a shambling walk, catching our breath, an untidy mob of men making for safety, not a formed military body.'

A few camouflaged helmets could be made out just above the line of soil, then the sight of a couple of red berets quelled all doubts. Last night there had been 200 of them, now only 50 men penetrated the forward positions of the Borderers A Company. Some of them stopped without permission to ask the Borderers for cigarettes or water. Powell halted them a moment, and 'still half-hysterical from their exploit, they started to tell their tale'. The Borderers were an intact company, well dug in and in pristine condition compared to the mob of vagabonds that had just streamed through their positions. 'Take this filthy lot away before they contaminate my men,' demanded the Borderers' captain. Powell understood; there was no point trying to explain. 'Our tale could hardly improve the morale of the listeners, even if they believed it!' The last survivors of the 4th Parachute Brigade to enter the perimeter were led into a garden where men dropped to the ground with exhaustion and relief, conscious that they were now safe. Powell saw that 'others, after a swig from a water bottle, lay supine, unconscious in instant sleep.'[184]

General Urquhart's 1st Airborne Division had landed with 8,000 men; now there were only about 4,500 left, mainly division troops. The two parachute brigades were shattered, so just 1,500 of the remnants were infantrymen. The division commander grimly appreciated that there was no chance of reinforcing the force hanging on at the bridge. Only intermittent gunfire was audible from the eastern end of the street. Resistance at the bridge petered out during the day and was extinguished that night, ironically just as the relieving ground force captured the bridge across the Waal at Nijmegen. The recapture of both bridges cancelled each other out. The Germans could not reinforce the bridge they had lost at Nijmegen while the opportunity to relieve Frost at the Arnhem bridge was equally lost. Huge sacrifices had been made by both sides.

Despite the unsatisfactory outcome, the Germans had the remnants of the 1st Airborne Division precisely where they wanted them. From the very beginning they had instinctively appreciated that this force was dangerously overextended. They proposed to deal with it before it could be rescued, a simple case of splitting the division in two along the line of the street and reducing the parts. The airborne soldiers they would face had come to terms with an indignation bordering on insubordination at the level of 'cock-ups' they had endured, and an ingrained stoicism took over. Whatever the mistakes, they resolved not to be held to account for the failures of others. They were quietly determined to hold their ground, if only to make the sacrifice of their mates worthwhile. If the Germans wanted them out, they would have to come and get them. It was the attackers who had to expose themselves.

'What will Wednesday bring us?' wrote Anje van Maanen in her diary. Much had changed for the Dutch inhabitants of the street – the Liberation was not going to happen. Daylight came at 6 o'clock and 'the cellar population awakes,' she recalled. They blinked at each other in an early morning daze before a rude awakening:

'We hear a crazy, shrieking and whistling coming nearer
– growing louder. It is horrible. We huddle together like

frightened chickens. Then there is an enormous smash, in the direction of the Hartenstein.'

They looked at each other with a frightened realisation. Shells! What were they, heavy artillery or tanks?

At the Police Station at No 107 Utrechtseweg, Mr G. Huijgen gave breakfast to Lotte Wagner and Alphonse Geltrüde, the two young interned German girls. Two other brief reports about evacuations from burned-out houses on the Molenweg were written up, then there are blank pages, no entries after 10.30am. Huijgen had finally decided to leave the Police Station and join his family in the cellar of their house on the Ploegseweg near the river. Not once during all the entries covering the Sunday to the Wednesday was any mention made of the air landings. Throughout the battles the citizens of Oosterbeek came or telephoned through to report houses on fire, ownerless bicycles and ammunition discarded in back gardens. A wishful desire to report normality rather than calamity fills the pages of the Municipal Police Daily Reports book.[185]

Von Tettau's ad hoc division had reached as far as No 279 Utrechtseweg near the Koude Herberg crossroads to the west, while from the east Möller's Kampfgruppe was closing on No 128 at the opposite end of the Utrechtseweg with Harzer's 9th SS. Calamity there would now be, because the street was under siege. As war correspondent Alan Wood at the Hotel Hartenstein, relaying dispatches to the BBC, described it:

'Of the last five bullets overhead three were from left to right, and two were from right to left.'[186]

They could be hit by small arms from any direction.

CHAPTER 6

The Siege of the Street

Cellar life: the Dutch

The two figures writhing beneath the dirty blanket in the dark stuffy cellar in the Pietersbergscheweg could have been mistaken for casualties. But the gasping moans suggested pleasure rather than pain. When they were exposed to the light everyone was shocked. The cellar was just south of the Hotel Schoonoord and barely 250 metres from the advancing German line on the street. It was a place for the wounded, not love. Whether interpreted as lust or love, the scene anywhere else would be regarded as normal, but in Oosterbeek under siege the norm had become the bizarre.

Doctor Gert van Maanen was treating the wounded here, and his 17-year-old daughter Anje described the reaction: 'Daddy is furious and he sacks the girl.' Many of the young Dutch girls had developed a crush on the paratroopers, but Anje felt this was beyond the pale. 'I don't know what has happened to them both,' she confided to her diary:

> 'But I wonder whether they have gone mad. Fancy, making love in a hell like this, they must be mentally disturbed.'[187]

Yet they were surrounded by hundreds of people trying to kill each other outside on the streets just beyond the confines of the cellar.

Nine-year-old Wil Rieken lived only 250 metres further east at No 178 Utrechtseweg. Her father Johan ran the bakery and had confided to his family that 'it is going wrong'. There was little point relying on structural support from the corridor any longer – it was time to shelter in the cellar. 'It was a very old house,' Wil recalled, 'with a good cellar, but it was full of bakery things.' It had to be shared with the grocer's family, a mother and two daughters, from next door. Like many of the street's inhabitants, they had now to intimately cohabit with relative strangers, which could prove embarrassing.

'The thing I felt very ashamed of, being a little girl, was to go to the toilet. There was just a little bucket or something and it was placed under the open steps leading down. I do remember I had to go desperately and finally my Dad said he would stay in front of me and that no one could see; but for me, the worse part was that they could hear! I felt ever so upset.'

She felt ashamed, being the first to admit she was a 'Daddy's girl'. Nevertheless, Wil did derive comfort from her straw play-dog Bota, and had been clutching him for five days now. She would do so until the end – indeed, he is around today. The young girl, like everybody else in the cellar, had no idea they were on the front line. The vanguard of the assaulting German soldiers from Möller's SS Engineer Battalion 9 was only a few streets away along the Utrechtseweg.[188]

'My parents had their bedroom on the same level as the living room and there were two big windows facing south,' tactically advantageous when the house was engulfed in fighting. 'There was a lot of fighting because the Germans were at the back,' Wil recalled. Möller's Kampfgruppe was pushing west. 'It moved around, sometimes the Germans and sometimes the Tommies in the house.'

Private Harry Boardman from C Company 156th Parachute Battalion had chased two Germans from No 178, then occupied it with two other stragglers. They had been machine gunned in a house further along the street, vacated it and, after being 'shelled from house to house', ended up in the bakery. 'I went into the cellar to have a look around,' he recalled, 'and I found the baker and his young daughter in hiding. I told them it was OK, we were Paras.' Johan Rieken had heard noises. 'My father had run up the steps and opened the door to see what had happened to the house,' Wil remembered,

'…and that time the Tommies were there, three young boys, who we later found out belonged to the 156th. They had lost their group and were in our house. They met my father and exchanged a few words and they advised him to go back down the cellar.'

Boardman and his men covered the gardens at the back of the house to the south. Germans were trying to infiltrate the length of the Utrechtseweg using the allotments behind as a back-door entry, and they began to pick them off. 'It was beginning to get dark and the Germans started to attack again,' Boardman remembered. There were fierce exchanges of fire through the two back windows. 'We held on as long as possible, and then had to leave,' he recalled. 'We got orders to move into the woods again before it got too dark. We were being machined gunned and mortared; it was not easy getting out.'[189]

Johan Rieken and his wife Jacoba were uneasy that night. They had seen the distinctively sinister glow of a flame-thrower belching down the street. The noise and hammering machine gun fire and the clumping around of boots up above completely unnerved them. Unseen and unseeing, they had no idea what was going on. They heard running and shouting. 'As long as I was with my Dad, I was OK,' Wil recalled.

Years later Wil was to meet a British gentleman at the Schoonoord Hotel, a few doors away, during the 40th Arnhem Veterans' commemoration. She became uncomfortable in the presence of one stranger, who persisted in staring at her when her young daughter arrived. The man approached and, apologising for his interest, claimed, 'I knew your father in 1944.' Wil Rieken was a little dubious about this until the veteran took her outside and along to her old house at No 178, which had since been converted to a ladies' fashion shop. 'This is where you were in the cellar,' he said. It was Harry Boardman, one of the defenders, who had returned and recognised her father's face in her daughter. 'He was very friendly,' Wil recalled fondly, 'and adopted my daughter as his grandchild.'[190]

War on the Utrechtseweg was being fought at three levels. At rooftop to first-floor level the British were defending. Forced into open spaces and moving along the streets and gardens at ground level were the Germans. They were now the most vulnerable. Below ground there were paratroopers in trenches, and beneath them were the Dutch in cellars. Each environment had its own peculiar characteristics. In terms of what could be seen, physical discomfort and vulnerability, the British, Germans and Dutch might have been living on different planets.

Moving into the cellars had been a gradual and reluctant process. Wil Rieken remembered her father saying 'stay in the corridor near the toilet' when the firing started, because of the structural support. By the third day he had gathered the family in the living room and decided they should all go down into the cellar. This was not welcome; cellars were claustrophobically small, unventilated and dark, packed with stored items and jars of food preservatives. There was very little room. War appeared to be arriving almost by stealth.

Schoolboy Cees Meijer lived at No 20 Weverstraat, no more than 100 metres south of the Utrechtseweg. He thought his cellar was large, covering the entire base of the house, but ground variations in Oosterbeek influenced the space available in other cellars. 'Our opposite neighbours, whose cellar had only a wooden ceiling, thought that too dangerous and so came to stay with us,' he remembered. This was happening all along the street as family or cut-off individuals sought admittance to havens offering greater safety. 'In the meantime,' Cees recalled, 'we have also given shelter to a relation, my grandmother's cousin, so in the end our small cellar sheltered 11 people, grown-ups and children.' Oosterbeek had been a wealthy leafy suburb untouched by war; it was full of people who had not fled with the Liberation. Why leave at the moment the dream had been fulfilled? There had been few indicators that the Germans might return.

Twenty-two-year-old Resistance helper Harry van Gorkum recalled that 'nobody wanted to leave', a typically human response – 'people always tried to stay'. Once the fighting started, people found themselves cut off from home. 'Our neighbours had even 12 people in their cellar,' Cees recalled.

> 'They had given shelter to some relatives who had gone down to the Benedendorp [at the bottom of their road] to welcome

the English, and who now found that they could no longer go
all the way to their own home.'

There was no room for mattresses for everyone, so people slept in rotation. Nobody slept much at night, with the fighting creeping inexorably nearer and nearer. 'Cooking was done on an oil stove,' Cees remembered. 'It was too dangerous to use the stove in the kitchen because of the risk of fire if a shell should explode nearby.' Light was provided by an oil lamp, adding to the sultry stuffiness, because the power had failed. All they were able to do was sit, talk and gaze at rows of bottled preservatives lining the walls.[191]

As life became increasingly dangerous, more and more people abandoned the uncertain protection provided by rooftops for the dismal security of cellars. Not everyone had one. Netje Heijbroek, living at 'Valkenburg' near the Koude Herberg crossroads to the west on the Utrechtseweg, remembered that 'it was so dangerous on Wednesday that we had to stay seated in the little corridor', which granted some structural support. 'We were not allowed outside any more' and 'the Englishmen were very concerned for us.' Then the house was hit by three shells. 'A grey cloud of dust rolled through the house,' she recalled, 'and strongly advised by the Englishmen we tumbled into the cellar.' In the panic of the moment 'nobody remembered their suitcase and blanket', painstakingly prepared before for just such an emergency.

The Heijbroek family could hear 'a lot of shooting going on, including from snipers in trees.' Lippert's SS NCO School Arnheim was attempting to push eastwards down the Utrechtseweg.

'Every time a shell struck, the cellar door was opened. "Is all OK
in the cellar?" "Yes." "Stay in the cellar, it is still dangerous".'

There were six of them, the immediate family and Mr and Mrs Pekelharing. Netje was 17 years old and her young sister 15. Fortunately the cellar was spacious. There were some barred grilles to look out, but for the most part all they could do was sit anxiously on the few chairs and, like everyone else, look at the rows of vegetable jars filled with preservatives on the shelves opposite. They spent an uncomfortable first night, sharing their spartan surroundings with the three Englishmen, who slept with them.

'It was a difficult, emotional night and nobody slept much. There was a lot of gunfire and a tremendous clamour. We lay or sat on the cold boiler room floor.'

At about 10 o'clock the next morning on 21 September the coal-chute lid opened and 16 more refugees from Oosterbeek slid their way down to the bottom. Four families now occupied the cellar, seven adults and nine children 'including some toddlers', which brought the number of civilians crowding into the cellar to 22 with the three British soldiers. The new arrivals had all fled the Mariaweg on the east side of Oosterbeek and told Netje all about the bitter fighting that was raging through neighbourhoods familiar to them all.

'Shots were being fired through baker Riksen's house [at No 40] and they had become so frightened that they had walked in the direction of Heelsum. Utrechtseweg was covered with tree branches [brought down by the intense firing] and was difficult to negotiate.'

There was no good news. 'At Mr Poort's house [No 236] a large white parachute was being used to cover many dead lying in the road.' The British, fearful for their safety and with the situation becoming progressively worse, had decided that they should join them in the cellar. 'Fierce fighting continued above our heads,' Netje recalled. It seemed only a matter of time before it would be Germans opening the cellar door.[192]

Cellars had become all-important in the changed environment. Resistance helper Harry van Gorkum remembered that cellars might have been small, but they were 'about the safest place to get away from the shooting and bombing'. Gert Maassen, living north of the Hotel Hartenstein, came to the same conclusion; he needed protection for his wife and seven-week-old baby. 'Our cellars would not give much protection,' he realised, 'as they were not vaulted,' and digging pits outside amid the increasing shelling was useless. 'Fortunately we were offered shelter by Mr Janssen, an upholsterer, who lived on Paul Krugerstraat.' This was 200 metres north of the Utrechtseweg, where the northern border of the British perimeter was forming. Maassen's back garden was fortunately adjacent to Janssen's property so, taking baby clothes, he and his wife crept through the back garden carrying the baby. To his surprise he found that 'there were now 14 people in Mr Janssen's cellar, but we managed to make everybody find a place to sit down.'[193]

Jan Voskuil, a 38-year-old chemical engineer, moved his entire family, parents-in-law, wife Bertha and nine-year-old son Henri into the cellar of Dr Onderwater's house at the corner of Annastraat and the Utrechtseweg next to No 192. He had no idea it had been identified as a future German objective. The sandbag-reinforced cellar seemed safer.

Traditional tolerances became strained amid the new bleak surroundings. Seventeen-year-old Anje van Maanen's cellar was so stuffy that they took the door off 'so we do have more fresh air for us all', and the window was blacked out. Sharing with family could be uncomfortable enough, but exposure to strangers, old men and young girls, jammed together with teenagers and children of both sexes, could be embarrassing. Time and growing tension, however, steadily peeled away any inhibitions, leaving survival as the primary concern. People became indifferent to unsanitary or objectionable habits. 'With so many people in the cellar, sleeping eating and drinking soon became a problem,' recalled Maassen on Paul Krugerstraat. 'If we wanted to visit the toilet upstairs, we had to warn the English; we soon learned to call "doubbel-joesie!"' 'Beside my pillow are Daddy's feet – I can bite his toes,' Anje wrote in her diary. Stirring and fidgeting around in the confined space made it difficult to sleep properly. Her aunt dozed nearby on a chair, while others snored away lying on wine bottle sacks, 'and the rest of the party lies everywhere, like skittles thrown away.' Nobody had enough room. They existed inside a fragile bubble, suspicious and often alarming noises outside contrasting with 'the more peaceful noises inside our cellar, the snoring and breathing,' Anje recalled. The fighting crept ever closer:

'We have not a clue that this street, the Tafelberg and Hartenstein [hotels], are really the only spots that are British. We don't realise the Schoonoord [hotel] is German again.'[194]

The front was barely 100 metres away from where she lay.

Cees Meijer, at No 20 Weverstraat, remembered that water came from the pails and zinc tubs that had been hastily filled when it was rumoured the water supply might be stopped. Word was passed from house to house. 'As a result of this, the water supply got overburdened,' he remembered. 'So we ended up with brown and rusty water.' Even this was being drunk now. The children, like Cees, had been delighted to hear they would not have to go back to school after the summer holidays, because the retreating Germans had requisitioned all the school buildings for accommodation. Youth and immaturity sanitised them from the tensions that were endured by their parents. Cees remembered:

'The grown-ups had only one thought in their heads: how to survive all this and how to keep the families safe. We, as children, thought these unusual circumstances rather thrilling; we did not realise the deadly danger we were in, at least not all the time.'

Birthdays and all the other vestiges of normality remained important.

'I remember one of the boys in the cellar being disappointed when nobody congratulated him on his birthday on September 20th. "I don't suppose I will get any presents now!" he said.'[195]

Cellars became increasingly packed as German pressure remorselessly constricted the British airborne perimeter defence. To the north of the Utrechtseweg, Maassen, sheltering with the Janssens, recalled two old people laboriously descending the steps into the crowded cellar. They were Mr Terlaag and his wife, whose house near the Oosterbeek-Hoog railway station, 500 metres up Stationsweg from the street, had been burned down.

'We could not understand how they had managed that very dangerous trek' but 'we found room for them in the cramped space that was all we had.' Shelter was not a guaranteed option. Just 200 metres on the other side of the street, at No 20 Weverstraat, young Cees told a different story:

> 'From time to time we would hear civilians passing through the street. They were trying to find shelter in a cellar and they called out to us if we could take them in. However, our cellar was so crowded that we could not give shelter to any more people. Besides, we dare not leave our cellar during the heavy fighting.'[196]

The Dutch could only read the battle by sounds and, being civilian, they were unable to interpret what they heard. Anje van Maanen wrote in her diary that 'there have been rumours of street fighting, of fights in the Weverstraat, where one side of the street is British, the other side German.' But this was already history as she wrote it. The fighting had passed over the heads of those sheltering beneath No 20. 'The night from Wednesday to Thursday September 21st was very tumultuous,' recalled Cees Meijer. 'We heard some bumping noises over our heads.'

A German soldier came down in the early morning and asked if only civilians were in the cellar. 'We asked him if he thought our cellar was a safe place and he answered that it would do as long as it would not be bombed.' The next trip upstairs revealed that the Germans had mounted a machine gun in their shop window; their curtains were on the floor, having clearly been used as blankets by the Germans. When the small house behind theirs suddenly blew up after a sudden 'shrieking noise' the rest of the shop window was blown in, showering the kitchen with glass. 'Not to worry,' the SS troopers reassured them, it was simply their own artillery registering the range.

Weverstraat and the Meijer family were now behind the front line, which had only moved 100 metres further west. The German high tide was washing around the edge of No 178 on the Utrechtseweg. In the cellar beneath, the Rieken family heard boots clumping over the floor boards and loud voices. 'As long as I was with my Dad I was OK,' Wil, the youngest daughter, recalled. 'There was lots of running and shouting and the house changed to the Germans.' Two SS troopers suddenly stumbled onto the top of the cellar steps and shouted, 'Raus! Come out!'

'One took a hand grenade and went halfway down the steps. I think he did not want to go into our cellar, so he came back and said, "It's OK". So the hand grenade wasn't lobbed and we were told to go back down again in the cellar. I am sure if we had hidden someone, we would have been shot.'

'Nobody was killed in the house,' Wil remembered, 'but many were outside – you had to step over them.' They were desperately short of food. 'The grocery shop next door had a back lane,' Wil recalled, 'so my father went into that shop and tried to find some food for us, some ham and things.' The German flood was flowing past all around.[197]

Bleeding: the Germans

Having securely boxed in the British, command of the battle to reduce the Oosterbeek perimeter passed to Obersturmbannführer Harzer's 9th SS on 21 September. As von Tettau's Division was taken under operational control, it was ordered to redirect its less experienced units to the rear, and primacy handed over to the SS-Standartenführer Lippert's SS NCO School consolidated control of all the multi-various groups, including the newly arrived Hermann Göring Battalion. Lippert's SS battalion commanders took over and regrouped the sailors and the ad hoc Fliegerhorst Luftwaffe ground crews acting as infantry, and moved them to quieter parts of the front.

Bittrich, the SS Corps commander, called for concentric attacks to begin at 08.00 on 21 September. It was clear that the 'Schwerpunkt', or main point of effort, would be spearheaded by Harzer's veteran units advancing east to west. Pressure was still applied in the north and west, but Harzer anticipated any breakthroughs would come from the 'narrow but deep penetrations' he ordered in his area as the remainder of the British perimeter was compressed to destruction.[198]

The shape of the Oosterbeek street network served the British defence effort well. Side streets ran broadly north to south across the line of the German east-west advance, providing ready-made obstacle belts from house rows converted into strongpoints. Thick woods hindered Lippert's infantry advancing from the west, leaving only two primary thoroughfares for tanks: the Utrechtseweg in the centre and the Oosterbeekseweg near the river. Both were blocked by the Borderers. Harzer's eastern approach was trident-shaped, channelled by three streets running broadly east to west. Möller's Engineer Kampfgruppe attacked along the Utrechtseweg, the main approach, while two diagonal streets offered subsidiary approaches on his left. The Kampfgruppe Harder used the Klingelbeekseweg, which merged with the Benedendorpsweg alongside the river. The Kampfgruppe von Allwörden tried to penetrate the confused network of streets and parkland in between. Key to dismembering the perimeter was the need to crack resistance around the Oosterbeek crossroads.

SS-Hauptsturmführer (Captain) Hans Möller pursed his lips with frustration as he scanned through binoculars the long line of the Utrechtseweg stretched out before him to the west. Nothing could move along it. It was a virtual free-fire zone. He had just lost his 3rd Kompanie commander, Gerhard Engel, virtually cut in half by a British anti-tank round that had suddenly spat down the street. The occasional red glow of a tank projectile fired in return abruptly streaked along its length, sweeping masonry and brickwork from the house facades it brushed before rocketing skyward on impact. Dimly visible ahead was a crossroads, where the big hotels were located, maybe 600 metres away. They seemed to be marked with Red Cross flags; he could not be sure, but a hindrance if true. The crossroads was the objective, dominated by the two-storey Hotel Schoonoord to the left and the Hotel Vreewijk on the right. Burned-out vehicles could be seen littering the approaches.

Although the Germans did not appreciate the true significance of the crossroads up ahead, they did realise that if they captured this approach road it would isolate the paratroopers to the north of it. Only 250 metres beyond the crossroads was the Airborne Division headquarters located at the Hotel Hartenstein, the nerve centre of resistance and another unknown.

Möller formulated the plan as he observed. His left avenue of approach had fairly densely packed houses, whereas the right was more open, the wooded Dennenkamp Park with a few houses dispersed inside. Any advance down the road, marked here and there by a sprawled body partially covered with the leafy branches that had been scythed down by 20mm cannon fire, was out of the question. The only conceivable avenue of approach might be through the back gardens of the houses to the left of the street, fired into by self-propelled guns and heavy weapons established in the parkland to the right. He rapped out brief orders to his assembled company commanders observing alongside.

Möller was uneasy – the outcome of this battle hung by a thread. Two enormous Allied air armadas had twice inverted the odds that had been successively fought off as the pendulum had swung both ways. Möller and his men had been shaken by the ferocity of the initial attacks, barely contained during the first two nights. These men appeared to have respect only for flame-throwers and tanks. Only the fortuitous arrival of Sturmgeschütz (Assault Gun) Brigade 280 had broken the attacks, and Möller and his men were on the crest of the returning wave, washing back up the Utrechtseweg for the third time. They had to fight every inch of the way.

There was still a tenuous link with the Hohenstaufen Division of sorts, and Möller knew more than he was letting on to his men. SS Hauptsturmführer (Captain) Wilfred Schwarz, the division operations officer, recalled that 'the situation only started to stabilise once the Oosterbeek ring was closed and the Arnhem bridge was retaken.' But the men suspected otherwise. The tall smoke stacks of the Nijmegen power station, a mere 10-kilometre drive to the south, could be clearly seen at night across the flat polderland. They were illuminated by the glow from the fires in the town behind and by intermittent flashes of crackling artillery. As Schwarz saw it, 'the soldiers saw unceasing reinforcements from the air' leaving a nagging suspicion. 'Would our forces in the south also hold out?'[199] In the very short term they had to continue the fight and snuff out this resistance enclave as soon as possible.

Möller methodically scanned the houses left and right with his binoculars, storey by storey, and those up ahead. 'Möller was a careful man,' remembered 19-year-old SS Rottenführer Wolfgang Dombrowski. 'He was a very experienced soldier and very selective where he sited his HQ.' Dombrowski, not over-fond of officers, regarded his commander with grudging respect. They had been through a lot together – Tarnopol in Russia, Hill 112 in Normandy and Saint-Lô, fighting constant rearguard actions. It was Möller who found the 2-kilometre-wide hole that enabled them to break out of the Falaise gap. 'He kept his battalion together throughout these halcyon days,' Dombrowski observed. Panzer Pioneer (armoured assault engineer) Battalion 9 was severely mauled; only five of its 140 vehicles got out. They were down to about 100 men and five armoured half-tracks when they got to Holland, and had to hand three of these to another unit. 'Bittrich and Harzer might view the battle from a tower or high point with binoculars, but Möller would observe from the cellar,' commented Dombrowski approvingly.[200]

Möller was searching for a shape, shine, flash or moving silhouette, anything that might give away the British positions. There was nothing specific. The order was clear enough: mop up the street. But where to start? Every one of his three company commanders was dead or severely wounded. The battalion was literally bleeding to death. Only seven of the original men who had formed up for the basic engineering course at Dresden in 1943 were left. Apart from a cadre of veterans, the battalion had completely changed character; they were nothing like the men he had led as an SS Scharführer (Sergeant) with the Der Führer Regiment, coming down this very road, the Utrechtseweg, clearing it of Dutch snipers in May 1940. Hendrika van der Vlist, the daughter of the owner of the Hotel Schoonoord – in Möller's sights – had already identified 'how much the German army has degenerated in these years'. They were no longer regarded as the 'born soldiers' that had arrived with the 1940 Blitzkrieg. Living in Oosterbeek since the German invasion, she had seen:

> 'They had become lax. They would no longer sit down on a hard chair. They wanted the most comfortable easy chairs in the house. Their wash-hand-stands were full of all kinds of toilet powders and creams.'

Dutch Resistance helper Harry van Gorkum was equally derisory:

'You think they were masters of their trade, but they weren't – they shot at everything that moved. You stayed away from Germans at all costs.'[201]

With nothing positive to identify the British positions, Möller had little choice but to attack based on where, if he was British, he would site the defence. This meant anti-tank weapons would have to be sited to fire down the Utrechtseweg. They would break into the houses left of the street and climb over the garden fences while clearing the parkland on the right. He was convinced that the line of houses on the Stationsweg, right of the crossroads and facing the park, would be occupied by the British.

Veterans never ask irrelevant questions, and Möller's freshly appointed company commanders had few – they knew what to do. The problem was getting the scheme across to the mix of 'alte hasen' ('old hares') and youngsters under command. Möller's men were operating at street level, where movement courted retribution from the ever-observant and unforgiving British. Venturing too close to a window sill instead of observing from the shadows in a room's depth was immediately punished. 'Unterscharführer (Corporal) Tornow, a brave and circumspect leader of men,' Möller recalled, was found with a hole in his head, 'paying dearly for just one moment of carelessness'. A salutary lesson to all – there could be no mistakes.

Street fighting required methodical control and coordination. Möller directed and laid on the heavy weapons, while company commanders one level down had to physically execute the attack. The battalion commander opted for an echeloned advance along the Utrechtseweg. A Sturmgeschütz III assault gun, with its 75mm weapon, and two tanks were to fire along the street with the 3rd Kompanie half-tracks at a distance, crushing fences and front gardens on the left and hugging the parkland on the right. The 2nd Kompanie, under SS Hauptscharführer (Staff Sergeant) Sepp Schmatz, began to wind its way through the gardens behind the houses on the left while Steinart, with the 1st Kompanie, struggled further behind linking in with the entire left wing of the 9th SS Division advance, breaking against the eastern edge of the British perimeter.

Möller's men had a few flame-throwers and panzerfaust bazookas to blast entry holes and flame the opposition. It took a brave man to wear the cumbersome flame-thrower cylinder pack. The effective range was only a few score metres, so they had to get close. Few tended to be taken prisoner because of the fear and dislike the weapon engendered; even less survived a strike on the cylinder, which would transform them into an instant screaming fireball. The difficulty was to direct fire support to cover the selected forced entry point to a fortified house. This had to be breached, then forcibly entered. Every man had to know what to do, which window or door to enter. The SS assault pioneer veterans who knew their job were outnumbered by those that did not.

Twenty-four hours earlier, Möller's Engineer battalion had been reinforced by replacements from the Reichsarbeitsdienst (Labour Service), Navy and Luftwaffe ground personnel. Möller recalled that 'the replacements had no combat experience whatsoever and were absolutely inexperienced in street fighting.' Stress had already afflicted the veterans, who had barely recovered from the mauling received in Normandy weeks before. 'Our nerves had been shot to pieces after six days of this,' confided Wolfgang Dombrowski with the 2nd Kompanie. 'As soon as we heard an aircraft everyone would immediately dive into a ditch.' Comradeship bonded the survivors, even to the extent that long-term hospital treatment would be foregone rather than risk being later redrafted, like the newly arrived replacements, in a strange 'ersatz' (spare) unit. Survival chances were better with those you knew. Möller admitted that the new arrivals 'were rather sceptical and reluctant at the beginning, which was far from surprising.' In time they blended in, if they lived.

The Reichsarbeitsdienst formed part of the progression from civilian school-leaver to Wehrmacht conscript. These were 16-year-olds who had exchanged a spade for rifle and grenade. They were not 'Mummy's boys', as they often said in the Hitler Youth, because that had also included an element of military conditioning. Labour Service was conducted under military conditions in a barracks away from home. A few may have practised target-shooting with sports rifles in the Hitler Youth. Having been issued with an outsize SS camouflage smock, they were expected to fight elite parachute soldiers with virtually no preparation.

The official Hohenstaufen Division report on these men from Schiffstamm (Naval) Abteilung (Battalion) 14 and another naval unit from Zwolle was that the standard of weapon training and morale was 'satisfactory', but that the officers and NCOs were untrained and should not be employed in the attack. These were naval gunners and technical air force personnel whose base locations had been overrun in Normandy. They had fled during the retreat and been picked up at specially constituted reception points. 'The infantry training is for the main part bad,' assessed the report, and 'as the officers and men hardly know each other, they cannot be regarded as a unit.' These were the men struggling across the garden fences alongside Möller's SS troopers at the back of the Utrechtseweg or advancing in the open parkland. The Germans were moving at street level – and to move was to invite fire.

Möller's advance, supported by squeaking and trundling assault guns, was bearing down on a group of houses around No 192 Utrechtseweg, where it intersects with the side street at Annastraat. To get there, Sepp Schmatz's 2nd Kompanie had to cross the Weverstraat, passing Cees Meijer's cellar beneath No 20. For the first time Cees began to appreciate the perilous nature of their situation. His attention was caught by 'a deafening fire from anti-aircraft guns', until:

> 'Later we heard the crunching sound of caterpillar tracks. They belonged to armoured vehicles, which stopped every 20 metres in order to fire a shell. They did this right in front of our cellar, at a distance of about 2 metres. The oil-lamp flickered and went out because of the air pressure. Everything shook. That was the first time I was really afraid that something awful was going to happen.'[202]

Behind the barricades: the British

On the morning of 21 September the British reorganised the perimeter defence so that the east side was under the commander of the 4th Parachute

Brigade, and the north and west under the Air Landing Brigade. The remnants of both parachute brigades held the south-east with 300 men, with the survivors of the 10th and 156th Battalion groups holding the east end of the Utrechtseweg, with brigade headquarters elements in depth, totalling some 165 men. C Company the Border Regiment was holding the west end of the street, with the remainder of the surviving battalion left and right of it; the north side was manned by 7 KOSB, down to 250 men, glider pilots, engineers and the 21st Independent Parachute Company.

The perimeter measured about 1 kilometre wide by 2 kilometres deep, down to the lower village and river. It encompassed a sector of dispersed family housing from just north of the Utrechtseweg to the Koude Herberg crossroads in the west and the Oosterbeek crossroads to the east. By chance the area included most of the solidly built villas and houses built during the 19th century by Dutch entrepreneurs who had benefited from the lucrative Dutch East Indies trade. They were solid substantial masonry constructions with cavity walls, wood or reinforced concrete floors and well-constructed roofs. The one- or two-family houses were structurally sound and well dispersed, with large gardens and green areas in between. There were also some solidly built factory and infrastructure buildings included inside the perimeter, like the gasworks by the river.

After the war, during the Cold War, a number of NATO military surveys were conducted in Europe to identify the defensive value of areas covered by urban sprawl in north-west Germany, Holland and Belgium. Dispersed family housing, like that at Oosterbeek, which has not changed much since, was considered favourable for the defender and not particularly suitable for tanks in the event of a Soviet-led Warsaw Pact invasion.[203] The ceilings and walls of the majority of houses offered good protection and resistance to tank and artillery fire. Moreover, they offered numerous fire positions with good mobility in between provided by alleys, back yards and substantial gardens. These avenues and byways conferred as much, if not greater, advantage to defenders as to attackers, providing mobility for counter-attack and escape options. The onus was on the attacking Germans, who had to expose themselves to fire on approaching. By chance, the British had been obliged to occupy positions that were as good as any they might have selected, able to offer maximum resistance value. Dispersed family housing on both sides of the street gave an average of 30 yards line-of-sight for shooting, with a 50% probability of being able to engage the Germans from whatever direction they approached. Numerous family rooftop and loft conversions had created ready-made sniper lairs. Open shop windows along the south side of the Utrechtseweg enabled good machine gun positions to be established, able to dominate the open Dennenkamp parkland opposite, a primary German approach. Wide shop-window openings enabled good fields of fire for guns lurking in the deep shadow of shop interiors. Oosterbeek's houses were solidly built with wooden latticework strengthening both walls and rooftop linings, providing excellent potential for strongpoints with an innate capability to endure punishing mortar and artillery fire.

These tidy pleasant houses had still to be converted into fortified points. Streets and alleyways in between needed to be reconfigured by road blocks, and strewn with mines and booby traps to create killing areas, ensnaring tanks and unwary infantry. After a courteous knock at the door, soldiers would rapidly enter and begin systematically to trash house interiors to erect defensive positions, invariably under the incredulous eyes of depressed owners. More damage was caused to cosy domestic interiors within hours, preparing them for defence, than during the days of subsequent enemy action. The cold realities of modern war began to touch the inhabitants of the street, often for the first time. Breaking homes and hearts produced a despair worsened by an appreciation that broken bodies would likely follow. Within 72 hours the Dutch transitioned from the inconvenience of broken windows and discomfort to the horrifying realisation that their families were now in mortal danger, and it all started with a polite knock at the door.

Anje van Maanen's door bell rang early on 21 September. 'Daddy comes down to tell us, our house will be a fortress, there will be about 50 Tommies in the house.' Despite the crackling rumble of conflict all around, this seemed unbelievable, that someone would wish to barricade themselves among their belongings, where they slept, ate and existed as a family group. 'We ask if it is possible for the Tommies to go somewhere else. Must this house be used as a fortress?' A banal question in a bleak scenario. 'Is it really necessary?' Anje asked. 'The answer is Yes, they need this house badly.' This is accepted with some resignation. 'Well, all right, we think, so be it.' At which point the doorbell rang again and the already familiar British soldier is emphatic. He tells them they had better leave, because 'he is sure there will be a fight'. The house had been selected as the headquarters location for the 21st Independent Parachute Company.

> 'If the Germans find out, and we are still in the cellar, they
> will be furious and we will all maybe be killed.'

The soldiers started to come in. 'It will not be for long,' the Tommy said, seeking to reassure them. 'Tomorrow you can come back into the house – Monty will be here any moment now.' Anje was not so sure:

> 'Monty can go to hell. He will never come!'

The interior of the house was systematically wrecked as it was prepared for defence. Private Candine-Bate recalled Anje's mother saying, 'Make yourself at home,' after wishing them 'Good morning'.

> 'It was heart-rendering to see the tragic look of pain and
> bewilderment that this Dutch lady was unable to keep from
> her eyes as she watched her beautiful home being pulled to
> pieces.'[204]

Many of the British soldiers entering the houses had fought four to five days outside, in the open. They had a roof over their heads for the first time and also daily contact with Dutch civilians. This oddly brought back memories of their own homes, being abruptly confronted with domestic norms, albeit transacted between the ground floor and cellar. Sergeant Ron Kent, with the pathfinder company on the Utrechtseweg, recalled how 'it was a relief and a novelty to be inside a house again and to see and talk to civilians.'[205]

Major Geoffrey Powell, with the 156th Parachute Battalion, was defending a group of houses along the Stationsweg, 100 metres up from the street and facing Möller's impending approach. For the first time in this battle he felt a modicum of safety. 'There was a comfortable sense of security in this house,' he recalled. Many of the houses they were occupying were rather grand, well built, turn-of-the-century constructions. His battalion had been caught and decimated in the open, fighting running battles across fields and woods north of the airborne pocket. A bayonet charge had been necessary to gain entry into the perimeter. 'Now it was our turn to sit tight and hit the enemy floundering about in the open,' he recalled with some satisfaction. But to do this, the houses had first to be barricaded.

'It took only a moment to smash the glass out of the frame with the stock of my rifle,' Powell remembered; otherwise a shell or bullet fragment coming through 'would slash my face into rags of flesh'. Soldiers rapidly transformed their new habitats into defensive strongpoints, rubbishing rooms to improve their survival prospects. Only a few sensitive souls reflected on what this would signify to the occupants, if they had inflicted the same damage on their own homes. The Dutch seemed uncannily like the British in both appearance and attitude – there was a natural rapport. The homes might even have been mistaken for well-to-do properties in England. Powell watched the process of transformation:

> 'Fifteen minutes later, the trim Dutch house had been wrecked. Every pane of glass had been smashed, and every picture and mirror knocked from the walls; there was no time to be careful. In the centre of each room barricades had been built, well back from the windows out of sight of the Boche, but sited so every scrap of ground outside was covered. Sideboards and chests-of-drawers stuffed with books or bedding made the barricades, the contents of the furniture flung in heaps into the corners of the rooms. Mattresses were rolled down to the basement, ready for use, if needed, by the wounded men. More books, crammed into drawers, were blocking those windows not required for shooting through.'

When it was finished Powell commented that 'manic vandals might have swept through it, some woman's life work ruined in the time it took to drink a cup of coffee.' They had been lucky; the house owner, likely a doctor, had a fine library, in effect the equivalent of a supply of sandbags. Books were important to Powell, who recalled that 'the wrecking of the library had been particularly unpleasant'.

Suddenly, briefly standing before them was a little old Dutch man. His behaviour and the look of abject despair written across his face marked him out as the owner. There he stood, Powell recalled, 'the books spilling out of the windows into the garden mud, the shattered roof, and the filthy soldiers gazing at him from the murk of smashed furniture.' With a strangled cry of misery he clumsily stumbled off down the path. 'He was visibly upset,' Powell observed.[206]

The barricading and preparation in and around the strategic hotel crossroads location was literally conducted behind closed doors. Möller's approaching soldiers saw nothing. They were more intent on picking out their approach route. Sergeant Ron Kent remembered that often,

> 'To gain a better field of fire, ground-floor windows were ignored, shutters closed and front doors locked and bolted, a sentry placed on the back door; then the first floor frontage was prepared as a Bren gun position, with all glass shattered and removed and furniture and bedding wedged into window frames as some sort of cover behind which to operate.'

Snipers were placed in attics to cover both front and rear. There was no front garden – it was the street outside the front door. Their immediate neighbours were normally the enemy, lurking in and around the houses opposite. 'We barricaded the front windows so that Jerry could not throw hand grenades into them,' remembered Kent. Sergeant Louis Hagen with the Glider Pilot Regiment described how the 'main idea was, that if any house could not hold out, the occupants could fall back upon the next house and reinforce it.' Branches were put up to screen movement and 'we did everything possible to have safe, invisible communications along the whole street.'[207]

An odd form of domesticity was observed in one of these fortified houses. The glider pilots along the Stationsweg had kept one furnished room called the 'officers' room'. 'Nobody could escape the spell of this room,' recalled Sergeant Louis Hagen. 'The shutters were closed, and the candlelight, bed, couch and easy chairs gave it a homely atmosphere.' Bizarrely it provided the setting for a lot of war-like planning and orders. 'It needed great willpower to leave this room and carry on with any job,' Hagen maintained, because 'it made you feel that somewhere there was still peace and homeliness.' The soldiers had a different view of such sentimental domesticity. Private 'Taff' Bert Wilmott was one of the few surviving soldiers from the 10th Parachute Battalion defending the key group of houses around No 192 Utrechtseweg, above the Voskuil family in one of the cellars below. Like Möller's battalion advancing towards them, the 10th Battalion was bleeding to death. Only 70 or so soldiers were left from the 582 men who had jumped in five days before. They had their own distractions. Wilmott recalled Sergeant George Hughes visiting their positions with glasses of wine, 'chanty ones', precariously balanced on a silver salver, ostentatiously offering them a sip.

'We had a Bren mounted well back in the room on the snooker table,' Bert recalled, describing an otherwise cosy household scene. They shot at any German soldiers running past. Sepp Schmatz's 2nd Kompanie had closed up and was beginning to hug the position. 'The Jerries at the back kept having a go at us,' Wilmott remembered:

> 'The proprietor and his family were in the cellar below. He came up occasionally and boiled a saucepan of eggs to take down to his family.'[208]

The pressures on the British defenders were building up. Constant wake-up calls and the physical exertion needed to crawl in and out of trenches and climb countless stairwells was wearing out the young officers and NCOs, who had little or no sleep. They were carrying the main strain. Company commanders were one remove from this, directing rather than physically executing. Unremitting physical activity and the lack of sleep engendered a general sense of ill-being. Such cumulative strain might be eased for young private soldiers, who could momentarily sleep and regenerate without the nagging worry of constant security checks. Simple actions required inordinate effort. It became difficult to formulate thoughts and pass on the woolly results through speech slurred with fatigue. Benzedrine tablets kept them awake, but like any drug a reaction set in after a period of time, doubling the torpor with a form of hangover.

For days men had only catnapped. There might be as many as six 'stand-to' alerts in one night. The paratroopers were fighting on, even though they were down to 25% or 50% of their normal strengths. Normal troops would have surrendered long ago. Obstinacy and the bond each man had with his 'mate' or 'mucker' kept them going. Men operated in pairs, eating, on sentry, on patrol and often in death, as they were reluctant to leave each other. One man stood watch in the trench while his mate tried to sleep. Uncomplicated loyalty transcended the fear of death and mutilation that still remained pervasive. Soldiers appreciated the operation was a 'cock-up', but the blame would not be laid at their door. They would never give up.

Despite exhaustion, the paratroopers were proving ever more resourceful and skilful adversaries in the complex business of street defence. This required steady nerves, instant aggression, positions in depth and good coordination between the respective house strongpoints to ensure all-round defence. 'One got skilled in avoiding being hit,' remembered Sergeant Louis Hagen, 'and as time went on our casualties became fewer,' while for the Germans they became progressively larger. Street fighting had only been haphazardly covered by the airborne units. Major Geoffrey Powell, with the 156th Parachute Battalion, recalled that 'back in England we had fired our weapons, thrown grenades, and exploded charges among the pathetic, shattered working-class houses of Battersea.' They were warned not to cause too much damage because other units were following. 'I was grateful for that week in South London. At least we knew the theory,' Powell reflected. This was in contrast to Sergeant Louis Hagen's irritation at their lack of preparation for their current predicament. 'Petty-minded officers and Sergeant Majors' had focussed on pointless 'bull' rather than the business in hand. 'Why couldn't they have taught us about house-to-house fighting and the PIAT gun?' he asked. 'But then, drill, and lining up of beds and blankets, occupies the greatest number of men with the least effort.' All Hagen had to fall back on was Wintringhams's *Picture Post* magazine descriptions of street fighting in civil war Spain, which 'proved invaluable later on'.[209]

The British were feeling the strain. Sergeant Ron Kent remembered moving the few hundred metres from safer positions around the Ommershof down to the Utrechtseweg. 'One man was reluctant to leave the comparative safety of his foxhole and had to be encouraged out of it with his section sergeant's Colt automatic in his ear.' There were few signs of lack of resolve in the Parachute pathfinder company, but 'when they did show, it came with a sense of shock to those who observed them'. Little was said; everyone struggled with their individual demons. In the darkest parts of the Hotel Hartenstein cellars along the Utrechtseweg and beneath the gardener's cottage in the grounds, Louis Hagen saw men who had given up the fight:

'They looked like people who had been seasick for days. Nothing in the world would coax them up. Down there they vegetated; ate, slept and relieved themselves in a world where only their fear was reality.'

One of them was his close friend, a volunteer glider pilot who 'knew what the war was about'. He was conscientious, hard-working, and unsparing with himself, and Hagen could not grasp the psychological changes that had occurred. 'He was obviously going through hell', but there was no way he was going to be coaxed out of the cellar. 'He simply could not make himself move and, short of using force, there was nothing I could do.' Swearing had also petered out. Many of the so-called 'tough guys' promoting an aura of apparent self-confident courage through streams of expletives had lost it.

'To hear, "I wonder when the Second Army will come and get us out of this mess", simply stated, without a four-letter

word used at least four times, gave me the same surprise as if
they had suddenly expressed themselves in Ancient Greek.'

The arrival of the relieving XXX Corps was at the back of everyone's
mind.

Expletives were reserved for the Germans, as Hans Möller, closing in
with his SS troopers, explained:

'All appeals for them to surrender either received no response
at all or were answered with biting remarks such as "focken
Germans" or with taunts.'[210]

Storming the crossroads

The Utrechtseweg was the main arterial road going through Oosterbeek
to Arnhem. The intersection by the two British medical dressing stations
at the Schoonoord and Vreewijk hotels was vital ground, dominating the
north-east corner of the British pocket. It was Möller's primary objective.
The roads, increasingly cluttered by wreckage, were crucial, the only
way that self-propelled guns and heavy-calibre weapons mounted on
armoured half-tracks could get between houses. The paratroopers were
boxed in by the shape of the subsidiary street network emanating from
the Utrechtseweg, but the heavily constructed 19th-century mansions and
houses were proving their saviour, because they boxed out the panzers.
This meant a cat-and-mouse game between British anti-tank guns and
self-propelled guns on the few roads when the Germans needed to move
their armoured vehicles to cover infantry attacks.

The British developed an ear for the start of any German attack by the
sound of growling tank engines, jockeying for fire positions amid the
incessant shouting from accompanying infantry. Many of the attacking
soldiers did not know what to do and had to be bullied into position. Eighteen-
year-old Johannes 'Jan' van Zonnenveld lived at No 76 Utrechtseweg. He
took a risk crossing the Weverstraat looking for water and saw a Sturmgeschütz
III lining up to move and shoot through back streets in the direction of
Annastraat and the Utrechtseweg crossroads beyond. The SS soldiers

gathering for the advance were 'as usual, letting everyone in the neighbourhood know they were near one another – how different from the British!' he reflected. All the excess shop merchandise had been thrown out into the street at the corner of Annastraat and Weverstraat, to clear the fields of fire for the German machine guns mounted in the shop windows. A fight was about to break out, and the Germans shouted at him to disappear.

Sergeant Louis Hagen vividly recalled the revving engines and shouted commands that seemed to precede all attacks. The German 'was desperately afraid of us', Hagen had long concluded. Their attacks tended to stall at the first sign of resistance and wait for tanks or direct-fire artillery to sort it out. 'Against 10 of us, nearly 50 of them in a strong position almost gave themselves up,' he recalled derisively, 'then their constant shouting and bawling at night, for no reason than to give themselves confidence!' The new SS replacements needed it. 'No body of men, with only small arms as we had, could possibly have withstood a German Panzer [Division] of the old material,' Hagen commented.

The snub-nose businesslike Sturmgeschütz IIIs with their tortoise-like protective side plates growled around the streets on the eastern side of the airborne perimeter. They appeared to drive around before emerging from side streets to post a shell inside an identified British strongpoint. There were regular visitations every few hours. A sustained assault was an entirely different proposition, and SS Hauptsturmführer Möller's battalion stormed the group of houses around No 192 Utrechtseweg, just short of the crossroads. Jan van Zonnenveld watched such an attack going in at about 2 o'clock during the afternoon of 20 September:

> 'What had begun as an occasional exchange of sniper fire turned into an out-and-out inferno. The Germans attacked British positions in Annastraat with Sturmgeschütze screened by panzer grenadiers with machine guns. It was about 5 in the afternoon before the dreadful din came to an end.'[211]

Captain Stuart Mawson, the 11th Parachute Battalion Medical Officer looking after the wounded in the Hotel Schoonoord, watched the anti-tank duels soon in progress. One of Möller's self-propelled guns cautiously emerged from a side turning 100 metres down the Utrechtseweg:

'The anti-tank gun had got the first shot in, which went across its bows and ploughed into the road, throwing up a large splash of dirt and cobbles. The self-propelled gun had withdrawn sensitively like the horns of a snail and, moving through back gardens, had established itself in a position from which it could advance, fire a shot, and retire again behind the corner of a house.'

The overshoots caused pandemonium in the medical wards of the Schoonoord. Mawson recalled a tough glider pilot lying helplessly on a mattress having sprained both ankles landing his glider. He was already out of action without having struck or received a blow,

'Until a piece of metal flashing through the window practically severed his right hand from his wrist. And there were others: a man lying face downward because of a wound in his buttock, having his shoulder sliced open as though he had been struck with a razor-sharp whip; and the medical orderly, standing over a stretcher, who suddenly collapsed on the wounded man beneath him, and lay there dead with a hole in the back of his head, until others pulled him off.'[212]

SS Rottenführer Wolfgang Dombrowski remembered that they had been making really good progress with their assault gun, until they came under fire from an anti-tank gun supported by paratroopers. He had not been overly impressed with the Sturmgeschütz gun crew, a 'motley mix of a Wehrmacht NCO in charge with a Luftwaffe loader and two more army men'. The clunk of the glancing blow blew off loose equipment and swept debris across the front plate. 'The crew, which had virtually been thrown together,' Dombrowski remembered, 'panicked when they were hit by an anti-tank weapon.' The gun jerkily reversed back into the side street, the fearful driver gunning the motor, 'and although the damage was only superficial, the crew bailed out over the rear.' The disgusted NCO remained remonstrating in the turret until he too climbed down.

Almost immediately a group of paratroopers broke cover and sprinted across to the abandoned assault gun. One of them, Lieutenant Pat Glover with the 10th Parachute Battalion, had previously served in an armoured unit. They tried to get the gun working. The vehicle was simply a 75mm gun mounted on tracks; it had only a 10-degree traverse, so a track had to be locked and the vehicle swivelled to lay on target. Try as they might, the British could not work this out. 'We heard them test the engine and it started,' Dombrowski recalled, 'and soon the gun elevated up and down.' This scene was viewed with growing unease. 'We were very nervous about this.' Then the NCO exclaimed 'Good God!' as the barrel was pointed at them. The paratroopers managed to spray them with machine gun fire from the fixed mount, but to Dombrowski's relief 'they did not get the main armament working'. The deadlock continued until 'eventually, the engine was turned off and they came out,' Dombrowski recalled with some relief, 'but it still remained there, a constant potential threat to both sides.'[213]

Artillery preceded the attack on the crossroads, supplemented by self-propelled guns firing directly into the houses from the Dennenkamp Park, and through the houses on the Weverstraat. Inside the cellars, the only way to interpret the battle was through sounds. Cees Meijer heard the artillery:

> 'One often heard first the firing, then a kind of whistling sound and then the noise of the shell-burst. One was constantly wondering where the shells came down, and if the next one would be nearer or further away.'

Cees was especially frightened when:

> 'We heard a wounded German soldier who was lying in the street. He kept calling, "Willy, Willy, Willy!," but his voice got weaker and weaker and after half an hour it stopped.'

Möller's SS engineers doubled forward into the assault after blowing entry holes in the houses around No 192. The experienced veterans led. Forcing an entry was the critical moment. SS Untersturmführer Linker with the 3rd Kompanie got his men close up to the garden walls and house corners. 'When we got there,' Möller recalled, 'hand grenades were dropped down on us.' They had to get inside. 'Bitter isolated and hand-to-hand fighting ensued as the men fought their way from room to room, from the ground floor up, from garden to garden and from tree to tree.'

'One shell and a grenade exploded in our window barricade,' remembered Private 'Taff' Wilmott from the 10th Parachute Battalion, fighting from within, 'and knocked the barricade down.'

> 'A couple of seconds and two grenades came through the window. The pair of us dived for the door. Hell of a bang but no one was hurt.'

Wilmott has fleeting memories of the struggle for these houses, which went on for hours. He saw the attack develop. 'There was a lot of them on the move to our front in the direction where Oosterbeek Town Hall is now,' he remembered. He fired at them with the Bren on the snooker table. Spandau machine gun bullets slapping into the walls behind them released clouds of plaster dust. Further bursts tore sharp flakes of plaster off the walls and ceilings as bullets ricocheted all around. A single burst alone was sufficient to rip out the best part of a window frame. Defenders and attackers were soon enveloped in blinding, choking palls of white plaster and brick dust.

> 'The Jerries at the back kept having a go at us. We held them off. They used to fire on us from the bedroom windows, but as they were end-on to us, it meant they had to lean right out of the window to fire… One Jerry character used to run out of a house, quickly throw a "tater-masher" grenade and run back in. It never reached us but he had a charmed life as I don't think we hit him either. There was quite a bit of shelling and one hit the upstairs room and somebody fell through onto the snooker table.'

Tumbling down with the avalanche of debris from the ceiling was Lieutenant Pat Glover. 'I had accounted for three Germans when the house was hit by shells and I fell into the front room.' This 10 Para enclave, down to the final 50 or so surviving battalion members, was fighting for its very life. Very few officers were left. Captain Clegg's jaw had been shot away during the bayonet charge into the house. After overseeing its hasty defence, he collapsed through loss of blood. Glover saw Major Warr, the last company commander left, 'and some of his men dashing about from house to house and putting up such good fire that the Germans could not approach,' until he too was badly wounded.

Schmatz and the 2nd Kompanie had swept over No 20 Cornelis Koningstraat in their flanking movement 150 metres south of the Utrechtseweg, heading for the crossroads. Schoolboy Willy van Zanten was sheltering in the air raid shelter outside, built for four but packed with nine members of his family. They could sense the fighting ebbing and flowing up above; 'one moment we were British, the next German'. At one point a German brandishing a machine gun appeared at the entrance and shouted, 'Tommies?' His mother fiercely retorted, 'No! Go to hell, no Tommies here!' In frustration the German shot up all the tobacco plants that were growing over the shelter. 'The situation got so bad that you could have a German soldier behind a machine gun at one side and, about 30 to 40 metres away, the British,' Willy recalled.[214]

'Schmatz's 2nd Kompanie had kicked off their attack at the same time to cover the right flank of 3rd Kompanie,' Möller explained.

> 'He attacked the surprised paratroopers from the rear with flame-throwers, which enabled Untersturmführer Linker to catch his breath and to retain and consolidate the new position. The Red Devils still fought back and battled for every room and every house, for every piece of ground or garden, no matter how small it was – like cornered tigers.'

'Suddenly there was a burst of flame and someone shouted that they were burning us out,' recalled 'Taff' Wilmott. 'Sergeant Hughes ordered us to get out and we crossed the lane to the house next door.' Inside this house was 'quite a number' of B Company with Sergeant Hollebone and a Royal Artillery Lieutenant, but the officer was soon killed by a sniper. They took it in turns to sit with a Sten gun in an open porch, shooting any Germans who came around the corner at the back of the house.

'One thing I will always remember,' recalled Robert 'Paddy' Stewart from D Company:

> 'When I got shot the Germans made a bayonet charge and one of them came for me and was just about to stab me when one of the boys must have seen what he was going to do and managed to shoot him. He landed with his feet in my side and his rifle carried on and stood against a tree.'

The Germans picked him up later that night. 'A German officer gave me a cig and asked what town I came from,' Stewart recalled, 'and I told him Oxford.' The German responded, 'We are still enemies, because I was at Cambridge.' Stewart lost his left thumb and right arm and excused the quality of his subsequent notes outlining his experiences. 'Sorry about the scribble,' he wrote, 'but with four fingers I find it rather hard.'[215]

The 10th Parachute Battalion was steadily dying in this tangle of burning, shattered houses and alleyways strewn with debris. 'Things got very hectic,' Pat Glover recalled:

> 'The Germans got into the house that the CO had vacated and subjected my house to terrific machine gun fire and we fought back – holding them back. I then heard that Lieutenant Saunders was dead, Major Warr and the CO badly wounded. About half an hour later I was about to fire on a creeping German when I was shot in the right hand from behind by a sniper, which cut two veins and I soon lost a large quantity of blood.'[216]

Not a single 10 Para officer now remained on his feet. In No 2 Annastraat, Lieutenant Colonel Smyth's battalion headquarters, the wounded were taken down into the cellars. They were crammed in with 20 Dutch people, which included the Voskuil family. Mrs Bertje Voskuil remembered the previously 'buoyant' Peter Warr being carried down seriously injured with a thigh wound. He lapsed in and out of consciousness, grumbling and swearing with the pain. 'Oh for a pint of beer!' he once exclaimed. Colonel Smyth followed, badly wounded and paralysed from the waist down. 'I think he had been shot in the stomach,' Mrs Voskuil recalled. 'There was a lot of blood, but it was so dark, with one candle in the cellar, that you couldn't see properly.'

Following behind the 2nd Kompanie entry force was Steinart's 1st Kompanie, 'lagging behind on the left of the Utrechtseweg,' Möller recalled. Muthmann, one of his platoon commanders, led the vanguard, methodically clearing all resistance. He was 'advancing in bounds and committing assault platoons that wrested possession from the enemy, house by house, room by room, garden by garden, metre by metre in a damned tenacious struggle requiring the utmost courage from every individual.' Steinart was suddenly down, severely wounded, ending up in another cellar being cared for by the Dutch.

'Then I heard them fighting in the house above us – shots and screams,' recalled a fearful Bertje Voskuil. 'They made all sorts of noises when they were fighting, sometimes like animals.' The cellar door abruptly burst open and German grenades bounced down. A particularly tall British soldier, Corporal Albert Willingham, jumped up to shield them and took the full force of 'two terrific explosions'. Mrs Voskuil was hit in the legs by shrapnel, and her son Henri, sheltering next to her, had his face and stomach raked by splinters. Lance Corporal George Wyllie in the cellar saw the gaping wound in Willingham's back as he slumped across Mrs Voskuil. There was total bedlam in the pitch blackness; the blast had blown out the candle and deafened everyone. Many in the cellar had been hit; Bertje's husband was struck in the hand and knee, and Major Warr again on the shoulder, having raised himself on one elbow to call out that they were surrendering. Somebody was shouting 'Kill them! Kill them!'

It was pandemonium. 'You have no idea how much people scream in such circumstances,' Mrs Voskuil remembered. 'Silence!' she yelled in

English, 'Silence!' Everyone was crying out or sobbing as the trauma of the realisation of what had happened set in. One of the English boys had got up 'shaking visibly', Mrs Voskuil remembered, steadying himself with his rifle and bayonet. 'Low animal-like sounds – almost like a dog or a wolf – were coming from him.' Mrs Voskuil started to translate for the Germans, 'although I believed my son was dead'. 'Perhaps it was utter despair,' she recalled, 'because a year before I had lost my younger son from a blood disease.'[217]

'It seemed now that the only leader we had left was Sergeant Barry Hollebone,' 'Taff' Wilmott with 10 Para recalled. They carried on fighting:

> 'Just as it was getting dark there was a lot of commotion out the back. You couldn't see for undergrowth, but we got the impression there were a lot of Jerries there and they seemed to be shouting and arguing. It seemed as though they were being made to attack us and did not really want to. We could hear them quite close and we all lined up along a long window with a wire mesh screen. We opened up a barrage of fire and they seemed to break and run.'

Wolfgang Dombrowski, with Möller's 2nd Kompanie, recalled how 'our front line stabilised at the crossroads, and we remained lying on this line until virtually the end of the battle.' There is little or no mention of Möller's battalion amid the surviving battle reports from the Hohenstaufen Kampfgruppe after this stage of the battle. As Dombrowski states, 'the focus of pressure was to the left and right but never again with us.' The truth was that, like 10 Para, whom they had just fought, the battalion had ceased to exist as a cohesive military unit. Möller states in his after-action report that 'my 2nd and 3rd Kompanie stayed put in and around the hotel and hospital area,' suggesting that the existence of the Red Cross marker precluded any further advance. The dressing stations represented the high-water mark of the SS advance from the east along the Utrechtseweg.

Private 'Taff' Wilmott recalled that 'later the next day we were relieved by members of the 21st Independent Parachute Company and had to make our way back to the Hartenstein [the division headquarters].' All their officers were gone. 'We were told to rest and we lay on the floor.' Only 36 men were left from the 582 that had parachuted in six days before. Of 31 officers, 15 were dead or later died of wounds and none were to get back to the British lines.

Two battalions from opposing sides had fought themselves to virtual extinction at the east end of Oosterbeek's Utrechtseweg. The only difference, an important one, was that Möller at least had some officers left, so more reinforcements were fed to him. His battalion was to be later reformed and re-equipped in the Reich in time to participate in the later December Ardennes German counter-offensive. Lieutenant Colonel Ken Smyth, the 10 Para CO, shot and paralysed from the waist down, was to linger on for another month before he died in captivity. The battalion's losses were so heavy that it was never reformed until after the war. Thirteen Sergeants and 96 men were killed, an unusually high 15.8% fatality rate; the remainder of the original 582 were wounded or prisoners, and only 36 were going to get out. 10 Para was reformed after the war as a Territorial Army unit. Ironically, having survived the worse the Wehrmacht could level at it, the unit would join its former adversaries as a footnote in history when the battalion was disbanded as part of a Ministry of Defence cull in 2001.

CHAPTER 7

Concentric Attacks on the Street

'Continuation of the attack along the whole front':
Von Tettau, west and north

Corporal Jim Swan, observing the Utrechtseweg in the west with C Company the Borderers, recalled the morning of 21 September:

> 'There was a slight haze on the ground and a wee bit of rain, which cleared. It was damp. We still had some tea cubes left in our section and with some water supplied by one of the lads who had found a tap with water in a greenhouse, we had a brew-up. Peace did not reign for long though; mortars and shells came … they'd got our range. It was a case of keeping to your slit trench and keep your eyes open. Bullets kept zipping through the trees above our heads.'[218]

The Division von Tettau announced 'continuation of the attack along the whole front on 21.9 beginning at 08.00 hours'. Concentric attacks from the west and north were started in concert with 'the left neighbour', Harzer's 9th SS Kampfgruppe, already probing with deep attacks against the perimeter from the east.[219] The less-experienced 10th Schiffstamm Abteilung had been replaced by the Wossowsky Battalion from the Hermann Göring Training Regiment. They were directed to attack the high ground at the Westerbouwing feature occupied by B Company the Border Regiment, south of the street alongside the river. Spearheading their advance were four flame-thrower Char B1(R) tanks from Alfred May's Panzer Company 224.

The Division von Tettau advances east along the street from the west while the 9th SS Hohenstaufen commanded by Harzer pushes east to west, forming the airborne perimeter at Oosterbeek.

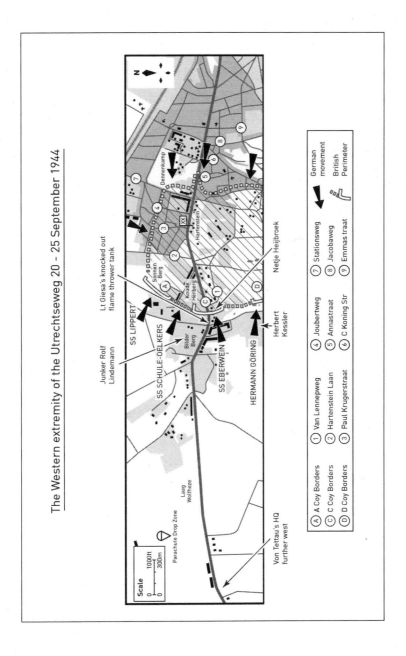

The Western extremity of the Utrechtseweg 20 - 25 September 1944

Scale

0   1000ft
0 300m

Parachute Drop Zone

Laag Wolfheze

Von Tettau's HQ further west

Junker Rolf Lindemann

Lt Giesa's knocked out flame thrower tank

SS LIPPERT

SS SCHULE-OELKERS

Bilder Berg

SS EBERWEIN

HERMANN GÖRING

Herbert Kessler

Netje Heijbroek

Sonnen Berg

Kneuk Herberg

Hartenstein

Dennenkamp

A A Coy Borders
C C Coy Borders
D D Coy Borders

1 Van Lennepweg
2 Hartenstein Laan
3 Paul Krugerstraat

4 Joubertweg
5 Annastraat
6 C Koning Str

7 Stationsweg
8 Jacobaweg
9 Emmas traat

German movement

British Perimeter

215

Herbert Kessler's bicycle-borne 3rd Company had approached the 90-foot bluff riding along a wooded trail with the company commander's staff car up front. 'There was no trace of the enemy far and wide,' he recalled. Two of the flame-throwers had already crawled onto the high ground. 'The soldiers were sitting on their bicycles without a care on their minds when they were surprised by murderous machine gun fire from the flank,' and bedlam ensued. Nobody had spotted the outline of the British defensive position, ensconced among the hedges and trees around the edge of the Westerbouwing Inn. The Germans' approach had been stealthily monitored by the British from the tourist observation tower. Kessler remembered the impact on the 'closely packed' cyclists, who had paused on the track. 'Some were hit before they had time even to throw themselves to the ground, let alone take cover.' The initial shock paralysed the column, which sought sluggishly to react. 'The heavy train had already set up their machine guns and were busily returning the fire,' Kessler recalled.

> 'The soldiers snapped out of their surprise and started to go forward into the brush and open fire, so that we could now hear our own weapons in action. In this way, single groups penetrated the low wood, moved towards the hotel, and occupied the building in which the enemy still was.'[220]

One of 224 Company's tanks knocked out a 6-pounder anti-tank gun on the position, and two of the Border platoons were overrun after a fierce firefight. The third platoon was forced to fall back on the reserve platoon at the foot of the hill. Three of the four flame-thrower tanks were knocked out by PIATs, including one trundling down the road that joined the Benedendorpsweg running alongside the river, outflanking C Company on the Utrechtseweg. Leutnant Heinrich Höser, the 30-year-old panzer section commander, was killed and his turret blown clean off by the resulting ammunition explosion. Three Borderer counter-attacks by the remnants of B Company with HQ and Support companies failed to throw the Germans off the position. B Company was utterly depleted and the

Germans were left in control of the high Westerbouwing feature, which overlooked the airborne perimeter almost in its entirety. The base of the enclave had been narrowed by more than a half and the vital ferry site lost. 'Breeseforce', under Major Charles Breese, the Border second-in-command, was formed to plug the gap alongside a group of hastily formed ad hoc remnants. This local success for the Germans came, however, at a price. 'Regiment Lippert reports some 800 metres of ground gained against strong resistance,' Von Tettau reported, but 'especially heavy losses are reported for the battalion Hermann Göring.'[221]

D Company, between B alongside the river and C on the Utrechtseweg, was hit next when two more of Alfred May's 224 Company flame-thrower tanks pushed in among the platoon positions, shooting up the trenches. Only the rear of two 6-pounder guns defending the position could be brought to bear, and this had to be manhandled into position under fire. Corporal Tommy Langhorn was killed by a burst of machine gun fire swinging the barrel from the front, incensing his crewmates. 'They've got the Corp, let 'em have it!' they shrieked in frustration and loaded with sabot armour-piercing shot. Anxiously they waited, enduring a storm of enemy small arms and mortar fire before the tank broke cover. The first 6-pounder round smashed in at 2,700 feet per second, causing the obsolete French tank to lurch to a halt and burst into flames. Five more rounds followed in as many seconds before the visibly enraged gunners were dragged off the gun. None of the panzer crew got out as the burning hulk spat and hissed on the track.

German recriminations followed this costly series of attacks. The 26-year-old Leutnant Artur Wossowsky, who led the attack, was an anti-aircraft artillery officer, inexperienced in leading infantry in combat. He was cut down. His commander, Oberst (Colonel) Fritz Fullriede, later described the debacle in his diary:

'The Wossowsky Battalion lost all its officers with the exception of one Leutnant, and half its men in this attack on Oosterbeek. These insanely high losses were caused by a certain Oberst Schramm, who was in command there, and forbade the use of too many heavy weapons so that his own men would not be endangered. This idiot preferred to allow hundreds to be cut down.'[222]

Lippert meanwhile sacked Sturmbannführer Helle, the commander of the Dutch SS Wach Battalion 3, for being unable to maintain 'the desired forward momentum'. The hapless Helle was torn off a strip and 'told he had no tactical nous and, as he had no idea of the enemy situation, or his own, I had to relieve him of command.' His men were dispersed among the SS NCO School Arnheim.

Fullriede was raising concerns echoed by many experienced commanders fighting around the perimeter. Many of the reinforcements scraped together to stem the crisis were simply unready for combat; like the Hermann Göring Battalion, they were recruits prematurely snatched from training. SS Obersturmführer (Lieutenant) Lebahn, commanding the 7th Stamm (Replacement) Company on the west side of the perimeter, complained that many of his recruits had arrived still wearing their civilian clothes. They put on their uniforms in the trenches and 'NCOs have to give instruction about how to load and prime grenades in their defence positions'. Those 'very few' who had received a modicum of military training were formed up in sections and sent into battle. Lebahn was even less impressed with his reinforcements. 'Most of the reservists had come from cultural or clerical pursuits and with few exceptions could best be described as a collection of "dish-cloths".' Many of them were from the Luftwaffe, 'who had retreated without orders, including some SS NCOs and men.' Lebahn accepted that in the circumstances, he needed to remain philosophical:

'Cowards among the recruits were not the norm, but these untrained soldiers acted the same way as their former military predecessors did, which was to stay alive, an inevitable part of the weakness of the human condition.'

Shooting the cowards to encourage the rest was hardly the solution, Lebahn accepted, because 'I would have to sentence every fifth man'. Nevertheless, during the subsequent days of fighting around the perimeter 'the majority of the replacements, some members of the Luftwaffe, reservists and replacement reservists acquitted themselves well.' On the first day that they went into action, 25 of them were killed and 60 wounded. 'Despite a ban from the OKH Army Headquarters (Oberkommando des Heeres), about 1,600 recruits were transported back to Germany,' added Oberst Fullriede. 'Their deployment would have been pure infanticide.'[223]

Leutnant Alfred May earned a personal rebuke from General von Tettau. 'All of the six operational tanks of Panzer Company 224 employed this day were lost during this day's heavy fighting,' he complained. One tank was even missing. May was told that 'we can no longer afford any losses', and his tanks were hereby placed under Von Tettau's direct command. The three still running were attached to Lippert's regiment. He imposed several inflexible safeguards, further undermining May's command and stifling any initiative. 'The company commander is ordered by me that when attacking and the infantry pull back, he is to do so right away, should any further advance result in the loss of any of his tanks.' Only Lippert's SS battalions commanded by Eberwein and Schulz were recognised as having the suitable expertise and weapons to protect the panzers. Von Tettau cajoled his command, insisting that 'everybody has to keep his eyes open to recognise enemy anti-tank guns as soon as possible.' Nobody needed telling. The SS resented the infantile advice, and the recruits were quickly learning.[224]

'The fighting became harder in the last phase,' recalled SS Junker 'Rolf' Lindemann, advancing with Lippert's regiment. 'We were static in defence positions in light woods with bushes and clearings.' They were dogged by the inexperience of the Schiffstamm sailor infantry under their command. 'I was sent as a messenger to tell the Navy unit what to do,' he recalled. 'They were all lying loosely packed next to each other on the ground, terribly vulnerable to artillery fire.' His experience against this enemy was totally at odds with what most veterans had endured in Russia, where 'medics, with or without weapons, and hospitals were fired at'. These men were different. He recalled a lost German ambulance that was apprehended by the British:

'The driver thought his number was up. A British officer asked him if he would be so kind as to take a heavily wounded British officer to a German hospital. The British even put the driver on the right road and offered him a gold watch for his trouble.'[225]

In the west the Border Battalion was holding on, but steadily disintegrating. D Company, immediately south of the Utrechtseweg, blocking alongside the newly formed 'Breeseforce', was down to two officers and 35 men. Corporal Jim Swan's C Company, blocking the street, had been pushed back further and reduced to 50 men, less than half its original strength of 131. Contact with D Company to their left was sporadic at best, with many Germans infiltrating between. Swan was with a patrol that identified a German attack forming on their flank. 'They were all creeping up through a small copse and bushes, and they were preparing to attack.' A small fighting patrol, liberally supplied with hand grenades, put in a spoiling counter-attack:

'We attacked and surprised the Germans and we really sent them flying. Quite a few got killed and badly wounded. We got back to our positions and settled down again. It seemed funny, although we caught them on the hop, when we started throwing grenades they really hackled back at us before running off, but remarkable that none of us got hit.'

Attacks along the line of the Utrechtseweg continued throughout the day. 'Later we could see that they were massing again,' Swan recalled. Major Neil, the C Company commander, formed a group of men with eight Bren guns, with No 2s carrying at least four magazines and riflemen with additional magazines, and lined them up behind a protective hedge. They suddenly burst through and struck the surprised Germans:

'After a couple of yards of rapid fire – the Brens had been fired from the hip – we carried on, it must have been 30 odd yards. We were getting near the forward German troops.

They were starting to run back – it was pandemonium – we
didn't run after them.'

They had to return swiftly to their trenches 'in time to get a right
barrage of mortar bombs again', which they suspected was the original
preparatory German barrage.[226]

Sergeant Gordon Walker, with the AFPU film unit, had positioned
himself in a house at No 17 Van Lennepweg, overlooking the Koude
Herberg crossroads on the Utrechtseweg. 'I established myself here,' he
recalled, 'so that I could film out of two windows,' which enabled him to
see both the Border positions and 'the Germans who were a matter of 75
yards away'. Walker witnessed one of Lippert's attacks along the
Utrechtseweg:

'We stopped firing and let him come to within 15 or 20 yards
of us, then gave him everything we had, including the firing
of PIATs to break them up. He broke and ran to get out of it,
but I doubt if many made it. I will photograph the massacre
when XXX Corps eventually – if ever – get to us.'

His companion Sergeant Lewis recalled how 'I have made attempts to get
action pictures but it is hard'. The problem was that 'our area is so constricted
that all of it is laced and crossed by mortars, shells and small arms weapons.'
Wherever they moved 'men are hit by strays and ricochets'. Their situation
was becoming precarious. Walker wrote in his 'dope sheet', accompanying
his pictures, that 'we have given up all ideas of photographs and are fighting
now for our lives, the worst I have ever been in.' It did not get any better; a
crisis suddenly erupted during one of the particularly determined German
attacks. 'Shortly afterwards,' Walker remembered,

'The house was hit and set on fire and about that time one of
the cameramen came down the road and into the house and
said, "You've got to get out of here, the Germans are coming
up very close, and we're all surrounded just about here".'

Walker shouted back, 'We haven't got much option – the house is on fire and we've got to get out.' As the German attack came pouring in 'I gathered my camera and what equipment I could, and film, and ran for it, losing my 16mm camera, tripod and all the other excess gear that was needed for the jobs we do.' He later wrote in his 'dope sheet', 'paratroopers moving to new positions, the sky is hazy and the light is poor.'[227]

As they pulled back, Netje Heijbroek's house, 'Valkenburg', just beyond the Koude Herberg crossroads, was overrun by the Germans. There were three British glider soldiers trapped, sheltering inside their cellar. Netje's family heard fierce fighting overhead followed by 'heavy footsteps, the cellar door opened and closed again'. Her father positioned himself at the foot of the cellar steps holding a white flag. 'There were 25 of us, including three English soldiers,' she recalled. When the cellar door opened again, Netje's father hopefully called up, 'Hello Tommy? Was Tommy?' The cellar door slammed shut again. 'There were Germans in our house,' Netje recalled. 'We were again German.'

When German jackboots clattered down the stairs, pandemonium erupted in the cellar. All the Dutch civilians dashed out of the boiler room as the British soldiers rushed in and slammed the door. 'It was amazing how everyone reacted,' recalled an astonished Netje. Everybody had thought the same thing. For the moment they were lucky, but tension rose. 'If we find a Tommy, this whole cellar will be wiped out,' threatened the Germans, 'including women and children.' It was a difficult predicament; overhead the fighting was clearly continuing and the Germans winning. The Dutch took stock. The assaulting German soldiers, who 'belonged to an elite corps', were augmented 'by lads from the Navy, some very young, aged 17 or so'. They knew the war was lost. 'The officers were difficult, unpredictable, disappointed, mostly drunk and very threatening.' The inhabitants of the overcrowded cellar were sitting on a highly combustible emotional powder keg.

Time and again the Germans appeared at the head of the cellar steps, always met and delayed by Netje's father. They would come down and search the cellar. 'The threat they radiated was enormous,' Netje recalled, but somehow or other the Dutch 'with might and main' always managed to effectively cloak the presence of the British behind the boiler room door. 'We narrowly escaped death on a number of occasions,' she recalled as the Germans eventually settled themselves in the cellar. 'Deep' conversations then followed with the terrified Dutch as they started to drink heavily, further ramping up cumulative and exhausting tension.

> 'With every check, that door remained an object of suspicion. Once a Feldwebel [Sergeant] gave the order to open it and see what was behind, but an officer said, "Let it be." How relieved and thankful we were.'

The ever-raucous Germans constantly niggled at Netje's father. 'Every day they found cause for putting my father before a firing squad, be it a radio, an odd uniform, a picture of the Queen, etc.' Their presence became unbearable. The British had been forced to move so quickly that all their equipment had been left behind in the main cellar. Nobody could get food or drink to them; they managed to extract a little water from a central heating drainage tap.

> 'The Germans continued to arrive, now with a gramophone and records, which they played loudly, then with more drinking. They were relieved every 2 hours, and everyone was woken up, especially at night.'

The British, left to fend for themselves in the dank boiler room, eventually caught colds and started to cough. 'My father organised a choir,' Netje recalled, to deaden the sound. 'We sang national songs while the shooting continued over us.' The pressure that Netje's father endured to protect the Dutch and the trapped British was to contribute to an eventual nervous breakdown. Arie van Veelen, a young Dutch lad sheltering with them, approached Netje years after the war and remarked 'that the singing had made a great impression on him'.[228]

The precarious cellar existence was beginning to wear down the frayed nerves of all the civilian inhabitants of the street. Fighting and the accompanying fires were starting to drive them out. Three hundred people were sheltering in the coach house of the Hemelse Berg nearby, one of the largest stately homes in Oosterbeek. Fifty were in the main house sheltering with some 25 British wounded. Twenty-one-year-old Julie Beelaerts van Blockland remembered her mother demanding that the Borderers move a gun set up next to the house, because 'it would be dangerous for all the people we had in the house'. Despite the growing intensity of the fighting 'they moved it for my mother's sake'. But such niceties could not continue. Corporal Jim Swan recalled evacuating everyone from the house, whose garden they had entrenched on the Utrechtseweg.

> 'We didn't want a repetition of what had happened earlier in the week. The house, which was just in front of our defence line, was set on fire and we could do nothing for the people trapped in the cellar.'

They wanted no more screams from helpless civilians caught up in the fighting. On Friday a group of airborne soldiers came into Julie van Blockland's cellar:

> 'They had blackened faces and were in a bewildered state, having had no food or sleep for several days. They just wanted to rest, but mother insisted that they took their weapons off. They were with us for a little while, then they had to go outside into the inferno, the hell that was outside – the crossfire and the "moaning minnies" that were going on all the time.'

The civilians from the coach house rushed the hall when they thought that those sheltering inside were getting better food, but shelling and burning forced them back into the coach house. 'The fires spread and our home became a shell,' Julie recalled. When she got out 'I kept my hair wet in case of sparks'.[229]

Herbert Kessler's 3rd Hermann Göring Company continued their attacks, having developed a healthy, almost intimidating respect for their adversaries. 'These were indeed elite troops,' he acknowledged, 'fellows tall as trees, well-fed and excellently equipped.' Half his company of some 300 men were either dead or wounded by nightfall, following the capture of the Westerbouwing feature. His men were 'completely shattered', he remembered, their problems compounded by the difficulty of reforming in the wooded area.

> 'Fighting amongst the trees made it particularly hard to recognise the enemy. Snipers up in the trees caused considerable losses, enemy automatic weapons changed their positions frequently and it was therefore very difficult to silence them and there were more losses.'

After a brief reorganisation the company attempted to continue the advance towards Oosterbeek, but to no avail. One of their assault groups reached an enemy-occupied row of houses and 'we advanced by making use of every possible opportunity for cover'. Just before they could cross the road to their front they were hit by a storm of fire 'with such intensity that the enterprise immediately collapsed'. The assault commander, a sergeant, was cut down and there were many casualties. 'The only thing to do,' Kessler recalled, 'was to retreat as quickly as possible.'

SS Standartenführer Lippert recalled that parts of his battle group reached the Oosterbeek gasworks, but were too weak to push on and join Harder's SS Kampfgruppe in sight on the opposite side of the perimeter. 'At noon,' Kessler recalled, 'the company was completely scattered and pulled back, while an adjacent unit continued the attack.' They were in such a sorry state, 'a small group, with missing comrades dead, wounded, or scattered as stragglers', that they were granted a brief rest before occupying a secondary line in depth, in the wooded area in front of Oosterbeek. Opposite them sat 'Breeseforce' and the remnants of the Border D Company on the slopes of the Helmsche Berg and around the gasworks by the river. The western German approach along the Utrechtseweg was effectively barred.[230]

To the north of the street, the 7th KOSB were finally driven from the 'White House' strongpoint at the Hotel Dreijeroord, after several days of fighting with Sten, grenade and bayonet. The losses incurred required the northern perimeter to contract. The Germans now occupied the line of the Joubertweg, with the British holding them back from the Paul Krugerstraat, running west to east just 250 yards north of the Utrechtseweg. Glider pilot Staff Sergeant 'Bunny' Baker, defending nearby, had chosen not to attend the final church parade prior to taking off. 'I knew we were out to kill, and somehow it seemed hypocrisy as the Bible taught us not to kill, and it was obvious that Dutch people would be killed.' He felt vindicated when his men took down a German sniper; 'his body lay from a church window'. 'I felt sure I had done the right thing in refusing to go to the church parade!' he reminisced.[231]

As in the west, the Germans were overrunning an increasing number of Dutch-occupied houses in the north. Geert Maassen had tried to get back to his house at No 32 Mariaweg to recover some things for his baby, having been forced out of its inadequate cellar for one on the Paul Krugerstraat, the forward British position. He was reassured to see a smiling paratrooper sitting on a chair with a Sten on his knee in the open doorway of his house as he went inside to recover his effects. The sudden rattle of Sten gun fire behind alerted him to the fact that the Germans were very close by. On emerging he saw three dead German soldiers sprawled across his garden hedge, calmly regarded by the paratrooper who was lighting up a cigarette. Maassen realised with a sinking heart that 'the Germans must already be in the Joubertweg – I don't like that at all.' He noticed that the paratroopers had vacated his garden and 'I had to crouch down for cover as I heard the bullets fly over my head'. He finally reached the Janssen cellar on Paul Krugerstraat 'where the others sighed with relief. They had heard the shooting and feared for my life.' The Germans, he told them, were very near.

> 'Then we heard a strange, grinding sound. It turned out to be a German motorised gun. It came from the north, down the Mariaweg. It set fire to Mr Crum's bakery and also damaged our house considerably.'[232]

Crum's bakery was at the intersection of Mariaweg and Paul Krugerstraat. As it burned both sides ceased fire as the civilians poured out of its cellar before renewing the fight.

This sector was held by the Division Reconnaissance Squadron, and one of its sergeants, James Pyper, has chilling memories of tank shells shrieking straight through the inner and outer walls of house strongpoints 'just as if the structure was made of cardboard'. 'The din was frightful,' remembered Lieutenant John Stevenson, also with the recce, enduring the punishment being meted out by self-propelled guns nearby:

'The explosions seemed to increase in violence. The air was driven painfully from my chest. At times I experienced momentary panic as I gasped, sucking breath into my lungs. Away to the left I could discern the elongated muzzle of the armoured monster that was seeking to destroy us. Then this seemingly impregnable menace was temporarily obscured by a stab of flame, belching clouds of smoke as another shell hurtled from the barrel.'

Then came the infantry. 'Of all my impressions of the battle,' Stevenson insisted,

'...the one that has been the most lasting has been the shouting of the German NCOs. Whenever you heard this loud parade-ground shouting and the answering "Jawohls", you knew that there was an assault of some kind about to be mounted.'

One of the defenders, Corporal Jim 'Spud' Taylor, remembers his companion Lieutenant Dougie Galbraith silently removing a pin from his grenade and holding it, grinning, while it sizzled in his hand for 3 seconds before dropping it on the attackers below. It was timed to go off just before it reached the ground and 'there was no chance of a smart German picking it up and throwing it back at you'. The bakery was abandoned amid a rush of assaulting German troops. The remaining A Troop defenders ran into the Janssen house next door. Trooper Alfred 'Gunner' Web shouted out the warning: 'They're coming down behind you, fucking hundreds of them!' as his companion, Corporal Taylor, shouted back, 'Watch your own side – they're coming round behind you too!' They breathlessly dashed into the Janssen house where they were confronted by a lady preparing vegetables in the kitchen, as if her family were coming home for the midday meal. There was no escaping the fact that their position was becoming increasingly precarious. They could not shift the self-propelled gun outside. 'The English soldiers who were staying in Mr Janssen's house did not say much,' remembered Geert Maassen, 'but we felt that they were not optimistic, one could read it in their eyes.'[233]

'Things went from bad to worse,' admitted staff Sergeant 'Bunny' Baker. He had lost a close friend, who was going to show him the north after the war, then one of his captains was killed by a sniper 'after I had moved to let him sit down'. Another pal was 'blown to pieces, and I do mean pieces,' he emphasised. 'Many years afterwards his wife asked me what had happened to him, but I could never put it in writing.' The remorseless death toll was corrosive to the human spirit, including that inflicted on the enemy. Baker was depressed by the senseless slaughter they had inflicted on 'a crowd of Germans, who were getting out of buses and preparing to attack'. They were clearly inexperienced. Dressed in black, they lined up faultlessly with automatic weapons and conducted a parade-ground attack in the face of concentrated fire from a group of Bren guns:

> 'It seemed stupid as they advanced, singing a rousing song – God forbid that I should ever hear that song again! We held our fire until they were close, then opened up. They went down like grass before a scythe. Another came on with similar results. Then the remainder lined up and the chap next to me cried, "For God's sake, go back!" Thank God, they did.'

Baker and the Bren gun crews 'withdrew in a kind of drunken stupor'. When he came to write it all down much later, he felt that 'it seems like I am writing about someone else'. The stench of battle pervaded his memory, 'a mixture of burning cordite and the sickly smell of death'. The second enduring emotion was a feeling of abandonment. 'We were completely on our own', fighting and dying in isolation. 'We were in a mess, but while furious with the people who we felt had let us down, we would not go down without a fight.' Years later he still feels perfectly justified skipping that final church parade.[234]

Jan Hol, who had been evading German forced labour at No 10 Stationsweg, had recklessly cycled past the British line into the German-occupied Joubertweg in order to find a missing person. 'I sensed something was wrong and that danger threatened', but ignored the warning waves from British paratroopers. In the Joubertweg 'ahead of me I saw masses of Germans walking in groups alongside the houses.' There was a tank and field gun beyond, and half a dozen Germans strung out loosely across the road were just as surprised to see him as he was them. 'Komm hier Mensch!' 'Come here you!' they shouted, but he was cycling back furiously and disappeared around the corner before a shot could be fired. The Germans were forming up for the final attacks.[235]

Geert Maassen in the Janssen cellar on Paul Krugerstraat remembered that 'early in the morning' on Friday 22 September 'there was again a lot of shooting going on'. Noise was the only indicator of what might be happening in the cellars, and this time it was 'unbelievable' and very near. A wounded Englishman was brought down, 'a bad omen'. As they tried to reassure the badly wounded man, 'over our heads we heard the English shooting'. It was getting worse, 'it sounded like a man-to-man fight', then silence.

> 'We thought it too dangerous to go and have a look. We felt
> the English could not hold their positions any longer, we had
> to say goodbye to our happy dreams. The shooting sounded
> further away and night fell.'

The following morning they heard 'heavy footsteps – German footsteps! We heard German voices – they had come back.' The Liberation was over.

Sixteen-year-old student Sjoert (Stewart) Schwitter's family, living nearby, were immediately turfed out when their home was overrun by the Germans:

> 'There were 13 of us. We had all our luggage ready for such an eventuality, but it happened so quickly – "Out! Get out!" – that we took practically nothing. Father went first, with a white flag and a pillow under his arm, and Mother carried an empty cake-tin; it was such a terrible situation that they just picked up the nearest thing without thinking.'

They were waved towards the British positions on the Steinweg. After the trauma of the German ejection, 'the British were very polite and allowed us to stay in the cellar' of a house previously occupied by National Socialists.[236]

SS dispatch rider Alfred Ziegler was still with the Kampfgruppe Bruhn pushing up against Joubertweg. He had first spent his nights sheltering in abandoned trenches with his motorcycle combination rolled over the top for protection. 'Our small unit was engaged in house-to-house fighting throughout the day and paid a terrible toll,' he recalled. In the evening, there were only 21 unwounded men left from the Panzerjäger, absolutely leaderless. Hauptmann Hans Bruhn told him to look for Von Allwörden, his commander, and advise him to withdraw the remaining dismounted SS assault gun crews, fighting as infantry, 'if he wanted to have any left'. Bruhn commanded the replacement Panzergrenadier Battalion 361, still training in Germany when they were called forward. He was a one-legged veteran of fierce fighting on the Russian front, where he had been decorated with the Knight's Cross. As such, he instinctively appreciated the worth of the technically trained assault gun crews. Ziegler made his way back to Von Allwörden's headquarters in Arnhem. SS-Hauptsturmführer Klaus von Allwörden's battle group was operating alongside a similar Kampfgruppe under SS-Obersturmführer Harder, pushing south-west into the eastern part of the perimeter alongside Möller's battle group on the Utrechtseweg.

'I found Von Allwörden in a large house on the edge of Arnhem with many officers, and also ladies,' an indignant Ziegler recalled. 'Enjoy the war while you can' was a popular SS refrain, 'because the peace will be terrible!' 'The victory was celebrated there with lots of alcohol,' Ziegler observed, 'which was certainly one way to get through a war.' Obersturmführer Harder's headquarters in the Van Gend & Loos building in Arnhem appeared to follow a similarly raucous philosophy amid the fighting. Five Dutchmen had been summarily executed at No 63 Bakkerstraat nearby. Dutch fireman Theo Scholten had visited Harder's command post to seek permission to fight the fires out of control in both Arnhem and Oosterbeek. Obliged to wait outside, Scholten saw

'All types of German soldiers are hanging about down here. They have bottles of wine which they drain after first knocking the necks off. This accounts for the noisy mood.'

Ziegler was told to get out. 'What do you want here?' he was asked. 'You belong at the front!' With clenched teeth he requested reinforcements for the depleted Panzerjäger. Only 10 men from Von Allwörden's defence platoon were dispatched. 'I was to tell Herr Bruhn that the Panzerjäger would not be pulled out of the line and that he could count on us as before.' Ziegler was unimpressed at this peremptory dismissal – 'sheer mockery,' he commented, 'only serving to reaffirm my opinion and attitude towards some gentlemen and their qualifications.' Bruhn was sympathetic on his return. 'He could only shake his head and promised we would not be committed again.' He kept the surviving Panzerjäger around his command post, but 'some of my mates were killed or wounded even there'.

After the war Ziegler claims that he physically assaulted Von Allwörden at an SS reunion over this. 'I hated his guts,' he commented bitterly. Harzer, his superior officer, was asked why he chose to do nothing, to which he drolly responded, 'He could be court-martialled, decorated or promoted out of the way.' What was the point of an altercation or a complicated court-martial at such a time? He pointed out that 'the war was not going to last much longer in any case'. Meanwhile, the battle of attrition carried on to the north of the perimeter between the Joubertweg and the Paul Krugerstraat streets. The Germans were barely 250 yards short of the Airborne Division headquarters at the Hartenstein Hotel on the Utrechtseweg.[237]

'We always believed our artillery was dropping short,' Ziegler often complained. He became suspicious when 'I noticed shell bursts landing in a distinct pattern before us.' They were deliberately registering around their positions, he realised, and shared this concern with his Leutnant. 'Don't be so imaginative, they're strays,' he responded. 'But they weren't!' A deluge of shellfire descended and Ziegler found himself evacuating the wounded Leutnant to hospital on his motorcycle combination. Major Geoffrey Powell, with the survivors from 156 Para on the Stationsweg, also saw a shell explode 100 yards ahead,

> '…much larger than anything so far seen, sending a pillar of dust and smoke into the sky and raining earth and stones into the road. My heart sank. This was medium artillery, large stuff.'

Another whistled overhead, exploding well inside the German line, and 300 yards away a huge column of smoke went up amid Germans, who appeared to be digging trenches. 'My spirits rose a little. They were shelling their own troops,' thought Powell. Looking out over the Dennenkamp Park, he heard the shrieking rush of several shells, accompanied by crackling multiple impacts and a forest of smoke pillars. 'Now I understood,' Powell recalled. 'They were British guns, not Boche.' For the first time in this battle they appreciated they were no longer alone. 'Around me rose the chatter, shrill and excited', as the soldiers realised that they were watching the medium guns from Nijmegen register then obliterate the targets to their front.

> 'All day, whenever they had a few minutes to spare, the men had been mocking the sloth of the Second Army, the grumbles being not the good-natured complaints flung as a matter of course at other units and formations, but harsh scorn for troops who had let them down.'[238]

All the Second Army had to do ostensibly 'was motor up the road from Nijmegen'. Seeing was believing; something was at last happening. Would they now, after all, escape this trap?

Nemesis: the Poles

After passing Nijmegen, some of the aircraft started to buck. Inside, the Polish paratroopers felt thumps reverberating against aircraft walls, and puff balls of smoke could be viewed through windows. Expended shell fragments rattled off the aluminium skins of the Dakotas. Lance Corporal Marcin Henzel, looking out of the open door, viewed an uninterrupted trail of wreckage on the ground, 'a horrible sight', broken aircraft, gliders, vehicles and tanks. Vicious fighting had been raging along the Eindhoven-Nijmegen 'airborne corridor' for five days now. Tension had risen throughout the Polish Brigade as postponement followed anxious postponement for troopers marooned in aircraft on fogbound English airfields. 'They were getting pissed off,' recalled pilot Lieutenant Robert Cloer with the US 34th Troop Carrier Squadron, due to fly them,

> '...and the rest of us couldn't explain to them what's going on. When it was cancelled a second time, they were really pissed. They wanted to fight, they wanted to go over there and fight. Some of them thought we didn't want to take them or something.'

Warsaw was burning amid the Polish underground uprising, unsupported by the Russians, and the Polish paratroopers had not been allowed to go to their assistance. They thirsted for revenge. 'They scrubbed the flight for the Poles on September 19th,' recalled Lieutenant William Bruce, a pilot in the same squadron, 'and the Polish paratroopers were very upset.' So much so that a knife was pulled on one of the American officers, and the two had to be pulled apart. 'He was not making an idle gesture,' Bruce commented; the officer had represented authority and 'there was blood in his eye'. Another over-anxious paratrooper was so distraught that he shot himself next to the aeroplane. An amazed American bystander described the scene:

> 'I couldn't believe what I saw next – there's this dead guy
> lying there, and his comrades didn't even look at him, except
> to throw cigarette butts and trash at him.'

It was a case of third time lucky, but 41 of the 114 aircraft earmarked to drop had to turn back because of the weather.

The 73 remaining aircraft arrived over the drop zone next to Driel at 17.00 hours on 21 September and thundered in, exhibiting yet another demonstration of unmatched Allied technical superiority. There had been substantial resupply sorties that afternoon, but German soldiers from Nijmegen to the Lower Rhine looked up open-mouthed at the huge flypast of aircraft, flying in faultless 'vic' formations with open doors. Another substantial drop was imminent, inverting odds on the street for a third depressing time. Polish paratroopers started to tumble out between Driel and the Nijmegen railway embankment just south of the Lower Rhine. Although clearly visible from the Utrechtseweg, few of the inhabitants of the street battened down inside cellars witnessed the majestic drop, but they certainly heard it. Heavy German guns across the river joined with light flak from Elst and the railway bridge, throwing up a storm of anti-aircraft fire. Around the drop zone machine guns and rifle fire opened up against the over-flying Dakotas. Puffs of smoke burst amid the aircraft stream, soon interlaced by flashing webs of tracer fire.

The heavily encumbered Poles were dropping on their first combat mission of the war and made slow exits, extending run-ins for up to 45 seconds. As the normal procedure for pilots was to reduce power and prop-wash to assist stable exits, 'my aircraft lost considerable altitude,' recalled Lieutenant Colonel Henry Hamby piloting a 310th Carrier Wing aircraft. 'I must have been at 300 feet when the last one got out', which closed the range to the advantage of the German gunners. He turned sharply left to escape the drop zone and 'started getting hit almost as soon as the last paratrooper was out'. Thumping impacts signified hits from 20mm cannon fire, one through the port engine, which shielded him, another into the fuselage, and a third that exploded inside the cargo compartment. 'Everybody but me was wounded,' Hamby recalled. 'The worst was the crew-chief, who had his butt blown off.' He managed to nurse the aircraft back to Brussels.[239]

'Hail Mary,' murmured Private J. Zbigniew Raschke, responding to the whispered farewell of the man in front of him. There was a severe jolt followed by a shouted 'We got it in the wing' from a nearby Corporal, who then exclaimed, 'The wing is on fire!' They carried on jumping from the burning aircraft. When Lieutenant Albert Smaczny cleared aircraft No 65 he could already pick out individual rifle reports amid bursts of machine gun fire, which sent up arcs of yellow tracer that 'seemed unreal'. Looking up, two bullet holes appeared in his canopy. One descending paratrooper had his helmet shot off the top of his head, taking away part of his skull. Fountains of dirt erupted around landed paratroopers struggling to disentangle themselves from their harnesses. Second Lieutenant Zbigniew Bossowski landed in a water-filled ditch that immediately spat up fountains from spandau fire. 'Stop shooting at us, you horse's ass!' he heard one of his troopers shout in perfect colloquial-Wehrmacht German, and to his amazement the gun stopped. Driel proved to be the paratrooper's nightmare: a 'hot' drop zone. 'Everything erupted,' recalled navigator Second Lieutenant James Wilson with the 310th Troop Carrier Squadron:

> 'I mean fire from every direction. That DZ had mortar fire hitting the ground all over the place. I looked up and saw flak cars on that railroad track, and they had 40mms, and they were firing directly at us. Well, the troopers got out, and it looked to me like that there was a mortar landing every 6 feet. I couldn't believe that any of that Polish outfit could survive from what I saw.'[240]

The Germans were equally shocked. 'This was all we needed,' recalled 19-year-old Rudolf Trapp with the 10th SS watching from the Onderlangs 'low road' beneath the Utrechtseweg. 'When we saw fresh paratroopers landing we lined up along the Rhine edge and shot for all we were worth.' Hitting parachutists oscillating from side to side in the air, at an undetermined distance, is difficult, even for experienced riflemen and machine gunners. 'I set up my machine gun and quickly fired protracted bursts,' remembered Trapp, 'because there is so little time before they get on the ground.' Tests have since revealed that it takes an average of 1,708 rounds fired at 350 metres to hit a single paratrooper in the air. Even at 150 metres, much closer, it can still take as many as 185 rounds to be on target. The idea is to wait until the man is down and struggling to get out of his parachute harness. Nevertheless, the Germans were deeply dismayed by the appearance of yet another mass parachute descent. 'This was a shock,' Trapp declared. 'A second front.' They knew that the freshly landed troops would seek to cross the river and reinforce the bridgehead perimeter. 'We stood under the trees and fired in the air,' Trapp recalled, but Polish casualties were to prove surprisingly light.

In all five Poles were killed and 36 wounded, not the bloody slaughter the Germans and many witnesses thought they had seen. Some 1,003 of the 1,568 paratroopers had arrived. 'It looked worse than it was,' navigator James Wilson assessed. 'All the Gooney Birds ahead of us did a hard right' to avoid the flak. 'It looked like everyone of them was being shot down.' Two aircraft went down in flames over the drop zone and five were destroyed altogether, mainly picked off by low-level fire as they turned for home, looking like 'elephants rolling around in the sky,' as Wilson described, having disgorged their loads.[241] Thirty-three aircraft were damaged, 14 so severely that they were turned over to service groups for repair. From the point of view of the embattled paratroopers in the perimeter, the drop appeared as catastrophic as it looked. They were cynically disposed after ceaseless fighting to believe in reinforcements only when they saw them, and in this case they were on the wrong side of the river.

The Germans, however, were badly rattled. Nobody felt safe with enemy paratroopers in their rear. Obersturmbannführer Harzer immediately switched all his newly formed reserves, due to participate in a full-scale concentric attack against the perimeter and the street the following day, into a blocking force, the Sperrverband Harzer, which was sent across the Lower Rhine to contain the Poles at Driel. Five battalions, numbering 2,500 men, were taken out of their reserve positions around the perimeter and put in place along the railway embankment facing the new threat to the west. The Dutch on the south bank were alarmed by this sudden influx of German troops. Jan Hendrik Esvelt, living near the recaptured Arnhem road bridge, recalled the rapid deployment of the Sperrverband Harzer. They were awoken at 07.00 by major troop movements. 'The whole street is surrounded by soldiers,' he wrote in his diary, 'all new recruits of six weeks,' who had been driven up from Zutphen, 'telling us they are expecting an attack and are spreading out into the fields in the direction of Elden.' This was unsettling news. 'Now we are really getting scared,' he wrote. He asked a German officer what was happening and was told, 'Get out fast.'[242]

Von Tettau instructed Lippert's regiment to place the newly arrived Fliegerhorst Battalion 3 to secure the area around the Heveadorp ferry. 'It must be assumed,' he wrote in his report, 'that these [Polish] forces are to relieve the encircled British Airborne Division.' Standartenführer Lippert had been shaken by the Polish landings, which 'for my mission was one of the most critical situations that emerged,' he admitted. He remained perpetually concerned about 'my greatest worry', which was potential British break-out attempts into his area to link up with the Poles across the Rhine ferry at Heveadorp. By simply appearing, the Poles extended the life of the embattled airborne perimeter and the transitory Liberation of the street for a few more days.

Very few Poles were actually going to get across the river in the course of the next three days to realise these very real German concerns. During the night of 22/23 September only 52 men from the Polish 8th Company got over using a string of six rubber recce dinghies and improvised rafts. Attempting to negotiate the swift flow of 1.4 metres per second with shovels instead of paddles was ambitious enough before a succession of flares popped over the Lower Rhine and machine gun and Nebelwerfer rockets bracketed the river and banks. Two boats were sunk on the third trip, the survivors managed a fourth, but only one dinghy re-emerged after the fifth attempt, so the Poles had to give up.

Sixteen canvas and plywood assault boats came up with the 43rd Division on the Saturday night. Private Chwastek, aghast at how flimsy they were, waited his turn 'sick to his stomach' as his company crossed beneath the tracer arcs ominously reaching out from the north bank. They appeared to form fiery crosses over hapless boats that appeared to vanish at their touch. There was much delay and confusion and only 250 determined but terrified Poles managed to set off. 'We clearly saw a large, clumsy boat break away from the opposite bank and steadily, quite rapidly move in our direction,' recalled Polish war correspondent Marek Święcicki observing from the perimeter bank. 'Above it spread a coloured, flashing irregular umbrella of twinkling points of light.' These appeared to hover around each boat until finding the correct height before lashing and scything about the dark mass of the boat in spurting fountains of spray, until it disappeared without trace. Święcicki observed:

> 'A large mill on the river's southern bank was ablaze, and the great wings swung impotently and aimlessly. They had a strange, nightmare appearance, like an apocalyptic cross that now rose high into the air, with arrowing straddling arms, then dropped to the dark blue line of the forest.'

This was where the Polish paratroopers were shoving off, lit by the blazing suburbs of Arnhem and Oosterbeek on the opposite bank, an intimidating spectacle for the paratroopers journeying across a mythical River Styx to gain access to the perimeter, 'passing from one fire into another', as wi cicki observed. By morning just six of 14 boats remained. Of the 250 Poles that set off, only 153 – mainly from the 3rd Battalion – actually entered the perimeter.[243]

The Germans rated the Polish contribution to the perimeter far more highly than the British themselves. General Sosabowski's Polish Parachute Brigade was not battle-inoculated and was inserted piecemeal into an unknown and desperate situation with no intelligence. Many of its men had not fought since 1939, an entirely different tactical and technological scenario. Some had not fought at all. Having jumped into a 'hot DZ' at only two-thirds of their strength, they were immediately launched as a rapid reinforcement across a fast-flowing river with inadequate boats, suffering appalling losses in the process. One British Sapper officer on the river bank remembered that 'the Poles did not seem to have any idea where they were meant to go, what they were meant to do, or when they were meant to do it.' The confusion of the river crossing resulted in men, often separated from their commanders, being inserted into the fighting as soon as they arrived. One officer receiving them on the perimeter bank recalled that 'I had to meet them, organise them into squads and send them off with guides to the sections of the perimeter to which they had to go.' Not an easy process. 'It was very unpleasant for we were under fire all the time.' Many did not reach the Stationsweg and Oosterbeek crossroads until nearly the middle of the day on the 24th, completely reliant on guides to negotiate a tangle of unknown sniper-dominated streets under heavy mortar and shellfire.[244]

Captain Gazurek, with soldiers from the Polish 3rd Battalion, arrived at the Oosterbeek crossroads, where the 21st Independent Company was covering the Utrechtseweg from houses at the foot of Stationsweg. British veterans were grateful for any succour, but the cold unforgiving veterans did not rate the survival chances of these fresh arrivals too highly. The unblooded Poles could be overbearing and temperamentally unpredictable, an impression exacerbated by language difficulties. Like the British, who also initially mistrusted the Dutch, ingrained suspicion of Polish collaborators at home played a part. Jan Hol, living in the Stationsweg, remembers the language problem, recalling that they were 'tough fanatical men who kept themselves to themselves'. An exasperated Sergeant Ron Kent with the Independent Parachute Company recalled that 'the Poles tended to stand around in large groups quite oblivious of the danger from snipers and took ten casualties in this way in as many minutes.' For their part, the sensitive Poles thought the British condescending. Prevented from assisting a burning Warsaw, they were instead hastily inserted into a suspected trap. Then they were suddenly launched into a hotly contested perimeter following an ineptly conducted and costly river crossing. Little wonder that the Poles hardly felt reassured that they were part of a considered team enterprise.

Captain Gazurek haughtily brushed aside the advice of his guide, Private Harold Bruce, that he should get down to ground level for his own safety.

'A Polish officer does not crawl in front of the enemy,' he retorted, and was promptly felled by a single shot as he walked through a garden gate. Lance Corporal Kuzniar behind him was shocked to see his helmetless head lying on a stump, the skull laid open by a bullet. Gazurek's grisly jaw moved twice before the fiery captain expired. This was the familiar instructor, who had never permitted the Polish paratroopers to remove their uncomfortable helmets during training. Bruce gave up pointing out the German positions when a sniper's bullet pierced his groin. It was deflected by a shilling piece in one trouser pocket into another in his smock that contained a hand grenade, which shattered without exploding. Two grenades fell from the same pocket, also without exploding. Bruce lay prostrate, panting with shock, with grenade splinters in his thigh and hands and a bullet wound to the groin, but still alive, his third close call with death.[245]

It was to prove a similar predicament for Poles arriving on the west side of the perimeter, in the Borderer positions. At dawn on 22 September B Company positions next to the Lower Rhine were alerted by a call: 'Don't shoot, we're Poles!' They held their fire and 20 reinforcements who had crossed the river during the night came through their positions, the first tangible indication of relief. Sadly, by mid-morning 16 of them had become casualties, most caught by a particularly fierce morning 'hate' of German mortar and shellfire. The exasperated Borderers could not understand why the new arrivals would not immediately dig slit trenches for cover.[246]

Once established, the Poles were bitter and uncompromising fighters. 'They fought like demons,' remarked one British officer. 'They didn't have to be told to get snipers, they just went out after them and got them.' German soldiers taking for granted the protection afforded by Red Cross flags around the Schoonoord and Vreewijk hotels on the Utrechtseweg were taken under fire by Lieutenant Kowalczyk's 3rd Battalion men on the Stationsweg. Any armed German taking liberties with the Laws of Armed Conflict was picked off as fair game by the Polish paratroopers, and a vigorous fire was directed at any field-grey or mottled SS camouflage that exposed itself. Little time was taken in the heat of battle to differentiate whether the objects being carried were stretchers or Mausers. German soldiers who had insistently poked their weapons from the crossroads dressing stations, despite protests from the British medical orderlies, pulled them back in abruptly on hearing the word 'Poles'.

Hauptsturmführer Hans Möller detected 'the grimace of the east' when 'the nature of the fighting drastically changed when a Polish unit was committed opposite my 1st Company under Steinart.' Möller described that they fought under the 'Poland is not lost yet' motto, which was a German Landser euphemism for 'cheer up' in an especially bleak situation. The Poles were bad news, with their 'distorted mask of sheer violence, never willing to display fairness,' he complained. They were an uncomfortable reminder of the uncompromising realities of the Russian front because the Poles 'fought with such a cruelty and hatred that it became impossible to recover the wounded and dead from the combat zone'. The SS hated Poles with a venom that was heartily reciprocated. They added uncertainty to what had been a previously predictable outcome of the fighting on the Utrechtseweg. The British were receiving reinforcements – how long did they have to reduce the pocket before the ground forces arrived? 'The Red Cross did not mean anything to them!' declared a clearly exasperated Möller. 'Several of my engineers who tried to help their wounded mates had to pay for this with their lives.'

'I remember a wounded machine gunner,' recalled Rottenführer Wolfgang Dombrowski, fighting on the street.

'We waved a white flag and two stretcher-bearers went forward to get him. They were immediately fired upon and disappeared ashen-faced into a house. What's the matter with them? Have they lost their nerve? It was all right to pick them up before now!'

Try as they might, they could not get near the wounded man. 'The Poles fired at him and kept the medics at bay until he was dead.' Having fallen behind a wall, he could not be dragged out. 'As far as the Poles were concerned, you could forget fairness,' recalled Dombrowski. They were an unforgiving enemy. 'You didn't take any chances with the Poles.' To deal with an occupied house, they approached with boots wrapped in rags to deaden the sound. 'Once the house was surrounded, hand grenades would go in from all sides until they had had enough.'[247]

Unknown to the British, the Polish arrivals had a disproportionate impact upon the extent of the German squeeze on the perimeter. Very few penetrated as far as the street, but they did preserve the tenuous British hold on it for a few days longer. Many of the Poles, bitter at not defending Warsaw and finding it difficult to communicate with their reserved Allies, died a lonely death. Flying Officer Reginald Lawton, a shot-down Stirling navigator sheltering in the grounds of the Hotel Hartenstein on the Utrechtseweg, recalled that 'among the inhabitants of our little group of trenches was one Pole'. He had the deepest trench of all and was enduring the battle in isolation, probably unable to speak with anyone:

'He was down there with two or three 24-hour ration packs, and was never seen to come up. Unfortunately for him, he was one of the unlucky ones, for he was hit badly.'[248]

Cutting out the 'sore thumb': Utrechtseweg east

On the morning of 22 September Brigadier 'Shan' Hackett, commanding the east side of the perimeter, was surprised to discover that the last survivors of the 10th Parachute Battalion had managed to hold on to some of the houses east of the Schoonoord dressing station. None of their officers were left. Nearly all the houses had been demolished by short-range shellfire from Möller's assault guns. The crossroads on the Utrechtseweg was vital ground. Möller had identified that 'the enemy had established a blocking position, especially in front of and around the Hartenstein Hotel, which was a little further away on the left of the Utrechtseweg.' A breakthrough here could overrun the Airborne Division headquarters, still unknown to him, and split the perimeter in two. Hackett therefore decided to replace

Some of the heaviest fighting along the street occurred at the Oosterbeek crossroads. For two days the 'sore thumb' position protruded into the German line until cut off and eliminated by the Germans on the 24th.

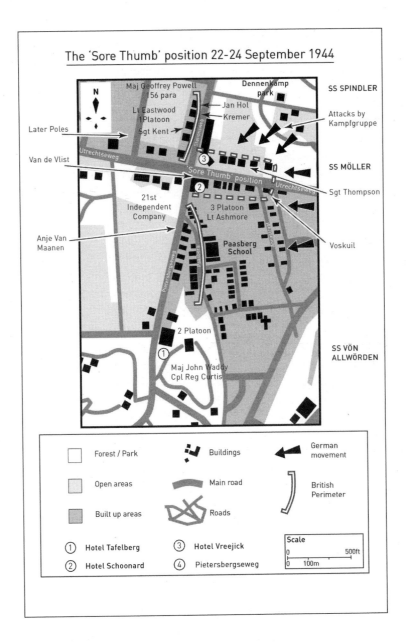

The 'Sore Thumb' position 22-24 September 1944

N

Maj Geoffrey Powell 156 para

Dennenkamp park

SS SPINDLER

Lt Eastwood 1 Platoon

Jan Hol
Kremer

Attacks by Kampfgruppe

Later Poles

Sgt Kent

Utrechtseweg

Van de Vlist

③

'Sore Thumb' position

SS MÖLLER

Utrechtseweg

②

Sgt Thompson

21st Independent Company

3 Platoon
Lt Ashmore

Anje Van Maanen

Paasberg School

Voskuil

2 Platoon

①

Maj John Waddy
Cpl Reg Curtis

SS VÖN ALLWÖRDEN

Forest / Park

Buildings

German movement

Open areas

Main road

British Perimeter

Built up areas

Roads

① Hotel Tafelberg
② Hotel Schoonard

③ Hotel Vreejick
④ Pietersbergseweg

Scale
0   500ft
0   100m

the virtually destroyed 10th Battalion with the 21st Independent Parachute Company under Major Bernard 'Boy' Wilson. Wilson strongly objected to occupying such a vulnerable position, but was overruled by Hackett.

'The company's casualty rate increased considerably after moving into the houses,' recalled Sergeant Ron Kent. They were just 'east of the crossroads,' he remembered, 'in a position that was becoming more and more isolated as it stuck out from the edge of the perimeter like a sore thumb.' It was at the mercy of marauding half-track self-propelled guns. 'It seemed that every house the company occupied received one or more shells from these guns during the day.'

No 3 Platoon under Lieutenant Hugh Ashmore had taken over the 'sore thumb' position during the drizzly dawn of 23 September. Private Dan Hobbs, occupying one of the houses on the Dennenkamp side, muttered an apology on finding the upstairs toilet occupied. On going back he found on closer inspection that there was a dead paratrooper seated on the loo, probably from the 10th Battalion. A missile had come through the back wall and exited his body through the toilet door, killing him instantly – not a good omen. Ashmore was backed up by Lieutenant David Eastwood's 1st Platoon occupying the southernmost houses on the Stationsweg. 2 Platoon, under Lieutenant Joe Speller, completed the defence triangle, defending the school and houses along the Paasberg, south of the street. The most exposed house was 'Quatre Bras', No 2 Stationsweg, because with a Bren in the trench outside it covered the visible length of the Utrechtseweg. As such it attracted the most intense enemy fire. Private Tommy McMahon, well appreciating this, dumped the 'Welcome' mat just inside the front door, announcing, 'I don't think we want them to see this.' 'This began a grim day for the whole company,' Ron Kent recalled.

Each house normally sited a Bren gun, lurking in the gloomy interior behind a first-floor window, behind furniture and rolled carpets piled up against the forward walls. Section snipers were up in the attic, watching the rear gardens alongside riflemen in upstairs rooms spotting for him with more Bren gun teams. The Bren, stably mounted on a bipod, was also an exceptionally accurate single-shot weapon. Down below, men with Sten guns covered entry points at doors and windows. Decorator's stepladders were often pressed into service for soldiers to man observation points through half-opened skylights. Virtually every strongpoint had trenches dug in the surrounding gardens. Hackett had already identified that 'houses are a snare unless you can keep the self-propelled and anti-tank guns at arm's length and round the corner.' The German tactic was to reduce houses to rubble, then infiltrate with infantry. 'Frequent destruction of houses meant frequent breakages of weapons,' Hackett pointed out, 'and there were no replacements.'[249]

Obersturmbannführer Walter Harzer, commanding the 9th SS Hohenstaufen Kampfgruppe, was feeding in ever more reinforcements to the battle as they arrived. Panzer Abteilung 506, equipped with Königstiger 'King Tiger' tanks, was anticipated to arrive by rail on 22 September and would be ready to administer a coup de grâce within 48 hours of unloading. The night before, elements of the Pioneer Lehr Battalion, an engineer training unit from Glogau in the Reich, was landed by Ju 52 transport aircraft at Deelen airfield just to the north. These especially trained assault pioneers equipped with flame-throwers were parcelled among the three SS Kampfgruppen attacking west to east along and south of the Utrechtseweg. Other engineer detachments had already been earmarked to join them.

Twenty-one-year-old sapper Wolfgang Dinkel had hastily been incorporated into Pioneer (Engineer) Battalion 26 at Höxter and taken by lorry to Kleve near the Ruhr. He did not even know his new company commander, Leutnant Andel. He hastily dashed off a quick note to his parents in Stuttgart-Bad-Cannstatt, to let them know he was going into action:

> 'My old company, which was raised with great difficulty in Stablack, has so to speak fallen apart. Yesterday a company was hurriedly cobbled together in Höxter and sent west. I belong to this new combat company, which will be deployed at the front very shortly. We can already hear the sound of artillery and machine gun fire from the western front.'

He had formed up and reformed with a strange unit inside 24 hours. Another soldier, an Austrian Sapper, Josef Forstner, was also hastily included within Dinkel's company. He too hastily wrote home. 'Dearest Parents…'

> 'Must quickly scribble a few sad lines to you, am since yesterday in the Ruhr area. Today the 22nd [September] at 6 o'clock this evening we leave to do battle in house-to-house and street fighting. So, if these are the last lines, again a thousand best wishes. Your Josef.'

These were indeed his last lines. Leutnant Anders's engineer company was to be incorporated within the SS Kampfgruppe Harder's thrust into the eastern suburbs of Oosterbeek.[250]

On 23 September German attacks came crashing into the 'sore thumb' position, in an attempt to break the impasse at the east end of the street. Möller recalled that the 'Kampfgruppe Spindler to my left with its recently reformed battle groups, Von Allwörden and Harder, near the edge of the Lower Rhine started to attack on the entire front towards Oosterbeek.' They were liberally supported by tanks and self-propelled guns. 'During these fights the Engineer battalion got ahead quite well initially.' Left of the Utrechtseweg Möller remarked that 'the Tafelberg and Schoonoord hotels were well within reach of Schmatz's 2nd Company and Linker's 3rd Company sectors.' They had to pause to avoid friendly-fire confrontations 'as they might be drawn into our own field of fire and into the main line of resistance'. While tanks and self-propelled guns stood off and blasted entry holes for the assault pioneers, Möller's half-tracks roared up and down the road, peppering doors and windows with heavy cannon.

Lieutenant Hugh Ashmore's platoon was overwhelmed by the superior barrage, and suffered heavy casualties trying to fight back with stuttering small arms fire. The self-propelled guns trundled up and began to systematically reduce each house to rubble. Corporal Bill Price in the Burgerlust Hotel next to No 186 Utrechtseweg found that if he stayed on all fours the shells simply shrieked overhead. He considered crawling inside one of the large sturdy ovens for protection, only to see it disintegrate before his eyes. Showers of stick grenades heralded the approach of infiltrating infantry, and bitter room-to-room fighting developed. Outside trenches saved men from being completely trapped by armoured vehicles shooting in with their accompanying infantry. One tank drove into the garden fronting the Utrechtseweg, firing continually with its hull machine gun, but the crew were unable to depress the muzzle to ground level. Ashmore's platoon was severely mauled, suffering 14 casualties before the men were finally ejected from the houses.

Sergeant Ron Kent, receiving the overflow of attacks on the Stationsweg, was powerless to assist his pals defending Nos 155 and 153 on the highly vulnerable Dennenkamp side of the Utrechtseweg. 'Sergeant Jerry Thompson, with the remains of his section, rushed wild-eyed into No 1 Section's position, without helmet and looking for Germans.' His blood was up:

> 'He had been blasted out of his house by SP guns on the main road. The house had literally been brought down about his ears. Before leaving, Jerry hurled a Gammon bomb of his own concoction into a mob of Germans, who in arrogant confidence had entered his garden. Jerry had killed a lot of Germans and now, quite berserk, was looking for more.'

He was killed later that day. Many of the platoon had died or been 'put in the bag,' Kent announced, 'and the "sore thumb" position that the 10th Battalion had previously established was snuffed out.' The line had been straightened behind the Hotel Schoonoord, which was overrun again. The core defence was now along the Stationsweg, north of the street at the crossroads, and the school and cluster of houses along the Paasberg to the south.

The two German PK (Propaganda Kompanie) photographers, Jacobsen and Wenzel, had trailed Möller's advance up the Utrechtseweg, taking pictures of the British wounded being evacuated from the Vreewijk and later the Schoonoord hotels. They took images of paratroopers, hands in the air, being quickly disarmed and questioned behind an advancing Sturmgeschütz assault gun. Jacobsen took one iconic photo of the stationary armoured vehicle, its commander grinning broadly into the camera; a 'happy snap' with splashes of blood in the foreground on the street and a discarded 75mm shell case lying where it had been ejected onto the cobblestones. 'We're winning' was the obvious slant of the propaganda shot.

Wounded Company Sergeant Major George Gatland watched from a window in the Schoonoord as the assault gun drew up and lurched to a halt outside. 'The turret hatch opened and a German poked his head out and began taking pictures of the Schoonoord.' It was bizarre. 'He couldn't have clicked off more than one or two when there was a burst of fire, a Bren, and he slumped over.' Was this Jacobsen or Wenzel? A sequential examination of their frames appears to suggest Wenzel may not have taken any more pictures after the preceding scenes of destruction and the evacuations. Gatland watched the camera clatter off the assault gun and hit the ground. 'The tank withdrew with the German still hanging on top of the turret.' Gatland, propped up against the chimney inside the Schoonoord, found that he could stare right into the lens of the fallen camera.[251]

Dutchman H. van Veelen, helping inside the Schoonoord dressing station, remembered that 'some of the wounded who were brought in looked dreadful' with 'deep flesh wounds from shrapnel, huge gunshot wounds, broken arms and legs, and torn-off limbs.' The building was already considerably damaged. 'The rooms on the first floor were hit,' Van Veelen recalled, and 'the casualties lying there were wounded again, sometimes more seriously, or even killed.' Hendrika van der Vlist, the hotel owner's daughter, remembered bodies 'lying in our garage, in a row, one beside the other'. An overflow was created 'on the lawn behind our house'. Desperate fighting around the 'sore thumb' position outside was both heard and felt inside the hotel. 'All the time the din is so heavy that we keep the blackout as long as possible in front of the windows,' she recalled, as 'it helps to prevent the shell splinters and glass from coming in.' Sergeant Major Gatland remembers the wounded being reduced to lying 'apprehensively on their stretchers or mattresses with their blankets drawn over their heads', as many were killed. 'It was sheer unrelieved hell.' They were completely helpless. 'The only thing we could do when we were lying in the Schoonoord was talk, and I will tell you many stories went around.'

When the Germans overran the hotel for the final time they posted armed guards at the windows. 'This resulted in the fact that the MDS was shot at, in spite of the Red Cross signs,' Gatland recalled, and 'the man next to me was shot in the head and killed instantly.' Inside, the Dutch helped where they could. Gatland recalled a white-haired old lady who came round with a china cup with water when the fighting decreased. 'She was shaking so badly, the water splashed all over the men.' The battle flowed all around. Once Allied artillery began firing into the pocket, they knew relief was close, 'but they never came,' Gatland reflected. 'I'd wake up in the morning expecting the Second Army to be there, but they never were.' The situation of the wounded steadily deteriorated. 'Colour had drained from their faces, from which it had not recently been possible to remove the stubble. Their eyes were red-rimmed and bloodshot,' he recalled. 'I wonder what I must have looked like.' They lay and endured the stench 'from the urine buckets, pus-soaked dressings and sweat-soiled clothes'. All they seemed to talk about was, 'Where was the Second Army? When would they come? How much longer could this go on?'[252]

Company Sergeant Major James Stewart from the Independent Company used to take advantage of the lax German security around the dressing station. 'We were very short of ammunition,' he recalled, 'and used to creep along and see if we could whip any,' because it was always left outside when the wounded were taken in. He turned up on the Thursday 'to see if there were any British wounded well enough to sneak out.' Unfortunately this time he was jumped by two Germans as he walked in:

'There was nothing for it but to hand over my rifle, which I did to one of them. To the other I gave my grenade, but as I pulled it out of my belt I pulled the pin out. I knew what I was doing, so I had 3 seconds advantage over them. We all dived. The two Germans were killed, but I wasn't even wounded.'

By this stage of the battle fortune favoured the canny and quick – the others were dead. Anje van Maanen remembered a huge refrigerator opposite their house near the Hotel Tafelberg. 'At any hour of the day and night you could see a man and a woman sitting in it, arms around each other, and the door ajar.' Whatever it took to stay alive, she reflected. 'It is not without a touch of humour, in spite of all the misery.'[253]

Having cut out the 'sore thumb' position, Hauptsturmführer Möller's Engineer battalion awaited the outcome of the intense conflict going on to the south, 'where the entire left wing all the way to the banks of the Rhine, Von Allwörden and Harder, were engaged in heavy fighting.' Attacks were going in against the Hotel Tafelberg, just 250 yards from his positions on the Utrechtseweg:

> 'The noise of battle was coming back to us, especially near the banks of the Rhine where the fight raged on unabated. There were gun reports and impacts. When they were farther away they sounded dull, but very often they were damned close, leaving the broken windows vibrating. The hectic chatter of machine guns and reports of hand grenades bore testimony of bitter fighting.'[254]

Twenty-one-year-old Wolfgang Dinkel and Sapper Josef Forstner, who hours before had scrawled quick notes to their parents, were both killed outside No 7 Ploegseweg by a shell blast, quite likely from a medium artillery shell fired from Nijmegen. Some 16 days later Leutnant Anders notified Frau Dinkel that her son 'died a hero's death'. This was scant consolation, because her other son Lothar had just been declared missing in Normandy. 'One of my best soldiers,' Anders had written, part of the standard phraseology offered to all the grieving parents by the over-taxed company commander. 'He gave his life,' Anders routinely concluded, 'for his loved ones at home, for his beloved Führer, and for the Fatherland of us all.' The Dinkel family were unimpressed with his sentiments. Contrary to popular practice, the standard words 'Gefallen für Führer, Volk, und Vaterland' were omitted from Wolfgang's obituary text. The local newspaper dared not do this, so the Dinkel obituary was published in a Kunzelsau paper 100 kilometres away on 13 November 1944. With the war so clearly lost, his parents were less prepared to accept meaningless sacrifices.[255]

The situation of the helpless patients in the Hotel Tafelberg, coming under these fresh attacks, was if anything worse than that of the occupants of the Schoonoord. Corporal Reg Curtis, wounded earlier with 1 Para, remembers that two English medics and a Dutch nurse were killed tending patients. He had a disturbing grandstand view of the fighting 'through a gaping hole in the wall, where once was a window' at the rear of the hotel:

> 'I noticed the ominous sound of an approaching tank; I couldn't see it, but the squeaking of its caterpillar wheels grew ever louder as it trudged and edged nearer.'

It was feeling its way, moving from right to left until it changed direction, coming into view at 150 yards, creeping inexorably forward to within 100 yards of the hotel.

> 'I went quite cold. The SP gun slewed around and came to rest for what seemed hours instead of minutes. I appeared to be face-to-face with this awesome-looking gun. Its gargantuan barrel was pointing right at me. The gun bellowed out – I froze and shut my eyes.'

The shell shrieked so close by that 'I certainly felt the draught as it sallied by. Sod that, I thought,' and he called for a medic to move him to a safer place.[256]

Major John Waddy, wounded with 156 Para, was operated on lying on the Tafelberg billiard table, and wounded again afterwards. Like most of the dressing stations in the shrinking perimeter 'we were in fact being shot over and shot through'. When the Germans broke in they set up firing positions against the glider pilots that were defending further on.

'Conditions were pretty basic' and got worse, he remembered. With no water or food 'the only water could be got from putting buckets out in the garden and waiting for it to rain.' Now they were behind the line and occasionally subjected to their own artillery fire from Nijmegen. 'Mediums,' Waddy recalled, 'and boy is that heavy.'

> 'We got another direct hit on the room and the German who had been firing from the window was killed. I woke up; half the room had collapsed. There was a glider pilot who'd had both his legs broken in a glider smash on the first day and I'd never heard anybody scream so much because the explosion had lifted up a piano and had dropped it on his broken legs. Anyway, the house caught on fire and we were pulled out.'

He ended up in the garden lying next to a pile of 30 bodies, which were all the men that had been removed from the dressing station who had died of their wounds. The situation of the wounded on the east side of the perimeter was becoming untenable. After tortuous negotiations between the British and German medical staffs, a 2-hour ceasefire was negotiated for Sunday 24 September, to get them out.[257]

Hans Möller had already visited the Schoonoord dressing station with his Division Surgeon, SS Sturmbannführer Egon Skalka. He discovered paratroopers lying next to German soldiers amid civilians and was to be haunted by 'feverish, sometimes fearful eyes expressing a silent, yet urgent questioning' that followed him around the room. His Pioneer Battalion 9 was the unit responsible for the strict adherence to the ceasefire along the length of the Utrechtseweg, his sector. At 15.00 the convoy decorated with white and red cross flags that had passed through his lines that morning moved through under escort to begin the recovery of the wounded.

The ceasefire was viewed with distrust by both sides. Major 'Boy' Wilson, defending just behind the Schoonoord with the 21st Independent Pathfinder Company, was reluctant but ordered to participate. One of the British medical officers had been required to pass on a German threat to blast a house 30 yards from the dressing station with two tanks, ostentatiously trundled forward, if Wilson did not vacate the position. 'Major Wilson did not take kindly to this threat,' Sergeant Ron Kent recalled. 'The house was, he considered, vital to the company's position.' One of the tanks was hit in the rear by a PIAT, which set off an ammunition fire, which settled the argument and the other withdrew. The ceasefire passed off 'observed from 15.00 to 17.00 as agreed,' recalled Möller, 'even though a few isolated shots rang out here and there.'[258]

An eerie silence descended on the street. 'We checked our watches and it became quiet,' Wolfgang Dombrowski recalled. 'A corridor was set up,' he remembered, 'and the truce was only valid within this corridor – fighting still occurred around it.' Both sides were not averse to deriving advantage where they could. Major 'Boy' Wilson was convinced the Germans would seek to improve their tactical positions. Despite the chivalrous treatment of the wounded, British stretcher-bearers from the Schoonoord were not averse to quickly scooping up German soldiers brought down at favoured sniper spots, so as not to warn unsuspecting future customers. When the German ambulances lined up, Captain Colin Harkers recalled that 'one of my troops drew my attention to the fact that the drivers were congregated outside our fences looking into our slit trenches.' They were also seen smoking Senior Service cigarettes from air-dropped tobacco tins. 'After further discussion,' he remembered, 'we went outside and indicated to the Germans that they were our property and to hand them over.' To their surprise 'we got three reasonably full tins – that made our day!' Hendrika van der Vlist, assisting inside the Schoonoord, noticed a group of German soldiers peering excitedly through the windows. 'In the distance they could see their enemies crossing the road,' discussing what they might do. 'They wanted to fire at them,' she recalled. 'They were boys of 17, 18 at most.' She reminded them about the wounded.[259]

Hans Möller remembered that 'it was deeply moving for all concerned to see how a seemingly endless column of wounded was taken through the Utrechtseweg by shuttle vehicles to the St Elizabeth Hospital.' The time came for Sergeant Major George Gatland to be moved. 'Silence. It was strange,' he recalled. As the man next to him was taken away 'we looked at each other, smiled and waved goodbye, but we didn't say a word. I felt a lump in my throat.' It was deeply frustrating for the British pathfinders to watch as 250 walking wounded started to make their way down the street towards Arnhem, especially when an injured friend was spotted in the painfully moving procession. 'A melancholy sight,' remembered Ron Kent. Möller became sentimental, relieved that 'the wounded and mangled people could receive qualified treatment.' Lives had undoubtedly been saved. 'Why do you wage war?' one distressed Dutchman asked him. 'Is it really necessary?' Möller could afford to be sentimental – they were winning. A more hardbitten Wolfgang Dombrowski echoed the opinion in the ranks. 'The pause to hand over the wounded really emphasised what a nonsense war is,' he reflected. The soldiers were more philosophical:

> 'The British paratroopers came out. Words were exchanged and a few cigarettes thrown across. We had plenty because many of their supplies had landed in our own lines. I looked at them and thought we have never seen each other before, had nothing against them, nor they against us. But then it will start up again.'[260]

Seventeen-year-old Anje van Maanen, assisting at the Tafelberg, was sceptical about the truce. 'If there is no shooting within an area of 200 metres of the hospital grounds they will stop shooting in an hour,' she recalled. 'Of course this is a nonsense,' she irritably declared. 'Nobody would ever find him, so everything goes on like before and the Tafelberg is continuously hit.' Anje was nearing the end of her tether. 'I have lost courage completely,' she admitted to herself. 'I can't bear it any longer, that shellfire and the knowledge that every shell kills.' The inhabitants of the street were hearing about a steady toll of friends, relatives and acquaintances appearing alongside the soldiers in the grimy dressing stations. 'Shall we be killed within the next hour or so and be buried underneath the rubbish and the corpses in the garage?' It made her even question her religion. 'How is it possible that God can allow this hell and why must soldiers like our airbornes die like animals?' She despaired in her isolation, convinced that 'the Germans will kill us all, if not bodily then surely mentally.'

'Those who thought that the 2-hour ceasefire would bring some change or even an end were disappointed,' Möller remembered. 'My 2nd and 3rd Companies stayed put in and around the hotel and hospital area.' The soldiers started to psychologically wind themselves up to fight again. 'Ten minutes before the end of the truce everybody would disappear,' commented Dombrowski. It only required one last effort and the street would be theirs. 'Depending on the situation it would slowly start up,' he recalled, 'or more suddenly as a German attack went in.'

'The Germans have come back!' announced a clearly rattled Anje van Maanen. 'Ausweis Zeigen! Identity papers!' bellowed the German soldiers. Everyone, soldiers, medics, the walking wounded and civilians were lined up against the walls of the Hotel Tafelberg. 'Everybody is panic-stricken, upset and afraid,' Anje remembered. This was her low point, 'the most miserable moment of the whole war,' she confessed. 'The monster, which seemed so far away, has come back. This is unbearable!' The defence of the street was teetering on collapse.[261]

CHAPTER 8

The Agony of the Street

Western Utrechtseweg: Heelsum to Helmische Berg

The earlier imaginary bicycle ride along the length of the street during the summer of 1944 provided insights into the impact of four years of German occupation. Eight days of battle had dramatically transformed this scene, physically and psychologically. To the west, Lippert's SS NCO School Arnheim regiment was lapping at the door of No 250 Utrechtseweg, by the junction with the Van Lennepweg. At the east end, Möller's SS Pioneer Battalion 9 had passed Wil Rieken's house at No 178 Utrechtseweg and had reached No 210, just past the Oosterbeek crossroads. Barely 1,000 yards of the street remained in British hands.

The only way to repeat that summer 1944 journey was to drive a German vehicle or captured English jeep. Parachute containers suspended drunkenly from trees were much in evidence as soon as Heelsum was passed, approaching from the west. Wrecked gliders were visible from the road, strewn across the landing zones to the north of the street. Some were still smouldering, most shot to pieces by successive low-level Luftwaffe fighter sweeps. Young NCO Herbert Kessler with the Hermann Göring Training Regiment recalled that 'by day the soldiers went on discovery tours', sorting through the abundance of treasures hanging from the trees like 'scrumping' for apples. 'The soldiers became their own suppliers and were not dependent on the unit kitchen any longer,' he remembered:

> 'The best and finest tinned foods, things of which one dared only to dream, complemented by cigarettes and chocolate, rained down on us. We even found a folding bicycle and, to make things complete, a copy of the London *Times*. We were flabbergasted.'

There was no clear front line and the vast proportion of this rich harvest had come down in the German-occupied areas.

Opposite the junction with the Wolfheze road was a simple makeshift cross denoting General Küssin's grave and the Arnhem town commander's staff, killed alongside. On Tuesday Padre Arnold Pare had got two German prisoners to bury the three broken bodies retrieved from the shot-up Citroen staff car, abandoned by the roadside. Two upended Lee-Enfield rifles stuck in the ground marked the resting places of Privates Hopwood and Chenell, killed when 3 Para passed by, with one of the first Dutch victims, Mrs van Veelen de Weerdhof. Just beyond the Wolfheze junction was the Koude Herberg crossroads, distinguishable by the destroyed Char B1 flame-thrower tank, which had belonged to Leutnant Siegfried Giesa from Panzerkompanie 224. It stood sentinel outside No 271 Utrechtseweg, next to the Koude Herberg Inn. Any Germans would need to debus from their vehicles at this point and move into the woods on either side of the road, because the way ahead was blocked by C Company the Border Regiment. Nothing could move directly along the street from this point; from here on, it was a free-fire zone. Herbert Kessler had advanced nearby with his 3rd Company. 'The surrounding terrain offered a bleak view with the debris of battle,' he described, with 'dead soldiers and disabled equipment scattered about.'[262]

Striking to any observer advancing along this stretch of the Utrechtseweg would be the amount of artillery fire going into the small area of the perimeter ahead. It extended about 1,000 yards beyond, and 2,000 yards south, down to the Lower Rhine. This small area was regularly ploughed over by 120 heavy German artillery pieces, ranging in calibre from 75mm to a substantial 150mm. In addition, several batteries of medium Allied artillery from XXX Corps's 64th Artillery Regiment were firing from Nijmegen, 10 miles away, ranging in on German positions all around the perimeter. German shells varying in weight from 10 to 43 kilograms were boring into houses inside the perimeter at regular intervals. Home defence static batteries had been towed from the Ruhr with agricultural tractors and wood-burning gas-powered lorries and set up around the perimeter. Father Hermanus Cornelis Bruggeman recalled the arrival of just such a battery on 24 September, near Johannahoeve Farm, 2 kilometres north of the street:

'Suddenly there was a lot of noise and shouting German soldiers. They came with some motorbikes and trucks full of cannons ... and beside the barn they positioned the artillery. They brag that they can fire 16 shells at once. With their coming the peace in the community was over. Everybody felt so uncomfortable with the Germans so close. The elderly were moved into the basement.'[263]

Starting with the arrival of the Flak Brigade under Oberstleutnant Swoboda, all heavy artillery batteries were eventually placed under the command of Artillery Regiment 191, which directed all artillery fire at Harzer's bidding. The guns were ranged in from the woods and copses surrounding the Oosterbeek perimeter and were constantly heard booming in the distance, if not directly seen.

The death and destruction meted out by this concentration of artillery fire was perhaps the primary agony of the street. Two batteries of Nebelwerfer rocket-firing artillery under SS Hauptsturmführer Nickmann from SS Werfer Abteilung 102 could unleash ripple salvos of 18 rounds at 2-second intervals. These launchers would suddenly shoot 72 150mm rockets into any chosen point inside the perimeter. Major Geoffrey Powell, in the Stationsweg, thought the six-barrelled launchers 'vicious' and more frightening than normal 'because they gave such a prolonged warning of their intentions'. From a distance:

'The multiple thump of firing was followed by the whine of the six descending bombs, which rose to a scream before they burst in shuddering patterns around the houses. All the hate of battle seemed to be packed into that scream; each cluster of bombs might have been a sentient being engaged in searching for its own living target among the houses and gardens.'

Robustly constructed houses sheltered them well, 'and the bombs did little more than eat further into our depleted reserves of courage'. The Germans were well aware of the psychological toll the fearsome weapons exacted. 'The whump-whump-whump of the "moaning minnies" was the most frightening experience,' SS-Rottenführer Wolfgang Dombrowski's prisoners told him. 'Many of them emerged from cellars with their nerves shot to pieces.' 'I went to look at a dud unexploded one and wished I had not,' admitted war correspondent Alan Wood in the grounds of the Hartenstein. 'I had not realised before the size of the stuff that was falling on us.' The multiple impacts often generated false gas alarms. Trooper Ray Evans with the Reconnaissance Squadron remembered one excessively smoky barrage around the Hartenstein when somebody blew a whistle. 'We all knew that this was the official signal for gas, but, immediately it sounded, right away someone piped up with the cry "Half-time"!'[264]

The agony of artillery fire was its apparent malicious intent to seek you out, which it would eventually do in the end. Flight Lieutenant Billy Williams, part of the Division PR Team pinned down next to the Hartenstein, remembers that 'I myself dug four slit trenches' of which 'two caved in through shell blast', one was taken over by a Bren gun team in greater need, 'while the fourth received a direct hit by a mortar bomb just before we left'. 'Early on I had my mouth shut viciously by a shell burst,' recalled shot-down Stirling navigator Reginald Lawton. 'I learned to hold something between my teeth, usually one of the small tree-root tendrils that stuck out of the side of the trench.' Many had been chewed in the course of the week, when 'we would spend the next 3 hours or more curled up as small as possible at the bottom of the trench.' 'I haven't words to describe the noise,' explained Bombardier Bob Christie with the 2nd Light Airborne Battery, except:

> 'It got worse and worse. It was difficult to think clearly, never
> mind carry out calculations in the troop command post.'

'From all the surrounding din you soon learned to distinguish the distant "pom-pom-pom" of the particular guns that were ranging on you,' recalled

Lawton. 'You just had time to tighten your fingers in your ears before the scream of the three shells was drowned by the explosions.' These were the sights and sounds of shellfire, pouring in from all directions, apparent to all approaching Oosterbeek via the street from the west.[265]

Just beyond Leutnant Giesa's shot-up tank, standing forlornly beside the road was Netje Heijbroek's house, 'Valkenburg', near the Van Lennepweg. Agony for the Dutch was not knowing what artillery fire could do. Sheltering inside cellars, they could hear but not see. H. van Veelen, a Dutch volunteer assisting at the Schoonoord, remembers rescuing a woman from an inadequate cellar, where a mortar bomb penetrated the roof and exploded. 'At least that's how it seemed to me,' Van Veelen explained. She 'had terrible injuries to the groin area and her hands; her hands had probably been folded in her lap when the explosion occurred.' She lost a lot of blood. 'I don't remember what happened later on or even if she survived.' Cellar life was becoming increasingly grim, once overrun by the Germans on this west side of the street, as Netje recalled:

'With 22 people in the cellar, calls of nature became a big problem. We had a large preserve jar which was full to overflowing after a few days.'

Rain then began to flood into the cellar and 'the mattresses which my mother had got the Germans to fetch in the meantime began to float.' Eventually her mother got the Germans to empty the pot, 'which was then used to catch the rain water'. The thin veneer of civilised convention was starting to slip as survival alone became the overriding concern. The intrusive German occupation finished off any lingering memories of a comfortable domestic existence:

'The Germans had a sumptuous dinner in our dining room; all round the table were easy chairs, and on the table was our beautiful damask tablecloth and the Chinese plates taken from my grandmother's cellar. We had already seen from the cellar stairs that they had slaughtered chickens and rabbits.

Upstairs we found everything in great untidy heaps, plus huge
piles of excrement. Around about, everything was covered
with dust and rubble.'[266]

The family's homely standards appeared to have been irretrievably trashed.

Corporal Jim Swan with C Company the Border Regiment, blocking
the Utrechtseweg, recalled first light on the eighth day:

'Morning with a slight mist and smell of burning and slight
mustiness. We missed our usual barrage of mortar and shells
but had a greeting of small arms fire first. We kept our teeth
clean with chewing small branches on the trees – they kept
the mouth fresh anyway.'

The day before 'A Company on our right seemed to be getting worse
than us.' Peering closely 'you could see the enemy in the distance
through the trees moving towards A Company.' All they were able to do
was fire a few Bren gun magazines in their direction, which was 'slightly
out of range for any real effect'. They were increasingly isolated and
steadily being whittled down by even more casualties, which meant they
could hold less ground. 'We lost contact with D Company on our left,'
he recalled, which meant that 'the Germans could infiltrate the gap and
we had to be on our guard in case we got surrounded.' It had started
raining, which was 'refreshing rather than a nuisance'. Recce patrols
were sent out to restore contact with D Company, but the men were tired,
reduced to 'ambling along, eyes and ears open of course', but still no
contact with D Company. Major Neil, his company commander, insisted
on dispatching fighting patrols to skirmish with the enemy. 'This was
to show that we were stronger than we really were.' All the time they
were under steady unremitting pressure. 'A week gone by and no link-up
yet,' Swan recalled. As soon as there was a lull they sought to get out
of their claustrophobic holes. 'We were just browned off being in slit
trenches and then down came a real stonk.' One of his friends, suspecting
his overhead cover may not be thick enough, was killed in the sudden

barrage. 'It was just a case of taking off his brown ID disc and covering him up beside his trench companion.' The grave was ready-dug, 'rather ironic when you come to think about it now,' he recalled.

Attacks interspersed with violent mortar stonks continued. 'The enemy were shouting and hollering at us all day; they even had a loudspeaker telling us we were doomed, or words to that effect.' Despite the wide gaps at the western wooded end of the Utrechtseweg, the Borderers' line held. Corporal Swan was convinced that they had achieved a form of moral ascendancy over their adversaries, because despite the unsustainable drain of casualties:

> 'Although the Germans got close within grenade-throwing distance, they just seemed to stop and melt away, leaving dead and wounded. We often found some of their grenades, a "potato masher", that had been thrown and failed to explode… The soldiers who were throwing them were not pulling hard enough on the bead at the end of the handle before throwing and they must have been nervous, which gave us a slight boost – that they had a fear of us somehow.'[267]

Standartenführer Michael Lippert could see bright flames and smoke trickling from the burning gasworks to the south of the street, which demarcated his front down by the Lower Rhine. The constricted area of the shrinking perimeter was contributing toward its survival because Lippert, attacking from this west side, commented that 'tactically planned full-scale attacks in this highly critical situation were not possible without endangering our own troops on the other side of the Cauldron, as also the German wounded and prisoners lying inside.' Restraint applied because they could hardly identify the British line. 'The enemy had dug in or had fortified houses and that was where you could hear the shooting.' The advance had stymied into a battle of attrition, 'from street to street, house to house, man against man'. Lippert pointed out that 'it was no longer ordered to achieve great area gains against the bitterly defending enemy.' Besides, there was no point, 'because the end was predictable'.

Lippert's major concern in the west was the growing threat from the Poles on the other side of the river. Heavy weapons behind his front line faced in 'all directions to cover every contingency'. Lippert later admitted that 'it remained a puzzle why the Polish Brigade did not come over the Rhine and attack the Kampfgruppe in the rear.' The German defence at Westerbouwing had repelled the attempted crossing by the Dorsets, spearheading the XXX Corps approach to the river, but Lippert chose not to comment on that achievement. He did point out that the north bank of the Lower Rhine between Heelsum and Wageningen was only held by scraped-together army reservists, 'and a crossing in this sector would have been a walk-over'.[268]

Hardly anyone noticed the final courier pigeon released from the 1st Border Battalion Headquarters just off the street. Lieutenant Joe Hardy had flown in with two carrier pigeons, one of which had gone missing with an earlier message. Food was scarce and covetous eyes had lingered over the small remaining bird, regarded more as a meal than communication. Major Cousens, the acting CO, had little to transmit – what was there to say in the midst of a catastrophic situation? Hardy was given carte blanche to write what he wished. 'About 8 tanks laying about in sub-unit areas, very untidy but not otherwise causing much trouble,' he wrote. Unintentionally the final message released by the battalion at 08.00 on 25 September demonstrated that morale was intact. 'Now using as many German weapons as we have British, MG 34s most effective when aimed towards Germany,' it announced; the 'Dutch people have been grand but Dutch tobacco rather stringy' and there was 'a great beard-growing competition in our unit, but no time to check up on the winner.' The bird miraculously made it back to Corps Headquarters, where it became a nine-day wonder.[269]

Central Utrechtseweg: Hartenstein to Weverstraat

The road ran straight on from the Van Lennepweg C Company block on the Utrechtseweg to the Hartenstein Laan, where the road bends in front of the Hotel Hartenstein. Beyond was a continuous straight road, past the Oosterbeek crossroads, running eastwards towards Arnhem. No vehicle or person on foot could negotiate this section of the street unscathed.

Lieutenant John Christie's wrecked Reconnaissance Squadron jeep outside the Hartenstein bore mute testimony to this fact and the need to be wary. Five days earlier Lieutenant Colonel Charles Mackenzie, General Urquhart's senior staff officer, had watched the drama unfold. Standing on the road he witnessed 'a loud explosion on the vehicle', but had no idea where it had come from. 'Whatever it was, it struck Christie full in the chest, and took an arm, as well as part of his shoulder and chest away.' Despite his terrible injuries John Christie staggered to his men nearby, dying in Trooper Bill Bateman's arms as he attempted to comfort him. 'Oh, my God!' he murmured as he expired. 'Oh, my God!'

There was also an overturned German lorry by the roadside, still there when the wounded Brigadier 'Shan' Hackett was evacuated by jeep to the St Elizabeth Hospital. Its demise had been another bizarre drama played out along this stretch of the road. Nobody knew how it had managed to evade the Borderers' block and drive straight down the Utrechtseweg. 'I remember a German supply truck coming up the main road,' recalled Sergeant Ernest Jenkins, dug in at the side of the Hartenstein, 'and the driver seemed suddenly to realise that he was in trouble, so he accelerated.' Until then he had enjoyed a charmed life, but then a 6-pounder anti-tank shell went through the driver and his companion in the cab. They found 'the front seat passenger had had his arm and shoulder blown away, although his hand was still left in his pocket' – a welcome kill because 'we got cigars and black bread from that truck'. Jenkins later witnessed an even odder incident when, shortly behind the lorry, 'a group of Germans came up the same road in marching formation'. The inevitable happened:

> 'Whether they didn't know their way around properly or not I couldn't say, but it was astonishing how everyone just waited and held their fire until the Germans could be taken on with maximum casualties… Then they were scattering in all directions, but mainly up the same road as the lorry had gone.'[270]

The once grand-looking Hotel Hartenstein, on the right of the bend going towards Arnhem, was the Airborne headquarters, the nerve centre of the perimeter. It lay barely 250 yards from the German line to the north, 500 yards from the SS Hohenstaufen Kampfgruppen advancing from the east, and 750 yards from Von Tettau's battle groups bearing down from the west. War correspondent Alan Wood, sheltering in the hotel grounds, pointed out that the 900-yard gap between the two formations on the street meant that 'Germans on our side must be going over our heads and hitting the Germans on the other side and vice versa, so maybe both lots think we are stronger than we are.'

By this stage of the battle the hotel building had been badly battered. 'At first I did not recognise our hotel' recalled Polish war correspondent Marek Święcicki:

> 'I was even inclined to think that at least I had come on it from the wrong side. But there it stood. The comfortable roofs, the soft mattresses, the windows with fine views onto the forest, the flower beds and the road were gone.'

Snipers regularly fired into the doorless hotel vestibule. 'There was rubble in the rooms, window frames with no glass in them hung uselessly, pieces of broken furniture were scattered over the floors.' The once majestic trees surrounding the site had been defoliated and reduced to stumps and the flower bed, with its pseudo-artistic sculpture in the middle, was gone. 'The white walls of the house were covered with a fine and plentiful riddle of holes from bullets and shrapnel.' Alan Wood thought the grounds were 'more like a hot-spot from the last war instead of something from this one.' Trenches were deep and becoming ever more extensive. 'I had seen photographs from the 1914-18 war,' recalled Trooper Ray Evans with the Reconnaissance Squadron, 'and of woodland completely stripped, but I never thought that I should actually see it happen.' Bob Coldicott, in a trench nearby, remembered that 'every tree in our area finished up as clean as a telegraph pole'.[271]

Inside the hotel the division commander, Major General Urquhart, was coordinating the perimeter defence with his two brigade commanders. They planned and considered its prospects, with Germans just a few hundred yards away. This short stretch of the street became vital strategic ground as a consequence, bitterly fought over for nine days. 'I think that greater resolution on the part of the Germans could have finished us off completely,' judged Major 'Boy' Wilson, defending its eastern road block with the much depleted pathfinder company:

> 'They could fire into us from the three sides of the oblong. They had all the space around which to assemble their strength at any one point and they had greater tank and artillery support. Yet they never broke the perimeter.'[272]

The achievement came at considerable cost. 'By day the Hartenstein park was sordid indeed,' remarked Major Geoffrey Powell with the survivors from 156 Para. 'Burned-out trucks and shattered equipment were scattered everywhere among a litter of severed branches and ploughed turf.' Observed from the road were 'heaps of earth' that 'marked the parapets of trenches; other mounds were topped with rough wooden crosses.' Those heaps of earth were manned by glider pilot soldiers. One of them, Sergeant Arthur Shackleton, had worked out that it was safer with 'stone walls around us' rather than a trench, but then found 'it didn't work that way'. Part of his daily routine was to check the line with his commander, Major Toler:

> 'Morning and evening we had to go round the sections of the glider pilots finding out in the morning who were killed during the night, or in the evening who were killed during the day, and making sure that the trenches in their sector were manned. Put in two here, put in two there, so that there was people in the trenches and no gaps.'

This was hazardous because of the need to dodge the constant shelling and mortaring. 'Since then we have both said how frightened we were but daren't show it at the time.'[273]

Everyone who could hold a weapon, including division staff officers with pistols, was taking a hand in the defence of the Hartenstein building.

This included the AFPU team with Sergeants Lewis, Smith and Walker, who had relocated from the Borderers' positions to the west and were sheltering inside the hotel. Smith took several pictures of soldiers with Stens and pistols peering out of windows boarded up with furniture. 'This picture shows the last strongpoint – Div HQ – being defended,' he wrote on his 'dope sheet':

> 'The shelling is hellish. We have been holding out for a week now. The men are tired, weary and the food is becoming scarce, and to make matters worse we are having heavy rains. If we are not relieved soon, the men will just drop from sheer exhaustion.'

One German sniper had his sights on the rear entrance of division headquarters and, apart from provoking strong language among those whose dignity he ruffled, he narrowly missed the division commander. General Urquhart was inside the hotel hall conversing with a staff officer 'when bullets from this familiar foe,' he recalled, 'started pinging into the walls... I had heard earlier reports about his prowess,' Urquhart remembered, and his ability to 'put several shots in one door and out of the other.' Sergeants Gordon Walker and Dennis Smith were sent out to deal with them.

'What we were looking for was the rifle flash as he fired, and on that we would fire back at that position,' Walker recalled. They tried to spot him in the trees from a window at the back. 'The only way we ever knew we was successful,' he remembered, 'was if the firing stopped, when we reckoned we'd got him.' At dusk they had to fetch water from a local well in the woods 200 yards away. 'It was the eeriest experience,' Walker remembered, 'lowering a bucket down the well to get water, expecting a bullet in the back any second.' Such forays were often suddenly interdicted with mortar fire:

> 'I came back under very heavy mortar and shell fire and I dived into a slit trench, which I thought was empty, but it wasn't.

There was a little squirrel in it, so I threw the squirrel out and got in myself. The squirrel came back, bit me and burrowed underneath me. There was the stupid position of me, a soldier, fighting a little squirrel for possession of a slit trench.'

Mortar fire was incessant and remorseless. 'After each bout of shelling there are just one or two killed and one or two stretcher cases to be taken away,' recalled Alan Wood. 'A jeep nearby is blazing… By some freak the shell closed the circuit on the electric horn, so the burning jeep hooted forlornly and continuously for 10 minutes as though it was in pain.' Prospects were looking increasingly bleak.

Sharing their misery were 215 German prisoners caged in the tennis courts at the back of the hotel with ten civilian collaborators. They came from as many as 48 different units. Cameraman Mike Lewis had filmed them forming up for roll-call during the early days. 'Fifty percent were non-German,' he noted on his 'dope sheet', and some 106 were Dutch SS from Helle's Wach Battalion 3, overrun on the Ginkel Heath during the 4th Parachute Brigade's second lift. By now they were in a sorry state. Like the British, having been handed shovels, they were well underground, but with no shortage of complaints. Seven were killed by their own shelling. They were running short of food and the British asked the Germans for more across the lines, but they were told they should take better care of their prisoners.[274]

An enduring agony for British soldiers fighting along the length of the street was to watch the resupply flights flying into the teeth of fierce German flak, to little purpose, as the containers often fell behind German lines. Photographer Sergeant Mike Lewis captured the looks of utter despair on the faces of men waving outstretched supply parachutes in the grounds of the Hotel Hartenstein as they witnessed yet another resupply fiasco. 'Perhaps the crews were so intent on driving through the flak to find the DZ and drop their stores that they never saw the waving men,' assumed Major Geoffrey Powell, or 'they thought that the Germans were trying to mislead them.' Whatever it was, the flurry of opening parachutes was always too far beyond.

From the air the perspective was entirely different. 'Good God, have we got to fly through that!' recalled Flight Sergeant Ken 'Kit' Carson, navigating a 512 Squadron RAF Dakota a few days before. 'You could see where you were to going to go by the trail of flak ahead.' The crews were beginning to appreciate the 'sinister' significance of the flak density, 'which suggested the operation was not going well'. They could clearly see the 88mm flak guns firing up from a great horseshoe shape around the drop zones. Radio operator Flight Lieutenant Stanley Lee, flying the lead Dakota of 512 Squadron, remembered another Dakota 'sticking to our wing tip as if by glue', which was quite disturbing because 'it had a fire in its starboard engine'. Moreover 'the fire was obviously out of control and I could see that the aircraft could not continue to fly for very much longer.' There was no point trying to warn the pilot, who continued along his perilous bearing. 'The fire was so big,' Lee recalled. 'There was no way the pilot could not have been aware that his aircraft was on fire.'

Down below on the Stationsweg 'even the enemy mortars had stopped shooting,' Powell realised, and regardless of the danger his men 'were on their feet, waving their weapons or helmets, or the small yellow squares issued for the purpose, trying to attract the attention of the pilots.' 'We did our best to show them where to drop,' remembered downed Stirling navigator Reginald Lawton on the Utrechtseweg, even firing yellow Very cartridges, 'but it was heartbreaking to see the containers begin to fall long before they were over us.'

Veteran BBC war correspondent Stanley Maxted actually made a sound recording of such a drop from his slit trench in the Hartenstein park. 'Everybody is cheering and clapping and they just can't give vent to their feelings about what a wonderful sight this is,' he reported, because he could see some containers drifting down on target. 'All those bundles and parachuted packages and ammunition are coming down around us, through the trees, bouncing on the ground, the men are running out to get them.' His actuality recording was to be one of the most dramatic BBC sound bites to emerge from the Arnhem battle:

'You can hear the kind of flak that those planes are flying through, it's absolutely like …[noise of flak]… hail up there.

> These enemy guns all around us are just simply hammering
> at those planes, but so far I haven't seen anything, I haven't
> seen any of them hit, but the bundles are coming down, the
> parachutes are coming down …[noise of planes and flak].'

Geoffrey Powell, like everyone else, including the Germans, was watching the lone Dakota flaming like a bright torch. Everyone could see the khaki-clad RASC dispatchers in the open doorway, already too low to jump, pushing out panniers of supplies. 'I could see their faces,' Powell recalled. 'The fire was on their side of the plane; the wing was burning before their eyes.' General Urquhart remembered that hundreds of soldiers stopped what they were doing to gaze skyward. 'We were spellbound and speechless,' he recalled, 'and I daresay there is not a survivor of Arnhem who will ever forget, or want to forget, the courage we were privileged to witness in those terrible 8 minutes.' Powell watched the starboard wing crumple and 'the flaming plane disappeared beyond the trees, the panniers still falling from the open door.' Anje van Maanen, looking up from the Pietersbergscheweg opposite the Hotel Tafelberg saw a burning aeroplane. 'Those RAF boys are great,' she wrote in her diary:

> 'One aeroplane leads, the rest follows, the first one drops his
> stores and the rest have to do the same, on the same spot, and
> this of course is an easy target for the Germans.'

Watching from above, Flight Lieutenant Lee saw only one white parachute come out, just one survivor from seven amid the coloured supply parachutes. The aircraft appeared to slow down and falter, then he saw a terrible spectacle as it 'quite slowly folded in two'. In seeming slow motion 'the two wing tips came up to meet each other and just as they touched the starboard wing broke off.' The wreck crashed into the ground just beyond the railway embankment north of the street, by Reijers-Camp farm, the scene of the earlier catastrophic 4th Parachute Brigade retreat. The pilot, Flight Lieutenant David Lord, was awarded a posthumous Victoria Cross. Harry Chatfield, a pilot in the same squadron, was to later wryly comment:

'You always think of the poor buggers in the back – they did not have a ruddy chance, and they did not get a medal. The ruddy pilot gets something, but the others in the back get nothing.'

Powell watched the place where the Dakota had vanished long after the last plane had gone, 'mourning the futility of the self-sacrifice we had just witnessed'. Of about 1,500 tons dropped, the division recovered only 200 tons, at a cost of 66 transport aircraft lost and 345 men, of whom 222 were killed and 123 taken prisoner.[275]

The enduring agony for the Dutch on the street, pinned between the constricting perimeter, was a dangling hope for eventual Liberation, which the disastrous supply flights and punishing Allied artillery firing from Nijmegen pitifully sustained. 'When will Monty come?' was an enduring conversation in dimly lit cellar interiors. The British, never occupied during the war, were unable to appreciate the significance of the emerging reverse staring them all in the face. One of the Independent Company soldiers asked Mrs Kremer at No 8 Stationsweg 'if the things they had heard about the Germans were really true.' Ans Kremer, one of the daughters, recalled that 'mother started to explain, but the soldier couldn't believe it'. Hans Rosenfeld, really John Rodley, one of the native-born anti-Nazi Germans serving in the company, angrily responded, 'Don't even bother to try to explain – they'll never understand.' Gloom at their prospects was exacerbated by the awful destruction. Eighteen-year-old J. A. van Hofwegen at No 154 Weverstraat had watched as all his mother's crockery was smashed inside their small glass-covered cabinet. 'Should we have been sitting there, we would at least have been wounded,' he recalled. Shellfire burst a hole in the roof 'and standing in the hall we could see the clouds' so that 'in the hall it rained just as hard.' A black horse, having fled the pastures near the river, pathetically stumbled by the back of the house. 'Her neck was bleeding and part of her front leg was hanging off.' She collapsed and died just beyond the house. Soldiers tried to comfort them. 'Tomorrow the Second Army will be here,' they said. 'Listen, that is the sound of their guns in the distance.'[276]

The British themselves were coming to terms with the reality of their situation. 'We kept on saying, when are XXX Corps coming?' recalled

Private Johnny Peters with the Borderers, 'and an officer said, "Oh they'll be here tomorrow," and again "be here tomorrow" and that's all we heard and tomorrow never came.' Anje van Maanen angrily wrote in her diary:

'The English still say "Monty comes soon!" Are they really so naïve to think that we still believe that? I wonder, or do they believe it, or do they just say it, to comfort us? And suddenly I furiously think, "That blasted Monty, he can have the measles, why does he not come to relieve these poor chaps who fight themselves to death?"'

It was all too much. 'It makes me very cross.'[277]

The Hotel Schoonoord was immediately distinguishable on the street just beyond the Oosterbeek cross roads with its fluttering Red Cross flags. Outside was the wreckage of a civilian Ford car that had been driven up by two Dutch volunteers to deliver water in milk churns. It was hit by a German mortar bomb. H. van Veelen, a volunteer working inside, saw it 'immediately transformed into a ball of fire':

'The driver, who was wearing a leather suit, rolled out of the car but he must have been killed instantly. He burned like a torch. Someone else came out through the rear door, also enveloped in flames. One of the RAMC men, who was standing at the front of the Schoonoord as I was, had the presence of mind to throw a blanket over the stumbling man, thus smothering the flames.'

The suddenness of the catastrophe, the explosion and piercing screams had paralysed Van Veelen. 'I just stood there as if my feet were nailed to the ground.'

Hendrika van der Vlist regarded the same scene much later, peering from behind one of the hotel curtains. 'Big boughs are lying on the ground,' she remembered. 'The jagged stumps of the trees point towards the sky and at every explosion leaves whirl down.' She looked at the wreckage of the Ford. Wim Gerritsen, the boy who survived, was upstairs. 'He has lost the sight of one eye. The other eye is also wounded. Will it heal?' Outside the partly burned body of the driver was still lying in the garden, where a thick chestnut tree had been split in two by the shellfire. She looked around the crossroads and the Stationsweg opposite, the British front line:

> 'How on earth is it possible that all the houses around us are still standing? Yes, they are there, but they look like different houses. No human being is seen behind the broken windowpanes of course; the inhabitants are in their cellars. Tatters of curtains are fluttering outside, like phantoms. Shutters are hanging askew, there are holes in the walls. The roofs have been hit and damaged. Broken tiles are lying on the ground.'[278]

Little is generally seen during street fighting. Hundreds of combatants disappear in an urban environment as they take cover and covertly move between countless rooms, nooks and crannies. Attackers are obliged to break cover more often than defenders. Trapped inside their cellars, the civilian inhabitants of the street had psychologically transitioned from accepting destruction to the realisation that they were down to simply surviving. Above them British soldiers were fighting and dying, and not always in isolation. Glider pilot Des Page was startled by a young 21-year-old Dutch woman, who had screamed out, 'Don't shoot, I'm a woman!'

> 'But this is about 2 o'clock in the morning and we're trigger-happy and somebody let go and her toe got shot off. My officer ran up and we've got trouble; there's firing going on and we've got a girl we can well do without.'

She was recovered and hushed just as a German patrol went past 'behind us, which shows us how close we were'. She was carried to a First Aid

Post, but Page felt helpless; there was little they could do for her. 'I did the only gallant thing,' he recalled. With 'dirty face and blood running down, I kissed her hand and said, "You'll be all right, dear."'[279]

Jan Hol at No 10 Stationsweg was sharing a room with a British Bren gun team. The firer and Bren 'was placed on some furniture, a bit back from the window for extra cover', while the No 2 kept careful watch on the houses opposite 'reporting in curt sentences what he saw'.

> 'The first short bursts of fire were my signal to flatten myself on the floor, because it was seldom that the Germans didn't reply immediately to this fire. A lot of Arie's beautiful furniture in this room was damaged. Poor Mrs van Halem would be horrified to see the mess that was her living room.'

German pressure eventually drove out the civilian inhabitants, who had to evacuate to a better cellar at No 8. The very old and young suffered most in these trying conditions. Young men such as Jan Hol, hiding from German forced labour, helped where they could. He assisted by leading groups of people through the communication trench the British had dug to connect with No 8:

> 'A dear old lady with a not inconsiderable backside became stuck in the muddy trench. With the milkman pushing and me pulling, we slid her ageing frame along on her huge, old-fashioned bloomers until she reached the end of her unceremonious though necessary journey.'

The conditions in the crowded Kremer family cellar at No 8 were little better and their numbers swelled to 15 people. Eleven-year-old Sander (Alexander) Kremer recalled that 'for the toilet we used the coal bunker and covered "it" over with coal.' Cellar life was claustrophobic and cramped, with little food and water. There were ten civilians and six soldiers in Roelie Breman's cellar in the Benedendorpsweg. 'Pieces of the wall are coming down' from the reverberations from artillery fire, 'but we see no fire,' she remembered. They were awfully cramped. 'We sit on our heels and keep trying to make more room. There are people sitting on the stairs as well and we get very stiff.' She preferred not to drink the 'very nice' English tea because 'there is no toilet in the cellar and it is very dangerous upstairs from time to time.' J. A. van Hofwegen, living in the Weverstraat nearby, did find water in a central heating boiler. 'Wonderful, I felt like Moses!' he recalled. Sander Kremer remembered how every now and again the door opened and British soldiers 'threw in handfuls of sweets for the children'. Cellar companions could not be chosen, and trust was not a feature amid strangers haphazardly thrust together in intimate surroundings. One old lady 'had her bag of jewels stolen by one of our less popular "guests",' Sander recalled.

The spectre of death was all-pervasive. Sander befriended some members of the Independent Company who came into their sector. 'We got to know them all extremely well during those four days and they became lifelong friends,' he recalled. One of them was Rodley, alias Hans Rosenfeld. He showed Sander his trench in the front garden and told him that 'the Germans would never see him there'. There was some truth in this statement because 'later in the day a soldier came to the cellar and said, "Rodley's dead," and told them he had been hit by a ricochet in the neck. Eleven-year-old Sander had no idea what a 'ricochet' was and the soldier spelled it out. His mother wrote it up on the wallpaper, where it remained for 20 years.

The stretch of road from the Oosterbeek crossroads to No 128 Utrechtseweg, next to the junction with the Weverstraat, was the primary conflict zone along the street. The front line at the east side of the perimeter followed the line of the Stationsweg and Pietersbergscheweg from north to south, although it was hardly discernible as such on the ground. Gaps were closed by fire, patrols regularly skirmished either side of the line, and German snipers and small groups regularly infiltrated through. Weverstraat was generally where the German self-propelled guns lurked and formed up for probing attacks. Wrecked British Bren gun carriers were knocked askew in the street in this area, seemingly ensnared by the downed overhead tram cables. Wil Rieken's house at No 178 had already been abandoned.

The Rieken family were escorted out eastwards by some German soldiers through the back gardens paralleling the Utrechtseweg. 'On some rooftops we saw parachutes hanging with baskets and large cylindrical drums,' remembered schoolboy Cees Meijer. He and his friends had been chased away by German soldiers who 'had taken some white sheets from our shop and had spread these on the street'. Cees 'thought they had done this in order to mislead the supply planes.'[280]

This straight section of the Utrechtseweg was a favoured sniper hunting ground, liberally deployed by both sides. 'Boy' Wilson's pathfinder company had its own snipers dominating this stretch of the road, whereas each company of German infantry fielded two specialist snipers for each rifle company. The skill was less about being a good shot, rather about being a resourceful, canny hunter who regarded the enemy dispassionately as prey. A good sniper could achieve a head kill at 300 to 600 yards, and effectively harass beyond that. Ranges such as these were occasionally conceivable along the straight length of the street or around the Dennenkamp and Hartenstein parks. Effectiveness required a remorseless attitude and excellent fieldcraft for an approach, and cannily prepared concealed positions set up in time for dawn. A particular skill was the ability to create 'angled shoots', which involved the sniper taking position in deep shade or behind cover to shoot inside a very restricted arc, generally through confined gaps between houses out to a good range. Such firers were the hardest to locate because building angles, trees and walls cloaked both their muzzle flash and the opening report of the rifle. A sniper could be located by 'crack' and 'thump', the calculation in seconds between the round cracking as it passed by, breaking the sound barrier, relative to the 'thump' of the rifle firing in the distance. The calculation required a particularly cool head.

The Germans employed tree snipers, utilising planks or tying themselves to trees. The British dismissed this as reckless fanaticism or inexperience, because the sniper should always have an escape route, or at least change position after a few shots. 'Even when they had been shot and killed' tree snipers 'did not fall from their position,' recalled Private Noel Rosenberg. 'At first glance they still appeared to pose a threat, attracting further fire from following troops.'

Fleeting targets were fired at from 'mouse holes' knocked through brickwork and plaster to cover isolated gaps between buildings or a wall. Trooper Ken Hope, with the Reconnaissance Squadron, remembered Germans that 'ran full pelt between the gaps in the houses, and it was rather like the appearance of the target in a funfair pot-shot range, when one tries to anticipate the appearance of the target and open fire.' On one occasion he recalled that 'unbelievably, the biggest German I have ever seen ran into the alley.' He paused to stand there and 'must have been about 6 feet 4 inches tall'. He was felled and 'screamed for what seemed ages'. Remorse was not part of the sniper's psyche, or that of soldiers who had fought non-stop for eight days. As German snipers prevented them from assisting the victim, 'they gave him a lullaby of *Lili Marlene* through the window,' recalled their troop commander Lieutenant Stevenson, 'the sort of mad thing that people were doing.'

Patience was a virtue possessed by both sides. Private Frank McCausland, with the 21st Independent Company, watched a man for 20 minutes until he was able to get a clear shot, leaving him slumped from a window further up the street; professionals might wait half a day. Private Tony Crane, with the same company, notched up 16 kills, which he recorded on the wallpaper at No 34 Pietersbergscheweg, Anje van Maanen's street, still preserved today in the Oosterbeek Airborne Museum. His tally consisted of lines of swastika crosses for each day beneath a defiant message of 'Never Surrender. Fuck the Germans'. The wallpaper record shows that he waited three days with 'nothing' scrawled up, until six swastikas appear on the 24th, followed by ten on the 25th. Crane was as persistent as he was remorseless. One of the men he hit was wounded and evacuated to the Schoonoord dressing station. When Crane saw him emerge with a bandage covering his wound but still carrying his weapon he decided the dressing station had fallen into German hands once again. This made him a legitimate target, so he shot him again and killed him.

The Germans were equally skilled. Trooper Stanley Collishaw with the Recce Squadron recalled his Glasgow friend Alf Odd trying to spot a sniper with binoculars near the Hartenstein. 'I can see the bastard,' he murmured, before collapsing in the trench. Reflected light from his binocular lenses had given the opposing German sniper the pinpoint guidance he needed. Nineteen-year-old Alfie Odd was the youngest man from the company to die. German snipers were patient and could demonstrate a macabre sense of humour. One waited while Corporal McWilliams on the Paul Krugerstraat went from house to house gathering scraps of food before getting a clear shot. Private Noel Rosenberg saw him raise the stew pot in the air and shout with some relish, 'Look what I've got lads!' before the German sniper put a bullet through the pot, splashing the contents all around. 'We went hungry for another day,' Rosenberg glumly recalled. He could more easily have shot McWilliams, 'but instead chose to have a bit of fun'. Snipers were rarely so charitable.[281]

More than snipers, the spectre of flame was an enduring agony for British paratroopers on the street. There was no defence against it and the SS increasingly used flame-throwers along this eastern stretch of the Utrechtseweg, to get them out. 'I think it was that which frightened me more than anything,' admitted Trooper Jimmy Cooke with the Recce Squadron:

'It fired out of the wood, and those great tongues of flame, about 20 feet long, travelled over our slit trenches and landed at the back of us. These things struck fear and terror into everyone.'

They survived because they were dug in below ground. 'We reckoned that they only had to dip down a little, and that would be it.' Glider pilot Staff Sergeant Ronald Gibson heard the rumble of tracks and the toc-toc-toc of a heavy machine gun engaging their flank section. 'A moment later I saw a series of flashes through the leaves, or rather the blurred reflection, like a sheet of lightning hidden by a heavy screen of cloud.' Not until later did he realise the section had been pushed back 'leaving two of my friends sprawling in their holes burned to death'. Flame consumed all the oxygen in a confined space and could kill through asphyxiation, even if the burning petroleum liquid could be avoided.

The impact was awful. Platoon Sergeant Val Allerton with the 21st Independent Company described what it was like to be subjected to such an attack, when a jet of flame was splashed against the walls and windows of their occupied house:

> 'It seemed to him that a great ball of fire filled the whole of his vision, blotting out the houses and the sky and everything around him. He felt heat such as he had experienced only once before, when he had stood well back at the opening of a furnace. He felt his breath catch and dry up in his lungs; he was flat on the bedroom floor, his hands clawing at the floorboards, his mouth open and his throat choking.'

He steeled himself for what he might find following the faint cry he had detected, which had 'become a continuous wailing succession of sobs'. Looking inside the still smouldering room with burning curtains and paint bubbling on the window ledge, he came across one of his own badly burned men.

> 'Where his fair fastidious face had been was something of horror. It was impossible for him to take in and appreciate what had been done to the other man. He simply looked at the smouldering smock, at the shrivelled veil around the neck, and at the hand, twisted and crooked like a chicken's claw, which groped and jerked on the chest.'

He tried to administer morphine. 'The long broken succession of sobs had stopped, and out of the lipless cavity came a word repeated over and over again: 'Please ... please ... please'. RAF navigator Reginald Lawton, sheltering in the grounds of the Hartenstein, remembered a group of men on Saturday afternoon who came running through the trees and leaped into their trenches. 'The one who had jumped into our trench told us that a tank, using a flame-thrower, had cleaned out his section of trenches.' The men were fearfully agitated. 'He was pretty shaken and stayed with us the rest of the day.'[282]

Eastern Utrechtseweg: Weverstraat to the St Elizabeth Hospital and beyond

When the British were overrun they went to a hospital or prison camp. There was nowhere for the Dutch to go – German soldiers simply waved them towards Arnhem. Captured soldiers were swept up by the German organisation, but civilians received scant attention. The truce to evacuate the British wounded, who were carried or escorted, lasted 2 hours. Dutch civilians, ejected by the fighting into a very active no-man's-land along the Utrechtseweg, had to fend for themselves. Germans were largely indifferent to the Dutch; they had sided with the British so deserved what they got. Some individual officers and men were compassionate, maybe sympathetic, but this was not translated into any official assistance. In any event, the civilians had to get out. The journey along the eastern stretch of the Utrechtseweg was therefore essentially by jeep or truck for the wounded British and on foot if you were Dutch.

Brigadier 'Shan' Hackett's wounded evacuation experience from the perimeter was typical of most. Seriously wounded in the thigh and stomach from a mortar tree burst, he had to wait outside the Hartenstein, enduring the 'huge rending clang' of a shell burst nearby 'without trousers, shivering with cold'. His hardly competent jeep driver whisked him along the stretch of the Utrechtseweg beyond the Hartenstein, which had him wincing all the time because he was aware 'how it was usually swept with machine gun fire'. Familiar sights passed him by en route. Major Wilson's pathfinder company was still fighting from its positions short of the crossroads, then he was past the Schoonoord and Vreewijk hotels, 'where ragged Red Cross flags still hung,' he recalled:

> 'The confused uproar of the battle grew louder as we drove on into it under our own Red Cross. I could see around me German troops in action behind cover.'

Nobody shot at the Red Cross jeep. This noise of battle was an enduring memory for artillery officer Lieutenant Peter Wilkinson, who described what Hackett had likely heard:

'There were constants: mortaring, small arms fire, shelling and the thump of our guns firing. Other components emerged from time to time: the clatter of tank tracks on cobbles, the roar of tank diesel engines, the explosions of burning vehicles and ammunition. Sobs and shrieks. It went on and on!'

Hackett passed the prominent upturned German lorry in the street, blown up by mines before reaching the safety of the German line. It had survived until then because it was by chance following a Red Cross jeep. 'We had watched that happen, and no one got out,' he recalled.

Soon Hackett was in the unprecedented situation of seeing German soldiers standing plainly in the open. 'Helmeted heads were peering out of houses here and there' as they drove past. Just beyond the Weverstraat 'by the roadside one of those accursed self-propelled guns, our greatest bane, was moving into position.' Before long he saw more and other supporting vehicles. 'It was like seeing wild animals outside their cages,' Hackett remembered.

Schoolboy Cees Meijer had already been shelled out of No 20 Weverstraat, a street turning off further along. 'We saw more and more buildings on fire,' he recalled, 'some very near our house, and we tried to find a safer place.' They snatched up some hand luggage and fled a few streets further west to his grandparents' house on the Molenweg. 'It was a dangerous journey, there was shooting everywhere, but we arrived alive and well' to take shelter with three others already burned out of their houses. Further down the Utrechtseweg, at No 76, Johannes van Zonnenveld remembered that 'there was a Sturmgeschütz outside Steemer's door' on the Dennenkampweg on the other side of the street:

'During the morning it fired three shots. It then made off, which was lucky for the crew because in half a minute two shells landed exactly where it had been standing; a third shell went through Steemer's shop window.'

Parallel to this stretch of the street on the south side was No 20 Cornelis

Koningstraat, where from the basement schoolboy Willy van Zanten recalled that 'you could hear everything'. It was ironic for Hackett driving past to see Nijmegen across the polderland 10 miles away, burning and crackling out artillery fire, so near yet so far. XXX Corps was now lapping up to the river bank south of the Lower Rhine. 'If you heard the artillery in the Betuwe firing, everyone was quiet,' Willy remembered. 'A whoosh meant the shell had passed but, hearing a bang and not a whistle, we took cover because that meant we might be hit.'

Fewer German soldiers were visible as Hackett's vehicle drove on. The only movement along this stretch of the street was replacements and resupply moving up to reinforce Hans Möller's SS Pioneer Battalion 9. Van Zonnenveld remarked:

> 'German catering corps personnel passed by regularly, carrying food in metal containers on their backs. They were on their way to the centre of the village with food for distribution to their own units.'[283]

'We were on cobbles now, moving fast and roughly,' Hackett recalled. 'Every bump gave me acute discomfort. It was bitterly cold and my teeth chattered.' Drizzle and rain obscured smouldering houses in steam. The desolation from continuous Allied artillery strikes provided little satisfaction as Hackett was driven past. 'By the roadside I saw half a body, just naked buttocks and the legs joined on and no more of it than that.' There was no elation to be had from the accurate long-range pounding from 64th Medium Regiment. 'It was like being in a strange and terrible nightmare,' Hackett remembered, 'from which you longed to wake and could not.'

Hackett's jeep passed beneath the railway viaduct. On top the battered and abandoned diesel train still stood forlornly waiting on the embankment, leading to the collapsed railway bridge. To the left was the distinctive 19th-century Koepel prison dome, long vacated by the Dutch, who had been driven out of the shattered Lombok district by the advancing Germans. Just before the junction of the high and low roads, tram No 54, shot up during the 2 Para advance a week before, was still there, ensnared by tangled downed cables with bodies by the roadside. The pock-marked façade of the St Elizabeth Hospital came into view after the left fork, distinguishable by the huge Red Cross sheet draped over the entrance porch. Outside were the remains of burned-out lorries shot up during the advance. The red oxidisation on the metalwork made them look as though they had weathered years rather than days. Hackett was disgusted to see German SS soldiers looting through the local houses. 'I felt a deep and personal hatred for every one of them,' he recalled. An SS Unteroffizier stepped out to bar their progress. 'Everything about him was cocksure and beastly, his nose, his mouth, his tunic, his manner.' 'Here's an officer!' the SS man remarked sardonically, regarding the wounded Hackett without his trousers. Hackett's driver was pulled out of his seat as the SS NCO gesticulated with a triumphant thumbs-up gesture to his friends that it was now his. Hackett was dropped off at the entrance, laid on a stretcher and carried inside. Compared to the average lot of the civilian refugees struggling east along the street, he was eminently fortunate.[284]

When the Van Maanen family was ejected from their house opposite the Hotel Tafelberg, they had no idea where to go. 'There will be no armistice,' they were told – just get out. 'It is unbelievable, but it has to be,' the family appreciated. With no military guidance, it was going to be extremely hazardous to move civilians along a virtual free-fire zone. They were disorientated by the ruins and rumours and alarmist reports of what was happening. Nerves were stretched to breaking point. The family appreciated they must go now. 'I am desperately longing to get away, out of this mess,' remembered 17-year-old Anje, but they were surrounded by Dutch civilians moving in all directions. 'Some of them appear screaming,' she remembered, while others 'can't make up their minds which way they will go.' In the middle of the small alley they had chosen was a German corpse, which they had to step over, 'with open eyes – horrible'. Machine gun bullets slapped into the wall beside them and they had to turn back, passing the ghastly corpse once again, to find a way out. Anje stumbled upon a German inside the nearby woods. 'The man answers very nicely which way is the best.'

But how could they traverse the fighting zone, visibly under fire with their band of 14 anxious fugitives?

Somebody at the head carried a long stick with a white handkerchief at the end, 'our white flag, but a tiny one,' Anje recalled. They struggled along with outsize suitcases bulked out with blankets tied around with parachute cord. Movement was especially tricky for the very young and old. 'We creep and climb across destroyed trees and branches and all sorts of rubbish,' Anje remembered. The pause in artillery fire was only momentary and started up again as they passed a stable. 'Dunghill or not, I fall flat on my stomach and with my nose right into it!' she recalled. Her companion Ettche Smit could not walk properly because of a wounded heel. She was helped along with her coat over her pyjamas supported by others in the group. 'How will she walk to Arnhem?' Anje wondered.

The topography of the street was completely transformed by the devastation. Glider pilot Des Page remembered that 'you could not put your foot down without treading on either shrapnel, busted glass or whatever – it was literally shattered everywhere.' The Van Maanen band moved through unrecognisable side streets next to the Utrechtseweg; badly shelled houses were burning along the Overzicht and Paasberg. 'Everything is in a horrible mess,' Anje observed, 'and I can hardly recognise the place where I was five days ago.' A white sheet was substituted for the white handkerchief but elicited scant sympathy from any German soldiers they passed. The 'Moffen' laughed and smirked at them. 'Oh – I loathe them,' she wrote in her diary. Once past the Weverstraat they found two prams and loaded up the suitcases. It began to pour with rain:

> 'Auntie Auke is wearing a soaked dinner jacket on top of a summer dress, which she has borrowed from Paul [Anje's brother]. She has torn stockings on her legs and her hair falls around her head like string.'

Their appearance mirrored their desperate predicament. 'Paul looks like a scoundrel, unshaved, unwashed and his hair is all over the place,' observed Anje, while she looked like a 'gipsy'. 'I just had a new perm the other day and after this week and the rain it looks unbelievable, like some sort of sheep,' she thought. She wore an old raincoat, socks with holes and a summer dress torn from the waist to the hem, 'but I couldn't care less really'.

The Utrechtseweg, which they joined, was 'a terrible mess'. 'All the tramway poles are thrown over the road and everywhere there are the remains of tanks, cars, baskets, containers and every possible thing you can imagine.' They moved further eastward before being directed by a Dutch SS soldier north-east onto the Mariendalsweg. Corpses were lying around. Anje thought she saw someone hiding behind a tree before recoiling at the sight of 'a dead farmer with black socks and wooden shoes'. Under the railway viaduct was another body 'with an entirely black face'; she realised as they entered the Den Brink Park that 'the fight here has been terrific'. Any lingering hopes they may have entertained about a positive outcome to this battle were dashed by the sight of the huge Tiger tanks, standing silent sentinel beneath the trees. 'We see an enormous tank buried there with all its guns pointing in the direction of Oosterbeek,' she remembered. 'We quickly pass the murderous thing.'[285]

Schwere Panzer Abteilung 506 under Sturmbannführer (Major) Eberhard Lange had entrained with Königstiger (King Tiger) tanks at Ohrdruf in the Reich three days before. After a two-day journey they unloaded at Zenvenaar. Two companies, or 45 of the 68-ton monoliths, were allocated to Harzer's 9th SS command by Field Marshal Model, to finish off the British pocket. There were delays getting them ready for action. The special narrow tracks that enabled the tanks to negotiate rail tunnels and bridges on flat cars had to be changed over to the standard wide links. The huge but grossly underpowered King Tiger IIs were equipped with the same engine that propelled their predecessors, the Tiger I, which was 11 tons lighter. This resulted in numerous breakdowns en route because the drivers had been urged to sustain high speeds. Lange marshalled his 2nd Company, commanded by Hauptsturmführer (Captain) Wacker, to Harzer's Hohenstaufen to finish off the pocket, while the 3rd Company was sent across the river to the 10th SS Frundberg to block the approaching XXX Corps at Elst.

Wacker's 15 King Tigers began to assemble for the final assault. They were to attack in concert with the assault guns of Sturmgeschütz Brigade 280, which, like the British, was exhausted after eight days of fighting. Gefreiter (Corporal) Wilhelm Rohrbach, with its 3rd Battery, had begun to despair. 'There were even children in the Arbeitsdienst labourers fighting alongside us.' Rumours had abounded about Tiger tanks 'coming at the last minute', and thankfully here they were.[286]

The further east the despairing refugees moved along the street, the more obvious the outcome of this battle appeared. On reaching the St Elizabeth Hospital they found it 'crowded with Moffen, who scream and laugh, and we feel lost and scared,' recalled a very dispirited Anje van Maanen. Hackett had also observed the arrogant, drunken behaviour outside the hospital. Just the day before Captain Brian Lanscombe, a South Staffordshire Medical Officer, had been shot in the head on the hospital steps by a drunken Danish SS-Oberscharführer Karl-Gustav Lerche, in the company of an equally drunken SS Viking war correspondent. There was no obvious reason. It was a grim reminder of what the return of the 'monster' identified by Anje van Maanen meant.[287]

Beyond the hospital the formerly hated and feared Gestapo offices at No 85 Utrechtseweg were now empty and deserted. Outside No 63 the decomposing bodies of Lance Corporal Loney and Private Norman Shipley from the 2nd Parachute Battalion had finally been taken away. The two corpses encapsulated the ultimate agony of the street. It had been liberated and now the Germans had come back. Both bodies were robbed.

CHAPTER 9

The Evacuation of the Street

Break-in: the Hohenstaufen East

Early on the morning of 25 September Major General Urquhart, commanding the remnants of the 1st British Airborne Division, sent a 'phantom' encoded message to General Browning, the deputy Airborne Corps Commander at Nijmegen:

> 'Must warn you that unless physical contact in some strength is made with us early 25 Sep consider it unlikely that we can hold out any longer. All ranks are now completely exhausted as the result of 8 days continual effort. Lack of food and water and deficiencies in arms combined with high officer casualties rate has had its effect. Even comparatively minor enemy offensive action may cause complete disintegration. Should this become apparent all will be told to break towards the bridgehead if any rather than surrender. Controlled movement from present position in face of enemy is out of the question now. We have done our best and will continue to do so as long as possible.'

The decision for Operation Berlin, the airborne withdrawal across the Lower Rhine, had already been taken. The street was to be evacuated that night. 'The thing that kept us going was the fact that we were expecting to be relieved any minute by the British Second Army,' remembered Flying Officer Reginald Lawton, dug in next to the Hartenstein. There were many rumours. 'If we don't see tanks tonight we will tomorrow morning for sure,' and they were self-perpetuating. 'There's a chap down there who's just come from the river and he's seen them,' but as Lawton bitterly recalled, 'nothing ever came'. Prowling German tanks were mistaken by experts who claimed 'that those sounds were made by Churchills'. They were positive, but always wrong. It was the same conversation from east to west, as Corporal Jim Swan with the Border Battalion observed: 'A week gone by and no link-up yet.' Glider pilot 'Bunny' Baker remembered:

> 'On the last day everyone was in low spirits. My pal Joe had the lobe of his ear shot off and my right arm was painful from all the firing. We were hungry, wet and tired out. It was only a matter of a short time before we would run out of ammunition and food and would have to surrender.'[288]

Many were oblivious to the concept of relief – either XXX Corps arrived or they were going to be overrun. 'My little world was that wood in front of me,' recalled Trooper Bill Cook with the Recce Squadron, just north of the Utrechtseweg. 'I don't know yet why the Germans didn't come over, because I could see nothing to stop them.'

'And then it came out,' Major Geoffrey Powell, with the remnants of 156 Para, recalled. 'It was hard to believe, harder still to understand.' They were to withdraw that night. 'So the operation had failed! Everything had been in vain! It was all a waste!' When he told his men 'the muttered chorus of protest rose to a spontaneous babble, full of bitterness about the troops in the south who had failed to relieve us.' One of his sergeants insisted that 'we were far from finished and could still hold the bastards off for days'. Glider Pilot Arthur Shackleton heard General Urquhart explain: 'We will pull down from the north like a balloon bursting,' he said. The glider pilots were to recce and mark the routes down to the river, lay white tape and guide the rest of the division down when it got dark. 'Our withdrawal from the wood after standing firm for five days had come as a sudden shock' to glider pilot Staff Sergeant Ronald Gibson. 'It seemed that we would hold for ever.'

Up on the Utrechtseweg, the 21st Independent Company had 'mixed feelings', according to Sergeant Ron Kent. 'No one had thought of a withdrawal.' Sergeant Allerton vehemently insisted that the pathfinders should remain to kill the 'bloody Hun' even if the remainder of the

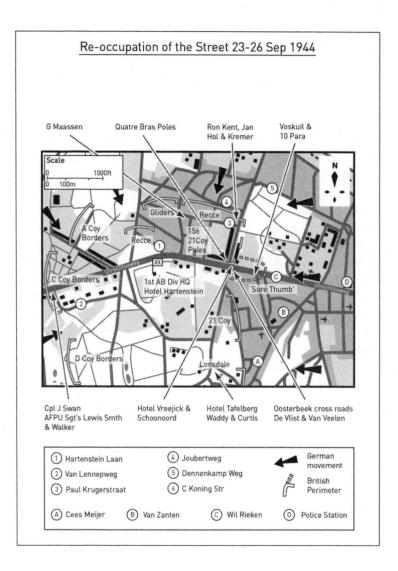

Re-occupation of the Street 23-26 Sep 1944

G Maassen

Quatre Bras Poles

Ron Kent, Jan Hol & Kremer

Voskuil & 10 Para

Scale

0 _____ 1000ft

0 ____ 100m

N

Gliders

Recce

A Coy Borders

Recce

156 21Coy Poles

C Coy Borders

1st AB Div HQ Hotel Hartenstein

'Sore Thumb'

D Coy Borders

21 Coy

Lonsdale

Utrechtseweg

Utrechtseweg

Cpl J Swan AFPU Sgt's Lewis Smth & Walker

Hotel Vreejick & Schoonoord

Hotel Tafelberg Waddy & Curtis

Oosterbeek cross roads De Vlist & Van Veelen

① Hartenstein Laan

② Van Lennepweg

③ Paul Krugerstraat

④ Joubertweg

⑤ Dennenkamp Weg

⑥ C Koning Str

German movement

British Perimeter

Ⓐ Cees Meijer   Ⓑ Van Zanten   Ⓒ Wil Rieken   Ⓓ Police Station

After nine days of continuous fighting, this final segment of the street was re-occupied by the Germans.

division should withdraw. Retreat was a startling change of focus, unwelcome to men who had accepted as a matter of course that they were expected to stay and fight. Having expected to die, now they might live. Sergeant Ron Kent remembered:

'The men consequently became nervous as kittens. It was hardly to be wondered at – the strain of the last eight days had been terrific and now that safety was only a few hours off, no one felt inclined to take chances.'

Geoffrey Powell's men felt the same way. After grief came disappointment, followed by anger that it was all for nothing. 'Now there was at least a chance that we might escape,' he reflected. 'Although the prospects of surviving the rest of the day and then withdraw across the river in our present state seemed slim.'[289]

The street was regarded as the most dangerous conduit for a German approach. Amazingly a concentrated armoured thrust aimed at division headquarters, just 250 yards from the edge of the perimeter, had never materialised. It was also the main thoroughfare out – to the St Elizabeth Hospital – for the wounded. Dressing stations further away from the street had deteriorated more rapidly, such as the Ter Horst house next to the old church and river, because it was too difficult to get casualties out and medical supplies in. It might take hours to transport a casualty across 1,000 yards of snipers, mortar and shell fire to reach division headquarters or the dressing stations on the Utrechtseweg. Sergeant Bill Hayden from 1 Para, treating casualties down by the river, recalled that 'the house was surrounded by a ring of dead men we had to throw outside':

'Only twice during very short lulls in the bombardment were we able to bury the dead. Each time a communal grave was dug for about 15 men with the help of a burial party from the artillery regiment… Every morning found three or more dead amongst our patients and as soon as these had been taken outside their places were filled by other wounded.'[290]

Sturmbannführer Eberhard Lange selected his ground well. Wacker's 2nd Company was attached to the Kampfgruppe von Allwörden, which had not posed a particular threat before now. The King Tigers rumbled down the Grintweg moving south-west, assembling around the green area to the south of Emmastraat, which because of its tangle of minor streets had never been considered a likely approach by the British. The Germans were aiming to snap off the perimeter at its base, near the river. Wacker's crushing assault, spearheaded by the biggest tanks in Europe, suddenly broke through the glider pilot positions on the Weverstraat, coming in behind the South Staffords defending to their left.

'German battle groups tried to cut off the enemy from the banks of the Lower Rhine,' recalled Hans Möller on the Utrechtseweg with Pioneer Battalion 9:

> 'The division had reinforced the left wing, especially the battle groups Allwörden and Harder, attacking with their Tiger tanks between the Utrechtseweg and the road along the bank of the Rhine.'

The British were caught unawares. Before they knew it, German tanks and infantry were in among the 2nd Airlanding Artillery battery positions and destroyed their command post. With no additional anti-tank weapons to hand, gun crews were ordered to stay in their trenches and engage the tanks over open sights when they came into view. Sergeant McLeod, caught up in the midst of the attack with A Battery, recalled:

> 'We were shocked as no order had been given for "tank alert" or "take post", and because of the terrible din of firing and mortaring we did not distinguish the tank noises. In no time Jerry infantry was upon us and the whole troop was overrun. It was a sad day for us.'[291]

German panzers were nosing beyond Weverstraat and down the Bildersweg deep into the perimeter toward the Kneppelhoutweg. There was barely 600 yards to go before linking up with Lippert's regiment attacking from the west. Harzer was on the verge of breaking through, but had to admit that 'the narrower the defence area of the perimeter became the more bitterly the British hung on to every ruin and rise in the ground.' Möller, observing from the flank, could see resistance tightening. 'Many knocked-out Tiger tanks and new and heavy losses on both sides testified to the ferocity of the fighting on this day.'

The 68-ton Tigers were slowed as much by their inability to motor through the ruins as the tenacity of resistance. 'In the constricted streets the cobblestones were breaking up beneath the weight,' Harzer remarked. 'In fact the tanks had difficulties in any case even to move forward in narrow avenues.' The King Tiger mounted the 88mm KWK 43 gun, the most powerful this war had seen, but the 11-foot-long turret with a further 9 feet of gun overhang snagged on obstructions, impeding the traverse of the super gun between houses. Lightly armed paratroopers sought to counter these monoliths, which were 33 feet long and 12 feet wide. All-round sloping armour 10 feet high coated with a crust of 'zimmerit' anti-magnetic paste made it all but impossible to scramble aboard. Even so, its lack of urban mobility meant that it could still be 'stalked' from the flanks and rear.[292]

'There are few more terrifying noises than the whine and rattle of an approaching tank,' remembered Lieutenant James Blackwood with 11 Para, fighting down by the river when 'the enemy drove in a tank and infantry attack in an attempt to split our position in two.' Private Ivor Williams with the South Staffords felt completely helpless. 'One of the German tanks headed for us and drove over our slit, flattening the Bren, which was now useless,' he recalled. 'When the attack was over I rearmed myself with a German Mauser rifle'. All that could be achieved was to separate the infantry from the tanks in the hope of making the tanks more vulnerable. Blackwood remembered:

> 'Once I thought we'd had it. The tank stopped and his great 88mm gun slowly, very slowly, moved round and faced us. For some unknown reason he did not fire and as soon as he

traversed his turret again to move away, we came up and had another whack at the Hun [infantry]. Good shooting too. Something grimly humorous seeing a frantically scurrying Hun legging it in vain with the bullets kicking up the mud at his heels.'

Private Ron Etherington and the Staffords intelligence section was overrun and captured by one of the gigantic King Tigers:

'This tank was Germany's biggest and I can still see the commander standing up in his turret dressed in black and smiling with an expression of complete superiority, satisfaction, but at the same time giving us a glance which to us seemed to say "Hard luck", or so I thought.'

Lieutenant Donald Edwards with the Staffords C Company, trying to get the wounded out in a Red Cross jeep, suddenly encountered a Tiger tank blocking his path. 'Toot your horn when you come back and I will let you through,' the compassionate tank commander said. Meanwhile a signals officer with direct contact with the 2nd Army had spotted the incident, and brought down artillery. The jeep went up in flames 'with the ammunition going like fireworks'. Edwards remembers that 'a wounded German dragged himself along on his elbows toward us shouting abuse in German before dying.'[293]

British troops hated the PIAT, far more ungainly and clumsy than its German panzerfaust counterpart. Cocking the spring was difficult, and it took a cool head under fire to push back the spring firing mechanism by standing on it. A certain hit was only achievable from about 30 yards. Glider pilot Walton Ashworth watched one lone firer kneeling to engage a tank. 'I was absolutely certain he was going to die there,' he recalled. Richard Long, witnessing the same engagement, saw him shout 'Load, load!' and fire at the tank, 'and you could see the track of the tank come away and lob on its side.' Major Robert Cain faced another tank that had emerged, but was hit by a blow-back explosion when his PIAT shell clipped a wall near him. 'There was a flash,' Long recalled, 'and he immediately fell over.' 'It was horrifying,' Ashworth recalled. 'When I got to him his face was totally black, with little spots of blood – what, 30 or so – all around, and he was shouting "I'm blind! I'm blind! I can't see!"' Cain was carried away by his companions with Ashworth staying with him for a few paces 'holding onto his hand'. Yet 45 minutes later he was back and Ashworth was 'staggered, absolutely staggered'. Long saw

> '...this chap came out of the copse with his face blackened, and he immediately got down with the PIAT gun. I thought he must be a very brave man to be knocked out probably and then to come back and take up the same position, and still hit tanks. He was still firing when we left.'[294]

To Harzer's immense surprise, one of Wacker's King Tigers was knocked out near the Klompen School on the Weverstraat near the Benedendorpsweg. It was hit by a 6-pounder, which bounced off, and also a number of 75mm artillery shells, fired by desperate airborne gunners over open sights. 'At the exact moment that we fired the gun,' remembered Lance Corporal Harry Smith with the South Staffords anti-tank platoon,

> 'A German dived into the centre of the main road with a machine gun. The shell hit the machine gunner instead of the tank, and he just disintegrated into thin air.'[295]

The gun telescope was out of alignment. Nevertheless, after this flurry of shots the King Tiger caught fire and two more PIAT rounds were fired into it to ensure that it could not be recovered. Harzer was becoming increasingly discouraged. 'The terrain for this attack was in my opinion not favourable, because the infantry had to advance over completely open ground, where there was absolutely no cover.' On the other side of the perimeter 'Von Tettau's battle group had elements pinned down in the area of the gasworks for the same reason.' The final straw was the knocked-out Tiger 'set on fire by a mortar round that hit the air-intake lid on the petrol tank.' At the time they could not be certain what the British were shooting and Harzer was reluctant to lose more tanks.

'The fighting grew fiercer and fiercer,' Möller commented, 'man against man, with bayonets and knives.' One dismaying report claimed that two paratroopers attacked an SS unit armed with only knives. This was not blood-lust; the intimidating aspect was that one of the paratroopers was clearly drawing fire to enable the other to close. Private Benjamin Pick from 10 Para described the tenacity of resistance on that day:

> 'We kept down till the tank passed us, as we were on a bit of a rise, and we pinned down the Jerries with grenades and revolvers till we had none left. They were throwing grenades into our trench so we picked them up and threw them back at them. Then they started throwing Mills grenades and they only have a 3-second fuse. After about the fourth one, one went off in my hand, blowing it off, so we had to surrender.'

The Germans were in awe. Pick walked right through them 'with my revolver still in my left hand as the right had been blown off.' They were taken to the German headquarters where 'an officer came to me and said, "Will you give me your revolver Tommy?"' Pick reluctantly handed it over. 'I still had a Luger in my smock and they didn't search me.' German casualties had been high that day and the British were clearly unlikely to surrender.[296]

Harzer pushed halfway across the perimeter before the British sealed off the advance by bringing down heavy artillery fire from Nijmegen onto their own positions. Möller's men were intimidated by 'the impacts of the enemy heavy artillery':

> 'Reports and detonations followed almost without let-up, the earth was trembling and a curtain of fire and dirt of unprecedented dimensions rose over and between our positions. We ducked down and sought shelter, but still remained exposed to the blind raging of the shells.'

The SS infantry could take no more. 'It was sheer carnage!' Möller remembered. Lieutenant Jim Blackwood with 11 Para recalled being under fire from both sides. 'The crack of passing shells and the violent explosions made our eardrums bleed, and when for good measure he called down heavy mortar fire, the whole crest quivered and smoked.' The line had been held, but only just. 'It was almost an hour before we risked climbing out on that exposed forward slope.' The attack had been blunted by concentrated artillery fire from XXX Corps. 'It was a study to hear the boys when later they crawled out of the trenches,' Blackwood remembered, 'and viewed the huge craters around our position.'[297]

Model continued to press Harzer for results, but after the failure of the King Tiger attack he conceded, as Harzer recalled, that 'with "Alarm" units from all parts of the Wehrmacht, they were not going to quickly or successfully eliminate a British elite division and brigade so easily.' Model therefore decided 'that in order to spare more blood, the British Airborne Division would be subjected to heavy artillery fire until the rest had given up.' The task was in effect handed over to the commander of Artillery Regiment 191, who was coordinating the fire of more than 100 heavy guns onto the 2-kilometre-square pocket. He was told to 'cover the length and breadth of the small enemy-occupied territory with heavy barrages.' Harzer meanwhile regrouped to ensure that 'veteran units' rather than 'big battle groups' were readied for the decisive assault. The British had barely held on during 25 September; the next morning should see the final attacks. Harzer sat back and observed as

'The artillery fire was escalated from harassing to killing fire into the isolated island of resistance. This systematic grind against the British paratroopers, who had been fighting for 8 days now without interruption, resulted in a rapid deterioration in their fighting spirit. Many crossed the lines and the numbers of prisoners rose steadily.'

'The houses burned brightly and collapsed and the treetops splintered,' recalled Möller, watching 'new impacts that dealt death and destruction'.

In the middle of the escalating artillery fire 'terrified civilians ran for their lives, sought cover, wept and cried.' More and more refugees took cover in the grounds of the Schoonoord and Vreewijk hotels, 'behind our demarcation line, which remained unscathed like a miracle'. Outside was a veritable Dante's Inferno:

'All around us, to our left and right and also further west towards Heelsum, the bombardment continued. The detonation of the shells mingled with the cries for help of the wounded who were lying out there in the driving rain or among the rubble of collapsing houses, desperately awaiting an uncertain fate. And so it went on … without let-up!'

Sturmbannführer Sepp Krafft, on the east side of the perimeter near the river with his reinforced battle group, recalled that 'towards the end of the fighting, many gave themselves up because of hunger and other privations, including breakdown of morale.'[298]

'By now the wounds of some men were gangrenous,' recalled Sergeant Bill Hayden, treating the wounded down by the Lower Rhine, 'and limbs had begun to turn black.'

'The stench was awful and we could not combat it. The Doc saw all this and it nearly broke his heart, because we were rapidly becoming nothing more than a mortuary. Water was scarce, the mains had been cut, and all day and all night, particularly at night, the poor devils cried out for water. We doled it out to them almost in sips.'

The intensity of fighting around them meant that 'we had no Red Cross flags to fly, Bren and anti-tank guns were in our back garden, and there was a mortar position behind us.' When the Tigers attacked, three of them 'broke through and lay broadside on to the house about 60 to 80 yards away in a field.' They fired into them at point-blank range and 'in no time they had blown two rooms to pieces and killed a number of patients in both rooms.' This could not go on. The Medical Officer was seriously wounded and Hayden and another medic, Corporal Roberts from 2 Para, assisting him, were injured. The panzer commander was persuaded to stop when Bombardier Golden approached him under a white flag and told him what he was doing.

> 'Snipers were active all the time. One man died trying to bring in some compo to us, and another poor chap was shot clean through the head, right in our open door, with in his hand the tin of cigarettes he was bringing for the patients.'

One sniper fired through the kitchen windows the whole afternoon, with bullets whining off the passage walls. 'We had to attend the fresh cases as they came in by lying on our stomachs as a result of this.' Soldiers gritted their teeth and bore it, counting off the hours and minutes, willing the onset of darkness and possible escape from the impossible situation to which they felt they had been abandoned.[299]

We'll be back! The British departure

A withdrawal in contact with the enemy is one of the most difficult phases of war. The street would have to be abandoned in secret and any movement cloaked by deception measures. Any pull-out had also to be concealed from the Dutch. Success was dependent upon gradually thinning out the front line via a series of rendezvous and forming-up points linked by guides, all the time covered by artillery fire from XXX Corps across the Lower Rhine. Disaster would result if the Germans at any stage detected what was going on. However, the bloody fighting that had blunted the previous day's attempt to break through the perimeter had tangibly demonstrated to the Germans that the British intended to stay. Harzer's King Tigers had, however, driven in a wedge into the horseshoe-shaped perimeter near the river, which would have to be avoided and bypassed during darkness. That wedge could equally be exploited at first light to apply a concerted coup de grâce to finish off the enclave. Sergeant Ron Kent, with the pathfinder company, described the typically terse orders being issued to all units around the perimeter that day:

'We're getting out across the river tonight. Get your boots covered with strips of blanket and see that none of your equipment is loose or rattles. We move out by sections starting at 21.15 hours. Assemble in the open patch behind the wood near 4th Brigade HQ. Company will act as rearguard and move off at 21.45 hours – No 1 Platoon leading. Glider pilots are taping a route down to the part of the river where Canadian REs will have some boats to take us across. A pair of Bofors will be firing two streams of tracer at intervals from about 21.30 onwards. They will give you some indication of the direction to head for if you go astray. Any questions?'

Crucial to the plan was the successful negotiation of the Utrechtseweg. As the main arterial east-west road going through the top of the perimeter, it was the most intensely observed section of it. Any regular movement spotted going across it from north to south would give the game away.

As darkness fell, the northern edge of the perimeter, like Urquhart's description of a balloon bursting, began to thin out first. By 20.00 hours the Reconnaissance Squadron began to slip across the Utrechtseweg in twos and threes. Corporal 'Tommy' Trinder recalled that 'we would leave slit trench by slit trench, at 3-minute intervals'. He explained, 'As each lot moved off, they were to tell those in the next trench to the right that they were going.' After 3 minutes they were to do the same. 'In our case, the trouble was that no one bothered to tell us.' Finding that nobody was about, Trinder told his platoon commander, who said, 'Oh well, we'd better just stay where we are.' That was not how Trinder saw it. 'You stay if you like,' he responded. 'I'm off!'[300]

Major Geoffrey Powell's 156 Para Battalion survivors made their way down to the Utrechtseweg, past the Polish positions on the corner of the Stationsweg. It was a dark night with pouring rain, and for once nobody was complaining about the weather, which was effectively cloaking movement by reduced visibility and the sound of running water. 'First we had to cross the main road,' he recalled. Crossing in ones and twos would have been reckless, quickly alerting the spandau crews that covered this length of the street. They were 'ready to rush across in a tight mob'. At a hissed command:

> 'We burst across the road in a compact bunch and threw ourselves in a heap on the other side behind the shelter of some trees. As the last few men dropped, two spandaus found the range; a second too late the stream of scarlet tracer all but brushed our heels before floating lazily away into the darkness of the woods beyond the Hartenstein.'

They left the Utrechtseweg behind them. Just ahead and to their left the 21st Independent Company nervously waited in the houses and the school along the Paasberg for the order to move out. 'Nervously,' Sergeant Ron Kent explained, 'because with deliverance now so close to hand everyone was acutely conscious of the danger of being killed or wounded at the last minute.' Inside the school Sergeant Stan Sullivan chalked up a last defiant message for the Germans, and hopefully a departing encouragement for the Dutch. 'We'll be back!' he wrote. By about 21.30 the Poles, holding the corner at the Oosterbeek crossroads, were the only coherent rearguard, still able to block the Utrechtseweg to the east. Lieutenant Smaczny with the 8th Company was told he could withdraw at half past midnight, but only on orders from a runner. Smaczny was unimpressed with what he considered 'a virtual sentence of extermination', but kept these thought from his men.[301]

At the west end of the street the survivors of C Company the Border Regiment were still holding their blocking position short of the Koude Herberg crossroads. A company to the north came struggling down to the road through the darkness and rain; they were now down to 42 men, only 22 of whom were still unwounded. This represented three assault boat loads if they made it to the river. The men had felt humiliated at the prospect of withdrawal, greater than the relief of getting home again, because their wounded were to be left behind. C Company was of similar strength. It was arranged that A Company would thin out from the street 10 minutes before C at 23.00 hours. They would cover each other. 'We got our tackle ready that we were going to take,' recalled Corporal Jim Swan with C Company, 'and settled down to wait.'

This was no textbook withdrawal. The survivors were implementing a plan of staged withdrawals through check points along the minor roads and tracks to the river. Contact with D Company south of the street had been lost for two days. D Company was unaware the withdrawal was on that night. Having watched the bloody repulse of the attempted river crossing by the Dorsets the previous night, the 19 soldiers left were sitting and awaiting the arrival of an even stronger Allied reinforcement from across the river. All the signs seemed to indicate this was happening, with the heavy XXX Corps artillery bombardment crashing down around the German lines. Pouring rain made it impossible to distinguish any movement between the trees. In the D Company cellar the wounded were heartened by the constant thump and crump of shellfire. Tomorrow they were likely to be relieved.

As the first men began to melt away from their positions on the Van Lennepweg, Major Neil's C Company put in an aggressive deception attack along the street. Corporal Jim Swan remembered:

'Around 23.00 hours we were going to get out of our slit trenches and advance towards the enemy firing as rapidly as possible and making as much noise as possible then, on order, get back to our trenches as quick as possible.'

This was effectively carried out. 'Then, as the company peeled off from the right flank, platoons each fired a parting shot.' The Germans appear to have been suitably intimidated. 'Our time came,' Swan recalled. 'We fired, got up and left along the front of the house and down the driveway and onto the road.' The blocking position to the west of the street was dismantled by 23.15. 'We were last in line,' Swan remembered. The shadowy figures moved off the Utrechtseweg into the woods following a white tape, sloshing through driving rain. 'We had to keep together and we'd keep getting separated.' Now and again they halted to close up. 'Planes were coming over and occasional bullets and tracers zipped through the air.' D Company never got the message and was left behind.[302]

Unteroffizier Herbert Kessler was lying that night with one of two Hermann Göring outposts on the Rosander Polder in the pouring rain, facing the Polish positions on the far bank of the Lower Rhine:

'We had hardly arrived in the place, and were still lying in the damp grass not daring to move, but watching in great suspense for any movement near us, when a short distance away we saw the silhouettes of people in motion.'

As they were the only German troops in the vicinity, it had to be the enemy. 'To hesitate was pointless, and very soon wild shooting at short range began.' Despite some casualties, Kessler and his men thought they had the better of the engagement. 'It seemed, however, we had the stronger nerves, for the enemy retreated.'

All around the perimeter, the Germans sheltering from both the rain and shellfire had no real inkling of what was happening. Standartenführer Michael Lippert, responsible for Kessler's sector, later remarked that 'the English break-out to the south in the night of 25th/26th was actually my luck, because a concentrated break-out toward the west could not have been held by my units.' Heavy losses over the preceding few days had meant that 'the front line in my sector was full of holes and there were no reserves available.' Von Tettau remained clueless. He was more intent on ensuring that the aftermath of the Dorset's attack the night before was tidied away. Three companies of Fliegerhorst and reserve infantry had been committed to the area that morning. During the evening, regrouping and attack orders 'for the continuation of the attack for the 26th' as before, were set in train. Von Tettau was also busy relocating his command post. He replaced the overcritical and troublesome Lippert with Wehrmacht Lieutenant Colonel Wagner, who arrived from Army Group B. Lippert remained under SS control. No thinning out of the British line was detected, although it was observed that 'the enemy's resistance seems to slacken', which was assumed to have been 'caused by high losses and dogged assault force operations'. Boats were spotted during the night 'in the sector of the Regiment Knoche on the Lower Rhine front, where the enemy made renewed crossing attempts.' Kapitänleutnant Zaubser's sailors, fighting as infantry, reported that they 'were repelled mostly by concentrated fire'. Von Tettau was able to satisfactorily report that 'only individual boats succeeded to cross and infiltrate'.

On the Rosander Polder Herbert Kessler's men were soaking wet but quietly satisfied that they had seen off the enemy. Suddenly they were startled by a voice shouting, 'Don't Shoot!' A shot-down English Flight Lieutenant stumbled into view. 'We breathed a sigh of relief when at last the sky began to turn light, for this was the sign to return to our rest positions.' What they observed that night appeared in no way unusual. Hundreds of withdrawing British paratroopers had passed them by in the night. The Germans saw what they expected to see. Having witnessed British resupply aircraft flying through curtains of fierce flak to supply the perimeter and seen so much blood expended on the ground, nobody expected the British to give up.

Hans Möller's Pioneer Battalion 9, focussing on surviving a battle of attrition, continued to send fighting patrols to probe the eastern end of the Utrechtseweg. They were similarly blind to what was taking place. Möller, reflecting on the dismal fate of his decimated battalion, regarded the rainy street that night:

> 'A wall of fire shining in shades from bright yellow to violet brightened the rainy sky over a long distance. The large gasometer had been hit, and the flames cast a sinister light on a scene of useless destruction.'[303]

The street was being vacated right under their very noses. 'After nightfall,' he recalled, 'the artillery bombardment intensified,' as he anticipated it would. Counter-battery fire was attempting to nullify the German attempts to pound the perimeter into submission. Schoolboy Cees Meijer, sheltering in his grandparents' cellar on the Molenweg, just south of Möller's positions, remembered:

> 'In the night of Monday September 25th there came the most horrendous shelling and bombardment we had till then

experienced. The noise came from the south and was ear-splitting. Nobody could sleep and we all thought that this was the prelude to the arrival of the large army from the south, which would come across the Rhine and destroy the Germans.'[304]

Polish paratroopers, feeling their way along the communications trench to No 8 Stationsweg, just north of the street, were startled by a terrific outburst of small arms fire behind them. One of their Bren gunners, positioned above the gardens, shot back in the direction of the racket, but was stopped by their platoon commander, Second Lieutenant Kula, who explained that it was the British covering their retreat. Soon the shadowy forms of glider pilots moved by to be swallowed up by the black night as they crossed the street heading for the river.

Suddenly the Germans 'went mad', Lance Corporal Kuzniar recalled, throwing grenades and shooting up one of the abandoned houses they had encircled nearby. Gaining no response, the German firing died away. Then at 21.30 the Germans attacked the corner house, 'Quatre Bras', at the Oosterbeek crossroads, where Stationsweg joined the street. This time the Poles fired for all they were worth, raining grenades down onto the intersection and raking it from left to right with Sten guns. As the flares spluttered out, peace returned to the street. The Germans were close but confused; some houses were silent, whereas others offered incredible resistance when disturbed. The German fighting patrols withdrew. 'Quatre Bras' could be more easily subdued at daybreak.[305]

In the cellar of No 8 Stationsweg, 33 hungry sheltering Dutch refugees endured the quaking reports of large-calibre British shells working over the German positions to the north of the perimeter. They instinctively kept away from the cellar door, with no desire to see or expose themselves to the storm of fire outside. 'The last night brought an artillery bombardment that continued for a long time,' recalled Jan Hol, 'but the paras were nowhere to be seen or heard.' He felt uneasy. 'Where could they be? Were they all dead, or prisoners of war?' Like the Germans 'I couldn't believe that the answer to these two questions was yes.' Between 11 o'clock and midnight the Poles gradually slipped across the Utrechtseweg into the grounds of the Hartenstein.[306]

Glider pilot 'Bunny' Baker sprinted across the triangular green between the Hartenstein Laan and the street with a group of seven other glider pilots towards the Hotel Hartenstein. 'We decided to disregard the order that we had to wrap our boots with cloth to muffle our movements because we thought it possible we would have to run and these might trip us.' They dodged a mortar burst, then, 'gasping for breath', reached the division headquarters. 'There was no sign of Joe,' nobody had cried out, but his close friend was missing. He was surprised at what he found inside the headquarters:

> 'This was a scene of unbelievable misery – the stench of bodies awaiting burial, the stink as the wounded were sick, the smell of medications, the groans of dying men, the words of padres as they gave the last rites – no words of mine can convey the utter desolation that existed.'

The small group of pilots had to keep moving. 'I allowed myself to be rushed out and down to the river,' Baker recalled, to his enduring regret. 'Should I have tried to go back and find Joe?' he interminably asked himself. 'This question I can never answer to satisfy myself.' Despite exhaustive enquiries after the war and the constant efforts made by his friend's wealthy father, 'not a trace of Joe emerged'.[307]

German prisoners in the tennis court 'cage' behind the Hotel Hartenstein were a further concern. Operational security was vital and thus far the withdrawal from the Utrechtseweg area had not been compromised. Flying Officer Reginald Lawton recalled the unfortunate man who drew the 'short straw' of looking after them until the last minute. 'His instructions were to make himself as conspicuous as possible to the prisoners and to stay as long as he could before abandoning them and joining the tail end of the evacuation.' The demoralised prisoners, who were, like the Paras, short of food and subjected to eight days of artillery fire that had already killed a number of them, simply sought to stay out of the pouring rain and avoid the intimidating shellfire crashing all around the perimeter. Major Geoffrey Powell, passing the high mesh fence, saw a face pressed up against the wire 'alert with a mixture of anticipation and fear'. Powell appreciated that 'the Germans had seen what was happening, and the man knew that he would soon be free if he managed to survive the night.' Lawton later heard that the man left behind 'stuck it out until 10.30 when the tension got too much for him.' Actually, the Airborne Provost kept a watchful eye on them until 01.30 hours.

Shortly after midnight both the western and eastern blocks on the Utrechtseweg had been dismantled. 'The thin rain which had been falling when we started had grown into a harsh, windswept downpour,' Powell recalled, 'and the stars were hidden by a canopy of black rushing clouds.' Unbeknown to both the Germans and the Dutch, the street had lost its short-lived Liberation status, a situation that would endure for nearly eight months.

'To the right of Arnhem a stream of tracers was coming across the river from the south side,' Corporal Jim Swan could see as they closed on the river, having abandoned the west end of the Utrechtseweg. 'We guessed this was the demarcation line for the boats coming over the water.' As they settled down in the darkness to wait, the ragged files of more than 2,000 withdrawing British paratroopers were stealthily moving down from the high line of the Utrechtseweg to the river, under fire in the pouring rain. Despite appearances, Powell felt the plan 'seemed to be working well'.

> 'The line of men was now jerking in a staccato and tiring manner. Every pause by the leaders because of some hold-up in front brought the column to a juddering halt. Then, when it started again, those in front seemed to move too fast so that the ones at the back were all but running to keep up.'

The men in front swung wide to avoid something lying across the footpath outside the gateway of a small villa. It was the body of a young woman, 'slim and handsome', totally out of place and in fact the first civilian body he had seen. 'She was so neat,' he recalled, 'her skirts arranged decorously about her legs, her face calm and unmarked, so different from the torn and bloodied corpses to which he had grown accustomed during the past week.' She had not been dead long and the discarded jug at her side suggested she had come out to collect water for her family.[308]

The withdrawing paratroopers had to negotiate the totally flat and featureless ground of the Rosander Polder at the foot of the slope, where water-filled ditches and marsh led down to the river. There was not a lot of cover; mercifully they were cloaked by darkness and rain. 'It was a night of fireworks, bangs I had never before heard going on before,' remembered glider pilot Sergeant Arthur Shackleton. 'The Germans thought the army was assaulting to get to us, so they started firing indiscriminately.' They waited for 2 hours, and when no boats were seen for half an hour they moved further along the river bank. 'A spandau or some machine gun opened up – they must have seen us or something,' Shackleton remembered, because it went 'right down the line of men':

'I got shot in the shoulder. When I sort of picked myself up off the ground, these 12 or maybe 14, were all dead, or they had run away. There was nobody there except the dead ones. So I thought, "Well, I'm not staying here."'

'For the first time during the whole action I panicked,' recalled glider pilot Sergeant Louis Hagen, when he came across wounded strewn across his path. He could hear subdued cries and made out body shapes, dragging themselves toward the track. 'Feverish pleading eyes looked up towards me, arms clutched around my legs. It seemed all the wounded were frenzied by the fear of being left behind.' Hagen ran about in circles to get help, to find who was in command. 'I vomited and felt faint,' he remembered, until an authoritative voice called up from the river to leave them alone. 'They could not be got over the river just now.'

The crossings were a tense desultory affair. The 23rd Canadian Field Company supported by three other companies with 21 power boats and 16 paddle boats had 6 to 7 hours to transport more than 2,000 men across the river. The paratroopers saw them as 'whispers and shadows in the night'. At any moment the Germans might realise what was happening. The power boats could carry 16 men but were sometimes overloaded to as many as 36. Chattering sinews of spandau tracer converged on those unlucky enough to be illuminated by flares, and columns of water abruptly rose up among boats motoring or paddling stealthily across. Crossing under power might take 4 to 5 minutes, or three times as long for increasingly tired engineers paddling against the swift current to avoid the German riverside positions downstream, then having to drag their boats around the groins to get back upstream. 'There were 14 knots in that current,' recalled glider pilot Des Page. 'You couldn't swim across it, you had to swim at an angle.' Still the Germans did not see that the British were slipping away. It took about 150 boatloads at a rate of about 20 to 30 an hour to complete the crossing, in the face of constant engine failures and casualties from enemy fire. Nobody knows how many perished between the two river banks. It was a costly withdrawal for the survivors of the 21st Independent Company, who lost another five men that night, three of them missing, never to be seen again. Private Johnny Peters with the Borderers remembered:

'The boats were getting shot at, blokes were screaming. If you got hit and the boat turned over, or the blokes panicked in that boat, you just drowned, and that happened to loads of people.'

'I'd made it,' he later reflected on getting across, 'but my mates hadn't.'

Arthur Shackleton's boat was hit, 'a kind of "phut",' and the boat disintegrated, tossing them all into the water. 'I think the air in my smock kept me afloat,' he recalled, because he was completely dazed. 'I could see these flashes, but couldn't hear it, and I couldn't use the arm or the leg.' He felt like he was drowning until his dangling leg touched something solid. A Canadian voice said, 'Oh, there is a body coming, help me out with it.' Shackleton responded, 'I'm not a body, I am alive,' and screamed when the Canadian grabbed his wounded shoulder to get him out of the water. He was taken away by an ambulance.[309]

At 04.00 hours Sturmbannführer Sepp Krafft's battle group, down by the Lower Rhine just the east of the crossing points, was under heavy artillery fire. His later obsequious personal report to Himmler, the head of the SS, claims that he had in fact appreciated that the British were withdrawing. His nearest company laid down a heavy fire, likely on those boats unfortunate enough to be picked up by the strong current and sent their way. 'Under the fire of its heavy weapons, only two or three boat loads got across,' he claimed.

Major Geoffrey Powell got to the other side and quickly climbed the 8-10-foot-high dyke wall, 'all tiredness now gone, running almost gaily down the other side. The rest of the boat joined me in a scurry.' They had made it. 'The bank shut out the battle like a curtain dropping behind us. We were safe!' As the sky lightened and Herbert Kessler's Hermann Göring soldiers made their way back to their own lines with some relief, about 300 or so British soldiers huddled against the north bank regarding the same lightening sky with trepidation. The boats stopped coming.[310]

The street was completely evacuated. Only a few wounded soldiers kept up a desultory fire as dawn broke. An injured signaller kept radio traffic going inside the ruined Hotel Hartenstein. A total of 1,485 British and Polish troops perished along or within earshot of the Utrechtseweg, and 6,525 were taken prisoner. By morning 1,741 men from the 1st British Airborne Division, 422 glider pilots and 160 Poles, together with 75 men from the failed attempt by the Dorset Regiment, had been ferried or swum across the Lower Rhine.

It took the Germans some considerable time to work out what had happened. At 09.30 General von Tettau was reporting that the 'II SS Corps announced that the enemy made another attempt to break out to the east in the early morning hours but was repulsed.' And that 'during this fighting 170 were taken prisoner and 140 German prisoners freed.' Meanwhile Lippert's regiment, taken over by Wagner, 'reports assault force attacks along the whole front'. Lance Corporal Harry Smith with the South Staffords recalled that 'there was about a hundred of us in a hollow in the bank of the river' facing German tanks and infantry up the slope:

'An officer said that it would be useless carrying on as we would not stand a chance if the Germans attacked us; all of us

disagreed with him. But as he stood talking to us he was hit
by a 20mm shell in his hip, blowing a piece of his hip away.
We then realised that it was hopeless as the Germans opened
up heavy fire on our position.'

To the north of the abandoned perimeter Alfred Ziegler with the
Kampfgruppe Bruhn recalled the last night. 'As the Paras were
withdrawing there were break-out attempts – patrols attacked us.' They
continued to be wary until 'these withdrew and finally gave up in the
morning'. At 10.25 Von Tettau announced that the Battalion Eberwein
had cleared the area north of the Utrechtseweg and had linked up with
the SS at the Hartenstein. As the self-propelled guns of Sturmgeschütz
Brigade 280 nosed up to the entrance, Gefreiter Wilhelm Rohrbach's
enduring memory was of 'our captured comrades marching at the head
of the remaining surrendered British and Polish paratroopers coming out
of the tennis courts.' All units to the west, Von Tettau reported, advanced
east to 'join in the attack'. Even this took time – nobody wanted to die at
this stage of the fighting. Junker Rolf Lindemann pushing forward with
Oelker's Battalion, one of the Lippert SS NCO School units, claimed
that 'it was not a real attack, the Paras had gone already, we only found
weapons and dead people.' It appeared that Schiffstamm Abteilung 10,
the infantry sailors, still had much to learn. 'During the final attack, the
navy unit on our right simply got lost on the way,' he caustically observed.
Lance Corporal Harry Smith's small enclave was swept up in these final
advances. By 12.00 the German link-ups were complete. 'The Battalion
Eberwein and elements of the Battalion Oelkers had broken through to
the Rhine and established contact with the Hermann Göring Battalion
at the gasworks and our eastern neighbour, the 9th SS Division.' 'What
happened then made us feel so disgusted,' recalled an indignant Harry
Smith. 'We were captured by men who must have passed the 60 mark
with big "Kaiser Bill" moustaches.'

'Come on,' Hauptmann Bruhn said to Ziegler. 'We might as well
mount up and drive over to take the surrender. It's over.' It still took until
14.00 to mop up resistance before Von Tettau felt able to report 'the

remainder of the encirclement had been cleared of enemy and the encirclement battle finished.' Hauptsturmführer Hans Möller recalled that 'it stopped all of a sudden, the silence appeared suspicious to everyone, it was almost painful.' His SS assault pioneers were relieved, but remained uncertain. 'Was it over? Would it start again?'[311]

In some cases it did. Eighteen-year-old Dutchman J. A. van Hofwegen emerged hesitantly from No 154 Weverstraat to see a gigantic King Tiger rumble past:

> 'The tank was completely closed and making a lot of noise, and in front of the tank a horse was running in panic with flying mane. This droning monster coming right at us was a terrifying sight and we stood at our doorstep with our hands up.'

Following behind the tank was German infantry shouting 'Raus! Raus! Out! Out!' They were very nervous. The leading NCO told them that 'the Tommies had crossed the Rhine during the night'. His unit of 60 men had been reduced to 15 overnight, so they were not prepared to be understanding. Van Hofwegen's back door suddenly swung open and a rifle and bayonet appeared, followed by a German soldier asking, 'Are there any Tommies here?' Startled, he responded in English, 'No sir, there are no Tommies here,' which was not what the German wanted to hear. 'Was, bisst du auch ein Tommy?' he demanded, wanting to know if he was an English soldier and insisting on seeing his identity pass. Outside two Germans driving past on a captured jeep came under fire from German positions further east 'and bullets flew around our ears'. Everybody hit the ground and a German NCO struggled to his feet and stood in the middle of the road shouting, 'Damn it, can't you see we are Germans?'

Incidents like this occasionally punctured the eerie silence reigning along the length of the street. Dust-covered Dutch civilians emerged from their cellars, blinking in the unaccustomed daylight. They, like the Germans, gradually began to take in what had happened. It was over. The street was back in German hands again. J. A. van Hofwegen observed:

'It was staggering to see how our familiar neighbourhood, where we used to play as little boys and had grown up, had, in nine days, changed into a wilderness of dead men, burnt vehicles, destroyed and burnt houses and buildings, demolished trees, dead animals. Everywhere we looked we saw ammunition, weapons, all kinds of equipment and debris.'

The Utrechtseweg had been completely devastated. Oosterbeek village lost 226 houses and shops, 46 cottages and 39 villas totally destroyed. This represented about one-eighth of the total buildings and there was practically no house undamaged.[312]

'After two days of fierce shooting and worried German faces, we awoke on Tuesday to relative quiet,' recalled Netje Heijbroek at 'Valkenburg' by the abandoned Borderer positions near the Koude Herberg crossroads. 'How strange it was, "the quiet" after all the noise of the shooting.' The battle had been lost, the Heijbroek family appreciated, and Netje wrote in her diary that 'it is over, we are German again. Today for the first time I cried.' To the north of the street Geert Maassen at No 32 Mariaweg saw a dead Englishman lying on the lawn behind his house 'with his head on a cushion and his gun beside him'. On the garden path of his neighbour's house was a dead German. 'He looked elderly, lying on his side, his left arm upright, pointing to the sky,' he recalled. 'It was a gloomy sight.' To the south of the street schoolboy Cees Meijer noticed when the shelling stopped in the early morning that 'it became deadly quiet'. His family carefully climbed the cellar steps and 'to our disappointment and shock' discovered German soldiers in the neighbourhood; they were drinking from a pail standing beneath a rain-pipe. 'It became clear to us that the long-awaited army from the south had not come.' He dismally watched a group of British prisoners of war being marched past, guarded by German soldiers on bicycles. 'Some of the English soldiers were wounded, but in spite of that they were singing.' It made him feel very sad.[313]

At the Oosterbeek crossroads, scene of some of the fiercest fighting on the street, Jan Hol emerged from the cellar of No 8 Stationsweg and regarded the Utrechtseweg. 'It was dead still,' he remembered:

'At first I thought that my hearing had been affected, that my eardrums had given up as a result of the explosive attacks they had been subjected to over the last few days. I quickly realised that the Paras were gone.'

The sun appeared, but the landscape, bathed in its watery light, offered little joy. 'It was as if the world had ended and I was the only survivor.' 'No birds sang,' but in his mind's eye images of the battle still raged. He regarded what had 'once been such a peaceful, clean and tidy street', but now:

'In the middle of the road stood the upper half of a man, cut in two just below the ribs. One arm was missing and the other pointed to the sky, where his eyes also stared. He was still wearing his spectacles.'

In the background the metallic voice from an abandoned Polish radio set sounded out from the badly battered 'Quatre Bras' house on the corner. 'Hello Co-del-co. Hello co-del-co,' a tired monotonous voice kept repeating. Three SS troopers approached him, heavily armed with automatic weapons at the ready and 'potato-masher' grenades protruding from their boot tops and belts. 'Wo sind die Engländer?' 'Where are the English?' they demanded. Hol responded hoarsely 'from an emotion they would never understand': 'No more,' he said. 'No more.'[314]

Shall we ever come back? The Dutch

The Germans had an ambivalent attitude towards the Dutch. They were a fine people, big-boned with blond and brown hair, not unlike Reichsdeutsche. Oosterbeek would not have been out of place as a leafy suburb of the Ruhr. The transformation on crossing the border was more cultural than physical. Fighting in Oosterbeek was perhaps more unsettling than the vicious conflict most veterans had conducted in Russian villages. Holland was uncomfortably like home, yet it was better to fight a war on a Dutchman's doorstep bordering the Reich rather than your own. The Dutch were hardly supportive: only 80,000 of them, a mere 1% of the population, had ever signed up for the National Socialist Party, even when Germany was winning the war. They protected their Jews and, like the French Marquis in Paris the previous month, they would stab you in the back as soon as the Allies appeared. Now, with the British defeat, Oosterbeek was the front line and, like Arnhem, was to be cleared of non-combatants. The German soldier was not noted for his tendency to let compassion get in the way of military rationale.

The two German PK (Propaganda Kompanie) war photographers, Jacobsen and Wenzel, had already taken pictures of refugees fleeing the fighting. Piles of belongings can be seen piled on a tricycle being wheeled along near Arnhem station at the entrance to the Utrechtseweg during the early days of fighting to the east of the street. Civilians can be seen nervously shading eyes and squinting into the sun behind the cameramen. Later, well-dressed families, fathers carrying children and others struggling with suitcases or carrying haversacks can be seen crossing the Bergstraat further along. The young lad wearing shorts and long socks carrying his raincoat over his arm made an appealing propaganda picture. The perfidious British can be seen driving the civilian populace before them, while German soldiers correctly pause, to let them pass through to the rear.

By Tuesday and Wednesday Dutch civilian patients were being forced to evacuate the St Elizabeth Hospital on the Utrechtseweg. Jacobsen and Wenzel were on hand to record this initial German policy, which was to get non-combatants out of the way – they were impeding military operations. Moreover, space was needed at the dressing stations and the hospital to take in the influx of military casualties. It was, however, a pre-emptory action, as recalled by Dr Laterveer leading the Red Cross column to remove the civilian patients from the St Elizabeth Hospital, 'enforced ... by order of the German authorities because it lay too near the front line'. Compassion was not a distinguishable feature of the photographs that Wenzel took. 'It was ordered so precipitately,' Laterveer recalled, because 'while we were still preparing the motor cars, the first group of patients, accompanied by nuns and nurses, and protected by a large Red Cross flag, already came walking along.' Wenzel took pictures of a nurse carrying a baby, the mother in pyjamas with a coat worn on top. Other women are pushing prams and elderly ladies are struggling along behind with oversize suitcases and bags. 'It was a sorry sight to see these patients with coats thrown over their nightclothes, stumbling through the streets' on their way to the Deaconnesse's nursing home outside the battle area. Its normal capacity of 220 beds swelled quickly to between 600 and 700.[315]

As the fighting intensified, a steady exodus of civilians forced out of their cellars began to straggle northwards with pathetic columns of men, women and children pushing overloaded bicycles, barrows and baby prams with their few remaining possessions. All were looking for shelter. Rumours began to circulate about a general evacuation, but were disregarded. 'That is something we refuse to believe!' confided Mrs J. Glazema van Altena in her diary, living on the northern outskirts of Arnhem. 'Just imagine, Arnhem with 90,000 people! One can't just throw them out like that!' At this stage sympathy was extended more liberally than hospitality. Some of the refugees found shelter, others were rejected by people who had no desire to accommodate unknown guests with hungry mouths.[316]

At 4 o'clock on 23 September Dr J. N. van der Does, heading the Gelderland Regional Red Cross, was summoned to appear at the SS Hohenstaufen HQ at Apeldoornseweg. SS-Obersturmführer (Lieutenant) Helmut Peter, commanding the Hohenstaufen's Feldgendarmerie (Military Police), pointed to a map on his wall and brusquely told Van der Does that everybody living south of the railway line between Arnhem and Ede had to leave before 8 o'clock that evening. The rest were to follow within 24 hours. Van der Does's protests were cut short. 'If any man, woman or child is found in town after tomorrow night,' Peter snapped, 'it will be the worse for them. Save your breath and empty your town.'[317]

This was not an evacuation, which is an assisted process, but an expulsion. Where these civilians should go and how they ought to travel was, it was made clear, not the concern of the occupying power. 'You went to friends,' explained Harry van Gorkum. 'There was not a displaced persons organisation, you went to where there was no fighting.' Civilian

315

transport modes – fire engines or trucks – were invariably confiscated by German soldiers and redirected to military service. Obersturmführer Peter tried to reconcile some of the maverick confiscations but was informed that 'the Fuhrer has said even the best is not good enough for the German soldier, so even when these vehicles are found, they can be confiscated by the Wehrmacht.' Since the war much criticism has been levelled at the validity of the evacuation order and Van der Does's over-ready acceptance of it. SS-Obersturmbannführer (Lieutenant Colonel) Spindler's command post on the Amsterdamseweg was consulted, but he was busy fighting the battle. He was very correct, knew nothing – including Peter – pointing out that he had many Obersturmführers under his command. Whatever the legality, it was too late to revoke the order; the exodus was under way and nobody was minded to change it. British resistance had stiffened, the Dutch were obviously supportive, so they were better off out of the way. Compassion was not an issue; indifference was the primary factor, verging on vengeful – the Dutch had asked for it. Obersturmführer Peter meanwhile slipped away, allegedly with a car full of loot.[318]

As the inhabitants of the street stumbled into daylight on the morning of 26 September to survey the catastrophic damage done to their homes, the disturbing evacuation rumours were confirmed. They were to depart from the Utrechtseweg and join the mass exodus that had already begun from Arnhem. Fifty thousand followed the recommended northern route to Apeldoorn, 22½ miles away. Another 30,000 opted for the unofficial stream heading towards Velp, 7 miles east. Three thousand would never come back. Oosterbeek was declared 'a forbidden area'. Not everyone was convinced. Most people began to pack, while others tried to fit out their cellars as temporary accommodation, insisting they would not go.

Geert Maassen had first to pick his way through the Utrechtseweg, moving east towards the station with a group of three families. 'We had to battle our way through an enormous amount of debris; the roads were full of wood, glass, fallen tiles, ammunition and abandoned vehicles.' As they moved across the small railway bridge into the Dreyenseweg they passed dead English soldiers and more discarded vehicles. The silence was almost tangible – 'unbelievable, this silence after all those days of immense noise'. They joined the refugee stream from Arnhem, heading north towards Apeldoorn. Light rain began to fall, the gentle sound interrupted only by crying children strapped on top of the luggage on hand carts, cold, tired and hungry. 'It made no difference if one was rich or poor,' one witness recalled. 'They all marched slowly on with the same miserable belongings, like outcasts.'[319]

Schoolboy Willy van Zanten left the same day, 26 September, after 'the Germans eventually came and ordered us out.' They had not realised the British had gone. 'We struggled with our carts and delivery bicycle borrowed from Mr Köhler, a poulterer, over the mess in the Weverstraat and Utrechtseweg.' They watched as a British plane was shot down by German batteries in the Mariëndaal Park. 'I remember the Germans congratulating each other, shaking hands.' Bread was passed out to them when they went by the German army camp that had been set up on the football pitch next to the Apeldoorn road. 'We saw old soldiers,' he recalled. 'It turned out they were Austrian, really old ones, distributing bread with tears in their eyes. I will never forget.' They met other acquaintances from Oosterbeek on the road, including 'a young neighbour of mine, Martin Derkson'. He had been wounded and had shouted to Willy's mother, 'Aunty Kee, help me', but he was to die in the Juliana Hospital at Apeldoorn.

Cees Meijer's parents on the Weverstraat decided, alongside their neighbours, that it would not be safe to stay. 'There was no way in which normal life could be continued. All facilities – water, gas, electricity – had stopped and many people had lost their homes.' As was the Dutch way, departures were often undemonstrative. People walked around their homes for one last time, carefully locking everything up; others simply left their cupboards open. Lost in thought and depressed, the door would be finally shut. Shall we ever come back? What shall we find if we do come back? Cees saw that the streets were full of debris, glass and soldiers' equipment:

'We saw a goat walking in the street, sniffing the contents of a parachute container. Some German soldiers were walking

around, carrying flame-throwers. People were opening rabbit
hutches to set the animals free.'

When they reached the Utrechtseweg it was impassable 'as the masts and
overhead lines of the trams were lying across the road'. As they crossed
the railway bridge leading to the Dreyenseweg 'we looked down on the
railway lines; they were festooned with parachutes in many different
colours.' They also filtered into the columns heading north:

'People were using anything on wheels – wheelbarrows,
perambulators, bicycles – to carry whatever they had
managed to save from their homes. It was a silent procession
that went up the Dreyenseweg and it grew even more silent
when we reached the top of the road and saw in the woods
many dead English soldiers, some of which were still holding
their weapons in their foxholes.'[320]

Anje van Maanen constantly peered at the vehicles driving past the
columns, watching out for her father, the doctor, who had remained
behind to oversee the evacuation of the wounded from the Tafelberg. She
dolefully regarded aeroplanes flying over Oosterbeek in the distance 'and
then black smoke, this is our home,' she thought. Water and occasionally
even coffee and biscuits were given out by Red Cross volunteers on the
route. 'People are sorry for us and help us when they can,' she remembered.
The primitive living conditions inside cramped cellars, battle tensions
and shortages of everything had sapped their body resistance. 'Suddenly
I notice that it is very cold,' she recalled, and 'now I notice the rain and
the silence.' Soon their possessions were drenched, including a cat that
had been added to the cart. Occasionally a lorry carrying Germans with
rifles and prisoners with red berets would pass by and always cause a
momentary stir in the normally emotionally impervious column. 'V'
signs were exchanged and the paratroopers always smiled back with
encouraging self-confidence. 'I look at the Tommies and smile, they see
it, but I daren't say hello, for the Germans won't have it, just a smile.' Her

Auntie Auke quietly wept as they walked along, very worried about her father. 'We put our blankets around us, for it rains hard and it is cold.' Anje was too confused and upset to cry.

The Van Maanens were to be reunited, when her father came by with the final truck loads of wounded from the Tafelberg, heading for Apeldoorn. 'We kiss,' Anje remembered:

> 'We have never been so poor and yet so rich. We have lost
> our village, our home and all our things in it, but we have got
> each other and we are alive.'

The searing experience of the previous nine days had transformed everyone's priorities on the street.[321]

The exodus was the precursor to the forthcoming Dutch 'Hunger Winter', as it was to be called. Before them lay an uncertain future, behind them, on the Utrechtseweg, it was a mess. German soldiers were already beginning to strip out some 8,000 doors from the houses to fortify the overhead protection for their trenches, even now being dug in a zone of fortified strongpoints along the northern bank of the Lower Rhine. Soon only Red Cross volunteers were left. These, as Tonny Gieling recalled, were 'forced to help the SS with the identification and burial of the dead… I witnessed terrible things,' he remembered:

> 'In one house I found a dead man and a woman sitting under
> a table, locked in embrace… There were bodies everywhere.
> The German soldiers took anything of value.'[322]

The street now became the primary supply road feeding this stalemate of trench positions along the Lower Rhine for the next eight months.

CHAPTER 10

Phoenix from the Ashes

Abandonment and Liberation

On Sunday 1 October 1944 at Wageningen, 8½ miles along the street west of Oosterbeek, schoolteacher J. Douwenga was awoken by strange noises. 'It was like the slow shuffle of thousands of feet,' he recalled, 'but there was no sound of voices'. Pulling back the curtains to see

> '...we looked, we just looked. What I saw was so tragic, so terribly sad, that it overwhelmed us completely. My wife could not bear it any longer and burst out into tears. An endless stream of refugees ... walked past in the pouring rain ... they were soaked to the skin and silent.'

Autumn leaves falling from the trees completed the sombre backcloth. More refugees had been set on the march, having been found by the Germans trying to subsist in cellars along and about the street. They had hoped to repair their homes before the winter, but it was not to be, a particular blow because they had prevaricated with no place to go. The Breman family had stayed in their house on the Benedendorpsweg near the destroyed railway bridge by the river until the end of October. 'We were driven from our house by the Germans,' remembered 15-year-old Roelie. 'We found shelter in an old hen-coop at Harskamp on the Veluwe.' The 'Hunger Winter' beckoned. 'We often went very hungry and had to eat boiled nettles as there was nothing else to be had.' Netje Heijbroek's family also managed to stay until 28 October in their house 'Valkenburg' near the Koude Herberg crossroads. 'Feldgendarmerie military police arrived' that afternoon – 'we had to be out of our beloved house by 4pm.' They left for Ede 'with a little wicker cart, a small English hand cart and a big three-wheeled cart' accompanied by their goat, cat and dog. 'With hearts heavy with disappointment, we went forward into the long hunger winter.'[323]

There were still 300 to 400 fugitive British paratroopers hiding out, mainly to the north of the street, beyond the old drop zones around Barneveld and Ede. Two substantial groups of these evaders were to cross the Utrechtseweg again, bound for the Allied lines south of the Lower Rhine. The dislocation caused by further refugee evacuations due on 22 October from around the nearby villages was used as cover for the Dutch Resistance to get the first group of 138 men out under the operation code-named Pegasus I.

The consequences of helping the British were well known. More than two weeks before, a Dutch Resistance attack aided by a British paratrooper sergeant on a car load of German officers at Putten to the north-west resulted in horrific reprisals. Lieutenant Colonel Fritz Fullriede, with the Hermann Göring Training Regiment, was ordered by his superior General Christiansen to 'burn the whole place down and line the whole band up against the wall'. Hostages were picked up and, as Fullriede commented in his diary, 'eight civilians attempting to flee were shot', including a 28-year-old woman. 'Orders from Berlin,' Fullriede recorded. 'All men between 17 to 50 to be transported for forced labour in Germany, all the women evacuated and Putten burned down.' He was reluctant to fulfil the order to the letter; only 87 of 600 houses were burned, for which he had to explain himself to his superiors. Nevertheless, to the horror of the women 660 of their men were shoved into cattle wagons bound for Germany, of which only 49 were ever to return, five of whom died shortly after. In total 552 people perished as a consequence of a single act of resistance. Therefore, assisting 400 or so evaders hiding locally to the north of the street was an act of calculated courage and, for some, sacrifice.[324]

During the night of 21/22 October 138 paratrooper evaders rendezvoused in the woods north-west of Renkum and set off after 21.30. Some time after 23.00 they crossed the Utrechtseweg for the last time, just to the west of the ruined brick factory where B Company the Borderers had repulsed Kapitänleutnant Zaubzer's naval infantry on the second day of the battle. As the column moved down the pathway beyond the street to the river, they bumped into a patrol of 12 Germans. Aghast at the sudden appearance of such a large band of desperate-looking paratroopers, shooting them up with Brens and Stens, the Germans scattered. Amazingly, silence descended again on the river bank and by 02.00 'Easy' Company of the US 506th Parachute Regiment had paddled them across the Lower Rhine.

A second attempt, Pegasus II, attempted between 17 and 20 November, was less fortunate. These men had been on the run for longer and were weaker than the earlier escapers, with their body resistance further reduced in the freezing rain that covered the operation. The problem was how to avoid the heavy batteries of German artillery positioned in the woods north and south of the Ginkel Heath, the 4th Parachute Brigade's previously contested drop zone. The large group of 130 evaders was spotted by an alert German sentry, who opened fire. The paratroopers were fired on again as they attempted to cross the Amsterdamseweg. Obliged to bomb-burst in all directions, many were captured on and around the Ginkel Heath in the darkness. Eight were killed, three of whom were executed after capture; 50 got away, but only two small groups of three and four men crossed the street and managed to reach and cross the river. Ironically, they crossed the Utrechtseweg at the point where many had joined it from Wolfheze and the drop zones to the north during the heady days of its Liberation. They were the last British soldiers to walk on the street for six months.[325]

With the paratroopers gone and the inhabitants ejected, the street lay at the mercy of its German conquerors. 'Oosterbeek has become one big dunghill, and the Germans seem to be rooting about on top of it,' recalled Hendrika van der Vlist, who achieved a fleeting visit back to the Hotel Schoonoord. 'The hotel seemed to be more ruined than when they left it,' she recalled. 'Does any room, any hall still have its ceiling?' It was a total mess:

> 'Blood-stained mattresses are lying about everywhere in the house. My wardrobe has been forced open. All the decent clothes have disappeared.'

It was depressing. Any civilians who attempted to re-enter the forbidden zone were turned back by German patrols who threatened to shoot if they ever sought access again. Random and haphazard pillaging of the houses was superseded by the more systematic policy of 'Raumung' or 'emptying' them. This work was carried out by members of the German Nazi Party, who came with lorries and trailers from just across the German border. So-called 'Salvage Kommandos' came from other regions in the Reich to collect household goods and articles for down-and-out German civilians, made destitute by Allied bombing. Houses were stripped of furniture, bedding, mattresses, clothes, kitchen articles, radios, pianos and anything considered remotely domestically useful. If it could not be removed it was wantonly destroyed or fouled. Houses had already been liberally coated with excrement by defending soldiers. Trucks took all these sequestered goods to the railway station, where they were loaded aboard goods wagons marked 'Liebesgabe aus Holland!' – 'Gifts with love from Holland!'

Meanwhile the former inhabitants of the street were coming to terms with the trauma of enforced vagrancy. Finding accommodation was a premium and not necessarily easy. They were guests in strange houses. Relationships conducted under duress resulted in unpleasant or precious memories. 'There is discord between the evacuees and the inhabitants of Apeldoorn,' Hendrika van der Vlist, forced out of the Schoonoord, recalled. People were getting under each other's feet. 'At that time they did not know that it would be for so long.' Difficulties immediately arose because 'in many families potatoes are getting scarce, and the evacuees are sharing their food.' Hendrika appreciated:

> 'Even in normal times it would not do; two housewives in one house, in one kitchen. And now in these days of tension it won't do at all.'[326]

Geert Maassen went with his wife and baby to a family living in Apeldoorn. 'They were very kind and helpful to us,' he remembered, 'but it soon became clear that the house was too small for three extra people.' Eventually they moved in with the nephew of one of his neighbours who 'took good care of us' until the end of the war. 'We still think of them with much gratitude,' he commented. Others were not immediately so lucky. Jan Hendrik Esvelt, driven out of his home by the fighting around the Arnhem bridge, remembered that his wife Lotte tried for accommodation but was rejected. His daughter Berend suspected that 'the fruitless begging for shelter by my mother was probably caused by the fact that she still had a bit of a German accent.' 'Not very encouraging,' Jan Esvelt confided to his diary. 'We slowly are starting to realise what it really means to be war refugees.' It was not simply hunger that afflicted the street exiles during the terrible winter of 1944-45:

> 'People who have not been exiles from a deserted town can never know. Have not most of us, awaking in stormy nights and thinking of our deserted houses, where now the wind raged through the broken windows, and the rain was driven in, suddenly become filled with an awareness of affection, of attachment to that house and to what we left behind there? An awareness so intense that we were amazed at it. And did it not grow into a homesickness for our street, our neighbourhood, and our town, into a great longing to see once more the faces of well-remembered people?'

These people lived with their ghosts. They still saw in their mind's eye the bitter struggles that were fought through their back yards, halls and living rooms. Now many of them were to starve.[327]

Operation Market-Garden had captured the farmland of southern Holland. There were still 4½ million inhabitants left in the industrialised north, where the urban conurbations of Rotterdam, Amsterdam and The Hague remained in German hands. At the beginning of Market-Garden the Dutch national railways went on strike to impede German troop movements. Food supplies and fuel were immediately cut off from the western cities. Reichskommissar Seyss-Inquart retaliated by imposing an embargo on the movement of food and fuel along Holland's canals and waterways. Large areas of Holland were also flooded by the Germans as a defence measure, which resulted in a huge drop in agricultural output. Both the flooding and the failure of Market-Garden encouraged Eisenhower and Montgomery to give little priority to the next phase of the Liberation of Holland; it was nicely isolating a catchment of German forces that would otherwise be employed in defence of the Reich. Meanwhile fuel supplies quickly disappeared as Holland was plunged into its coldest winter in living memory.

'There was not a lot of food left,' remembered Harry van Gorkum in Apeldoorn, so:

> 'Hundreds of people went into the country to try and get something from the farmers. The farmers were very often pretty ruthless with the prices they charged. You paid the equivalent of £100 for ½lb of butter, or something like that, and that was a lot of money then.'

Supplies of coal, electricity and gas all failed. All that remained on tap was water. Coal waste was scavenged alongside the railway lines; even the wood between tram lines was slit out for burning as parkland was stripped of trees. Ruined houses were searched for anything combustible. 'There was a lot of pilfering going on,' recalled Van Gorkum. Within three weeks of the rail strike the calorie intake for the northern cities was reduced to 1,300, half that in rationed Britain. The German counter-offensive in the Ardennes 'Bulge' pushed back the Liberation date for Holland even further as the defeat of Germany became the overriding priority.

Food distribution centres had to be set up in the remaining cities, which distributed half a litre of watery soup containing just 900 calories per day. One official commented that when it dropped to 500 calories, food approved for human beings was being rejected by animals. 'When you have eight children and a ninth just born, it takes something to keep all those little mouths going,' remembered housewife Hendrica Wiersma, 'and the soup was more like muddy water – it was not up to much.' Starving city children became lethargic, taking on the haggard and lined faces of the old. Normal teen development became warped; an average 14-year-old Dutch girl in early 1945 was a stone lighter and 2 inches shorter than the pre-war norm. 'Our daily menu was a mix of fried tulip bulbs and sugar beets,' remembered schoolboy Arie de Jong in late March 1945:

'My mother made an invention that switched us from the awkward fried tulip bulbs to smaller fried crocus bulbs. They turned out to be delicious … rather like small fried onions but not that strong onion flavour. It filled your stomach for a couple of hours and it didn't give those awful hiccups tasting like soil.'[328]

If the Allies did not come soon, it would be too late. Thirty thousand Dutchmen had been taken to Germany for labour and 18,000 had already starved to death.

Liberation, when it came on 13 April, waited for the warm weather. Like the Blitzkrieg of May 1940, it began with an assault on Arnhem across the River Ijssel from Germany and the east. Operation Quick Anger, the last of three phased attacks to clear northern Holland, was mounted by the Canadian First Army. Spearheaded by the British 49th (West Riding) Division, it was supported by the tanks of the 5th Canadian Armoured Division and rocket-firing RAF Typhoons. It was a repeat of SS-Unterscharführer Hans Möller's approach march with the SS Der Führer Regiment in May 1940, with the same initial objectives, including the capture of the old Dutch Westervoort fort, prior to a dash on Arnhem. Here the parallels ceased. This operation was conducted more slowly, with immense firepower and backed up by masses of armoured vehicles. Arnhem was defended primarily by the 858th Grenadier Regiment and Dutch SS from the 34th Nederland SS Division.

'We were kept mucking about at first,' recalled Lieutenant H. Macdonald with C Squadron the 11th Canadian Armoured Regiment. 'Example of how not to win a war – 2 to 3 miles of armoured fighting vehicles, many of types I'd not seen before, all on one road.' Despite the odds, the Germans kept them at bay for more than two days of bitter fighting. 'There was so much stuff there, that all you had to do was line up and let it go.' Macdonald's view was 'why attack Arnhem at all?' He felt it should have been bypassed, 'all blood and guts like Stalingrad'. It was not the place for tanks. 'In streets, only the leading one or two can operate. You can't deploy the rest.'

'Inevitably Arnhem had come to occupy a particularly emotional place in the minds of tens of thousands of British soldiers,' recalled Major Eversley Belfield, manning an Air OP attached to the 1st Canadian Corps. Some 36 Spitfires and 83 Typhoon sorties had blasted the town alongside artillery the day before. 'This town had almost come to be the symbol of the unattainable.' They attacked on a sunny morning with bright blue skies and cumulus clouds, with 'a maze of spring blossoms hiding the ugliness of sandbagged houses and wrecked vehicles,' recalled Alexander McKee, also attached to the Canadian Corps. He was observing from the south bank near Driel, having come up the road from Elst, lined with wrecked vehicles and tanks, where 'bodies of dead cattle lay thickly in the fields, the sweet and sickly smell of death mingling with the scent of the blossoms.'

Only the eastern end of the Utrechtseweg saw fierce fighting over these two April days in 1945. British infantry from the West Riding Division skirmished with Bren, Sten and rifle fire along the same stretch of the street where Lance Corporal Loney and Private Norman Shipley from 2 Para had been killed and photographed by the two SS PK photographers, Jacobsen and Wenzel. Soldiers burst through the shut doors of the Gestapo Headquarters at No 21, now next to No 59 Utrechtseweg, and found them empty and deserted. They continued along the street obscured by phosphorus smoke grenades thrown ahead and covered by Bren gun fire. McKee observed the great dome of the 19th-century Koepel prison 'like the Albert Hall, with four shell holes in its green roof', alongside which 'great tongues of fire leap and play at the base of an immense column of black smoke.' In the vicinity of the 'low road', just beneath the Museum on the street, McKee watched a 'Canadian Sherman let loose with its 75mm turret gun and a cloud of grey-white smoke blossomed horizontally out from the wall.' Shermans accompanied by infantry smashed down any potential strongpoint. 'Both tanks blasted the house,' McKee observed, 'which almost disappeared in the blossoms of spurting smoke and the irregular rashes of machine gun fire.' 'Towards evening' of the second day, 'which was again a sunny one', Lieutenant Macdonald with C Squadron remembered 'enemy opposition collapsed, and we were ordered to climb on all the available vehicles, when we swept through the town, meeting only light sniper opposition.' Any there was, was blasted into oblivion. 'We rested comfortably that night in deserted shops,' he recalled. The rest of the town was to be cleared the following day.

It was a strange experience for the British and Canadian soldier advancing along the Utrechtseweg. No jubilant cheers this time to welcome the liberators, simply deserted and 'spooky' streets. 'I passed into the area where the Airborne Division made their final stand,' recalled Eversley Belfield, passing through Oosterbeek:

> 'It is a terrifying sight with wrecked houses, the trees still damaged, being slivered by the mortaring and shelling, with broken branches with their brown autumn leaves attached.'[329]

The scene resonated with a sense of forlorn sadness. 'Piles of equipment lie around, burnt and abandoned.' The advancing 49th Division infantry observed that 'the enemy had systematically and wantonly looted every house and building.' One observer likened the experience to 'entering an ancient tomb'. Another Canadian officer remembered that the area was 'entirely empty of civilians, and the doors of many houses were standing open.' 'It is the complete lack of any attempt to clear up the place which gives it this air of macabre unreality,' remembered artillery officer Belfield. Some of his men discovered a Stirling bomber that 'had gone in nose first, the crew still in the machine; the Germans had merely taken their parachute from them.' 'This city,' the Canadian officer judged, 'is one of the most saddening sights I have seen in this war.' It was like 'a ghost city, oddly pathetic and disturbing.'

The British 49th Division pushed on through Oosterbeek to Renkum and Ede, clearing the north bank of the Lower Rhine. 'We were going a fair clip,' recalled Lieutenant Macdonald, 'and had seen German infantry get up and run.' There was no concerted German resistance in Oosterbeek itself along the street. One brief rearguard action was fought near the railway embankment beyond Den Brink, with the abandoned train nearby. 'One [German] had the guts to stay behind with his bazooka near a railway embankment,' remembered Macdonald. 'He hit the infantry on top of my tank, not the tank itself' with devastating consequences to unprotected human flesh. 'Holy catfish!' All along the route Belfield saw 'little rough wooden crosses made of two sticks' adorned with Airborne helmets, German helmets and red berets. On the drop zones the grass had been seared in the shape of gliders, 'perhaps 40 in all'. Two of the wrecked gliders still contained jeeps and a 6-pounder anti-tank gun, 'all rusted up'. The whole area was permeated with an atmosphere of defeat. 'One can only realise vaguely the heroism with which the Airborne Division fought,' he recalled.[330]

On 5 May 1945, 8½ miles further along the street at a half-ruined hotel in Wageningen, the German General Blaskowitz surrendered to the Canadian Army. Seven days before, Lancaster aircraft had begun dropping food to the Dutch in northern Holland; in one day 900 bombers dropped 1,800 tons of supplies. 'These were the best bombs we have dropped for years,' recalled Flight Officer Ellis, the bomb-aimer of a Lancaster flying across Ypenburg civil airfield, south-east of The Hague. The way was clear for the inhabitants of the street to return.[331]

The return to the Street

The municipal authority for Renkum, administering the street, was set up in the Bilderberg Hotel, near the 'hollow' where the 156th Parachute Battalion had been practically wiped out. Inside, everyone sought the red 'permit', which, stamped by the military authorities, granted permission to re-enter the street and discover what was left. The Dutch penchant for administrative exactitude made the procedure a bureaucratic nightmare. Each application for readmission was examined and re-examined with information that needed to be gathered and registered to prevent any influx of 'undesirable persons'. Newly arrived refugees met up with former acquaintances. Earlier arrivals would be anxiously pressed for information about the state of their houses. Does it still stand? Was there anything left inside? Evasive answers generally indicated all was not well, which was very often the case. People turned silently away when they began to appreciate that scanty possessions piled high on bicycles was probably all that they owned.

The street was badly battered. In the lower village, south of the Utrechtseweg, 83 houses and shops had been completely destroyed as well as three factories, a school, two farms, the large laundry, the old church by the river and the concert hall, all gone. About 39 houses were severely damaged. Some 688 buildings were to be demolished in the municipality as a whole. This left 1,567 heavily damaged homes and 2,157 lightly damaged. Only 772 houses merely had their windows broken. Roelie Breman, living on the Benedendorpsweg, remembered that 'our house was in ruins so we went to live in the shed'. This was an upgrade from the old hen coop, where they had spent the winter at Harskamp. Hendrika van der Vlist returned to the Hotel Schoonoord. Even when her father left it after the battle 'it was so badly damaged that he couldn't think of a solution' to make it habitable again. 'I would prefer it to have disappeared to having it as it is now,' he had despaired during the evacuation period at Ede. The issue was settled when he heard that it had burned to the ground. Her mother and father regarded the ruin. 'Part of the walls were still standing, scorched,' she recalled, and inside there was only debris. 'Leaning both hands against the door posts of the front door, father stood there and looked and looked, without uttering a word.' He died a few years later.[332]

The first residents started to return in May and June. The indispensable municipal stamp was required to get past the various police posts. Some houses were reduced to rubble, others gutted, the vast majority pictures of desolation and ruin, front doors kicked open or removed to shore up nearby trenches. Familiar-looking furniture stood mouldy and discoloured by rain in front gardens. Many found their gloomiest expectations surpassed. Once tidy and cosy households, where each treasured possession had its allotted place, they were now found knocked and thrown about everywhere. Even wallpaper was torn off walls where it was suspected valuables may have been hidden. Quite often, as 13-year-old Ben Jansen found on returning home to Dedemweg, all their personal belongings had been piled high in the centre of each room and despoiled. Nothing could be retrieved, so everything had to be shovelled out of the windows before cleaning up the house again.

Life was initially harsh: no gas, electricity, fuel or oil. Water supplies were at least soon adequate and the cleaning-up process could begin. A central kitchen was opened on the street on 20 August 1945 until gas and water supplies could be restored. Whoever could possibly spend the night in his former house generally insisted on doing so because pilfering was so prevalent. Houses were made habitable, starting with the roof, then spaces were cleared of debris inside, starting with narrow paths from the door to a window. Bed spaces were created for old mats and worn rags to lie upon until blankets and pillows could be brought from the houses to which they had previously been evacuated. Starting with kitchens and bedrooms, some form of order was created out of the chaos, until within a couple of weeks all the floors of surviving houses were at least comparatively clean. Bare floors, windows without curtains and cardboard instead of window-panes was a start, and steady progress was made during the summer months of 1945 to re-establish 'home'. All along the street were rows of neatly stacked bricks, scraped clean for reuse. Useless debris was banked along the Lower Rhine, where it could be transported elsewhere by barge to reinforce water defences and plug breached dams. 'Very slowly the village was rebuilt,' recalled former schoolgirl Henny de Jongh-Langevoort. 'For years there were a lot of ruins, we were quite accustomed to them, they seemed normal.' The first shops were re-established where the present Post Office is today. The phoenix steadily began to arise from the ashes of the Utrechtseweg.[333]

'I had not gone to school since September 1944,' recalled Willy van Zanten, back at No 20 Cornelis Koningstraat. The school was destroyed. 'My friends and I have played on and inside German tanks, where there was live ammunition too, which was dangerous but we did not realise that as youngsters.' Then in August 1945 there was a ripple of anticipation felt along the street when it was discovered that the 'airbornes' had come back. Two hundred paratroopers had returned to film a docu-drama about the battle, produced by the legendary Ulster film director Brian Desmond Hurst. *Theirs Is The Glory* featured a large number of the original Arnhem veterans, many from the 21st Independent Parachute Company, who had so effectively blocked the Oosterbeek crossroads.

The acting Burgomaster of Renkum, Mr Jan ter Horst, had been sitting at the Bilderberg Hotel, doubling as the municipal offices, when he heard a message that 'the British were at the Airborne Cemetery'. He was determined to meet them, despite the fact that 'the official car was in use elsewhere'. He managed to arrange an appointment to meet with General Urquhart, who was with a group of officers to conduct a post-action analysis of the fighting for Oosterbeek. Willy van Zanten and his friends recalled that 'we watched the movie-makers for *Theirs Is The Glory* many times, because there was not any school available at first.' His enduring memory was of the 'chocolate bars given to us by the soldiers. That was a real treat for us.'[334]

Anje van Maanen's father had found a note in the wreckage of his library from Lieutenant John Horsley, the 21st Company Intelligence Officer. The house had been used as the company's headquarters. He had written:

> 'This is the most comforting book to look at. I hope we haven't made too much of a mess in your house. We desperately needed everything we took. I shall come back and thank you for us all when it is less noisy!'

Forty-eight hours after writing the note John Horsley was killed during the evacuation, crossing the Lower Rhine. His letter encapsulated the guilt felt by many of the airborne soldiers returning to the perimeter for the film re-enactment. Jan ter Horst recalled their anxiety, which was expressed by General Urquhart at their first meeting at the Bilderberg Hotel. 'We have taken so many lives here and caused all this damage, which we can't help to repair,' Urquhart explained, 'that we thought it best to stay together in our party and refrain from any official contact.' The British felt that they were potentially treading on eggshells. Jan ter Horst tried to respond 'in my best school English' that:

> 'We too mourn these losses. The contacts we had made [during the fighting] in those days were extremely valuable and that we had witnessed so many acts of bravery, sacrifice and suffering for many attempts to keep the civilians out of the battle. We were all full of admiration.'

Urquhart was taken aback. 'It was quite a relief for him I remember,' explained Jan ter Horst. 'He had not expected that.'

It was decided to run a joint Anglo-Dutch church service at the newly established Airborne Cemetery, ironically set up just at the point where Spindler's SS blocking force had barred the 4th Parachute Brigade's entry to Arnhem. Padre Dijker, the Dutch Minister who was going to preside, felt that the graves looked 'so dreary with all that black earth without grass or flowers' that he decided 'we should ask schoolchildren to lay flowers from the gardens of their parents.' This was the precursor to the present poignant tradition, started in September 1945 and carried out each year since. At a particular point in the ceremony the local children step forward and lay flowers at each grave, after identifying the name and age of the soldier on the headstone, after which the Last Post is played. In 1945 the children were simply attired, laying flowers against simple wooden crosses on freshly dug graves. Today they are colourfully dressed in every conceivable modern style, placing their flowers against beautifully maintained marble headstones.

The link between the 'airbornes' and the residents of the street and Oosterbeek was picked up in September 1945 and has been maintained by succeeding generations. In 1945 the Renkum Council started a collection to build the 'Needle' Airborne Monument on the triangular green opposite the former division headquarters at the Hotel Hartenstein. This was from a war-impoverished population with virtually nothing to give. When General Urquhart laid its foundation stone at the first commemoration, so many Dutchmen attended that they were balanced precariously in clusters on the damaged rooftops of the Hartenstein Laan behind, or what was left of them, to get a view.

'Airborne Specials' were the trains that came across via the Harwich Ferry during the early years as veterans began to return to the street each year for the annual commemoration. In 1947 the Renkum Police Sports Club instituted the 'Airborne Walking Tour' to raise funds to allow financially disadvantaged veterans to make the annual pilgrimage with wives and relatives. It has since grown into one of the largest annual walking rambles in Europe. Jan Rudolphie, who was an early member of the Dutch Airborne Committee, fondly remembered the 'Airborne Specials':

> 'The British and Polish veterans received their vouchers at the departure point at Liverpool Street station in London. The front page of the voucher showed the name of the veteran or Next of Kin, as well as the name of the host family. The vouchers also indicated whether the pilgrim had to disembark from the train at Oosterbeek or Arnhem, shown by an "O" or an "A".'[335]

The whole affair was conducted with typical Dutch painstaking thoroughness. Commemoration programmes and admission tickets for all the various accompanying social events were included with the tickets. Virtually every year the Parachute Regiment continues to stage a commemorative parachute jump on the Ginkel Heath nearby, where they are greeted by thousands of waving and greeting Dutch, before a short ceremony is conducted on the drop zone memorial – a far cry from the drop made in the teeth of German opposition on 18 September 1944.

The order of service has hardly changed since 1945, beginning with the hymn 'O God, Our Help in Ages Past', sung confusingly in Dutch and English at the same time. The mass laying of flowers by Dutch schoolchildren was very evocative in 1945 and remains so to this day. Those children that endured the battle had vivid and disturbing memories.

Roelie Breman from the Benedendorpsweg recalled that 'many of our English friends' she had got to know during the battle 'had in the meantime been buried in our garden.' Once the bodies were reinterred in the existing cemetery she participated in subsequent flower-laying ceremonies. 'I felt very sad, laying flowers on their graves and remembering how often I had given water from our pump to these boys… I remembered Len' who, she explained 'came from London and that is about the only thing we know about him', and 'wondered if he, too, was lying buried somewhere near.' Willy van Zanten, from Cornelis Koningstraat, just off the street, still remembers that he laid his flowers on the grave of 'Corporal William (Joe) Simpson of the Royal Engineers', who, he recalls, had been 'killed by a German shell on the 20th September' and that 'Joe was 29 years old'. Willy's parents contacted Joe's mother and sent a photograph of Willy standing by his grave. This was the start of a long relationship with Joe's family; the mother died, but Willy maintained contact with 'Aunty Mary', Joe's sister.[336]

'We lived through the battle of Arnhem in all its violence and it made a very deep impression on me,' remembered Jan Hartgers. His family lived in the Mariaweg, around the corner from the Oosterbeek crossroads, the heart of the battle to the east of the street. He also laid flowers as a child at the first commemoration in 1945. 'These boys, as it were, had laid [buried] in our gardens and streets and you saw the reburials,' he recalled, 'so you can imagine we were highly motivated to do this.' 'The first time I laid flowers I was 12 years old,' remembered Henny de Jongh-Langevoort, 'not an age when you think deeply about it.' She thought the first ceremony was 'rather thrilling' and 'exciting to take part'. But over the years she began to appreciate its significance and the importance of the ceremony's continuity:

'Now the feeling is different. When you are young the moment is thrilling and afterwards you go home and start playing again. But when you're older you think more about it and you realise what kind of boys lay buried there. That does not occur to you when you are a child.'

'The curious thing,' explained Jan Hartgers, 'is that the youth of today enter the cemetery in the same mood.' The link, the realisation of the significance of this event that changed the street for ever, has been maintained. Hartgers has watched over and guided the children of subsequent generations through the same ceremony:

> 'Just before, they stand talking, and it is difficult to keep them quiet. But as soon as they come in, holding their flowers and walking between the graves, it's exactly the same as in those [1945] days.'

General Urquhart, interviewed before his death in 1988, expressed his astonishment at the Dutch reaction to the battle and what has since happened:

> 'It was a great surprise to me, the whole affair; because when we left here and withdrew across the Rhine the local people had a hell of a winter. Most of them were evacuated from their homes, they had no fuel, a very severe winter, great privation, cold and no food. So we quite expected when we came back that they wouldn't be best pleased to see us; in fact, we didn't expect any cooperation at all. And blow me down, it was a terrific surprise to find that not only were they polite to us, they were asking us to come back!'

As the phoenix of the street emerged from its wartime ashes, both the residents of the Utrechtseweg and those who bitterly fought to defend their brief Liberation bonded together. Inextricably fused in the same searing crucible of experience, they have maintained their links across generations since. 'It was a great revelation,' Urquhart explained. 'We slowly appreciated what the battle meant in the minds of the local people':

> 'They regarded it as their battle as well as we regarded it ours.'[337]

Introduction

[1] Breman *The Tommies Are Coming*! (Association of Friends of the Airborne Museum Oosterbeek, 1988)

[2] Kershaw, R. J. *It Never Snows in September* (Ian Allan Publishing Ltd, 1994)

[3] The street is referred to as the Utrechtseweg throughout to avoid potential confusion, even though some parts of it are referred to as the Utrechtstraat, depending on the date of issue of pre- and post-war local Oosterbeek street maps.

Chapter 1

[4] Wil Rieken, author interview, 27 May 2011. No 160 is the 1944 address. The house has since been converted into a high street shop.

[5] Van der Vlist, H. *Oosterbeek 1944* (Society of Friends, Airborne Museum, Oosterbeek, 1992)

[6] Schulz *Sieg über Frankreich* (Verlag Wilhelm Undermann, 1940), pp 37-8

[7] Van t'Land (ed S. Gerritsen) Geschichten, die bleiben (Nat Bevrijdingsmusem, 1944-45), p13

[8] Railway yard destruction: Freedom Trail Arnhem, F. van Lunteren and W. Brouwer website, Arnhem Railway Station, notes 2-6 (Arnhem Council and Gelders Archive)

[9] Möller, *Chronik des SS-Pz. Pionier-Bataillons 9* (Author manuscript, p19)

[10] Rieken, author interview, 27 May 2011; Van Gorkum, author interview, 8 Jul 2009

[11] Van t'Land, op cit, p13

[12] Pijkeren, Freedom Trail Arnhem website, Arnhem Railway Station

[13] Jansen, *Uncommon Soldier*, p10

[14] Jan K. in Gerritsen, S. (ed), op cit, p47; Rieken, author interview

[15] Jan K., ibid; local paper *Arnhemsche Courant*; Freedom Trail Arnhem website, Arnhem Town Hall; Kilkens, interview, *The World at War: Occupation Holland 1940-44* (ITV, 1973)

[16] Van Gorkum, author interview; Boas-Koupmann, interview, The World at War, ibid

[17] Photographic evidence, P-A. van Teesling *Over and Over* (Kontrast Pub, Oosterbeek, 2000), pp13, 14 and 17

[18] Posters and signs, ibid, pp16-17

[19] Van der Vlist, op cit, Introduction

[20] Van Gorkum, author interview

[21] Jansen, op cit, p14; Van Gorkum, author interview; Van der Vlist, op cit, p1

[22] Rieken, author interview, 27 May 2011

[23] Minis-Dijkstra in Gerritsen, op cit, p31

[24] Van der Kamp, M. Klijn *De stille slag: joodse Arnhemmers 1933-45* (Westervoort, 2003), p188, mortality figures p233

[25] Van der Vlist, op cit, p1; Otten, Freedom Trail Arnhem website, Arnhem Railway Station

[26] Bolte, recorded conversation, E. A. Bolte, 3 Jun 1965, Gelders Archive Document Collection, Second World War, Item No 150, Freedom Trail Arnhem website

[27] Koepel Prison, Freedom Trail Arnhem website

[28] House numbers in 1944 differ from those today, so Gestapo HQ was at the current 53, and the 'Kraton' PGEM building at 55A

[29] Wunderlink, letter J. Kamevaar to P. Dijkerman, 9 May 2005, Freedom Trail Arnhem website: Nieuwe Kade-Badhuisstraat; Olivier's comments, ed F. P. M. Prick, Gelders Archive Document Collection, Second World War, Item No 281

[30] Penseel, Jan C. Kuiper, Arnhemse Courant article, 28 Sep 1966

[31] Abbink and raid details, C. Janse Blik Omhoog. 1940-45. Wolfheze ende Zuid-Veluwe in Oorlogstijd (Duiven, 2000), p337

[32] Jansen, op cit, p14

Chapter 2

[33] Fullriede, Diary, 31 Aug 44, Nijmegen City Archive; Lippert, Abschrift, hand-written notes, Erwin Heck archive

[34] Fullriede, ibid, 2 and 10 Sep 44

[35] Enthammer, author interview, Schweinfurt, 15 Jun 1987

[36] Fullriede, ibid, 13 Sep 44; Bruggeman, Diary, 5 Sep 44, Pegasus Archive

[37] Voskuil, Ryan, C. *A Bridge Too Far* (Hamish Hamilton, 1974), pp9-10

[38] Sequence of RAF reconnaissance photos, 6 Sep 1944

[39] Bolderman, R. Voskuil Wartime Adventures of an Arnhem Schoolboy (Arnhem Friends Mini-History No 75, Oosterbeek Airborne Museum – henceforth referred to as MH)

[40] Intelligence reports, Notes Lt Col (retd) Th A. Boeree, Nov 1973

[41] Ziegler, author interview and notes 23 Nov 1987; Enthammer, author interview, 15 Jun 1987

[42] Dombrowski, author interview, 23 Oct 1987

[43] Breman *The Tommies Are Coming!* (Association of Friends of the Airborne Museum Oosterbeek, 1988), 1-6 Sep 1944

[44] Van der Vlist, H. *Oosterbeek 1944* (Society of Friends, Airborne Museum, Oosterbeek, 1992), pp2-3

[45] Heijbroek, MH No 66, May 2000; Van t'Land (ed S. Gerritsen) Geschichten, die bleiben (Nat Bevrijdingsmusem, 1944-45), p14

[46] Breman, op cit, 9-10 Sep; Van der Vlist, op cit, pp4 and 6

[47] Van t'Land (ed S. Gerritsen), op cit, pp14-15

[48] Heijbroek, op cit; Huijgen, Maassen, G. H. Daily Reports from the Municipal Police of Oosterbeek (MH No XIII), 17 Sep 12.20 and 12.35. No 107 is the 1944 address.

[49] Rieken, author interview, 27 May 2011

[50] Van Maanen The Diary of Anje 17-25 Sep 1944 (Oosterbeek Airborne Museum), 17 Sep

[51] Hol, Memories of Oosterbeek September 1944 (MH No 52, Nov 1996)

[52] Schoolgirl, Mrs W. J. van Koldenhoven, and Wiertsma, Freedom Trail Arnhem, F. van Lunteren and W. Brouwer website, Provinciehuis and Rijnkade

[53] Breman, Diary, 17 Sep 1944; Esvelt, Diary, 17 Sep 1944, courtesy of Berend Esvelt

[54] Maassen, Daily Reports, op cit

[55] Breman and Van der Vlist, ibid; Hofwegen, J. A. van September 1944: *A Month We Will Never Forget* (*Eagle* Magazine, Vol 9, No 8, Apr 2001)

[56] Van Maanen, op cit, 17 Sep 44

[57] Jansen, *Uncommon Soldier*, pp14-16

[58] Lawton, Waddy J. *A Tour of the Arnhem Battlefields* (Leo Cooper, 1999), p48

[59] SHAEF Supreme Headquarters Allied Expeditionary Force, quoted in Green, P. Fragment of Life, p8

[60] Figures from Van Hees, A.-J. Green On!, p12

[61] Urquhart, R. Arnhem (Pan, 1972), p37; glidermen Patrick Devlin, 1st Bn RUF, and Hancock, Kershaw, R. J. Skymen (Hodder & Stoughton, 2010), p175

[62] Shackleton, interview, WWII Experience Centre, P. Liddle, Jul 2002; MacKenzie, Sigmond, R. *Off at Last* (RN Sigmond, 2009), p44; De Burgh, Liddle interview, Apr 2002

[63] Frost, J. *A Drop too Many* (Cassell & Co, 1980), pp198-202

[64] 7 KOSB orders for Market, Public Record Office WO 171/1323 Para 16, HQ RASC Airborne Division Top Secret MARKET, para A(11) dated 14 Sep 1944; Frost, op cit, p200

[65] Sims, J. Arnhem Spearhead (IWM, 1978), pp32 and 34; Killick, Liddle interview, Oct 2001

[66] Toler, Waddy, op cit, p50

[67] Allsop and Stevenson, Fairley, J. Remember Arnhem (*Pegasus Journal*, 1978), p36; Green, op cit, p11; Shackleton, Liddle interview, Jul 2002

[68] Urquhart, op cit, p37

[69] Jansen, op cit, p20

[70] Sims, op cit, pp34-6; Curtis R. *Churchill's Volunteer* (Avon Books, 1994), pp159 and 162

[71] Krafft, after-action report, 1330hrs, 17 Sep 1944

Chapter 3

[72] Möller, personal account, July 1980

[73] Dombrowski, author interview, 23 Oct 1987

[74] Harzer, Bauer, C. The Battle of Arnhem (Zebra, 1979), p92

[75] Ziegler, author interview, 23 Nov 1987

76 Van Maanen The Diary of Anje 17-25 Sep 44 (Oosterbeek Airborne Museum), 17 Sep 1944; Hofwegen, J. A. van September 1944: *A Month We Will Never Forget* (*Eagle* Magazine, Vol 9, No 8, Apr 2001)

77 Photos, A. L. A. Krema-Kingma; Hol, J., *Memories of Oosterbeek* (MH No 52, Nov 1996)

78 Krafft, War Diary, SS Panzer Grenadier Depot and Reserve Bn 16, 17 Sep 1944

79 Schwarz, author interview, 16 Sep 1987; Müller, personal account, Schneider collection; Ziegler, author interview, 23 Nov 1987

80 Lippert, personal account, Erwin Heck archive; Fullriede, Diary, 21 Sep 1944; Lindemann, author interview 11 Jun 1987.

81 Reimann, Tiemens, W. H. *The Only Female Prisoner of War in Arnhem* (MH No 39, Aug 1993); Sims, J. Arnhem Spearhead (IWM, 1978), p38

82 Barents photo, Margry, K. Operation Market-Garden: Then and Now, 2 Vols ('After The Battle', 2002), p205 – No 130 Utrechtseweg is the modern address; Green, P. Fragment of Life, p13

83 Cleminson, Waddy J. *A Tour of the Arnhem Battlefields* (Leo Cooper, 1999), p58

84 Heijbroek, N. *Three Englishmen in Our Cellar* (MH No 66, May 2000); Krafft, op cit, 17.00, 17 Sep 44

85 Curtis R. Churchill's Volunteer (Avon Books, 1994), pp163-4

86 Krafft, War Diary, 17.30 and 18.25 hours, 17 Sep 1944; Lathbury, Diary, Sun 17 Sep, Duyts, W. and Groeneweg, A. The Harvest of Ten Years (Oosterbeek Airborne Museum, 1988); Urquhart, R. Arnhem (Pan, 1972), pp50-1

87 Frost, J. A Drop too Many (Cassell & Co, 1980), p209; Flavell, author interview, 1987; Barry, Waddy, op cit, p61; Sims, op cit, pp42-3

88 Harmel, author interview, 27 Oct 1987

89 On pre-war maps the Utrechtseweg changes its name to the Utrechtstraat on the high road just beyond the St Elizabeth Hospital. Some maps also refer to other stretches as the Utrechtstraat. To aid simplicity the modern name Utrechtseweg is used throughout the

book. Street numbers have also changed since the war. Present-day addresses are used in the text and wartime numbers included in the notes, when it is deemed helpful.

90 Dover, V. *The Silken Canopy* (Cassell, 1979), p94

91 Möller, personal account, July 1980

92 Urquhart, op cit, p56; Lathbury, Diary, 17 Sep, op cit, p66

93 Walker, interview, *Forever in Our Memory*, video, Sep 1989

94 Curtis, op cit, p167

95 Becker, letter from A. H. Becker to Th Boeree, 30 Oct 1952, Gelders Archive, Inv No 18

96 Van Maanen, op cit, 17 Sep 44

97 Breman *The Tommies Are Coming!* (Association of Friends of the Airborne Museum Oosterbeek, 1988), 17 Sep 1944

98 Meijer, C. *War in the Weverstraat* (MH No XXV); Zonnenfeld, J. W. van *Volunteers Needed* (MH No 79, Aug 2003)

99 Hol, op cit; Bolte (wartime house No 48), recorded conversation, E. A. Bolte, 3 Jun 65, Gelders Archive Document Collection, Second World War, Item No 150, Freedom Trail Arnhem website; Bolderman, R. Voskuil, *Wartime Adventures of an Arnhem Schoolboy*, MH No 75, Sun 17 Sep 44

100 Bokhoven, letter to Th Boeree, 20 Nov 1952, Gelders Archive, Inv No 18

101 Harzer, Bauer, op cit, p128

102 Diary, 17 Sep 1944

103 This was the house at No 16 Utrechtseweg, which no longer exists today

104 Verkerk, letter to Th Boeree, 17 Jan 1953, Gelders Archive, Inv No 18c; Dover, op cit, pp97-8, 100-1. The Verkerks' wartime address was No 53, and the Henzens were at No 31

105 No 72 was No 38 in 1944

106 Dover, op cit, pp102, 104-5

107 Maassen, G. H. Daily Reports from the Municipal Police of Oosterbeek (MH No XIII), 17-20 Sep 1944

108 Berenden, interview, Return to the Cauldron, B. Rawlings, BBC

Wales 1984; Rieken, author interview, 27 May 2011; Versteeah, interview, Arnhem, *Forever in our Memory*, video, Sep 1989

[109] Hol, MH No 52, Nov 96; Maassen, G. H. *Anxious Days at Dreijen* (MH No XXXV)

[110] Zonnenveld, op cit; Zanten, 'Willy' van *The Arnhem Diary of a Dutch Schoolboy* (*Pegasus* Magazine, Summer 2008)

[111] Van Maanen, op cit, Mon 18 Sep 44; Urquhart, op cit, pp55-6

[112] Crum-Bloemink, Taylor and Marshall, Fairley, J. *Remember Arnhem* (*Pegasus* Journal, 1978), p77

[113] Van Maanen, op cit, 18 Sep 1944

[114] Daily Reports, op cit, 17-20 Sep 44, between 10.00 and 12.00

Chapter 4

[115] Lippert, handwritten notes, Erwin Heck archive; Steckan, letter dated 17 Sep 44, Timmerman, H. *German Field Graves in Oosterbeek* (MH No 84, Dec 2004)

[116] Lindemann, author interview, 11 Jun 1987

[117] Kessler, H. *Kämpfe im Raum Arnheim* (Die Weissen Spiegel, 2/85, 5/85 and 6/85)

[118] Hardy and Longson, Eastwood, S., Gray, C. and Green, A. When Dragons Flew (Silver Link, 1994, 2009), p115; Lippert, notes

[119] Swan, interview, Paradata, Duxford

[120] Tettau, H. von *Gefechtsbericht über die Schlacht bei Arnheim 17-26.9.44* (Bundesarchiv), 15.20, 18 Sep 1944

[121] Breman and Van Maanen, Diaries, 18 Sep 1944; Maassen, G. H. Anxious Days at Dreijen (MH No XXXV)

[122] Möller, personal account, July 1980

[123] Waddy, author interview, 9 Aug 2007; Gatland and Berry, Pijpers, G. and Truesdale, D. *Arnhem Their Final Battle* (RN Sigmond, 2012), pp53 and 58

[124] Zonnenfeld, J. W. van *Volunteers Needed* (MH No 79, Aug 2003); Esvelt, Diary, 18 Sep 44; Heijbroek, MH No 66, May 2000

[125] *Daily Mail*, Mon 18 Sep 1944; Waddy, author interview, 9 Aug 2007

[126] Moss, Pijpers and Truesdale, op cit, p57; Waddy, ibid

[127] Koepel Prison, *Freedom Trail Arnhem*, F. van Lunteren and W. Brouwer website, Koepelgevangnis

[128] Curtis R. *Churchill's Volunteer* (Avon Books, 1994), pp166-9

[129] Möller, personal account, July 1980; Müller, personal account, 1980

[130] Hawksworth, Edwards and Stretton, Junier, A., Smulders, B. and Korsloot, J. *By Land, Sea and Air* (RN Sigmond, 2003), pp93-4

[131] Cain, Hall and Lane, ibid and p102

[132] Salt, ibid, pp102-3; Moss, Pijpers and Truesdale, op cit, p66

[133] Dobie, Junier, A., Smulders, B. and Korsloot, J. *By Land, Sea and Air* (RN Sigmond, 2003), p95; Toler, ibid, pp105-6; Lea, Pijpers and Truesdale, op cit, p81

[134] Harvey and Edwards, Junier, Smulders and Korsloot, op cit, pp107-8

[135] 1 Para Arnhem War Diary, sheets 4 and 5; Bingly, MH No 9, 1985

[136] Gieling, personal account, *My Memories of Arnhem 1944*; Roberts, interview, Return to the Cauldron, B. Rawlings, BBC Wales 1984

[137] Müller, personal account, 1980; Willoughby, Middlebrook, M. *Arnhem 1944* (Viking, 1994), pp195-6, and F. van Lunteren Collection account

[138] Howes, Junier, Smulders and Korsloot, op cit, p110; Shackleton, interview, WWII Experience Centre, P. Liddle, Jul 2002.

[139] Wartime number 37, which was one of three PGEM buildings in the street, has since been replaced by a modern construction. The PGEM offices opposite, called the 'Kraton', were at No 55A, now No 85. The Verkerk family lived next door at No 53, which is now No 83.

[140] Verkerk, letter from H. A. Verkerk to Th Boeree, 17 Jan 1953, Gelders Archive, No 18c; Cartwright, Junier, Smulders and Korsloot, op cit, pp108-9

[141] Becker, letter to Th Boeree, 30 Oct 52, Gelders Archive, No 18; house No 72 was No 38 in 1944

[142] Howes, Junier, Smulders and Korsloot, op cit, p110; Gilchrist, Pijpers and Truesdale, op cit, pp82-3

[143] Koepel prison, Report Gemeente Police, Ede, No 124H/1947; De Soet, *De laatse dagen von het huis Vredenhof* (Arnhem, 1946), Gemeente Archive, Renkum; Letter, Jan ter Horst to G. Maassen, 1 Apr 96

[144] Van Maanen and Breman, *Diaries*, 19 Sep 44; Rieken, author interview, 27 May 2011; Hofwegen, J. A. van *September 1944: A Month We Will Never Forget* (*Eagle* Magazine, Vol 9, No 8, Apr 2001)

[145] Van Gorkum, author interview, 7 Jul 2009

[146] Scholton, Dec 76, Gelders Archive, WW II Collection, No 8; Maassen, G. H. Daily Reports from the Municipal Police of Oosterbeek (MH No XIII), 19 Sep 44

[147] Van der Vlist, H. *Oosterbeek 1944* (Society of Friends, Airborne Museum, Oosterbeek, 1992), pp11 and 13, 19 Sep, p15; Heijbroek, N. *Three Englishmen in Our Cellar* (MH No 66, May 2000)

[148] Van Maanen *The Diary of Anje* 17-25 Sep 1944 (Oosterbeek Airborne Museum), 19 Sep; Van der Vlist, ibid, p19

Chapter 5

[149] No 63 was No 27 in 1944, and No 83 was 53; Verkerk, letter to Th Boeree, 17 Jan 1953, Gelders Archive, Inv No 18c

[150] Cain, Junier, A., Smulders, B. and Korsloot, J. *By Land, Sea and Air* (RN Sigmond, 2003), p114; Cain mistakenly called them 'Ferdinands', a much larger SP, which was a derivative from the Tiger tank

[151] Edwards, Montgomery and Cain, ibid, pp115, 118-19

[152] Gilchrist, Pijpers, G. and Truesdale, D. *Arnhem Their Final Battle* (RN Sigmond, 2012), p89; Möller, personal account, July 1980

[153] Drew, Middlebrook, M. Arnhem 1944 (Viking, 1994), p205

[154] Rohrbach, C. van Roekel, *Sturmgeschütz Brigade 280* (MH No 70, May 2001); Mathes was posthumously awarded the Knight's Cross

[155] Dombrowski, author interview, 23 Oct 1987

[156] Reynolds and Parry, Junier, Smulders and Korsloot, op cit, pp121-2

[157] Van Lunteren Collection account, 11 May 2007; Verkerk, letter to Th Boeree, 17 Jan 53, Gelders Archive, Inv No 18c

[158] Coleman and Thompson, Junier, Smulders and Korsloot, op cit, pp124 and 126-7; Kerr and Blackwood, Pijpers, G. and Truesdale, D. *Arnhem Their Final Battle* (RN Sigmond, 2012), pp95-6

[159] Bankhead, H. *Salute To The Steadfast* (Ramsay Press, 1999), pp103 and 106

[160] Maassen, G. H. Anxious Days at Dreijen (MH No XXXV); Hol, *Memories of Oosterbeek September 1944* (MH No 52, Nov 1996)

[161] Powell, G. Men at Arnhem (Buchan & Enright, 1986), p46; Bankhead, p72

[162] Ziegler, author interview, 23 Nov 1987

[163] Waddy, author interview, 9 Aug 2007; Pott, O'Reilly *From Delhi to Arnhem* (Thoroton, 2009), p163

[164] Ziegler, personal account, 1980; Bankhead, op cit, p76

[165] Powell, op cit, pp86-7; Hanmer, Waddy J. *A Tour of the Arnhem Battlefields* (Leo Cooper, 1999), p106

[166] Hanmer, Waddy, op cit, p107; Hackett, Diary, from Sigmond, R. *Off at Last* (RN Sigmond, 2009), pp76-7; Powell, p84

[167] Halpert and Nosecki, Cholewczynski, G. F. *Poles Apart* (Sarpedon, 1993), pp111-12

[168] Esvelt, Breman and Van Maanen, Diaries, 19 Sep; Schwitters, Middlebrook, op cit, p271

[169] wi cicki, M. With the Red Devils at Arnhem (Max Love, 1945), p26

[170] Shackleton, O'Reilly, op cit, p172

[171] Hanmer, Waddy, op cit, p107; Krafft, after-action report, 1330hrs, 17 Sep 1944

[172] Dagwell, O'Reilly, op cit, p172; Holt and Coupland, R. Sigmond, op cit, pp77-8

[173] Kelderman, Voskuil, R. *Between Bombs and Gliders* (MH No XXVI); Van t'Land (ed S. Gerritsen) Geschichten, die bleiben (Nat Bevrijdingsmusem, 1944-45), p17

[174] Bankhead, op cit, pp79, 81 and 111-12; Powell, op cit, pp88-9; Page, O'Reilly, op cit, p175

[175] Doig, R. Sigmond, op cit, p83

[176] Lindemann, author interview, 11 Jun 1987; Green, Eastwood, S., Gray, C. and Green, A. *When Dragons Flew* (Silver Link, 1994, 2009), p130

[177] Swan, interview, Paradata, Duxford; Green, Eastwood, Gray and

Green, op cit, p147; Walker, AFPU 'dope sheets', Imperial War Museum (IWM), 19 Sep 1944, p3

[178] Steckan, Timmerman, H. German Field Graves in Oosterbeek (MH No 84, Dec 2004)

[179] Lippert, personal account, Erwin Heck archive; Lindemann, author interview, 11 Jun 1987

[180] Swan, interview, Paradata, Duxford; Giesa's action, P. Reinders *Panzer Kompanie C (No) 224 in the Netherlands 1943-5*, pp17-24

[181] Walker and Lewis, APFU 'dope sheets', IWM, 19 Sep 1944

[182] Krafft, combat report, 24.00hrs 19 Sep and 08.30hrs 20 Sep 1944; Lippert, personal account

[183] Lintern, Keating and Bankhead, Bankhead, op cit, pp124, 127-8 and 132

[184] Powell, op cit, pp127-31

[185] Van Maanen, Diary, 20 Sep 1944; Huijgen, Maassen, G. H. Daily Reports from the Municipal Police of Oosterbeek (MH No XIII), 17-20 Sep 1944

[186] Woods, Diary, 21 Sep 1944, Duyts, W. and Groeneweg, A. *The Harvest of Ten Years* (Oosterbeek Airborne Museum, 1988)

Chapter 6

[187] Van Maanen The Diary of Anje 17-25 Sep 1944 (Oosterbeek Airborne Museum), 22 Sep, p46

[188] Rieken, author interview, 27 May 2011

[189] Boardman, personal account, Air Assault Museum Archive, Duxford

[190] Rieken, author interview

[191] Meijer, C. War in the Weverstraat (MH No XXV); Van Gorkum, author interview, 8 Jul 2009

[192] Heijbroek, N. *Three Englishmen in Our Cellar* (MH No 66, May 2000)

[193] Maassen, G. H. *Anxious Days at Dreijen* (MH No XXXV)

[194] Van Maanen, op cit, Thu 21 Sep, p37

[195] Meijer, op cit

[196] Maassen, op cit; Meijer, op cit

[197] Rieken, author interview

[198] Harzer, personal account and battle report

[199] Möller, personal account, July 1980; Schwarz, author interview, 16 Sep 1987

[200] Dombrowski, author interview, 23 Oct 1987

[201] Van der Vlist, H. Oosterbeek 1944 (Society of Friends, Airborne Museum, Oosterbeek, 1992), 21 Sep, p28; Van Gorkum, author interview, 8 Jul 2009

[202] Replacement details, Kampfwert der Div Unterstellten Marine Einheiten, 9th SS Pz Div Abt 1a, 28 Sep 1944, Militär Archiv Freiburg; Meijer, op cit

[203] NATO survey, Area Type C, as identified by Shrivenham Royal Military College of Science Operational Reports OR/C/10, May 1978, and OR/C/13, Mar 1979; also Bundeswehr Gefecht der Kampftruppen im Bebautem Gelände, Handbook, 1976

[204] Candine-Bate, Gijbels, P. and Truesdale, D. *Leading the Way to Arnhem* (RN Sigmond, 2008), p94

[205] Kent, R. First In! (Batsford, 1979), p118

[206] Powell, G. Men at Arnhem (Buchan & Enright, 1986), pp138-9, 141-2

[207] Kent, op cit, p117; Hagen, L. Arnhem Lift (Hammond, 1945), p44

[208] Wilmott, personal account, Air Assault Museum Archive, Duxford

[209] Powell, op cit, p139; Hagen, op cit, p44

[210] Hagen, op cit, p70; Möller, personal account, July 1980

[211] Hagen op cit, p54; Zonnenfeld, J. W. van Volunteers Needed (MH No 79, Aug 2003)

[212] Mawson, S. Arnhem Doctor (Orbis, 1981), p101

[213] Dombrowski, author interview, 23 Oct 1987; Glover, Middlebrook, M. *Arnhem 1944* (Viking, 1994), p344

[214] Zanten, 'Willy' van *The Arnhem Diary of a Dutch Schoolboy* (*Pegasus* Magazine, Summer 2008)

[215] Stewart, Benest, D., *10 Para Research Notes*, Airborne Assault Museum Archive, Duxford

[216] Wilmott and Glover, personal accounts, Airborne Assault Museum Archive, Duxford

[217] Möller, personal account, July 1980; Mrs Voskuil, Middlebrook, op cit, pp345-6 and Ryan, C. *A Bridge Too Far* (Hamish Hamilton, 1974), pp393-4

Chapter 7

[218] Swan, interview, R. Milton, Airborne Assault Museum Archive, Duxford

[219] Tettau, H. von *Gefechtsbericht über die Schlacht bei Arnheim 17-26.9.44* (Bundesarchiv), 21 Sep, 00.40hrs

[220] Kessler, H. *Kämpfe im Raum Arnheim* (*Die Weissen Spiegel*, 2/85, 5/85 and 6/85)

[221] Tettau, H. von, op cit, 10.50 and 11.45hrs

[222] Fullriede, Diary, 21 Sep 1944

[223] Lebahn, *Gefechtsbericht der 7 (Stamm) Kompanie fur die Zeit von 17.9 bis 26.9.44*, dated 20 Oct 1944; Fullriede, op cit, 21 Sep 1944

[224] Tettau, H. von, op cit, 21 Sep, 19.00hrs, and Divisions Befehl Nr 15, Anlage 5, dated 22 Sep 1944

[225] Lindemann, author interview, 11 Jun 1987

[226] Swan, Milton interview

[227] Walker, interview, *Arnhem, Forever in our Memory*, video, Sep 1989, and AFPU secret 'dope sheet', 1st Airborne Division, 21-23 Sep, IWM; Lewis, 'dope sheet' D+5

[228] Heijbroek, N. *Three Englishmen in Our Cellar* (MH No 66, May 2000).

[229] Van Blockland, Middlebrook, M. *Arnhem 1944* (Viking, 1994), pp371-2

[230] Kessler, McKee, A. *The Race for the Rhine Bridges* (Stein & Day, 1971), p273; Lippert, personal notes, Erwin Heck archive

[231] Baker, E. B. *'Bunny' Baker's Arnhem Story* (*Eagle* Magazine, Vol 9, No 10, Dec 2001)

[232] Maassen, G. H. *Anxious Days at Dreijen* (MH No XXXV)

[233] Maassen, ibid. Pyper, Stevenson and Taylor, Fairley, J. *Remember Arnhem* (*Pegasus* Journal, 1978), pp167-8, 112-13 and 136

[234] Baker, op cit

[234] Hol, *Memories of Oosterbeek September 1944* (MH No 52, Nov 1996)

[236] Maassen, op cit; Schwitter, Middlebrook, op cit, p370

[237] Ziegler, author interview, 23 Nov 1987, and personal account, Abschrift, 1976

[238] Powell, G. Men at Arnhem (Buchan & Enright, 1986), pp144-5

[239] Cloer, Bruce, bystander and Hamby, Cholewczynski, G. F. *Spanhoe's September* (Walka Books, 2008), pp87-8 and 98-9

[240] Polish witnesses, Cholewczynski, G. F. *Poles Apart* (Sarpedon, 1993): Raschke, p3, Smaczny, p4, Bossowski, p7; Wilson, *Spanhoe's September*, op cit, p99

[241] Trapp, author interview, 17 Sep 1987; shooting at parachutists: contemporary Bundeswehr German Army data, Kershaw, R. J. Skymen (Hodder & Stoughton, 2010), p67; Wilson, Spanhoe's September, op cit, p99

[242] Esvelt, Diary, 21 Sep 1944

[243] wi cicki, M. *With the Red Devils at Arnhem* (Max Love, 1945), p26, pp71-2

[244] Sapper Officer, Eastwood, S., Gray, C. and Green, A. *When Dragons Flew* (Silver Link, 1994, 2009), p165; Officer on perimeter bank, Army Bureau of Current Affairs *Arnhem 2: Inside The Perimeter*, No 84, Dec 1944

[245] Hol, op cit; Kent, R. *First In!* (Batsford, 1979), p122; Kuzniar, *Poles Apart*, op cit, p228; Bruce, Gijbels, P. and Truesdale, D. *Leading the Way to Arnhem* (RN Sigmond, 2008), pp114-5

[246] Borderers, Eastwood, Gray and Green, op cit, p164

[247] Möller, personal account, July 1980; Dombrowski, author interview, 23 Oct 1987

[248] Lawton, Duyts, W. and Groeneweg, A. *The Harvest of Ten Years* (Oosterbeek Airborne Museum, 1988), p90

[249] Kent, op cit, pp118-19; Hobbs and McMahon, Gijbels and Truesdale, op cit, pp103 and 106; Hackett, Diary, Sat 23 Sep

[250] Harzer, Gefechtsbericht: Battle report and personal correspondence on the part played by the Hohenstaufen Division in the Battle of

Arnhem, edited with notes by Th. A. Boeree; Dinkel and Forstner, Timmerman, H. German *Field Graves in Oosterbeek* (MH No 84, Dec 2004)

[251] Jacobsen and Wenzel, proof shots, Bundesarchiv, Koblenz; Gatland, Pijpers, G. and Truesdale, D. *Arnhem Their Final Battle* (RN Sigmond, 2012), pp103-4

[252] Veelen, H. van Civilian Aid in the Schoonoord (MH No 64, Oct 1999); Van der Vlist, H. Oosterbeek 1944 (Society of Friends, Airborne Museum, Oosterbeek, 1992), pp32 and 35; Gatland, ibid, pp98, 100, 102 and 110

[253] Stewart, Gijbels, P. and Truesdale, op cit, p112; Van Maanen *The Diary of Anje* 17-25 Sep 44 (Oosterbeek Airborne Museum), 24 Sep

[254] Möller, personal account, July 1980

[255] Lothar Dinkel was actually to survive, captured by US troops, but the Dinkel family was not to be notified by the Red Cross until August 1945, after a particularly bleak 1944 Christmas. Lothar was eventually to locate his brother's grave at Oosterbeek in 1954; Timmerman, op cit

[256] Curtis R. *Churchill's Volunteer* (Avon Books, 1994), pp179-80

[257] Waddy, author interview, 9 Aug 2007

[258] Kent, op cit, p124; Möller, personal account, July 1980

[259] Kent, ibid; Harkers, personal account sent to Dr A. Groeneweg, Airborne Museum, Oosterbeek; Van der Vlist, op cit, p41; Gatland, Pijpers and Truesdale, op cit, p110

[260] Kent, Ibid, p124; Möller, personal account, July 1980; Dombrowski, author interview, 23 Oct 1987

[261] Van Maanen, op cit, 24 Sep

Chapter 8

[262] Kessler, H. *Kämpfe im Raum Arnheim* (Die Weissen Spiegel 6/85) and McKee, A. *The Race for the Rhine Bridges* (Stein & Day, 1971), p251

[263] Bruggeman, Diary, 24 Sep 44, Pegasus Archive

[264] Powell, G. Men at Arnhem (Buchan & Enright, 1986), p157;

Dombrowski, author interview, 23 Oct 1987; Wood, Margry, K. *Operation Market-Garden: Then and Now*, 2 Vols ('After The Battle', 2002), p667; Evans, Fairley, J. *Remember Arnhem* (Pegasus Journal, 1978), p162

265 Williams, Hees, A-J. van Green On! (Private Pub, 2007), p319; Lawton, Duyts, W. and Groeneweg, A. *The Harvest of Ten Years* (Oosterbeek Airborne Museum, 1988), p89; Christie, Wilkinson, P. The Gunners at Arnhem (Spurwing Pub, 1999), p121

266 Heijbroek, N. *Three Englishmen in Our Cellar* (MH No 66, May 2000)

267 Swan, interview, R. Milton, Airborne Assault Museum Archive, Duxford, Sep 23 D+6, Sep 24 D+7, and Sep 25 D+8

268 Lippert, Abschrift, personal notes, Erwin Heck archive

269 Hardy, Eastwood, S., Gray, C. and Green, A. *When Dragons Flew* (Silver Link, 1994, 2009), pp169-70

270 Mackenzie, Fairley, J. *Remember Arnhem* (*Pegasus* Journal, 1978), p118; Jenkins, ibid, p163

271 wi cicki, M. *With the Red Devils at Arnhem* (Max Love, 1945), pp50 and 62; Wood, Diary, 24 Sep, Duyts and Groeneweg, op cit, p183; Evans and Coldicott, Fairley, op cit, p162

272 Wilson, Army Bureau of Current Affairs *Arnhem 2: Inside The Perimeter*, No 84, Dec 1944, p4

273 Powell, op cit, pp185-6; Shackleton, interview, WWII Experience Centre, P. Liddle, Jul 2002

274 Walker, interview, *Arnhem, Forever in our Memory*, video, Sep 1989, and Margry, op cit, p678; Wood, Diary, 23 Sep, Duyts and Groeneweg, op cit, p183; German PoWs, Margry, op cit, p436

275 Resupply flights: Powell, op cit, pp79-80; Carson, author interview, 22 Sep 2007; Lee, Margry, K. *Arnhem VC Investigation* (*After The Battle* magazine, No 96, 1997, pp45-7; Lawton, Duyts and Groeneweg, op cit, p88; Maxted, ed D. Hawkins, BBC War Report: D-Day to VE Day, p203; Chatfield, author interview, 22 Sep 2007; resupply figures, Waddy J. A Tour of the Arnhem Battlefields (Leo Cooper, 1999), p126

[276] Kremer, Middlebrook, M. *Arnhem 1944* (Viking, 1994), p369; Hofwegen, J. A. van *September 1944: A Month We Will Never Forget* (*Eagle* Magazine, Vol 9, No 8, Apr 2001)

[277] Peters, *The Lost Evidence: Operation Market Garden* (Downing, T., Flashback TV, History Channel, 2006); Van Maanen *The Diary of Anje* 17-25 Sep 1944 (Oosterbeek Airborne Museum), 23 Sep

[278] Veelen, H. van *Civilian Aid in the Schoonoord* (MH No 64, Oct 1999); Van der Vlist, H. Oosterbeek 1944 (Society of Friends, Airborne Museum, Oosterbeek, 1992), pp25-6

[279] Page, The Lost Evidence, op cit

[280] Hol, *Memories of Oosterbeek September 1944* (MH No 52, Nov 1996); Breman The Tommies Are Coming! (Association of Friends of the Airborne Museum Oosterbeek, 1988), 21 and 24 Sep; Van Hofwegen, op cit; Kremer, Middlebrook, op cit, p368; Meijer, C. *War in the Weverstraat* (MH No XXV)

[281] Rosenberg, O'Reilly *From Delhi to Arnhem* (Thoroton, 2009), p247; Hope and Stevenson, Fairley, op cit, p170; McCausland and Crane, Gijbels, P. and Truesdale, D. *Leading the Way to Arnhem* (RN Sigmond, 2008), p122

[282] Cooke, Fairley, op cit, p168; Gibson, R. *Nine Days* (Stockwell, 1956), p76; Allerton, Zeno The Cauldron (Pan, 1966), pp202-3; Lawton, Duyts and Groeneweg, op cit, p91

[283] Hackett, J. I Was a Stranger (Sphere, 1977), pp21-2; Wilkinson, op cit, p121; Meijer, op cit; Zonnenfeld, J. W. van Volunteers Needed (MH No 79, Aug 2003); Zanten, 'Willy' van *The Arnhem Diary of a Dutch Schoolboy* (*Pegasus* Magazine, Summer 2008)

[284] Hackett, ibid, pp22-5

[285] Van Maanen, op cit, 25 Sep

[286] Rohrbach, C. van Roekel, *Sturmgeschütz Brigade 280* (MH No 70, May 2001)

[287] Lerche, despite changing his name, was found and put on trial at Munich in 1955, being sentenced to ten years hard labour. Nobody actually saw him shoot the victim. German War Crimes Affidavit MD/JAG/FS/61/2(D) Reg 30 Oct 1945

Chapter 9

288 Urquhart, Margry, K. *Operation Market-Garden: Then and Now*, 2 Vols ('After The Battle', 2002), p682; Lawton, Duyts, W. and Groeneweg, A. *The Harvest of Ten Years* (Oosterbeek Airborne Museum, 1988), p90; Swan, interview, R. Milton, Airborne Assault Museum Archive, Duxford; Baker, E. B. *'Bunny' Baker's Arnhem Story* (*Eagle* Magazine, Vol 9, No 10, Dec 2001)

289 Cook, Fairley, J. *Remember Arnhem* (*Pegasus* Journal, 1978), p169; Powell, G. *Men at Arnhem* (Buchan & Enright, 1986), p187; Shackleton, interview, WWII Experience Centre, P. Liddle, Jul 2002; Gibson, R. *Nine Days* (Stockwell, 1956), p83; Kent, Gijbels, P. and Truesdale, D. *Leading the Way to Arnhem* (RN Sigmond, 2008), pp123-4

290 Hayden, personal account

291 Möller, personal account, July 1980; McLeod, Wilkinson, P. *The Gunners at Arnhem* (Spurwing Pub, 1999), p138

292 Harzer, Gefechtsbericht: Battle report and personal correspondence on the part played by the Hohenstaufen Division in the Battle of Arnhem, edited with notes by Th. A. Boeree; Möller, ibid

293 Blackwood, Pijpers, G. and Truesdale, D. *Arnhem Their Final Battle* (RN Sigmond, 2012), pp140-1; Williams, Junier, A., Smulders, B. and Korsloot, J. By Land, Sea and Air (RN Sigmond, 2003), pp145-6; Edwards and Etherington, ibid, pp146 and 147

294 Ashworth and Long, *Victoria Cross* (Pearson, R., BBC Midlands presentation on Major Robert Cain VC). Cain lived and was awarded the VC

295 Smith, Junier, Smulders and Korsloot, op cit, p146

296 Pick, in Benest, D., *10 Para Research Notes*, Airborne Assault Museum Archive, Duxford. Pick was taken PoW and repatriated through Switzerland in Jan 1945, having lost his right forearm and been blinded by shrapnel

297 Blackwood, Pijpers and Truesdale, op cit, pp140-1

298 Harzer, op cit; Möller, personal account, July 1980; Krafft, Gefechtsbericht, 2: *The Enemy. Composition and Battle Value.*

[299] Hayden, personal account

[300] Kent, R. *First In!* (Batsford, 1979), p128; Trinder, Fairley, op cit, p191

[301] Powell, op cit, p195; Kent, ibid, p128; Smaczny, Cholewczynski, G. F. Poles Apart (Sarpedon, 1993), p260

[302] Swan, Milton interview, 25 Sep

[303] Kessler, H. *Kämpfe im Raum Arnheim* (Die Weissen Spiegel, 2/85, 5/85 and 6/85) and McKee, A. *The Race for the Rhine Bridges* (Stein & Day, 1971), p283; Lippert, Abschrift, hand-written notes, Erwin Heck archive; Tettau, H. von Gefechtsbericht über die Schlacht bei Arnheim 17-26.9.44 (Bundesarchiv), 26.9, 06.10 and 14.00 hours; Möller, personal account, July 1980

[304] Meijer, C. War in the Weverstraat (MH No XXV)

[305] Kuzniar, *Poles Apart*, op cit, p262

[306] Hol, *Memories of Oosterbeek September 1944* (MH No 52, Nov 1996)

[307] Baker, op cit

[308] Powell, op cit, pp196-7; Lawton, Duyts and Groeneweg, op cit, p94

[309] Shackleton, interview, WWII Experience Centre, P. Liddle, Jul 2002; Hagen, L. Arnhem Lift (Hammond, 1945), p106; Page and Peters, *The Lost Evidence: Operation Market Garden* (Downing, T., Flashback TV, History Channel, 2006)

[310] Krafft, op cit, 26 Sep 44; Powell, op cit, p202

[311] Von Tettau, op cit, 26 Sep 44, 12.00 and 14.00 hours; Smith, Junier, Smulders and Korsloot, op cit, p151; Rohrbach, C. van Roekel, *Sturmgeschütz Brigade 280* (MH No 70, May 2001); Lindemann, author interview, 11 Jun 1987; Ziegler, author interview, 23 Nov 1987; Möller, personal account, July 1980

[312] Hofwegen, J. A. van *September 1944: A Month We Will Never Forget* (*Eagle* Magazine, Vol 9, No 8, Apr 2001); damage, Maassen, G. Oosterbeek Verwoest 1944-45 (Private Pub, 1980)

[313] Heijbroek, N. *Three Englishmen in Our Cellar* (MH No 66, May 2000); Maassen, G. H. *Anxious Days at Dreijen* (MH No XXXV); Meijer, op cit

[314] Hol, op cit

[315] Laterveer, and Jacobsen and Wenzel photographs, Arnhem, September 1944 (Gemeente Archive, 1969), p70

[316] Van Altena, Jong, A. de War Evacuees in the Open Air Museum (NL Open Air Museum, Arnhem, 2004), p5

[317] Zee, H. van der *The Hunger Winter* (Jill Norman & Hobhouse Ltd, 1982), p46 and P. R. A. van Iddekinge, *Arnheim 44/45 Evacuatie, verwoesting, plundering, bevrijding, terugkeer* (Arnhem, 1981), p55

[318] Evacuation decisions, Van der Zee, op cit, p47; Van Gorkum, author interview, 8 Jul 2009; Spindler, letter G. A. P. van Helbergen to P. C. Heiser 23 Nov 4, Gelders Archive, Inv No 1240

[319] Maassen, op cit; witness, Van der Zee, ibid, p47

[320] Meijer, op cit

[321] Van Maanen *The Diary of Anje* 17-25 Sep 1944 (Oosterbeek Airborne Museum), 25 Sep

[322] Gieling, personal account, *My Memories of Arnhem 1944*

Chapter 10

[323] Douwenga, Zee, H. van der The Hunger Winter (Jill Norman & Hobhouse Ltd, 1982), p46; Breman The Tommies Are Coming! (Association of Friends of the Airborne Museum Oosterbeek, 1988), p51; Heijbroek, N. *Three Englishmen in Our Cellar* (MH No 66, May 2000)

[324] Fullriede, Diary, 1-4 Oct 1944; Putten, Van der Zee, op cit, p43

[325] Pegasus I and II, O'Reilly *From Delhi to Arnhem* (Thoroton, 2009), pp317, 330 and 336

[326] Van der Vlist, H. Oosterbeek 1944 (Society of Friends, Airborne Museum, Oosterbeek, 1992), pp70 and 61; confiscations and looting, Jong, A. de War Evacuees in the Open Air Museum (NL Open Air Museum, Arnhem, 2004), pp13-14

[327] Maassen, G. H. *Anxious Days at Dreijen* (MH No XXXV); Esvelt, Diary, 6 Oct 44; homesickness, The Battle of Arnhem, official post-war publication, Municipality of Arnhem, undated

[328] Wiersma and De Jong, TV interviews, M. Tosh, The Hunger Winter,

BBC Timewatch, Elstree, 1988

[329] Macdonald and McKee, *The Race for the Rhine Bridges* (Stein & Day, 1971), pp445, 447, 11 and 454; Belfield, private account of the liberation of northern Holland (Waddy collection)

[330] 'Ancient tomb', Whiting, C. *Bounce the Rhine* (Leo Cooper), p166; Canadian officer, The Canadian Army 1939-45, Chap XVI (Canadian Department of National Defense), pp281-2; Macdonald, McKee, op cit, p466; Belfield, ibid

[331] Ellis, ed D. Hawkins, BBC War Report: D-Day to VE Day, p339

[332] Damage, Maassen, G. *Oosterbeek Verwoest 1944-45* (Private Pub, 1980), Introduction; P-A. van Teesling *Over and Over* (Kontrast Pub, Oosterbeek, 2000), p71; Breman, op cit, p51; Van der Vlist, op cit, Introduction

[333] Jansen, Fairley, J. *Remember Arnhem* (Pegasus Journal, 1978), p206; Langevoort, interview, *Forever in Our Memory*, video, Sep 1989

[334] Zanten, 'Willy' van *The Arnhem Diary of a Dutch Schoolboy* (Pegasus Magazine, Summer 2008), p75

[335] Rudolphie, Pijpers, G. and Truesdale, D. *Arnhem Their Final Battle* (RN Sigmond, 2012), p164

[336] Breman, op cit, pp5 and 51; Van Zanten, op cit, p75

[337] Hartgers, Langevoort and Urquhart, interviews, *Forever in Our Memory*, video, Sep 1989